THE POLITICS OF TERROR

The Northeastern Series on Democratization and Political Development

The Politics of

EDITED BY WILLIAM CROTTY

TERROR

THE U.S. RESPONSE TO 9/11

NORTHEASTERN UNIVERSITY PRESS · BOSTON

Northeastern University Press

Library of Congress Cataloging-in-Publication Data
The politics of terror : the U.S. response to 9/11 / edited by William Crotty.
    p. cm.—(The Northeastern series on democratization and political development)
Includes bibliographical references and index.
  ISBN 1-55553-577-1 (pbk. : alk. paper)
1. United States—Politics and government—2001– 2. National security—
United States. 3. Patriotism—United States. 4. Civil rights—United States.
5. Terrorism—United States. 6. War on Terrorism, 2001– —Political aspects—
United States. 7. September 11 Terrorist Attacks, 2001—Influence. I. Crotty,
William J. II. Series.
  E902.P65 2004
  973.931—dc21   2003010692

Designed by Ann Twombly

Composed in Bodoni by Wellington Graphics, Hanover, Massachusetts. Printed and bound by Edwards Brothers, Inc., Lillington, North Carolina. The paper is EB Natural, an acid-free stock.

MANUFACTURED IN THE UNITED STATES OF AMERICA
08 07 06 05 04   5 4 3 2 1

Contents

FOUR INSTITUTIONS AND PUBLIC POLICY

Preface

This book concerns terrorism in the wake of 9/11, which represents a new kind of threat to America and demands a new kind of war. The basic issue addressed in this volume is how to balance legitimate national security concerns with the rights and freedoms that have characterized American democracy. There is, of course, no easy answer. Regardless of the alternatives considered and the paths chosen, the stakes are significant.

Governmental changes introduced in the aftermath of the terrorist bombings may have a fundamental impact on the character and operations of democratic government in the United States. The horrific events of 9/11 introduced a new form of external threat to the United States that prompted us to think about and discuss the ways in which a democracy can prepare to face such a challenge in the future. Equally important are contemplation and debate about how best to preserve the unfettered communications and interpersonal relations enjoyed by Americans in the open society to which we are committed.

For their parts in developing this book, I wish to thank each of the contributors as well as Amy E. Richey, my research associate at the Center for the Study of Democracy for her work on this book and her contributions to my essays; Bob Gormley, senior editor at the Northeastern University Press, and Ann Twombly of the Press who saw this book through from its inception to its publication; Shaheen Mozaffar and Mehran Kamrava for their helpful comments; and, finally, my wife, Mary Hauch Crotty, whose work in the field of biological terrorism and the official government responses to it was of critical assistance in sorting through the issues associated with the new terrorism.

WILLIAM CROTTY

Introduction:
Where We Are, Where We Are Going

The 9/11 terrorist attacks have changed the way America thinks about the world. Before these attacks, terrorism seemed to be a distant activity directed against isolated targets by fringe individuals carrying inexplicable grudges. It was of little immediate concern to this country. It was confined to little-known countries and fostered by unfamiliar groups in whom U.S. citizens had little interest. True, there had been bombings and terrorist attacks targeting American installations, embassies, and military bases. Then again, little was understood about the motives behind the attacks, and the government and media, as well as the public, gave them only passing attention. There had also been the terrorist attack on the World Trade Center in 1993, but it appeared to be a one-time event of limited success, not overly alarming. Political terrorism apparently was not perceived as a problem of national concern by President Bill Clinton's administration, whose attention was to be distracted by congressional investigations, accusations about fund-raising abuses, a sex scandal, and an impeachment. It was not a White House that could direct its energies to a threat whose seriousness and long-run consequences were yet to be recognized. George W. Bush, elected in 2000, seemed to display a similar lack of concern about the issue of terrorism.

America was a nation unchallenged in foreign affairs, the world's leader in finance, trade, and military might. The horror of the 9/11 attacks on the Twin Towers of the World Trade Center and the Pentagon changed everything. The collapse of buildings once recognized as among the most powerful symbols of the wealth of a great city and the might of a great nation was shattering to the nation's psyche. The televised pictures of the devastation; reports and pictures of people leaping to their deaths, and of technicians in the morgues trying to identify victims from body parts; the heroism of firefighters and police who responded to the attacks; and, most of all, the human face placed on the tragedy definitively brought home the dimensions of the international terrorist threat. Rather than being a series of lone attacks by individuals whose motivation lay in whatever fanaticism fed their anger, terrorism was now seen as a national threat—originating in groups that were highly organized and, as later investigations revealed, sophisticated in their training, planning, and execution. Political terrorism was to become the new American war, one to which an open society such as the United States was particularly vulnerable and for which the country was not psychologically or militarily prepared.

A curious war it would turn out to be. Americans were asked by their president to return to normal, to continue to buy and consume, and not to acknowledge disruption in their lives. New institutions were designed to coordinate the domestic response to potential terrorist acts, and the Congress passed broad empowering legislation in a matter of days. Afghanistan, the base for Al Qaeda leader Osama bin Laden, architect of the 9/11 attacks, was bombed into submission. New security precautions were devised for airports and other possible targets; security concerns, in fact, became internationalized. The total effects on American society, arguably the most open and democratic in the world, is not yet clear, but a price will certainly be paid in the freedoms enjoyed by citizens. The problem is to ascertain how great a price and how drastic the consequences for a democratic lifestyle—and, of even greater concern, for the future of democracy as we know it.

This volume examines these issues. It calls on scholars, each an acknowledged expert in his or her area, to assess the terrorist threats and the nature and adequacy of the American response. The essays herein evaluate the costs involved in reframing international relations in terms of universal terrorism and explore the impact of changes and policies implemented to deal with such threats. It could be reasonably argued that these concerns represent the single most compelling set of problems confronting the nation and the world in the contemporary period.

"Prerequisites for Morally Credible Condemnations of Terrorism," by

Stephen Nathanson, asks the troubling question: Are there any conditions under which terrorism can be morally justified? Regarding definitions of terrorism, there is a lack of clarity that is "an obstacle both to intellectual understanding and intelligent action." Nathanson adds: "Since 9/11, it has become urgent to escape the ill effects of confusion in thought and feeling about terrorism and other acts of violence." Nathanson raises issues seldom addressed about the ethics and morality of international behavior.

"Terrorism and the Remaking of American Politics," by John Kenneth White, assesses the ways in which Americans have rethought politics in the aftermath of 9/11 and the resulting effect on American values. As White says, "While Americans mourned their dead, they also grieved their loss of innocence. The sense of personal security that most citizens took for granted gave way to a somber reality that terrorism was now an integral part of the American way of life."

In "The War on Terrorism and the New Patriotism," Scott L. McLean writes that "not since 1942 has there been such an opportunity—or danger—of a massive civil mobilization of the U.S. population on the basis of American national identity." McLean explores the "powerful sense of unity and pride of country" in the wake of 9/11 and the consequences of the terrorist attacks on various forms of political and social behavior as well.

"America's Wartime Presidents: Politics, National Security, and Civil Liberties," by Jerome M. Mileur and Ronald Story, places the crises engendered by 9/11 in historical perspective. As they point out, every American president in wartime has had to "balance the interests of national security with the liberties of the people." Also discussed are the ways in which "the politics of their times," as well as "the personal predilections of the presidents" have affected the level of political dissent in wartime administrations. An examination of these previous eras of international threat sheds light on our own "war against terrorism." The authors assess, in turn, the presidencies of Abraham Lincoln, Woodrow Wilson, Franklin D. Roosevelt, Harry Truman, and Lyndon Johnson as well as, in a more limited fashion, George W. Bush.

In "Civil Liberties and the Judiciary in the Aftermath of 9/11," Daniel Krislov explores the likely responses of the judiciary to the legislation and administrative actions that have been initiated. Unfortunately, not enough time has passed for any definitive judgments to be made. Professor Krislov analyzes the issues involved and then, based on previous rulings, hypothesizes probable judicial reactions to cases involving questions of individual rights and legal procedure.

"Security versus Liberty: 9/11 and the American Public," by Lynn M. Kuzma, "explores the challenges an open society faces as it confronts the values trade-off between liberty and security brought about by the 9/11 terrorist attacks." The essay also examines in this context the support for newly developed antiterrorist policies. In doing so, it presents data collected from respondents in a small New England city, Portland, Maine, six months after the attacks. When possible, the Portland residents' opinions are compared to those found in national trend data. Professor Kuzma concludes that the post-9/11 consensus "has started to splinter and the dramatic support found for administrative policies in the direct aftermath of the attacks has begun to fade."

In "On the Home Front: Institutional Mobilization to Fight the Threat of International Terrorism," I discuss congressional reactions to 9/11 and the powers given the presidency. In particular, the congressional reaction is embodied in two major pieces of legislation, the USA Patriot ("Uniting and Strengthening America by Providing Appropriate Tools Required to Intercept and Obstruct Terrorism") Act and the legislation creating the cabinet-level Department of Homeland Security. As this examination emphasizes, there will be consequences for a comfortable and previously unquestioned American lifestyle as well as the possible transformation of an open, democratic society into some form of security state.

"Are We Safer Today?: Organizational Responses to Terrorism," by B. Guy Peters, makes the point that to date much of the analysis relevant to terrorism "has been dominated by the paradigms of military science or international relations." This is only one aspect of the problem. Also noted is the fact that the Federal Bureau of Investigation (FBI) and Central Intelligence Agency (CIA) have been faulted in not adequately protecting against the attacks. Professor Peters examines the reallocation of powers and the restructuring of the national government intended to meet the terrorist threat and considers the effectiveness of reliance on the bureaucratic approaches taken.

"The Presidency Responds: The Implications of 9/11 for the Bush Administration's Policy Agenda," by Richard J. Powell, points out that "the president seemed to grow in stature in the days and weeks following the attacks. Some have even argued that Bush himself changed." Professor Powell focuses "on the impact of the terrorist attacks on the manner in which the Bush administration has interacted with the broader political environment." His ultimate concern is the consequences for the institution of the presidency more than those for the immediate occupant of the White House; the reshaping of the institutional context of presidential leadership could be substantial.

The conclusion of the volume, "Terrorism, Security, and the American State," is an overview of the consequences of a "war on terrorism," the powers ceded the president by congressional action, and the public's level of understanding concerning the issues involved. How should the United States handle the real security threat? The questions are many, the answers few. Yet the actions taken in response to 9/11 could establish the framework for a new and different type of American politics and society.

Moral Dilemmas

STEPHEN NATHANSON

Prerequisites for Morally Credible Condemnations of Terrorism

My aim in this essay is to clarify the concept of terrorism and the moral status of terrorist acts. A lack of clarity about the nature of terrorism permits the word *terrorism* to be used in an inflammatory way, one that is an obstacle to both intellectual understanding and intelligent action. Likewise, a lack of clarity about the basis of moral criticisms of terrorism results in moral judgments that are widely seen as hypocritical and self-serving. Instead of reinforcing important values, moral condemnations of terrorism often generate moral cynicism and increased hostility between groups.

Since the days of Socrates, philosophers have sought clarity not just for its own sake but because its absence makes the rational interpretation of events and the sound assessment of policies impossible. Since 9/11, it has become urgent to escape the ill effects of confusions in thought and feeling about terrorism and other acts of violence.

Can terrorism be morally justified? Even asking this question can seem like an insult—both to the victims of terrorist actions and to moral common sense. Victims have suffered injury and death for actions and policies for which they were not responsible, and moral common sense resoundingly condemns terrorist acts as paradigms of immorality. One wants to say: if the murder of innocent people by terrorists is not clearly wrong, what is?

It is easy to condemn terrorism, and presumably any moral person will do so. Nonetheless, difficulties emerge when we broaden our focus and consider some of the other beliefs of people who issue such condemnations. While condemning terrorism is neither morally nor philosophically problematic for people who condemn all violence, very few of us take this view.

Most of us believe that some acts of killing and injuring people are morally justified. Moreover, most of us think that war is sometimes morally justified, even though we know that many people, both civilians as well as soldiers, are killed and injured in warfare. So, most of us think that even the killing of innocent people—though it is surely regrettable—is sometimes morally justified.

It is this fact that makes the condemnation of terrorism morally problematic. Can people who support wars in which civilians are killed consistently condemn terrorism? Or are such condemnations hypocritical and self-serving?

Judgments about terrorism frequently lead to hypocrisy for two reasons. Sometimes they presuppose self-serving definitions that make it analytically true that the acts committed by one's own country or group and its allies cannot be instances of terrorism. Sometimes they are based on biased, uneven applications of moral principles to the actions of friends and foes.

In order to avoid hypocrisy, we need two things. The first is a definition of terrorism that is neutral and does not prejudge the morality of terrorist acts by including the party or group who commits them as a defining condition. The second is a consistent application of moral criteria that apply to a broad range of actions that includes but is not limited to terrorist actions. Any serious inquiry on this subject, then, must begin with the right sort of definition and must apply moral principles in an evenhanded way. (For other philosophical discussions of the nature and morality of terrorism, see Primoratz 1990, 1997; Khatchadourian 1988; and Coady 1985, 2002.)

PART 1: WHAT IS TERRORISM?

Misconceptions and Confusions

We can see why a neutral definition and impartial application of principles are necessary by considering popular thinking about terrorism. Popular thinking appears to be dominated by two contrasting views of terrorism. The first view is a form of essentialism. It sees terrorism as a distinctive form of violence that is especially immoral. This view has been evident in remarks made by President George W. Bush and members of his administration since 9/11. Their assumption that terrorism forms a distinctive class of especially hateful actions underlies their view that combating terrorism must take priority over efforts to combat other evils.

A contrasting view is expressed in the cliché "one man's terrorist is another man's freedom fighter." This slogan challenges the first view by denying that there is a distinctive class of terrorist acts. Rather, it says, people call violent acts that they approve of "freedom fighting" and those that they condemn "terrorism." According to this view, there is no distinctive set or category of terrorist acts. Instead, the designation is subjective. The same actions will be labeled as terrorist acts by some people and not by others.

These two views share the assumption that *terrorism* is a negative term. The first view explicitly labels terrorism as vile and immoral. The second notes the selective way in which people apply the term *terrorist* only to acts that they disapprove of. Both views, then, see the term as negative.

Before trying to define terrorism, it will be useful to consider why both of these views are flawed.

"One Man's Terrorist . . ."

The most evident feature of the cliché "One man's terrorist is another man's freedom fighter" is that the very same actions can count as terrorism or freedom fighting. If we focus only on the relativity of this view, however, we miss another crucial feature—the positive connotations of the expression *freedom fighting*. An important feature of this designation is that it specifies a goal of the actions in question—the goal of freedom. Since freedom is a lofty, valued goal, the actions in question are raised in value by attributing to them the attainment of this goal. What looks like a purely relativist view depends in part on the plausibility of attributing objective value to freedom.

The slogan suggests that if people are freedom fighters, then their activities are justifiable. This reasoning, however, is flawed because it assumes that one can justify an act simply by citing the goal that it is supposed to achieve. Actions, however, can be morally wrong even if their goals are lofty and valuable. It is a central part of commonsense morality that the end does not always justify the means. There are morally illegitimate ways of trying to achieve valuable goals.

This same point is reflected in just-war theory, which contains two sets of criteria: one for determining the *jus ad bellum* (the justice of entering into a war) and a second set for determining the *jus in bello* (the justice of the means one uses in fighting). The *jus ad bellum* criteria focus in part on the goals of war. Aggression for territorial gain, for example, is ruled out as illegitimate, while the defense of one's own territory against attack counts as a "just cause."

The *jus in bello* criteria remind us that we must attend not only to goals but also to the means that we use to attain them. Even if one meets the just-war criteria for entering into a war, actions taken in the war can still be immoral. For example, a country that is fighting in self-defense may still act wrongly if it commits atrocities in the course of defending itself.

For these reasons, if we want to evaluate an action, it is not enough to know that it has been performed in pursuit of the goal of freedom. One can pursue freedom and still act wrongly. The "one man's terrorist . . ." slogan assumes that *terrorist* and *freedom fighter* are mutually exclusive, but people can be both. A person can strive for the legitimate goal of freedom while using means that qualify as terrorist tactics.

Virtually all of the plausible definitions of terrorism focus on means—i.e., actions taken—and not just on goals. Typical definitions of a terrorist action require that it be deliberate, violent, and harmful to innocent people. In addition, definitions often include the idea that terrorist actions have two targets: the people directly harmed and some broader audience or set of officials whom the terrorists are trying to influence (Khatchadourian 1998, 6).

While some freedom fighters use the kinds of means associated with terrorism, others avoid them. Mahatma Gandhi, for example, abstained not only from terrorist actions in his pursuit of Indian independence but from *all* acts of violence. The minutemen of the American Revolution fought directly against the British army. The means used by freedom fighters vary considerably, and whether a freedom fighter is a terrorist or not depends on these means.

The slogan "one man's terrorist . . ." rests on two distinct mistakes. First, it assumes that an individual or group cannot be both terrorist and freedom fighter. Second, it assumes that whether someone is a terrorist depends on that person's *goals*, whereas terrorism involves the *means* employed by a person or group. Both of these errors must be avoided if we are to reach an adequate definition of terrorism.

The Special Immorality of Terrorism

What about the essentialist view that terrorist acts are a distinctive class of acts that are especially heinous? This view is partly correct, but it oversimplifies important issues and thus encourages errors of both classification and morality. It encourages errors of classification by denying that the concept of terrorism is complex and unclear. It encourages distorted moral judgments as well. We need to remember that, as terrible as terrorism is, many nonterrorist actions are equally or more vile. If we forget this fact, we can lose our moral bearings and let the evil nature of terrorism blind us to the possible evils of counterterrorist responses.

A typical feature of terrorist acts is that they target some people in order to influence others. Hostages are taken, for example, in order to force officials to release prisoners. An airplane is bombed in order to convey to a larger audience the views, needs, or rights of a group that feels oppressed. Some citizens are killed in order to express hatred toward their country or its politics. Such acts use violence against a limited number of people to frighten or change the behavior of other people, who may be a large group or government officials.

To put the wrongness of terrorism in perspective, imagine a case in which attackers kill random members of a particular group in order to terrorize the whole group and cause them to depart from a particular area. In this case, terrorist attacks would be an instrument of ethnic cleansing, a way to expel a group from a territory. These acts are a form of terrorism according to most definitions and are surely worthy of moral condemnation.

Imagine a second case in which ethnic cleansing is achieved by massacring all the members of a group. In this case, the communicative aspect of terrorism—its tactic of harming some in order to send a message to others— would be lacking. There is no attempt to harm a small group in order to influence the decisions of others. Instead, the whole group is attacked directly, and the territory is emptied simply by killing them all. By most definitions, this would not be an act of terrorism, but it would certainly be a great evil and would be condemned by most people as worse than terrorism. After all, horrible as it is, the terrorist strategy described above kills a smaller number of people and at least allows others the option to flee and build a new life elsewhere. It is less destructive than outright massacre.

Or consider a case of nuclear retaliation that is aimed at enemy military installations; because of the proximity of some cities to military installations, this response might cause millions of civilian victims. Surely the magnitude of damage and the horror of the results of such an attack would be much greater than that of all the terrorist acts that have yet occurred. The fact that such an attack would not constitute terrorism per se does not mean that it would be less dreadful than terrorist acts or less important to prevent.

My point is not to put terrorism in a favorable light. Rather, it is to remind us that terrorist actions are not the only terrible deeds; nor are they necessarily the worst. This is important to keep in mind as people formulate strategies to combat terrorism. Those who seek to prevent terrorism can fall into a trap like the one we saw in the terrorist/freedom fighter issue. If terrorism is a genuine evil, then the goal of combating terrorism is a worthwhile goal. But it does not follow that any and all means of combating terrorism are morally permissible. If we take the just-war theory's *in bello* criteria seriously, we will want to make sure that our means of combating terrorism do not create an amount of harm disproportionate to the good we aim to achieve and that they follow the principle of discrimination, which requires that we aim to avoid harm to innocent civilians.

Biased Definitions

As the discussion so far makes clear, the attempt to define *terrorism* leads to a mix of contentious issues, both moral and classificatory. We can approach these issues through some remarks made by Conor Cruise O'Brien, who skillfully formulates a view that might be held by defenders of terrorism.

> Those who are described as terrorists, and who reject the title for themselves, make the uncomfortable point that national armed forces, fully supported by democratic opinion, have in fact employed violence and terror on a far vaster scale than what liberation movements have as yet been able to attain. The "freedom fighters" see themselves as fighting a just war. Why should they not be entitled to kill, burn and destroy as national armies, navies and air forces do, and why should the label "terrorist" be applied to them and not the national militaries? (Quoted in Kegley 1990, 12–13)

The passage expresses frustration that governments can get away with destructive activities while nongovernmental groups are labeled as terrorists and condemned for the very same kinds of actions. If governments can be justified in using force and violence, then so can nongovernmental groups.

O'Brien presents this argument in a forceful and appealing way. But what does the argument actually show? The intended conclusion appears to be that nongovernmental fighters have a right to commit terrorist actions because the same actions are carried out with impunity by governmental forces. As an argument for this view, it fails. At most, it shows that liberation movements are *as entitled* to commit terrorist acts as governmental armies are. This conclusion, however, is compatible with the view that no one, neither governmental armies nor liberation movements, has a right to commit terrorist acts. If the aim was to show that terrorist actions are permissible for "freedom fighters," this has not been shown at all. Instead, what the argument shows is the hypocrisy of those who condone terrorist acts when they are committed by government officials but condemn them when done by others.

The important lesson of this passage is that terrorism must not be defined in such a way that only some people can be guilty of it. A definition must be unbiased and sufficiently general so that actions exhibiting the features of terrorism will be labeled in that way—no matter who commits them.

The following definition from the U.S. Criminal Code would be ruled out by this point: "The term 'terrorism' means premeditated, politically motivated violence perpetrated against non-combatant targets by subnational groups or clandestine agents, usually intended to influence an audience" (Greenway 2001). According to this definition, the same actions done by *national* rather than *subnational* groups belong to different categories, and the negative term *terrorism* would never apply to actions done by governments. While it is understandable that such a definition might be part of a legal policy, it cannot be accepted for purposes of a political or moral inquiry.

Defining Terrorism

All definitions of complex concepts involve some element of stipulation. Since ordinary language is a hodgepodge, any definition that clarifies matters must conflict in some ways with ordinary language. The best argument for any particular definition is that it is helpful, that it clarifies issues in ways that promote understanding. Moreover, it may be that different definitions are useful in different contexts. A legal or military perspective may require a different definition from a political or moral inquiry.

The problem with the essentialist view about terrorism as a distinct category is that it ignores these messy facts about the definitional process. According to this view, terrorist acts constitute a ready-made set of actions that we merely recognize. This Platonistic approach will be frustrated by multiple definitions and by the fact that even adequate definitions of phenomena like terrorism will have blurry edges. A more Wittgensteinian view of meaning is helpful here: there are paradigmatic cases of terrorism and other cases that resemble terrorism in some ways but not in others.[1]

With these methodological thoughts as background, I offer the following definition of terrorist acts:

1. They are acts of serious, deliberate violence or destruction.
2. They are committed as part of a campaign to promote a political or social agenda.
3. They generally target limited numbers of people but aim to influence a larger group and/or the leaders who make decisions for the group.
4. They either kill or injure innocent people or pose a serious threat of such harms to innocent people.

The most obvious point about this definition is that it has a number of distinct parts, each of which highlights an important feature. The parts of this definition specify (a) the general type of action (violent), (b) the goals or motivation of the action (promoting a political/social agenda), (c) the strategy behind the action (harming some people to influence others), and (d) the victims of the action (innocent people).

How well does this definition fit with our common understanding? And how well does it satisfy the needs that I identified in my preliminary discussion? Does it avoid the pitfalls of subjectivism and bias? Could it be accepted by people with different political and moral aims?

Let us look at each part and consider how well the definition does.

1. *They are acts of serious, deliberate violence or destruction.* This seems quite uncontroversial. Though there are debates about the definition of violence, there is no doubt that typical cases of terrorism are violent, since they involve deliberate injury and death to people. Virtually no one would think there could be acts of nonviolent terrorism.

2. *They are committed as part of a campaign to promote a political or social agenda.* Terrorist acts are meant to advance a political or social agenda. In some cases, terrorists make political demands and threaten more violence if the demands are not met. Or they engage in violence to publicize their

cause. In other cases, they may act out of revenge—not so much to make others accede to their demands as to make others suffer because the terrorists and their own group have suffered. They may have multiple goals.

Igor Primoratz (1990, 134) has argued that while terrorism aims to get people to act as they otherwise would not, the goals need not be political. They can be social, religious, or criminal. My own sense is that the lack of some kind of social or political agenda moves a case away from the paradigm. People who engage in terrorist-like violence simply for personal gain are generally seen to belong to a different class of attackers. Kidnappers or extortionists, for example, threaten violence, but they seek to make a profit for themselves and have no interest in social or political change. Of course, if they imitate the methods of paradigmatic terrorists, then they will resemble them in important ways, and we may be tempted to lump them together with terrorists. This is one way in which the lines can become blurred in identifying terrorists.

A similar point can be made about terrorist-like actions that have no purpose. Walter Sinnott-Armstrong (1991, 118) offers the hypothetical case of Nancy, who "bombs buses simply in order to terrify people." She is a destructive individual who mimics terrorists in her methods, but her actions are a matter of individual pathology or criminality and thus they differ from paradigmatic cases of terrorism. Nonetheless, if terrorist acts stimulate copycat crimes by people who have no further purposes, we might feel that we were being threatened by a new kind of terrorism. So, while I would deny the "terrorist" label to Nancy, I think that we can imagine broadening our concept to include her. If we do this, however, we will need to draw other lines that help us distinguish different types of terrorism.

3. *They generally target limited numbers of people but aim to influence a larger group and/or the leaders who make decisions for the group.* In typical cases, terrorists commit relatively small-scale violence against members of a larger group that they want to influence. They count on publicity and the tendency of people to identify with victims who are like themselves in order to magnify the effects of the attacks and create a climate of fear. These features of terrorism often result from the terrorist's lack of access to weapons that states would possess. Terrorism is sometimes called the poor man's version of war. Individuals or groups who can't engage in large-scale violence carry out small-scale violence in ways that magnify its effects.

Access to powerful weapons, however, is increasing, and more terrorists may be able to acquire more potent weapons. The 9/11 attackers certainly upped the ante in death and destruction by using large passenger airplanes as explosive missiles and hitting targets that were themselves large and heavily populated. As terrorists acquire more powerful weapons, their attacks will look more like traditional acts of war.[2] The Al Qaeda bombings of embassies in Nairobi and Dar es Salaam were coordinated in the manner of a military attack. As the methods of terrorists increase in scale and destructiveness, the distinction between terrorism and traditional warfare begins to blur. After all, even in war, the aim is usually not to destroy the enemy entirely. Rather, the aim is to inflict enough damage to convince an enemy that it should surrender or otherwise comply with the opponent's demands. Warfare, like terrorism, often has both a target and an audience. Sometimes acts of war are meant *directly* to destroy people or weapons that are a threat; however, in the larger scheme of things, each act of destruction is also supposed to convince the opponent that surrender would be better than continued fighting.

Here again, we see the problem for essentialists, who view terrorism as a strictly demarcated category of action. While the communicative aspect of terrorism is cited to distinguish it from traditional war, various pressures lessen this distinctiveness. First, conventional war often has a communicative aspect, too. Second, terrorism that uses more potent weapons ceases to be "purely" communicative violence and starts to look more like the destructiveness of conventional warfare—that is, its purpose is simply to destroy objects or people. Given this fact, it is not surprising that the 9/11 attacks have been seen as acts of war, even though they were not carried out by governments.

4. *They either kill or injure innocent people or pose a serious threat of such harms to innocent people.* The key point here is that in paradigmatic cases, the victims of terrorist acts are innocent people. Terrorists do not strike members of an army in conditions of combat. Rather, they attack ordinary people riding on a bus, shopping in a store, or going to work. Why is this? Part of the answer derives from the idea of terrorism as poor man's warfare. Civilian targets are both plentiful and vulnerable. It is easier to harm them than it is to harm well-protected members of the military. Sometimes, these reasons make civilian targets attractive to national military planners as well. In World War II, military planners took advantage of the fact that it was eas-

ier to bomb a city than it was to bomb a particular factory or military facility within a city.

Condition 4 focuses on the fact that the victims of terrorist attacks are innocent people, but it is ambiguous because key terms can be understood in different ways. The issues raised by these different interpretations are complex and contentious. The first issue is whether the civilian victims must be intentionally targeted or whether indiscriminate attacks that kill innocent people unintentionally can count as terrorism. The second is how we should understand *innocence* in this context. What is it that distinguishes people who are innocent from those who are not? I will address the second question first.

WHO ARE THE INNOCENT?

Deciding who is innocent is a complex, much discussed issue, and several distinct views exist. People with different definitions of innocence can accept the definition of terrorism that I have proposed and yet apply it differently because they interpret the innocence condition differently.

One plausible view is proposed by Haig Khatchadourian, who interprets innocence as moral innocence. After noting that innocence can be a matter of degree, he defines a "perfectly innocent person" as one who "has no share in the moral responsibility . . . [and] no causal responsibility at all, for any wrong, if any, that gives rise to" the terrorist act (Khatchadourian 1988, 135). According to this view, a high degree of moral or causal responsibility for the legitimate grievances of the attackers is required if a person is to be a legitimate target of an attack. If this condition is satisfied, then the attack is not a terrorist attack. If a government official who initiates policies that severely violate people's rights is attacked by people protesting these policies, this act would not be considered terrorism because the official is not morally innocent. (This is not to say that such acts are necessarily justified morally; it is only to say that they would not be instances of terrorism.)

Terrorists who attack innocent people may define guilt in such a way that large classes of people are automatically guilty, independent of their actions. As Khatchadourian (1998, 135) notes, "Terrorists, driven by passion or paranoia, often baselessly enlarge, sometimes to a tragically absurd extent, the circle of alleged non-innocents."[3]

While Khatchadourian's point about baseless attributions of guilt and responsibility is certainly plausible, those who make these "baseless" judgments might well disagree about the innocence of those they attack. The moral conception of innocence invites this sort of disagreement. For this reason, one might look for a more neutral, objective way of defining innocence.

One such morally neutral strategy is proposed by Igor Primoratz, who suggests that we distinguish terrorism from political assassination by accepting the attacker's own perspective on guilt and innocence. While an assassin might hold his or her victims responsible for evil policies, genuine terrorists recognize that their victims have no responsibility for the evils they oppose. If we accept the attacker's own criteria of innocence and responsibility, then we can avoid getting bogged down in debates about who is truly innocent (Primoratz 1990, 131).

Notice that Primoratz is not saying that if an attacker believes the victim to be responsible for evil, then the attack is morally justified. Rather, he is addressing the question of how to classify actions as terrorist or not. If attackers, by their own criteria, recognize the innocence of their victims, then their acts are genuinely terrorist actions; if they hold their victims responsible, their acts are not terrorist.

While Primoratz's conception of innocence avoids the disagreements that Khatchadourian's moral conception invites, it has a more serious defect. The attackers themselves may believe that even people with the most tenuous connection to the policies or institutions opposed by the attackers are not innocent. Indeed, membership in an ethnic, religious, or political group by itself may be sufficient for the terrorist, even though the people attacked have no control over the policies that the attackers find hateful.

The reduction to absurdity of Primoratz's conception of innocence is a case of terrorists who deny that anyone is innocent. His perspective forces us to accept this conclusion. But if no one is innocent, then a central difference between terrorism and other forms of violence is effectively eliminated. Primoratz's view is defective because it gives authoritative status to the attackers' views. As a result, it opens up the possibility that the distinction between guilt and innocence will be completely obliterated.

A third strategy is to define innocence more legalistically in terms of people's role or status. This approach derives from the just-war tradition and standards of international law. In these contexts, the innocent are people who are noncombatants, while members of the military and certain public officials are seen as legitimate targets. Although Khatchadourian's moral criterion requires complex judgments, status-based conceptions are simpler and more objective. A particular soldier may not be morally or causally responsible for whatever the attackers oppose, but by wearing uniforms and serving in the military, soldiers forfeit the immunity that civilian, noncombatants enjoy.[4]

Drawing on this status-based conception, I offer the following criteria for those who are to be counted as innocent. People are to be considered innocent (in this context) if

1. they are not public officials or members of the military;
2. they are not responsible for the situation that the terrorists are protesting or seeking to change;
3. they lack the power to respond to terrorist demands or goals.

Of course, there may be terrorists who reject these criteria, but they are put forward as criteria that everyone should recognize. This is the perspective of international law, which draws such distinctions and declares the obligation of all to alter their tactics so as to avoid harming those who qualify as innocent in this sense.[5]

In my view, this third, status-based conception of innocence is best, though each definition has both its virtues and its problems. Whichever view one takes, I believe that people who emphasize the importance of civilian victims in defining terrorism are correct. While all war is dreadful in its destructiveness, there is something particularly repugnant about terrorism, and such repugnance is responsible for the plausibility of claims about the special immorality of terrorist acts (Primoratz 1990, 129). We can recognize this fact, even if we disagree about just how to define the concept of innocence in this context.

INTENTIONAL VERSUS INDISCRIMINATE ATTACKS

Condition 4 of my definition says that terrorist acts kill or injure innocent people or expose them to death and injury, but it is ambiguous about the question of intent. In paradigmatic cases of terrorism, innocent people are explicitly targeted as the attacks' victims. By contrast, many acts of war have innocent victims who are not intentionally targeted. Rather, their deaths and injuries are by-products of attacks on other people or objects.

The traditional just-war theory includes a principle of discrimination that is meant to rule out innocent people as legitimate targets of attack. At the same time, however, it makes a major concession to military realities, permitting deaths and injuries that are not intended, even when they are foreseen. The victims of such attacks—the so-called collateral damage—are as dead as the victims of terrorist attacks, but it is considered significant that their deaths are not desired or intended. Terrorists are thought to be especially dreadful because they seek civilian deaths, while others who kill civilians do so unintentionally.

This distinction creates further conceptual blurring because some actions that we are inclined to regard as terrorist acts are very like cases of collateral damage. Consider an example used by Tony Dardis to criticize Primoratz's definition of terrorism. Primoratz claims that terrorists know how to distinguish people who are legitimate targets from those who are not and that they deliberately attack innocent citizens. Dardis denies that terrorists are discriminating in this way. He thinks that terrorists are indifferent to whether people are innocent. He offers the example of a person who plants a bomb in the car of a police officer, knowing that it is possible that the officer's spouse and children may be injured or killed by the blast (Dardis 1992, 97). He sees this as a clear case of a terrorist act, even though the innocent people are not directly targeted. While Primoratz believes that terrorists are perversely discriminating, Dardis claims that they are indiscriminate. The contrast is between a person who ignores the principle of discrimination and one who observes it but does so in an upside-down manner.

Dardis's case has some persuasive force. Isn't the key characteristic of terrorists that they don't care whether they kill innocent people? If they are targeting others but show a callous disregard for civilians, isn't this enough to make them terrorists?

How we react to Dardis's example has implications for what we say about certain acts of war. For example, if we are sympathetic to his view and equate the indiscriminate car bomber with terrorists, then we might consider the use of weapons such as cluster bombs and land mines as forms of terrorism because these weapons are indiscriminate. The country that uses cluster bombs—as the United States has done in Afghanistan, for example—chooses to disperse a large number of "bomblets" over an area, knowing that a fair number of them will not detonate immediately and will pose a threat to people long after a particular battle or attack is over. Who will be injured or killed by the bomblets is completely unknown. The same is true of land mines (Human Rights Watch).

→ A similar point can be made about high altitude bombing of military targets. If the targets are near civilian areas, there can be a significant probability that civilians will be killed by the attacks. Bombing from lower altitudes might allow for greater precision and hence would be more discriminating, but low altitude attacks expose pilots and their aircraft to increased danger.

According to Primoratz, these military strategies would not count as terrorism because they do not intentionally target civilians. But Dardis's view suggests that these military strategies could qualify as terrorist acts if they met other conditions.

There are several possible views about this issue. First, one might claim that the difference between intentional targeting, on the one hand, and unintentional but foreseeable injury and death, on the other, separates terrorism from other acts of war and violence. As bad as indiscriminate weapons and tactics may be, intentional killing of civilians is definitive of terrorism. Second, one might say that cases like Dardis's car bomber show that the difference between intentional targeting and indiscriminate attacks is unimportant; both are cases of terrorism. Third, one could argue that the car bomber and similar examples are borderline cases that indicate the blurry edges of the concept of terrorism. If so, in this and other cases, there may be no definitive answer to the question whether a particular act is a terrorist act.

A fourth view is that it does not matter whether we call the car bombing a terrorist act. What is clear is that the car bomber is indifferent to innocent people, that he is prepared to see them die whether or not they are his targets, and hence that he is as morally culpable as a terrorist, whether or not we call his action an instance of terrorism. According to this view, we can answer whatever moral questions we have about this act independent of answering questions about how to label or classify it.

Do Definitions Matter?

Where has this inquiry gotten us? Do we know anything now that we did not know before? Have we answered the question "Can terrorism be morally justified?" The answer to the last question is "no," but my hope is that we are closer to knowing what we are asking when we inquire about terrorism's moral justification. We are asking: can an act that has the following features be morally justified?

1. They are acts of serious, deliberate violence or destruction.
2. They are committed as part of a campaign to promote a political or social agenda.
3. They generally target limited numbers of people but aim to influence a larger group and/or the leaders who make decisions for the group.
4. They either kill or injure innocent people or pose a serious threat of such harms to innocent people.

Indeed, our initial question is even clearer because the central moral issue involves condition 4—the killing and injuring of innocent people. If terrorism consisted only of the first three conditions, which are sometimes morally permissible, it could sometimes be justified.

The sticking point is condition 4, and this is entirely appropriate. The killing of the innocent is what makes terrorism repugnant to most people. And yet, the killing of the innocent cannot be invoked to show that terrorism is absolutely wrong because acts of war that many people accept as morally permissible often involve killing innocent people.

Here, then, is the central moral puzzle. If we condemn all terrorist acts because they involve the killing of the innocent, then we appear to accept the killing of innocent people as a sufficient condition of moral wrongfulness. But if we approve other actions that involve the killing of the innocent, then we cannot say that this form of killing is sufficient to make an action wrong. Further, if there are conditions that make the killing of innocent people morally permissible, then we may find that some acts of terrorism satisfy these conditions.

I noted at the beginning of this essay that it is easy to condemn terrorism but hard to devise a consistent, nonhypocritical way to judge it. In looking for a definition, I hope to have shown that the crucial moral question concerns the killing of the innocent and that the challenge is to find a consistent, nonhypocritical answer to this central problem.

If a blanket condemnation of terrorism is to be sustained, then one must either condemn all killings of innocent people or find a morally relevant difference between the killing of innocents by terrorists and the killing of innocents by others whose actions one finds morally acceptable. In what follows, I will consider several discussions of these difficult issues in order to see if a morally consistent position can be developed.

Primoratz on the Morality of Terrorism

Igor Primoratz argues that terrorism is never morally justified because (a) it always involves the intentional killing of innocent people, by definition, and (b) the intentional killing of innocent people is always wrong. He also defends the subsidiary thesis that moral consequentialism is false because, in principle, it could permit terrorism. By consequentialism, he means the view that the rightness of actions depends only on their results; actions are right if the results of performing them are better than the results of not performing them.[6] As Primoratz (1997, 222) notes, consequentialism has the following implication regarding the morality of terrorism: "When its consequences are good enough, terrorism, just like everything else, is given moral consecration."[7] In his view, any moral theory or principle that could "consecrate" terrorism must be false.

Primoratz offers a number of nonconsequentialist arguments against the morality of terrorism. The first two involve the nature of persons as moral agents and the high level of respect that is due to them. He writes: "Every human being is an individual, a person separate from other persons, with a unique, irreproducible thread of life and a value that is not commensurable with anything else" (Primoratz 1997, 224). Given the incommensurable value of individual persons, it is wrong to try to calculate the worth of their separate lives to determine if they can be destroyed in order to promote some greater good. This kind of political arithmetic violates the ideal of giving individual lives our utmost respect and concern. The emphasis of Immanuel Kant (1981, 36) on treating people as ends in themselves and not as means is the most famous philosophical expression of this ideal. Terrorists violate this central moral ideal. They treat innocent people as political pawns, giving no consideration to their individual worth but only seeing their deaths as useful to a cause.

In addition, Primoratz argues, terrorists ignore the moral relevance of guilt and innocence in their treatment of individuals. They attack not only those who are responsible for the alleged evils done to their own group or cause. They also attack people who have no causal or moral responsibility for these alleged evils; terrorists thus violate the principle that people should be treated in accord with what they deserve.

Terrorists, Primoratz tells us, also forsake ideals of moral dialogue and moral equality. They not only decide who will live and who will die, but also feel no burden to justify their actions in ways that the victims might understand and accept. Here he invokes a moral ideal of open discussion and publicity, subjecting one's views to moral debate with others. And, most powerfully, he invokes the point that harmful acts should be justifiable to the victims themselves.[8]

Though these ideas are sketched out rather than fully developed, Primoratz successfully articulates some important moral values. Drawing on these values, he concludes that terrorism is incompatible with "some of the most basic moral beliefs many of us hold" (1997, 225).

PRIMORATZ VERSUS TROTSKY

In order to further develop his argument, Primoratz describes and criticizes Leon Trotsky's defense of terrorism as a tactic of revolution. Trotsky argues that those who approve traditional warfare but condemn revolutionary violence are in a weak position because the differences between these actions are morally arbitrary. If wars that kill innocent people can be justified, then so can revolutions that kill innocent people.

Primoratz's replies to Trotsky are especially interesting because he wants to denounce all terrorism but not condemn all war, even though innocent people are killed in both. Primoratz (1997, 227) writes: "The suffering of civilians . . . is surely inevitable not only in modern, but in almost all wars. . . . But we must attend not only to the suffering inflicted, but also to the way it is inflicted."

To illustrate his point, he contrasts two imagined artillery attacks on a village. In one such attack, the intention is to kill the civilian inhabitants of the village. In a second case, the civilian deaths are foreseen but not intended. The artillery gunners' intention is not to kill civilians but "to attack enemy soldiers stationed in the village." Primoratz (1997, 227) adds: "Had it been possible to attack the enemy unit without endangering the civilians in any way, they would certainly have done so. This was not possible, so they attacked although they knew that the attack would cause civilian casualties too; but they did their best to reduce those inevitable, but undesired consequences as much as possible."

This is a case, then, of civilian deaths and injuries as collateral damage. Primoratz contrasts it with the first case in order to show that justified war fighting differs from terrorism in that terrorists intentionally kill the innocent, while justified war fighting does so only unintentionally. He also appeals to the principle of proportionality, which permits the destruction caused by military attacks only when the good achieved by them outweighs the evils they cause. Applying this principle to his hypothetical case of the artillery attack on the village, he notes that "military need . . . may have been so strong and urgent that it prevailed over the prohibition of killing or maiming a comparatively small number of civilians" (Primoratz 1997, 227).

Primoratz's conclusion is that Trotsky is wrong in arguing for the moral equivalence between war and terrorism. If those who fight wars avoid the intentional killing of civilians, then their actions can be morally justified, even when civilians die as a result of what they do. The key distinction lies in the intention. As long as soldiers and revolutionaries avoid the intentional killing of innocent people, they will not be guilty of terrorist acts.

PROBLEMS WITH PRIMORATZ'S VIEW

Primoratz's view has a number of attractive features. His condemnation of terrorism appears to be principled and firm, unlike consequentialist arguments, which can go either way depending on the circumstances. In addition, his view fits in with the widespread desire to allow for justified wars but to rule out terrorism as always being morally beyond the pale. Nonetheless, it has serious weaknesses.

First, by stressing the role of intentions, Primoratz appeals to the same beliefs that underlie the principle of double effect, which tells us that we should evaluate actions by their intended goals and not by their actual consequences. But this principle, while plausible in some cases, is defective. If the 9/11 attackers had intended only to destroy the Pentagon and the World Trade Center and had no desire to kill anyone, we would not think them less culpable. It would not be sufficient for them to say that they had intended only to destroy buildings and that, although they foresaw the deaths of people, these deaths were not part of their aim. On a smaller scale, the principle of double effect would not allow us to condemn the person who plants a bomb in the car of a police officer and unintentionally kills the officer's spouse and children (Dardis 1992, 97).

There are additional problems with Primoratz's attempt to differentiate morally permissible acts of war from impermissible acts of terrorism. In his example, the artillery gunners attack the village with full knowledge of the high probability of civilian deaths. It does seem morally relevant that they would rather not do this and that they might regret it afterward. Nonetheless,

Primoratz's approval of this attack does not square with the central values invoked in his discussion. Recall his statements about the incalculable value of individual lives and the moral demand that we respect individuals as ends, not means. Recall further his denunciation of those who engage in consequentialist calculations about the effects of killing versus not killing. Can his defense of collateral damage killings be made consistent with the ideals that he so strongly affirms? Is the killing of innocent people justified by the fact that the people who are responsible for these deaths would rather not kill their victims?

Consider Primoratz's claim that actions need to be justifiable to the victims themselves. He claims that the military need was "so strong and urgent that it prevailed over the prohibition of killing or maiming a comparatively small number of civilians" (Primoratz 1997, 227). Would the victims of the artillery attack accept the sacrifice of their own lives on the basis of this reasoning? Why should they?

Notice, as well, that in spite of the powerful denunciations of consequentialism by Primoratz, this crucial point in his argument is essentially an appeal to consequences. When he tries to justify collateral damage killings, he writes that the military need was "strong and urgent," which presumably means that the consequences of not destroying the military forces in the village would have been negative. When he says that only a "comparatively small number of civilians" would be killed or injured, he presumably means that the losses are not so numerous. His claim implies that the attack would have been wrong if the number of civilian deaths had been larger.

Unfortunately, this judgment requires the kind of calculation that he himself denounces so fervently: "It is precisely these calculations, in which human beings figure as units to be added and subtracted, that many find morally inappropriate and indeed offensive. Many will want to say, with Arthur Koestler's Rubashov, that 'twice two are not four when the mathematical units are human beings'" (Primoratz 1997, 224). Primoratz's own argument and his use of the principle of proportionality fit this description precisely and thus qualify as "morally inappropriate and indeed offensive" by his own criteria.

Suppose we accept his defense of collateral damage killings and reject his earlier claims as overstated. Then his argument against terrorism collapses because terrorists can use Primoratz's language to show that their actions may also be justifiable. If he succeeds in justifying collateral damage killings and if the distinction between these killings and terrorism cannot rest solely on whether the killings are intentional, then the criteria that he uses may be used to justify at least some terrorist acts. For example, suppose that terrorists could show that they have a "just cause" and that a particular attack on innocent people arose from a need that was "so strong and urgent that it prevailed over the prohibition of killing or maiming a comparatively small number of civilians." Consistency would require Primoratz to agree that the terrorist act was justified in this case. The only way to avoid this result would be to reject the criteria he uses to defend collateral damage killings.

In the end, then, Primoratz does not succeed in showing that terrorism is always immoral, while collateral damage killing can sometimes be morally justified.

Next Steps

One way to proceed at this point would be to try to repair Primoratz's view. I want to proceed in a different way, however. Because some acts of warfare that involve the intentional killing of innocents are widely regarded as justified, I want to see whether some defense can be given for the intentional killing of innocent people in wartime and what the implications of such a judgment might be for the moral evaluation of terrorism.

The Bombing of Cities in World War II

During World War II, Germany, Britain, and the United States all engaged in aerial bombardment of cities. While some bombings by the Allies were directed at military or industrial targets, the main targets were cities themselves and their inhabitants. If these attacks can be morally justified, then the killing of innocent civilians is sometimes morally permissible, even when it is specifically intended.

If these intentional killings of civilians were justified, then presumably a case can be made in defense of the unintended, collateral damage killings that I have been discussing. In addition, if they can be justified, we will have to consider whether they can be differentiated from the targeting of innocent people by terrorists. If not, we may have to accept that some terrorist actions might be morally justifiable.

I will now examine two works by authors who defend (some instances of) city bombing and who condemn terrorism: Michael Walzer's well-known book *Just and Unjust Wars* (1977) and Gerry Wallace's challenging essay "Terrorism and the Argument from Analogy" (1991, 149–60).

One of the central aims in Walzer's book is the articulation and defense of what he calls the "war convention," the set of principles that prohibits attacks on civilians. Stating his own version of the principle of discrimination, he writes: "A legitimate act of war is one that does not violate the rights of the people against whom it is directed. . . . no one can be threatened with war or warred against, unless through some act of his own he has surrendered or lost his rights. This fundamental principle underlies and shapes the judgments we make of wartime conduct" (Walzer 1977, 135).

Given Walzer's commitment to the war convention and his definition of terrorism as the "method of random murder of innocent people" for the purpose of destroying the morale of a nation or class, it is no surprise that he condemns terrorism. At one point, after describing a terrorist attack on an Algerian milk bar frequented by teenagers, he writes: "Certainly, there are historical moments when armed struggle is necessary for the sake of human freedom. But if dignity and self-respect are to be the outcomes of that struggle, it cannot consist of terrorist attacks against children" (Walzer 1977, 197, 205). Here and elsewhere, his denunciations of terrorism are strong and deeply felt (Walzer 1988, 237–47).

Nonetheless, when he discusses the aerial attacks on civilians by the British early in World War II, he claims that these attacks were justified, and he develops the concept of a "supreme emergency" to show why. Walzer (1977, 253) uses this concept to describe both the extremity of the threat that the British faced and its imminence. Nazism was no ordinary enemy; it was an "ultimate threat to everything decent in our lives." Moreover, in 1940 German armies dominated Europe and threatened to control the seas. Britain feared an invasion by a country that threatened both itself and the basic values of civilization. The only means that Britain possessed for inflicting damage on Germany was its air force.

According to Walzer, the combination of the enormity of the threat and its imminence produced a situation in which the war convention no longer held. In this extreme circumstance and in the absence of other means of defense, the prohibition against killing innocent people was lifted. If killing innocents served to ward off this dreadful threat, then it was permissible.

Walzer does not approve of all the city bombing that occurred in World War II. He approves only of what occurred while the emergency lasted. By late 1942 the threat of an invasion had diminished; the United States had entered the war; the Russians had weakened the Germans on the eastern front. In short, the threat was no longer imminent, and the constraints of the war convention should have been honored once again. But they were not. Most of the city bombing occurred after 1942, climaxing in the bombing of Dresden, the fire bombings of Japanese cities, and the atomic bombings of Hiroshima and Nagasaki. According to Walzer, none of these were justified by the supreme emergency rule.

In spite of this restriction, Walzer greatly enlarges the reach of the supreme emergency criterion, claiming that it applies not only to threats against all civilized values but also to threats against a particular nation. He asks: "Can a supreme emergency be constituted by . . . a threat of enslavement or extermination directed against a single nation? Can soldiers and statesmen override the rights of innocent people for the sake of their own political community?" (Walzer 1977, 254). And his reply is "I am inclined to answer this question affirmatively, though not without hesitation and worry." Walzer defends this extension of the supreme emergency concept to more limited threats by appealing to the role-based duties of a country's soldiers and statesmen. Even if they were willing to sacrifice themselves in the name of morality, they "cannot sacrifice their countrymen," who, Walzer assumes, are counting on them to defend the nation's interests.

The trouble with this position is that the relatively rare circumstance discussed with respect to Nazism appears to have expanded to encompass a somewhat common occurrence—the situation of nations threatened by others and faced with serious losses of life and liberty. Any such situation is sure to appear urgent to national leaders. Moreover, leaders are unlikely to wait until defeat is imminent and unlikely to stop attacks on civilians until victory is assured. The experience of World War II shows that it is difficult to reinstate constraints once they have been violated (Brown 1983, 6–15; Coady 2002, 17–20).

Given Walzer's argument for the justifiability of breaching the war convention, the question that needs to be asked is whether his argument also shows that terrorism might be justifiable. In spite of his own denunciation of terrorism, his discussion suggests that the answer is yes. Walzer (1977, 257) uses the expression "terror bombing" and in places refers to the Allied bombing campaign as "terrorism." Nonetheless, because Walzer never connects this part of his discussion with his earlier condemnation of terrorism, his position is ambiguous. Terrorism is unconditionally condemned, yet what appears to be its moral equivalent is conditionally approved.

Wallace's Argument from Analogy

The connection between the defense of city bombing and the defense of terrorism is addressed directly by Gerry Wallace in "Terrorism and the Argument from Analogy." Wallace believes that the World War II city bombing was morally justified, and he clearly articulates the reasons for this, writing that the bombing campaign was justified by the conjunction of four factors: "(1) It was a measure of last resort. . . . (2) It was an act of collective self-defense. (3) It was a reply in kind against a genocidal, racist aggressor. (4) It had some chance of success" (Wallace 1991, 155).

He then turns to ask whether terrorism "can mirror these features" so that acts of terrorism might be justified in a similar way. He imagines a defender of terrorism who draws an analogy between terrorism and city bombing: "The apologist [for terrorism] . . . is not holding that area bombing was terrorism but only that acts of . . . terrorism can be sufficiently like it . . . for the same conclusion to apply" (Wallace 1991, 155). That is, if city bombing—which directly targeted civilians—was morally justified, then terrorism can be justified, too.

Surprisingly, after constructing this powerful analogy and giving the appearance of providing a justification for terrorism, Wallace argues that terrorism cannot be justified because it cannot meet the four criteria that justified city bombing. He tries to show that while each of the criteria might be met separately, they cannot all be met together.

Wallace defends this claim by imagining a community that satisfies both criteria 2 and 3; that is, it is trying to defend itself and combating a brutal, oppressive regime. In these respects, its situation is similar to that of Britain in 1940. But, he claims, "Even if we allow that conditions (1) and (4) can be met separately, their joint satisfaction is impossible" (Wallace 1991, 155–56). If the community has a good chance of success through the use of terrorism (and thus satisfies condition 4), then terrorism is unlikely to be a last resort; other means might work as well. In this case, condition 1 is not met. But if terrorism is a last resort, then the terrorist tactics are unlikely to succeed, in which case condition 4 is not met. Thus, the terror bombing was justified in the British case, but terrorism is not.

Unfortunately, this comforting conclusion is extremely implausible at this point in the argument. Wallace's imagined apologist creates a powerful analogy between terrorism and city bombing. They share the relevant feature of intentionally killing innocent human beings in order to promote an important political goal. Both can be acts of collective self-defense against brutal regimes. But, Wallace objects, the confluence of features that justified city bombing could not possibly occur so as to justify terrorism.

Wallace might have been on firm ground if he had said that these circumstances are rare and unlikely to occur, but what he actually asserts is that the occurrence of circumstances that would justify terrorism is "impossible." There is no basis for this claim. The right circumstances occurred in the past for Britain, as he acknowledges, and so they might occur at other times for other groups. Wallace ought to conclude that if city bombing was justifiable, then terrorism is—at least in principle—justifiable, even if it will only rarely be justified.

THREE POSSIBLE VIEWS

If my arguments are correct, then Walzer and Wallace are both logically committed to acknowledging the possibility of morally justified terrorism. The view that I believe they are forced to concede is represented in table 1:

TABLE 1

Actions	Sometimes Justifiable	Never Justifiable
Intentional attacks on civilians	X	
Attacks causing unintended civilian deaths and injuries	X	
Terrorism	X	
War	X	

Walzer and Wallace defend direct targeting of civilians under some circumstances, unintentionally killing civilians in war, and the justifiability of war itself. The catch is that their overall view appears to require them to approve of terrorism under similar circumstances in spite of their shared reluctance to admit this.

Someone who condemns any attacks against civilians—whether intentional or not—will be in a strong position to condemn terrorism, but this person will also be required to reject war, since war almost inevitably involves civilian deaths as collateral damage. This view is represented as follows (table 2):

TABLE 2

Actions	Sometimes Justifiable	Never Justifiable
Intentional attacks on civilians		X
Attacks causing unintended civilian deaths and injuries		X
Terrorism		X
War		X

This pacifist view rejects all of the actions I have been discussing. Anyone who reveres human life and abhors the killing of the innocent will sometimes find this an appealing option, but it is generally rejected, even by morally conscientious people.[9]

A third possibility is the one that Primoratz tries to defend, which is represented in table 3:

TABLE 3

Actions	Sometimes Justifiable	Never Justifiable
Intentional attacks on civilians		X
Attacks causing unintended civilian deaths and injuries	X	
Terrorism		X
War	X	

It permits war and unintentional killings of civilians and condemns terrorism. The problem, however, is that Primoratz—like Wallace and Walzer—has trouble squaring the principles that he used to condemn terrorism with his own approval of attacks that produce foreseeable collateral damage deaths. His strong affirmation of the worth of every individual, his rejection of calculating consequences, and his demand that attacks be justifiable to the victims all seem to require him to condemn not only intentional attacks on civilians but even attacks that yield unintended civilian injuries and deaths.

I want now to sketch some arguments for the view that intentional attacks on civilians are always wrong but that attacks with civilian deaths and injuries as unintended consequences are sometimes morally justified. Since the typical and worst cases of terrorism involve intentional attacks on civilians, this view would permit the condemnation of terrorism while acknowledging that some acts of war—whether committed by governments or by nongovernmental forces—might be capable of justification, even though they create threats to the lives of civilians.

One problem with standard defenses of collateral damage deaths is that they lean too heavily on the distinction between what is intended and what is foreseen. This distinction, when used in conjunction with the doctrine of double effect, is simply too permissive. As I noted above, it would permit the 9/11 attacks if—contrary to fact—the attackers were targeting only *buildings* and did not actually aim to kill innocent civilians.

Walzer (1977, 155–56) makes a similar criticism of the double effect principle. "Simply not to intend the death of civilians is too easy," he writes. "What we look for in such cases is some sign of a positive commitment to save civilian lives." He calls his view the principle of "double intention." It requires military planners and soldiers to recognize the evil that is threatened by their attack (i.e., the civilian deaths and injuries that are likely to occur) and to take steps to avoid or minimize these evils, even if these precautions increase the danger to military forces.

Walzer's rule is a step in the right direction. Building on it, I would suggest the following set of requirements for just, discriminate fighting:

1. targeting attacks as narrowly as possible on military resources;
2. avoiding targets where civilian deaths are extremely likely;
3. avoiding the use of inherently indiscriminate weapons (such as land mines and cluster bombs) and inherently indiscriminate strategies (such as high altitude bombing of areas containing both civilian enclaves and military targets);
4. accepting that when there are choices between damage to civilian lives and damage to military personnel, priority should be given to saving civilian lives.

If a group acts in accord with principles like these, then it could be said to be acknowledging the humanity and value of those affected by its actions.

While attacks might expose innocent people to danger, adherence to these principles would show that it was not indifferent to their well-being. In this way, it might satisfy the demands of the principles and ideals cited by Primoratz in his critique of terrorism.

Why is this? Because the group is combining a legitimate effort to defend itself or others with serious efforts to avoid civilian casualties. Anyone who acted in accord with the type of guidelines given above could be described as "bending over backward" to avoid civilian deaths, and it is this degree of care that is required if collateral damage killings are to be justified. The "bend over backward" rule is superior to the principle of double effect both because it provides greater protection to civilians and because it can be applied in a more objective, realistic way. It would be less likely to approve sham compliance than is suggested in the doctrine of double effect.

In addition, the "bend over backward" rule might even be justifiable in a certain sense to the victims of attacks. No doubt, actual victims are unlikely to look favorably on attacks that will result in their death or injury. But suppose we could present the following situation to people who might be victims of an attack (a condition that most of us inhabit), for their consideration from behind a Rawlsian veil of ignorance.[10] We would ask them to consider the following situation:

- Group A is facing an attack by group B; if successful, the attack will lead to death or the severe oppression of group A.
- The only way that group A can defend itself is by using means that will cause death and injury to innocent members of group B.
- You are a member of one of the groups but do not know which one.

Would you approve of means of self-defense that will kill and injure innocent members of B in order to defend group A?

To put this question more precisely, if a people did not know whether they would be victims or beneficiaries, would they choose (a) a rule that permitted intentional targeting of civilians, (b) a rule that permitted indiscriminate attacks that fail to avoid civilians, or (c) the "bend over backward" rule that requires strenuous efforts to avoid harming civilians? I believe that they would approve the "bend over backward" rule and would reject rules that permit either intentional or indiscriminate attacks on civilians. By approving a rule that combined a right of countries to defend themselves against aggression with restrictions on means of fighting (such as those contained in the "bend over backward" rule), they would accomplish two things. First, they would ensure that they would have a right of self-defense if they were members of an attacked group. Second, they would ensure that if they were innocent citizens of the attacking country, the defenders would be required to take serious steps to avoid injury or death to them and other civilians.

If people generally could accept such a rule, that would make it justifiable to potential victims as well as potential attackers. That would not be the same as justifying an attack to innocent victims themselves, but it might be as close as we could get to satisfying that test.

It is worth emphasizing that the "bend over backward" rule does not justify all cases of collateral damage killings. Even if these are unintended *and* the attack springs from a just cause *and* we can differentiate such attacks from terrorism, attacks on military targets that fail to "bend over backward" to avoid civilian deaths are not morally permitted. Like terrorism, such attacks show an indifference to human life that is incompatible with humane, civilized values.

I believe that this sort of approach provides what nonpacifist critics of terrorism need: a principled basis for condemning terrorism, no matter who it is carried out by, and a principled justification of genuinely defensive warfare. Moreover, the perspective is unified in a desirable way. Terrorist actions fail to be morally justified because *intentional* targeting of civilians is the most obvious form of failure to comply with the "bend over backward" rule.

These principles both allow for the condemnation of terrorism and are immune to charges of hypocrisy. They provide a basis for criticizing not simply the acts of those who are called terrorists but also the acts of nations that fail to follow the "bend over backward" rule, either attacking civilians directly or failing to avoid civilian deaths. If condemnations of terrorism are to have any moral credibility, then these moral lapses by established governments need to be acknowledged and criticized. In some cases, acts of public repentance might be necessary to show that we apply our moral standards to our own acts and our own history.[11]

CONCLUSION

Can terrorism be morally justified? At the start of this essay, I suggested that while it is easy to offer a resounding "no" to this question, there are serious problems with this simple answer. First, it is not so simple to say what terrorism is. Second, it is not so easy to make this resounding "no" compatible with other widespread beliefs that approve of war and even of the killings of civilians during war. I indicated that making credible moral judgments about terrorism requires both a clearer sense of what terrorism is and a general set of impartial principles for judging acts of violence. My hope is that this essay gets us closer to achieving these goals.

NOTES

1. Wittgenstein 1958, sections 65–71. Recognizing problems like those I have cited, Khatchadourian 1988, 134, describes his own definitional approach as quasi-essentialist. Brandt 1979, 2–10, discusses the methodology of definitions and distinguishes "reportive" from "reforming" definitions.

2. On the growing concern about nuclear terrorism, see Keller 2002, 22 ff.

3. For a philosophical defense of an "expansive" conception of guilt, see Wilkins 1992, ch. 1.

4. This status-based conception of innocence is defended by George Mavrodes 1985, 75–89.

5. On the distinction between combatants and noncombatants, see, for example, Kalshoven 1991, 88–91. For an analytical history of thought about the distinction between legitimate and illegitimate targets in warfare, see McKeogh 2002.

6. For criticisms and defenses of consequentialist moral theories, see Scheffler 1988.

7. For a review of attempts by consequentialists to reject terrorism and a consequentialist defense of terrorist acts, see Wilkins 1992, ch. 2.

8. For a similar idea, see Nagel 1991, 23: "We are looking for principles to deal with conflict that can at some level be endorsed by everyone."

9. For thoughtful defenses of pacifism, see Holmes 1989; Norman 1995; and Yoder 1976.

10. Rawls introduces this idea in his 1971, 136–42.

11. On theses issues, see Buruma 1994; Shriver 1995; and Lifton and Mitchell 1995.

REFERENCES

Brandt, Richard. 1979. *A Theory of the Good and the Right.* New York: Oxford University Press.

Brown, Kenneth. 1983. "'Supreme Emergency': A Critique of Michael Walzer's Moral

Justification for Allied Obliteration Bombing in World War II." *Manchester College Bulletin of the Peace Studies Institute* 13, nos. 1–2: 6–15.

Buruma, Ian. 1994. *The Wages of Guilt.* New York: Farrar, Straus and Giroux.

Coady, C. A. J. 1985. "The Morality of Terrorism." *Philosophy* 60: 47–69.

Coady, C. A. J. 2002. "Terrorism, Just War, and Supreme Emergency." In *Terrorism and Justice*, ed. T. Coady and M. O'Keefe. Melbourne: Melbourne University Press, 15–20.

Dardis, Tony. 1992. "Primoratz on Terrorism." *Journal of Applied Philosophy* 9: 93–97.

Greenway, H. D. S. 2001. "The Trouble with Defining Terrorism." *Boston Globe*, November 26, A11.

Holmes, Robert. 1989. *On War and Morality.* Princeton: Princeton University Press.

Human Rights Watch. "Cluster Bombs in Afghanistan." On-line at www.hrw.org/backgrounder/arms/cluster-bck1031.htm.

Kalshoven, Frits. 1991. *Constraints on the Waging of War.* 2d ed. Geneva: International Committee of the Red Cross.

Kant, Immanuel. 1981. *Grounding for the Metaphysics of Morals.* Trans. James Ellington. Indianapolis: Hackett Publishers.

Kegley, Charles, Jr. 1990. *International Terrorism.* New York: St. Martin's Press.

Keller, Bill. 2002. "Nuclear Nightmares." *New York Times Magazine,* May 26, 22 ff.

Khatchadourian, Haig. 1988. "Terrorism and Morality." *Journal of Applied Philosophy* 5: 131–45.

Khatchadourian, Haig. 1998. *The Morality of Terrorism.* New York: Peter Lang.

Lifton, Robert Jay, and Gregg Mitchell. 1995. *Hiroshima in America: Fifty Years of Denial.* New York: Putnam.

Mavrodes, George. 1985. "Conventions and the Morality of War." In *International Ethics*, ed. C. Beitz et al. Princeton: Princeton University Press, 75–89.

McKeogh, Colin. 2002. *Innocent Civilians: The Morality of Killing in War.* New York: Palgrave.

Nagel, Thomas. 1991. *Equality and Partiality.* New York: Oxford University Press.

Norman, Richard. 1995. *Ethics, Killing, and War.* New York: Cambridge University Press.

Primoratz, Igor. 1990. "What Is Terrorism?" *Journal of Applied Philosophy* 7: 129–38.

Primoratz, Igor. 1997. "The Morality of Terrorism?" *Journal of Applied Philosophy* 14: 221–33.

Rawls, John. 1971. *A Theory of Justice.* Cambridge, Mass.: Harvard University Press.

Scheffler, Samuel, ed. 1988. *Consequentialism and Its Critics.* New York: Oxford University Press.

Shriver, Donald. 1995. *Ethics for Enemies: Forgiveness and Atonement in Politics.* New York: Oxford University Press.

Sinnott-Armstrong, Walter. 1991. "On Primoratz's Definition of Terrorism." *Journal of Applied Philosophy* 8: 115–20.

Wallace, Gerry. 1991. "Terrorism and the Argument from Analogy." *Journal of Moral and Social Studies* 6: 149–60.

Walzer, Michael. 1977. *Just and Unjust Wars.* New York: Basic Books.

Walzer, Michael. 1988. "Terrorism: A Critique of Excuses." In *Problems of International Justice*, ed. S. Luper-Foy. Boulder, Colo.: Westview, 237–47.

Wilkins, Burleigh T. 1992. *Terrorism and Collective Responsibility.* London: Routledge.

Wittgenstein, Ludwig. 1958. *Philosophical Investigations.* New York: Macmillan.

Yoder, John. 1976. *Nevertheless: Varieties of Religions Pacifism.* Scottdale, Pa.: Herald Press.

The Public Response

DEMOCRATIC VALUES, PATRIOTISM,
AND CITIZENSHIP

JOHN KENNETH WHITE

Terrorism and the Remaking of American Politics

Like so many other infamous dates in U.S. history, 9/11 will be notorious to generations who have only secondhand knowledge, through words and images, of the terrorist attacks on America: the charred steel and ashes of human remains at the World Trade Center in New York; the damaged portion of the Pentagon in Arlington, Virginia; and the smoldering airliner debris left in a wooded area of Somerset County, Pennsylvania. In the seconds it took the terrorists to hit their targets, the world changed. By nightfall, more than three thousand had perished. The death toll was especially staggering in New York, where the World Trade Center was transformed from a bustling hubbub of financial enterprise into a morgue of forbidding silence. So great was the number of fatalities that nearly one in five Americans claimed to have known someone who was missing, hurt, or killed on that fateful day, or to have had friends who lost loved ones (Princeton Survey Research Associates 2001). Reacting to the disaster, the French intellectual Dominique Moisi told the *Financial Times* of London: "All over Europe, not only in London but from Paris to Madrid, from Berlin to Rome, the terrorists who struck at America have recreated the strong sense of Western solidarity loosened by the end of the Cold War" (Apple 2001). The French newspaper *Le Monde* expressed the sentiments of many Europeans in a now famous headline that read "We're all Americans" (see Gibbs 2001).

While Americans mourned their dead, they also grieved for their loss of innocence. The sense of personal security that most citizens took for granted gave way to a somber reality that terrorism had become an integral part of the American way of life. By midday on 9/11, all commercial airliners were grounded, and President George W. Bush issued orders to shoot down any plane (even if it carried innocent civilians) that refused to land. A few weeks later, as the terrorist threat intensified because of the spread of anthrax through the U.S. Postal Service, the USA Patriot ("Uniting and Strengthening America by Providing Appropriate Tools Required to Intercept and Obstruct Terrorism") Act became law. This measure gave federal authorities enhanced powers to detain noncitizens, wiretap cell phones, intercept E-mails, and monitor Internet usage.

Following 9/11, Americans were tense, according to various polls: One in five believed that the terrorists would strike in his or her hometown, and one-third said they were either "a little nervous" or "very nervous" about boarding an airplane (Zogby International 2001g). Forty-two percent thought about another potential terrorist attack during the course of a "routine day" (Zogby International 2001f). Of course, "routine days" were something of the past. To take but one small example, the phrase *homeland security* suddenly became part of the vocabulary of the moment. Little more than a year after the terrorist attacks, Congress approved the creation of a Department of Homeland Security—the first cabinet-level department addition since the Department of Veterans Affairs was formed in 1988.

Repeatedly, Bush told the public that the war against terrorism would be long and difficult: "You will be asked for your patience; for the conflict will not be short. You will be asked for resolve; for the conflict will not be easy. You will be asked for your strength, because the course to victory may be long" (Bush 2001b). This sober reality was particularly jarring to the young. Across the country, students of all ages, most of whom had been unaccustomed to adversity, were suddenly and unexpectedly confronted with the face of death. Days after 9/11, MTV (the network for music television) received an E-mail from a viewer in Bowling Green, Kentucky, that read: "My generation has seen nothing like this in our lifetime, and it will be something that we will never forget. Our parents can remember where they were when President Kennedy was shot, and our grandparents can tell us what they were doing when Pearl Harbor was bombed. It is sad that our generation now will be able to look back in twenty years and say, 'I remember where I was when the World Trade Center collapsed'" (MTV.com 2001a). Chelsea Clinton (the daughter of Bill Clinton, the former president) was unusually expressive in recalling her memories of that fateful day:

I woke up that Tuesday morning feeling good about where I was in my life and happy about where I was going. Now that sense of security is gone, and since the 11th, for some moment every day, I have been scared. Not by a sense of immediate, immense danger, but by something more subtle and corrosive: an uncertainty about my place in the world—where I am emotionally, psychologically, and sometimes even physically. . . . I do not think it is out of place to divide my life into before and after the 11th. For the first time a single day now means more than just twenty-four hours—it implies a whole new world. (Clinton 2001/2002)

Across the country, random acts of kindness, compassion, and generosity became more commonplace. Seventy percent of the respondents to one poll reported engaging in some form of charitable activity following the 9/11 attacks, with 58 percent offering a financial contribution to those in need (Wirthlin Worldwide 2001). A nation that once "bowled alone" suddenly found neighbors who were becoming better acquainted (see Putnam 2000). This was particularly true in neighborhoods where families were grieving the loss of loved ones. In a Washington, D.C., community, neighbors baked food for a victim's family and arranged a photograph book for her funeral. Many had not known the deceased, but they became extended family members after the Pentagon attack. Amitai Etzioni, a longtime observer of American social habits, was struck by the rebirth of community spirit: "There has been an enormous return to community in every conceivable way. People simply need to be with other people more" (St. George 2001). According to one survey, 88 percent said the terrorist attacks highlighted what was really important in life, and 83 percent said that Osama bin Laden's dastardly deeds had brought the country closer together than ever before (*Time*/CNN/Harris Interactive 2001).

Television enhanced the growing sense of a national community, as millions gathered around the campfires of continuous network news programming. Not since the assassination of President John F. Kennedy in 1963 had the country been so rapt by the horrific events unfolding before its eyes. For four days, the major networks stuck to the tragedies in New York, Washington, and Pennsylvania with few commercial interruptions (see de Moraes 2001). Later, millions watched as the stars of music and film organized benefits that allowed the television audience to participate by contributing to those in need. The most successful of these was "America: A Tribute to Heroes," which was simultaneously broadcast on all the commercial networks and raised an estimated $150 million (CBSNews.com 2001).

The constant televised replays of the scenes of devastation reminded Americans that they were being tested in ways even more daunting than the challenges previous generations had faced. Dave Sirulnick, an executive vice president of MTV, believed there was a longing among the nation's young to measure up to their World War II forebears, hailed as the "greatest generation": "Through pop culture, through movies like *Pearl Harbor* and *Band of Brothers* on HBO, there was a sort of a sense of what other generations had gone through. And so it was very fresh in young people's minds that they didn't have anything like this. They didn't have Vietnam. They didn't have Watergate. I think instantly people understood that this [new form of terrorism] was going to define their generation" (CBSNews.com 2001).

"THE NEW NORMALCY"

The Transformation of the Popular Culture

After the 9/11 attacks, 85 percent of the individuals in one study said the United States should return to business as soon as possible (see Saad 2001). Despite such bravado sentiments, it was clear that while life would continue, it would be in an era that is best described as the "new normalcy" (see Sullivan 2001). One manifestation of this new normalcy was the immediate transformation of the popular culture. On 9/11, the alternative music group System of a Down had the nation's top-selling CD, *Toxicity*. One week later the group's standing on the pop charts precipitously dipped to the eleventh spot (see Segal 2001). Rising to replace it was a CD featuring Celine Dion singing "God Bless America" (see Moody 2001). Clear Channel Communications, which owns 1,170 radio stations and has 110 million weekly listeners, issued a list of 150 songs it considered inappropriate for airplay. These included the Gap Band's "You Dropped a Bomb on Me"; Soundgarden's "Blow Up the Outside World"; The Beatles' "Ticket to Ride"; the Drifters' "On Broadway"; all songs by Rage against the Machine; and even John Lennon's anthem, "Imagine" (see Strauss 2001). MTV took to playing what it called "comfort videos": Lenny Kravitz's "Let Love Rule," Bob Marley's "One Love," Sting's "If You Love Somebody Set Them Free," and U2's

"Walk On." Head Programmer Tom Calderone explained: "This is a weird word to use, but we're trying to find videos that are soothing and compatible with what the country is feeling right now" (see Segal 2001). The major network executives were also astounded when compilations of *I Love Lucy* and *The Carol Burnett Show* scored big audiences among young viewers. Almost immediately, television programmers began scouring the vaults for more old "comfort programs" to repackage and re-air. Meanwhile, the contemporary sitcom *Friends* was extended for another season in the wake of its overwhelming popularity following the attacks (see Wiltz 2001).

The Temporary Return of Confidence in Government

It was not only young people whose visions of the world were transformed by 9/11. All American citizens who once treated politics cavalierly suddenly found themselves listening to political leaders with attentive ears. According to one survey, 68 percent said politics had become "more relevant" to their lives (see Balz and Harris 2001). Writer David Brooks reported that politics was everywhere at Princeton University. On one corner of the campus, the Princeton Peace Network hosted teach-ins and rallies as students sang the civil rights anthem "We Shall Overcome," while nearby the Princeton Committee against Terrorism sponsored a rival event where students loudly sang "God Bless America" (see Brooks 2001).

As the horrific events of 9/11 became absorbed into the national psyche, confidence in government soared. Public opinion surveys found 60 percent saying they trusted the government in Washington to do what is right "just about always" or "most of the time" (Gallup 2001d). Vice President Richard Cheney marveled at the new support: "One of the things that's changed so much since September 11 is the extent to which people do trust the government—big shift—and value it, and have high expectations for what we can do" (B. Woodward 2001). Senator Hillary Rodham Clinton of New York agreed, saying, "Only the government can respond to what we've confronted" (Balz and Harris 2001).

While citizens were urged to be watchful for signs of terrorism, clearly the principal defense against it was indeed the federal government. According to a Gallup poll (2001d) taken shortly after the 9/11 attacks, 50 percent believed government should do more to combat the terrorist threat. The public desire for a more robust federal establishment was reflected in the actions undertaken by the president. Declaring a state of emergency on 9/11, Bush authorized $40 billion in emergency spending, with $20 billion earmarked for restoring New York City, and an additional $15 billion to bail out the faltering airline industry. Just as startling was Bush's sudden embrace of the call by Democratic Senator Joseph Lieberman of Connecticut for a new Department of Homeland Security, the largest reorganization of the federal government since the Defense Department was created in 1949. Also noteworthy was Republican Senator John McCain's proposal to quadruple the number of AmeriCorps volunteers to assist in homeland security. Interestingly, the program was begun by President Clinton in 1993 to promote a greater sense of public service among the young; McCain, still constrained by his antigovernment, conservative ideology, strongly objected to it at the time. These measures—all supported by President Bush—had more in common with Franklin D. Roosevelt's approach to governance than Ronald Reagan's.

Yet less than a year later, public trust in government had largely dissipated. In one poll, only 40 percent trusted the government in Washington to do the right thing just about always or most of the time (*Washington Post* 2002). Government had disappointed them, and their disappointment spread to other large institutions—including Enron, WorldCom, Arthur Andersen, Global Crossing, and Adelphia, whose corporate corruption had contributed mightily to the depressed stock market. Another poll showed that these regulatory failures took a toll: 75 percent had less confidence in the stock market; 74 percent had less confidence in corporate America; 53 percent had less confidence in the Republicans in Congress; 48 percent had less confidence in the Bush administration; and 46 percent had less confidence in the congressional Democrats (Greenberg Quinlan Rosner Research 2002).

An Altered Public Psyche

The events of 9/11 also exacted a severe emotional toll. Research indicated that seven in ten had either cried or shown greater affection for their loved ones in the days following the tragedy (see Gallup 2001c). Among the Christmas 2001 letters I received was one that described a Catholic priest asking his parishioners during a Thanksgiving homily to publicly give thanks for the things that mattered most to them. Among the more surprising responses was that of a man who said, "I know it sounds strange, but I'm grateful for September 11th because it put me back in touch with what is important to me." Pollster Stanley B. Greenberg (2001) found participants in his focus groups expressing similar sentiments: "I think it's darn time that finally this country got back to caring about what's important, which is, you know, your family and home and self, and, you know, stop being so materialistic."

Adversity also brought nontraditional families closer. In New York, Republican Governor George Pataki was persuaded to change that state's crime-victim assistance program, which required domestic partners to prove that these victims provided 75 percent of the household income before the state aid for their families would be forthcoming. Matt Foreman, director of Empire State Pride Agenda, found his agency swamped with requests to assist grieving gays and lesbians. He laments: "What's still unavailable to gays and lesbians and their non-biological survivors are the far-reaching government funds—Social Security, workers' compensation. . . . We're not in *Leave It to Beaver* land anymore. There are all kinds of families who don't fit the government's definition of family, who need help and won't be able to get it" (see Stuever 2001b).

Transformations within homes were accompanied by greater outward expressions of spiritualism and religiosity. Responding to a question about the American Dream after the terrorist attacks, 52 percent thought it could best be achieved through spiritual fulfillment; only 30 percent said it meant acquiring more material goods (Zogby International 2001e). As one MTV viewer wrote: "Life isn't about fancy cars, beautiful homes, and tickets to a great concert. It is about the wonderful people in this world. Live life!" (MTV.com 2001a). Part of this new living meant attending a church, synagogue, or mosque. Surveys taken after 9/11 showed church attendance spiraled to 51 percent—up ten points from a just a few months before—and 74 percent said they felt closer to God after the attacks (Zogby International 2001c). But like the burst of public confidence in government, church attendance fell to pre-9/11 levels just one year later. According to a September 2002 poll, only 39 percent said they attended church weekly (Democracy Corps 2002). The empty pews, at least at Catholic churches, resulted to some extent from scandals involving sexual abuse of minors by priests. Seventy-five percent of the respondents to one poll gave church leaders a negative rating for their handling of the scandals; two-thirds thought Boston's Cardinal Bernard Law should resign—and, eventually, he did (see LeMoyne College/Zogby International 2002; CBS News 2002). At a time when Americans needed the comfort and security of familiar religious leaders and institutions, the impact of the scandals was to threaten our sense of security as much as any terrorist attack could.

The New Patriotism

What *has* lasted is the rebirth of patriotism. The American flag, a controversial symbol in the 1960s, has been resurrected as a symbol of national unity. After 9/11, more than 80 percent queried by one organization displayed it in some form (*USA Today* 2001). Along with raising the flag came a national chorus of patriotic singing. One of the most moving scenes following the attacks occurred when a bipartisan congressional gathering spontaneously burst into a refrain of "God Bless America" on the steps of the U.S. Capitol. The song became something of a national anthem, much as it had been when the late Kate Smith sang it during World War II. Other patriotic tunes found favor with the public. A CD titled *Sing America*, which had been previously released in 1999, began climbing the charts; it featured Cher singing "The Star Spangled Banner"; Linda Ronstadt vocalizing on "Back in the U.S.A."; James Taylor performing the Stephen Foster standard "Oh, Susannah"; and the Mormon Tabernacle Choir with a rousing rendition of "God Bless America" (Segal 2001). President Bush quickly sought to capture the new patriotic spirit by urging veterans to speak to schoolchildren about duty and honor to the country. His wife, Laura, also urged children to be more patriotic. In a letter read in the nation's classrooms, the first lady wrote: "We can be proud and confident that we live in a country that symbolizes freedom and opportunity to millions throughout the world" (see Milbank 2001). Lynne Cheney (2002), wife of the vice president, published an alphabet book titled *America: A Patriotic Primer*.

Giving this new patriotism a lift were tales of heroism and courage from firefighters, police, and hospital emergency workers who were among the first to arrive at the World Trade Center and Pentagon. New York City Fire Department Chaplain Mychal Judge was killed by falling debris while administering the final sacrament (anointing of the sick, or last rites) to a dying fireman; grieving firefighters carried the Franciscan priest's body first to a local church and later to the firehouse where he lived before hurrying back to the World Trade Center to rescue others. Todd Beamer—the doomed airline passenger who, along with three others, foiled a hijacking attempt to crash a plane into the U.S. Capitol, White House, or some other Washington-area target—had his courage lauded posthumously in a best-selling book written by his wife, Lisa (Beamer 2002). Facing certain death, Beamer said the Lord's Prayer with an air-phone operator and told her of his intent to "do something" before ending the call with the words "Let's roll." The fact that one hero was gay (Judge) and another heterosexual (Beamer) no longer mattered (Stuever 2001b; Green 2001/2002). Nor did it matter that one of Beamer's helpers was gay. So celebrated were the heroics of 9/11 that rock musicians—not heretofore known to share many cultural affinities with police and firefighters—staged massive concerts to celebrate their heroism. Former Beatle Paul McCartney, who organized the "Concert for New York," wrote a song for the occasion entitled "Freedom" that celebrated this value and those who sought to defend it. Later, Bruce Springsteen released a poignant CD titled *The Rising,* which also honored the heroes of 9/11. Both musicians saw their fans respond favorably to their creative endeavors.

The presence of so many extraordinary heroes resulted in enormous national pride. President Bush told of receiving a letter from a fourth-grade girl indicating that she did not want her military dad to fight, but "I'm willing to give him to you" (Bush 2001e). Nowhere was the new patriotism more apparent than at that annual celebration of "the ideal American woman"—the Miss America Pageant. For the first time since World War II, the pageant took on an unusually militaristic tone in 2001. Those gathered in Atlantic City waved thirteen thousand flags, as the Jumbotron at Caesar's Palace flashed a sign that proclaimed, "One Nation, under God." Many cheered Miss New York, an air force reservist with plans to go into active duty (see Stuever 2001a). The eventual winner, a somewhat more tradition-minded Katie Harman, saw her role as that of a patriotic unifier: "This is an opportunity for Miss America to rally the hopes of the American public. I want to make sure that this tragedy does not bring America down" (Segal 2001). As Jamie MacDonald, a Boston dockworker, told a reporter on 9/11, *"This is the re-United States of America"* (emphasis added) (Auchincloss 2001).

GEORGE W. BUSH AND THE NEW "US VERSUS THEM" POLITICS

Nowhere was the transformation of life after 9/11 greater than at the White House. Like other presidents whose terms of office have been defined by historic challenges, Bush immediately realized that his response to this new strain of international terrorism would define his place in the history books. Showing his resolve, he employed a familiar baseball analogy, saying to friends that the terrorists were not "going to steal home on me" (Bruni 2001). Publicly Bush declared, "We wage a war to save civilization itself," and he repeatedly stated that overcoming the dangers posed by Osama bin Laden and his cohorts "is the purpose of my administration" (Bush 2001g).

The shedding of so much blood gave Bush an unparalleled opportunity to seize the bully pulpit. He did so with relish, as the struggle against bin Laden gave his presidency, to paraphrase Alexander Hamilton in the *Federalist Papers*, a new burst of energetic administration (Hamilton 1961).[1] No longer would *Time* magazine issue a cover with the headline "The Incredible Shrinking Presidency," as it did in the waning days of the first Bush administration (*Time* 1992). The amplification of the presidency back to its near-imperial cold war status was well suited to George W. Bush's *Father Knows Best* persona. Moreover, the secrecy needed to pursue the Afghanistan war and the upcoming conflict with Iraqi president Saddam Hussein—along with the demise of virtually all political opposition from Democrats—helped to mute Bush's instinct to stiffen when challenged. All of this proved to be a welcome balm to the president, since his policies had met with increased resistance prior to the attacks against terrorism. On September 10, 2001, the Gallup Organization (2001a) found Bush holding the lowest job approval rating of his presidency: 51 percent. Three weeks after the terrorist attacks, his approval rating stood at 90 percent (Gallup 2001b). This score exceeded the job approval rating (89 percent) posted by George H. W. Bush during the first Persian Gulf War, an all-time record (Moore 2001). Moreover, looking back at the 2000 election, few had feelings of buyer's remorse. A poll found 67 percent saying they did not believe the country would be better off with Al Gore as president (Zogby International 2001a). Similar percentages of respondents were happy that Bill Clinton was no longer in the White House, and that Dick Cheney rather than Joe Lieberman was vice president (Zogby International 2001d).

Republicans rejoiced in these numbers. Tom Davis, chairman of the National Republican Congressional Campaign Committee, saw an opportunity "to reshape the image of the party from the top down" (Dionne 2001). The party was certainly in need of an image makeover. During the cold war, Republicans portrayed themselves as muscular nationalists who would best protect the United States against the dangers posed by international communism. Their success in painting such a vivid portrait helped them to win seven of the ten presidential elections held from 1952 to 1988. The three Democratic winners—John F. Kennedy, Lyndon B. Johnson, and Jimmy Carter—were aberrations (see White 1998, esp. ch. 5). Following 9/11, many reasoned that what worked for the GOP during the cold war would do so again. They may be right. During the 2002 campaign, 52 percent of the respondents to one poll said they trusted the Republicans to make the right decisions when it comes to dealing with terrorism; a mere 20 percent picked the Democrats. Likewise, 66 percent said Republicans were more likely to make sure the U.S. defenses were strong; only 18 percent chose the Democrats (CBS/*New York Times* 2002). When asked about foreign policy, 47 percent told another polling organization they believed the Republicans would do a better job; 36 percent preferred the Democrats (*Time*/CNN/Harris Interactive 2002). These leads helped Republicans defy history by regaining control of the U.S. Senate and padding their slender majority in the House of Representatives.

Osama bin Laden also gave Republicans an unparalleled opportunity to recast U.S. politics by redefining "us" and "them." Republicans had been skilled practitioners of "us versus them" politics for years. During the cold war, the GOP helped create an image of the free world led by the United States (us), while those unfortunate enough to reside behind the Iron Curtain were led by the Communist-run Soviet Union (them). Now, President Bush could seize upon the American citizenry's love of liberty by turning the war on terrorism into the first "us versus them" conflict of the twenty-first century. Using the earthy language of the Wild West, he declared that he wanted Osama bin Laden "dead or alive" (Bush 2001c).

But Bush did more than simply make bin Laden the most wanted man in the world. Rather, he sought public support by turning the war against terrorism into a defense of traditional American values. Addressing the nation on the night of 9/11, he declared: "America was targeted for attack because we're the brightest beacon for freedom and opportunity in the world" (Bush 2001a). Later, before a joint session of Congress, Bush (2001d) drew a bright line between the twisted thinking of the terrorists and those who love freedom: "Every nation, in every region, now has a decision to make. Either you are with us, or you are with the terrorists. . . . Freedom and fear are at war. The advance of human freedom—the great achievement of our time, and the great hope of our time—now depends on us." As if to echo their commander in chief, Pentagon spokespersons dubbed the Afghan war "Operation Enduring Freedom." In numerous speeches, the president consistently portrayed the U.S. cause as one designed to enhance the values of freedom, religious tolerance, and a belief in progress, while castigating the terrorists as "evil-doers" who practice "a fringe form of Islamic extremism":

> The terrorists' directive commands them to kill Christians and Jews, to kill all Americans, and make no distinctions among military and civilians, including women and children. . . . Afghanistan's people have been brutalized—many are starving and many have fled. Women are not allowed to attend school. You can be jailed for owning a television. Religion can be practiced only as their leaders dictate. A man can be jailed in Afghanistan if his beard is not long enough. (Bush 2001d)

Interestingly, Osama bin Laden also saw the struggle with the Americans and their "infidel" allies in values terms. In a videotape released from his mountain hideaway, bin Laden sought to rally the Islamic world: "These events have divided the whole world into two sides—the side of believers and the side of the infidels. May God keep you away from them. Every Muslim has to rush to make his religion victorious. The winds of faith have come. The winds of change have come to eradicate oppression from the island of Muhammad, peace be upon him" (*Washington Post* 2001).

Not surprisingly, bin Laden's Afghanistan allies saw the American-led attack on their country as a clash of two cultures. Taliban leader Mullah Mohammad Omar contrasted the Western emphasis on materialism with the Taliban's religious piety: "Life can be led with just a few basics. The luxuries don't matter" (Dowd 2001). For years, the Taliban had been conducting its own war against modernity. Seizing power in 1996, Islamic clerics began their rule by hanging TV sets from trees and outlawing virtually all music and films (see Burns 2001). Noting these actions, Prime Minister Silvio Berlusconi of Italy cast the war against terrorism as one more episode in an ongoing struggle between Western modernity and Eastern antiquity: "We must be aware of the superiority of our civilization, a system that has guaranteed well-being, respect for human rights and—in contrast with Islamic countries—respect for religious and political rights, a system that has as its values understandings of diversity and tolerance" (*Newsweek* 2001). Americans saw the war from a similar perspective. As one participant in Democratic pollster Stanley B. Greenberg's focus groups put it:

> You know [in the United States] . . . you choose who you're going to marry, and you choose if you're going to have children, and you choose if you're going to go to school, and you choose to move out of state to get a better job, and you choose whether you get on a plane. And that's why a lot of people want to come here . . . because there's a lot of choices.
>
> You could choose your religion; you don't have to be one thing or another. If you're a woman, you can walk down the street; you don't have to hide under a veil. (Greenberg 2001)

THE GLOBAL REACH OF AMERICAN CULTURE

As Greenberg's respondent had noted, Osama bin Laden's crusade represented a clash between modernity and traditionalism. For decades, American cultural habits—especially changes that have given women and homosexuals additional rights—have long been derided in non-Western cultures. In 1998, bin Laden railed against the "American women soldiers" stationed in the Holy City of Mecca: "By God, Muslim women refuse to be defended by these American and Jewish prostitutes" (*New York Review of Books* 2001). The greater presence of women in the military—and in all other aspects of American life—ran counter to the traditional Muslim view that women should assume a secondary role. One of the terrorists even took a towel to cover the exposed shoulder of a woman in a portrait hanging in his hotel room (ironically, many of the attackers indulged in the hedonistic aspects of Western society, including drinking at sports bars and lap dancing at nightclubs) (Wilgoren 2001).

Yet, even as George W. Bush continued to cast the war on terror as a struggle between good and evil, Americans continued to wonder, "Why do they hate us?" Bush publicly professed "astonishment" that bin Laden, the Taliban, and their supporters could have such a profound antipathy for the United States (Bush 2001f). While part of bin Laden's animosity was rooted in long-standing U.S. support for Israel, much of it also stemmed from a deep dislike of U.S. popular culture. For some time, the extraordinary reach of American culture has been viewed by many Muslims as a threat to their religious beliefs and values. Back in the 1920s, Hasum al-Banna, founder of the Muslim Brotherhood, railed against the "wave of atheism and lewdness" that he saw engulfing Egypt—a wave that "started the devastation of religion and morality on the pretext of individual and intellectual freedom." Al-Banna assailed Westerners for importing "their half-naked women into these regions, together with their liquors, their theaters, their dance halls, their amusements, their stories, their newspapers, their novels, their whims, their silly games, and their vices" (Barber 1996, 210). Scott Appleby, a historian at the University of Notre Dame, believes that the difference between the Western industrialized nations and Islam centers on the role of religion in public life: "Islamists reject secular modernity with its pornography, materialism, drug dependency, and high divorce rate. They would respect the U.S. much more if we did not separate God from governance—if we were in fact a Christian state" (K. Woodward 2001, 68).

Today, the United States has been cast by a variety of Muslim clerics as representing "the great Satan" (see Bedlington 2001). Anthony Lobaido, an international correspondent for WorldNetDaily.com, describes how many Muslims see New York City as Satan's culture capital: "All that is evil in the world can be found in New York: MTV, the United Nations, the U.N. abortion programs, the Council on Foreign Relations, Wall Street greed, Madison Avenue manipulation, and of course more AIDS cases than the rest of America combined" (*New Republic* 2001a). Yet, even as American culture was being deplored by Muslim clerics, everyday Arabs still cherished their Marlboro cigarettes, wore Levi's jeans, played American pop music, watched American movies, and dined at fast-food eateries like McDonald's and Kentucky Fried Chicken (see Burns 2001).

So dominant is American culture that the popular sneaker company Reebok markets itself with the claim that on "Planet Reebok" there are no boundaries. Alfred M. Zeien, chairman of the Gillette Company (manufacturer of razors and other products), says, "I do not find foreign countries foreign." During the 1990s, Ted Turner, founder of the Cable News Network (CNN), forbade correspondents from using the word *foreign* in their newscasts. In a sense, these executives are right, as globalization has increasingly come to mean Americanization. In China, for example, one can easily see the long arm of U.S. culture in the growing number of McDonald's, Starbucks, and Kentucky Fried Chicken outlets (see Barber 1996, 24, 23, 5, 6).

Nowhere is the American dominance more emphatic than in its occupation of movie screens across the globe. For example, on the day that the Steven Spielberg film *Jurassic Park* opened in France, the film ran in nearly one-quarter of the country's 1,800 theaters. Iranian censors have tried without success to overcome the U.S. onslaught of films, banishing most of them as "banal, opportunistic, and pseudo-revolutionary." Nonetheless, movies such as *Driving Miss Daisy* and *Dances with Wolves* have found receptive audiences in Ayatollah Khomeini's home country (Barber 1996, 92, 94). In nearby Afghanistan, the Taliban tried to downplay the popularity of the film *Titanic*, even as many Afghan men restyled their hair to resemble Leonardo DiCaprio's locks (Burns 2001).

American television possesses a similar global reach. MTV, the American-invented music television cable network, reached approximately 323 million households in 2001 (MTV.com 2001b). But it is not only MTV that has enjoyed huge worldwide audiences. In Russia, the *Wheel of Fortune* game show, retitled *Field of Wonders*, features contestants who can win Sony VCRs into which they may load Hollywood films if they give the wheel the right spin. Poland has its own version of the wheel, dubbed *Kolo Fortuna*, which commands 70 percent of the Polish television audience on Thursday evenings. U.S. football has even spawned a French counterpart; during games an American-born announcer can be heard to exclaim: "Alors, quelle finesse! Regardez le quarterback sneak de Dan Marino, ça marche vraiment parfaitement, n'est-ce pas? Tiens! Touchdown! Eh, oui, je suis étonné! Quelle jeu! Quel grand show!" (see Barber 1996, 207, 102, 101). In most world capitals, no translation is needed to stay in touch with current events, as CNN is just a click away on the remote control. Across the globe, the U.S. media have succeeded in invading foreign lands in ways the Pentagon can only dream of doing.

Such dominance often breeds resentment. For years, Canadians have complained that their southern neighbor has exerted an undue influence on their country's culture. Back in 1986, Jeffrey Simpson, a columnist for the *Toronto Globe and Mail*, described the cultural behemoth the United States had become by envisaging its inversion:

Imagine a movie-lover in St. Louis who checked the local paper and discovered that 97 percent of the films showing in his city were foreign. Or how about a book-lover in San Francisco who found that in every city store foreign authors had written 75 percent of the titles and that American books were consigned to an inconspicuous display quaintly called "Americana."

Try to picture the vast record stores of New York filled with three foreign records for every American one. Think about watching television in Phoenix and finding three out of every four programs made not in the United States, but somewhere else. Consider the possibility that in Chicago three out of every four publications sold were foreign. This is what cultural life is like for Canadians. (Simpson 1986)

Simpson's complaint is an oft-heard one. Following the U.S. domination of the Cannes film festivals in the early 1990s, French Culture Minister Jack Lang proclaimed an all-out war against Hollywood. Lang got French legislators to approve a domestic content law that required 60 percent of video programming to be European and 40 percent of songs played to be French in origin. Likewise, an official in the Iranian Ministry of Culture and Islamic Guidance declared: "These programs, prepared by international imperialism, are part of an extended plot to wipe out our religions and sacred values." But the struggle against American dominance, dubbed *Jihad vs. McWorld* by political scientist Benjamin Barber, remains no contest. Even as France was passing its own domestic content laws, its government awarded Hollywood film star Sylvester Stallone the prestigious Legion of Honor (see Barber 1996, 91–93, 207).

Twenty years ago, Charles Z. Wick, a former talent agent who was tapped by Ronald Reagan to be the director of the U.S. Information Agency, said: "I would hope that American pop culture would penetrate into other societies, acting as a pilot parachute for the rest of American values" (*Time* 1986). Wick's wish has come true. In Arab states, visa-seekers crowd U.S. embassies and shout "America, free!"—even if these are the only English words they know (Burns 2001). They are hardly alone. One reason for associating the United States with freedom is the everyday products foreigners consume and the means by which they are marketed. Coca-Cola, for example, sells more than a soft drink; it sells a way of life. As one company executive in charge of sales in Kenya admitted: "There is a perceived way of life embedded in each bottle of Coke. Coke is modern, with-it." A young Czech concurred: "Coke equals America. America equals freedom" (*Time* 1986). McDonald's likewise sells more than hamburgers. Jim Catalupo, president of the company's international operations unit, describes the foreigner's encounter with McDonald's as a plethora of choices, each one the symbol of a free society: "It's the drive-thrus. . . . It's the Playlands. . . . It's the smile at the front counter. . . . It's all those things. . . . The experience" (Barber 1996, 128–29). For years, the Walt Disney Corporation sought to sell something more than a good time at its theme parks. As one early promotional piece for the first Walt Disney park in Anaheim, California, put it: "Disneyland will be based upon and dedicated to the ideals, the dreams, and the hard facts that have created America. And it will be uniquely equipped to dramatize these dreams and facts and send them forth as a source of courage and inspiration to all the world" (Barber 1996, 134). Today, the Disney Corporation's reach is thoroughly global, as foreign guests stream into its theme parks in California and Florida, while Euro Disney garners a somewhat smaller group of visitors in Paris. Moreover, its films are shown in movie theaters around the world, and its control of television markets has expanded, thanks to its own cable channel network and subsequent takeover of the American Broadcasting Company (ABC).

A PERSISTENT VALUES DIVIDE

But a culturally triumphant America overseas hardly mitigates the ongoing values divisions within the United States (see White 2002). Indeed, many Americans viewed the events of 9/11 through the looking glass of this divide. Former president George H. W. Bush denounced John Walker Lindh, the American who became a Taliban sympathizer, noting that he was the by-product of "liberal Marin County [California] hot-tubbers" (Grove 2002). On the other side of the values divide was Katha Pollitt, a columnist for the *Nation* who described having an argument with her thirteen-year-old daughter, a student who attends a high school located a few blocks from the World Trade Center. Her daughter, it seemed, wanted to fly the American flag, only to have her mother object: "Definitely not, I say: The flag stands for jingoism and vengeance and war" (Pollitt 2001). Others also saw the terrorist attacks through the prism of the values divide. Reverend Lou Sheldon, chairman of the Traditional Values Coalition, objected to the Red Cross and other relief organizations assisting gays and lesbians who lost partners in the 9/11 attacks: "They should be giving priority to those widows who were at home with their babies and those widowers who lost their wives. . . . This is just another example of how the gay agenda is seeking to overturn the one man–

one woman relationship from center stage in America, taking advantage of this tragedy" (*New Republic* 2001b).

Yet nowhere was the values divide greater than in the responses shown to two leading figures in the culture wars: Senator Hillary Clinton and the Reverend Jerry Falwell. Appearing at the World Trade Center ruins shortly after the disaster, Clinton found herself shunned by police and firefighters as she accompanied George W. Bush; he, on the other hand, was mobbed by admiring rescue workers. A few days later, the junior senator from New York confidently strode onto the stage at the "Concert for New York," which was organized by Paul McCartney with the help of several Clinton loyalists in the entertainment industry. Expecting a warm welcome from the rock-loving crowd, Clinton found herself loudly booed by police and firefighters sitting in the front rows, who also yelled, "Get off the stage! We don't want you here!" The former first lady could hardly be heard above the din. One fireman, Michael Moran, whose brother John was killed at the World Trade Center, said he jeered because of the "claptrap that comes out of her mouth!" Moran's disdain mirrored that of his colleagues: "She wants to spew her nonsense—she doesn't believe the things she says. She says what she believes will work in the moment" (Drudge 2001). Indeed, many police and firefighters were upset that Clinton had denounced the police brutality in the Amadou Diallo slaying two years earlier. But much of their dislike had little to do with policy. (In fact, Mrs. Clinton had successfully lobbied President Bush for federal funds in the wake of the disaster.) Rather, many police and firemen saw her as a pushy woman and carpetbagger whose independence, unconventional marriage, and acceptance of nontraditional lifestyles were abhorrent to them. During the 2000 senatorial campaign in New York, her Republican opponent, Rick Lazio, was endorsed by many of their representative groups: the New York Police Benevolent Association; the New York City Police Department Sergeants, Lieutenants, and Captains; and the New York City Correction Officers Benevolent Association, along with the Uniformed Firefighters and Fire Officers Associations. Backstage, the Clintons were upset at the poor reception, and Bill Clinton lashed out at John Sykes, the chief executive officer of VH1. According to news reports, the former president wagged his finger at Sykes and exploded, "We wouldn't have accepted your invitation to speak if we had known it would be this uncomfortable" (Grove 2001). One confidante of Hillary's exclaimed: "How could we not know this would be the wrong forum for Hillary?! These are cops and firemen who listen to right-wing talk radio. They still think she killed Vince Foster, for Christ's sake!" (Drudge 2001).

Just as divisive was a television appearance by the Reverend Jerry Falwell on Pat Robertson's *700 Club* two days after the terrorist attacks. On the program, the two evangelical leaders discussed the tragedies of 9/11 and speculated as to why they had occurred:

FALWELL: What we saw on Tuesday, as terrible as it is, could be minuscule if, in fact, God continues to lift the curtain and allow the enemies of America to give us probably what we deserve.

ROBERTSON: Jerry, that's my feeling. I think we've just seen the antechamber to terror. We haven't even begun to see what they can do to the population.

FALWELL: The A.C.L.U.'s [American Civil Liberties Union] got to take a lot of the blame for this.

ROBERTSON: Well, yes.

FALWELL: And, I know that I'll hear from them for this. But throwing God out successfully with the help of the federal court system, throwing God out of the public square, out of the schools. The abortionists have got to bear some burden for this because God will not be mocked. And when we destroy 40 million little innocent babies we make God mad. I really believe that the pagans, and the abortionists, and the feminists, and the gays, and the lesbians who are actively trying to make that an alternative lifestyle, the A.C.L.U., People for the American Way—all of them who have tried to secularize America—I point the finger in their face and say, "You helped make this happen."

ROBERTSON: I totally concur. (see de Moraes 2001; Niebuhr 2001)

The Falwell-Robertson exchange ignited a firestorm of protests. The Fox Family Channel, which broadcasts *The 700 Club*, said it "in no way shares the views expressed by Reverend Jerry Falwell" (de Moraes 2001). Lorri L. Jean, executive director of the National Gay and Lesbian Task Force, equated the attitudes held by Falwell and Robertson to those of the Taliban: "The terrible tragedy that has befallen our nation and indeed the entire global community, is the sad byproduct of fanaticism. It has its roots in the same fanaticism that enables people like Jerry Falwell to preach hate against those who do not think, live, or love in the exact same way he does"

(CNN.com 2001). In response, Falwell and Robertson said their remarks were "taken out of context" (de Moraes 2001). But both remained stubbornly defiant in their apologies. Falwell commented: "Our choices have consequences. Our rebellion has results. In many ways, the results of recent days are a reflection of the crumbling foundation of America. It is time to reflect and repent" (see Carlson 2001).[2] Later, Falwell repeated his long-held view that the ACLU and other organizations that "have attempted to secularize America, have removed our nation from its relationship with Christ on which it was founded" (CNN.com 2001). As the public disapprobation continued, Robertson resigned his post as president of the Christian Coalition—a tacit acknowledgment that he had become too controversial a figure to continue leading that conservative organization.

A REBIRTH OF TOLERANCE?

More than a year after the tragedies at the World Trade Center, at the Pentagon, and in Pennsylvania, it is clear that 9/11 changed the country in ways that are still far from clear. The 2002 midterm election results suggest that a revitalized Republican party has a chance to transform U.S. politics on the basis of its conduct of the war on terror and its appropriation of the value of patriotism. Whether this opportunity is one that will redound to the party's benefit remains to be seen. President Bush has gambled much on the war's outcome—including a strike against Saddam Hussein's Iraq that has the potential to decide his administration's fate at the polls and in the history books. Democrats, meanwhile, must find ways to convince voters that they can be trusted not only on domestic issues such as Social Security, Medicare, education, and health care, but in standing up for U.S. interests around the world. Some years ago, the political commentator Chris Matthews likened the Republicans to the "Daddy party" that holds a tough military posture, while Democrats were the "Mommy party" that fretted over education and health care issues. Voters, of course, wanted both their mommy and their daddy and compromised by splitting their ballots for Republican presidents and Democratic congresses.

It may be that the most important long-term political change caused by 9/11 is a deepening public commitment to the value of tolerance. This is particularly true among the young members of Generation 9/11. Judy McGrath, president of MTV, says of her youthful viewers: "One of the things this generation likes to say about themselves is that they are diverse and they appreciate differences. Now it's going to be like, 'Let's see how well you're going to deal with this'" (Rutenberg 2001).

Of course, this was not merely a test for Generation 9/11 alone. Following the terrorist attacks, there were instances of racial and religious discrimination directed at Arab-Americans and Muslim Americans. The Federal Bureau of Investigation (FBI) investigated ninety hate crimes committed in the days following 9/11. Representative John Cooksey, a Louisiana Republican who unsuccessfully sought to oppose Democratic Senator Mary Landrieu in 2002, said: "If I see someone come in that's got a diaper on his head and a fan belt [wrapped] around [it], that guy needs to be pulled over and checked" (*New Republic* 2001a). Several Muslim women who remained faithful to their religious tradition by wearing the traditional *hijab* became objects of public abuse. An Arab-American Secret Service agent traveling from Baltimore to President Bush's Texas ranch during the 2001 Christmas holiday was removed from a commercial airplane and detained for several hours. The pollster Richard B. Wirthlin found that an astonishing 40 percent of survey respondents believe that Islam advocates murder and terrorism, while 44 percent say that the 9/11 attacks represent the feelings of Muslim Americans toward the United States (*Wirthlin Report* 2001). In a 2002 *Commentary* magazine article, Norman Podhoretz captured the sentiments of many conservatives when he wrote: "Certainly, not all Muslims are terrorists. But it would be dishonest to ignore the plain truth that Islam has become an especially fertile breeding ground of terrorism in our time. This can only mean that there is something in the religion itself that legitimizes the likes of Osama bin Laden, and indeed there is: the obligation imposed by the Koran to wage holy war, or jihad, against the 'infidels.'" Reverend Jerry Falwell has referred to the prophet Muhammad as a "terrorist," a comment that earned Falwell renewed antipathy and for which he later apologized. Ibrahim Hopper, a spokesman for the Council on American-Islamic Relations, says: "At some times I feel like a member of the Jewish community in Germany in the latter stages of the Weimar Republic" (Milbank 2002).

At the same time, there were signs that Americans collectively decided to reject bin Laden's appeals to prejudice and embrace the value of diversity. Sensing the shift in mood, President Bush favorably cited instances where tolerance triumphed over prejudice:

I was struck . . . that in many cities when Christian and Jewish women learned that Muslim women, women of cover, were afraid of going out of their homes alone, that they went shopping with them, that they showed true friendship and support, an act that shows the world the true nature of America. Our war on terrorism has nothing to do with differences in faith. It has everything to do with people of all faiths coming together to condemn hate and evil and murder and prejudice. . . . I want to urge my fellow Americans not to use this as an opportunity to pick on somebody that doesn't look like you or share your religion. The thing that makes our nation so strong and that will ultimately defeat terrorist activity is our willingness to tolerate people of different faiths, different opinions, different colors within the fabric of our society. (Bush 2001f)

Bush's message was echoed by others in his administration. After Attorney General John Ashcroft had met with Arab-Americans who relayed incidents of intolerance, he told reporters: "The Justice Department has received reports of violence and threats of violence against Arab-Americans and other Americans of Middle Eastern and South Asian descent. We must not descend to the level of those who perpetrated violence by targeting individuals based on race, religion, or national origin." The secretary of education urged schools to preach acceptance of differences to schoolchildren, a message reinforced by First Lady Laura Bush. Even Democratic Senator Tom Daschle, whose office received an anthrax-tainted letter, pointedly observed: "The overwhelming majority of people understand instinctively that the way we get through hard times is by turning to each other, not on each other" (Zogby 2001). The media reinforced the plea for tolerance preached by Bush and unity-minded Democrats. Deploring signs of anti-Muslim, anti-Arab sentiments, MTV educated its viewers on the traditions embraced by the Taliban, followers of Islam, and Sikhs. The major broadcast networks likewise filmed public service announcements emphasizing the importance of accepting others with different faiths and cultural backgrounds (Rutenberg 2001).

It should come as no surprise that prominent spokespersons from both parties would advocate tolerance. In the book *Moral Freedom*, where tolerance is deemed *the* primary moral underpinning of our time, one of the author Alan Wolfe's interviewees explains: "I don't think anybody is better than anyone else. I really don't." This attitude is clearly some distance from the morality of Victorian England—not to mention the moral absolutism espoused by fundamentalist religious devotees of Judaism, Christianity, or Islam. Wolfe himself is emphatic: "Americans are not going to lead twenty-first century lives based on eighteenth and nineteenth century moral ideals" (Wolfe 2001, 82–83, 95–96).

It may be that the events of 9/11 have given tolerance an unexpected boost. Less than two weeks after the attacks, one poll showed that those holding favorable views of Arab-Americans totaled 63 percent, while 64 percent were favorably disposed toward American Muslims. Positive opinions of all Arabs and Muslims, whatever their nationality, held at 50 percent and 52 percent, respectively. In addition, 55 percent said they opposed any policy that would single out Arab-Americans for special scrutiny at airport check-ins, and 86 percent said they were either "very concerned" or "somewhat concerned" about the treatment that Arab-Americans and American Muslims might receive after the attacks (Zogby International 2001b). An October 2002 poll also bore witness to public tolerance: 56 percent said they had become more likely since 9/11 to respect cultures that do not share their values; only 27 percent said they were less likely to extend such respect (Ipsos-Reid 2002).

Throughout history, Americans have consistently portrayed themselves as possessing characteristics unlike those of their enemies. During the cold war, Americans drew a bright line between Soviet-style Communism and adherence to democratic values. The *World Book Encyclopedia* (1964, 724b) explained the general differences between communism and democracy not in terms of philosophical works by each ideology's leading advocates, but in the parlance heard around the dining room table: "In a democratic country, the government rules by consent of the people. In a communist country, the dictator rules by force and stays in power by force. A democratic government tries to act in a way that will benefit the people. . . . Under communism, the interests of the government always come first. . . . Communism violently opposes democracy and the democratic way of life." Thus, when Ronald Reagan (1983) dubbed the Soviet Union the "evil empire," most Americans agreed with him.

For many, 9/11 decisively answered the question "What does it mean to be an American?" As was the case during the cold war, being an American today means presenting oneself as the opposite of the country's enemy. *The decisive contrast between freedom-loving American patriots, on the one* hand, and Osama bin Laden and his Al Qaeda supporters, on the other, is the value of tolerance. If a greater public emphasis on tolerance is an unintended consequence of the terrorist attacks, the long-term effects are likely to enhance sociologist Wolfe's idea of a "morality-writ-small" politics that will predominate in the twenty-first century (1998, esp. 275–322). Such an enhancement of an individual values structure need not be at the expense of respect for more traditional values, nor need it discourage religiosity. Indeed, many Americans may conclude that these values should remain paramount in their personal lives. Yet, if more citizens are to embrace traditional married lifestyles—or attend a church, synagogue, temple, or mosque with greater frequency—those who advocate this way of living must present their case differently. In short, they must not argue for their way of life as one that is girded in absolute moral truths per se. Rather, they must make the point that adherence to tradition is consistent with a positive outlook on life and brings with it certain distinctive benefits to individual well-being. Even as we argue about how we translate our historic values in light of the new terrorist threats, a quotation from the introductory paragraph of this essay bears repeating: "We're all Americans now."

NOTES

1. Hamilton's famous line reads: "Energy in the executive is a leading character in the definition of good government." He continued, "It is essential to the protection of the community against foreign attacks."

2. Falwell's son, the Reverend Jonathan Falwell, wrote a fund-raising letter saying that "Satan has launched a hail of fiery darts at Dad." The younger Falwell asked for a special Vote of Confidence gift of at least $50 or $100. See Carlson 2001.

REFERENCES

Apple, R. W. 2001. "No Middle Ground." *New York Times*, September 14, 1.
Auchincloss, Kenneth. 2001. "We Shall Overcome." *Newsweek*, September 24, 19–20.
Balz, Dan, and John F. Harris. 2001. "Shock of War May Have Changed the Tone in Politics." *Washington Post*, October 14, A-3.
Barber, Benjamin R. 1996. *Jihad vs. McWorld*. New York: Ballantine Books.
Beamer, Lisa, with Ken Abraham. 2002. *Let's Roll! Ordinary People, Extraordinary Courage*. Wheaton, Ill.: Tyndale House.
Bedlington, Stanley. 2001. "Not Who You Think." *Washington Post*, October 29, B-2.

Brooks, David. 2001. "The Organization Kid Revisited." November 4. On-line at Newsweek.msnbc.com.

Bruni, Frank. 2001. "For Bush, a Mission and a Defining Moment." *New York Times,* September 22, A1.

Burns, John F. 2001. "America Inspires Both Longing and Loathing in Arab World." *New York Times,* Steptember 16, A4

Bush, George W. 2001a. Address to the nation, Washington D.C., September 11.

Bush, George W. 2001b. Radio address of the president to the nation, Camp David, Md., September 15.

Bush, George W. 2001c. Remarks to employees at the Pentagon, Arlington, Va., September 17.

Bush, George W. 2001d. Address to a joint session of Congress, Washington, D.C., September 20.

Bush, George W. 2001e. Address to the nation announcing the bombing of Afghanistan, Washington, D. C., October 7.

Bush, George W. 2001f. Press conference, Washington, D.C., October 11.

Bush, George W. 2001g. Address to the nation, Atlanta, Ga., November 8.

Carlson, Peter. 2001. "Jerry Falwell's Awkward Apology." *Washington Post,* November 18, F-1.

CBS News/*New York Times* poll. 2002. October 27–31.

CBS News survey. 2002. May 13–14.

CBSNews.com. 2001. "Millions from the Stars." September 26.

Cheney, Lynne V. 2002. *America: A Patriotic Primer.* New York: Simon and Schuster.

Clinton, Chelsea. 2001/2002. "Before and After." *Talk,* December/January, 100, 142.

CNN.com. 2001. "Falwell Apologizes to Gays, Feminists, Lesbians." September 14.

De Moraes, Lisa. 2001. "Wall to Wall Coverage Close to Setting a Record." *Washington Post,* September 15, C-7.

Democracy Corps poll. 2002. September 17–22.

Dionne, E. J., Jr. 2001. "A New and Improved George W." *Washington Post,* October 12, A-33.

Dowd, Maureen. 2001. "All That Glistens." *New York Times,* October 3.

Drudge, Matt. 2001. *Drudge Report.* October 23.

Gallup poll. 2001a. September 7–10.

Gallup poll. 2001b. September 21–22.

Gallup poll. 2001c. "Tuesday Briefing," press release, September 25.

Gallup poll. 2001d. October 5–6.

Gibbs, Nancy. 2001. "Mourning in America." *Time,* September 24.

Green, Jesse. 2001/2002. "Requiem of a Heavyweight." *Talk,* December/January.

Greenberg, Stanley B. 2001. "'We'—Not 'Me.'" *AmericanProspect,* December 17, 25–26.

Greenberg Quinlan Rosner Research poll. 2002. July 22–24.

Grove, Lloyd. 2001. "Hillary's Knight in Shining Anger." *Washington Post,* September 15, C-7.

Grove, Lloyd. 2002. "Who's Gonna Spill and Bill and Hill?" *Washington Post*, February 28, C-3.

Hamilton, Alexander. 1961. "Federalist 70." In *The Federalist Papers*, ed. Clinton Rossiter. New York: Mentor Books, 1961, 423.

Ipsos-Reid poll. 2002. October 15–17.

LeMoyne College/Zogby International poll. 2002. March.

Milbank, Dana. 2001. "Bush Makes a Pitch for Teaching Patriotism." *Washington Post*, November 2.

Milbank, Dana. 2002. "Conservatives Dispute Bush Portayal of Islam as Peaceful." *Washington Post*, November 29, A-4–A-5.

Moody, Nekesa Mumbi. 2001. "'God Bless America' Debuts on Top." Associated Press.

Moore, David W. 2001. "Top Ten Gallup Presidential Approval Ratings." Gallup press release, September 24.

MTV.com. 2001a. "Audience Response to the Attacks." September 12.

MTV.com. 2001b. "Cable Network Profiles."

New Republic. 2001a. "Notebook." October 8, 11.

New Republic. 2001b. "Notebook." October 22.

New York Review of Books. 2001. "Bin Laden's Obsessions." November 15, 4.

Newsweek. 2001. "Perspectives." October 8, 17.

Niebuhr, Gustav. 2001. "U.S. 'Secular' Groups Set Tone for Terror Attacks, Falwell Says." *New York Times*, September 14.

Pollitt, Katha. 2001. "Pull Out No Flags." *Nation*, October 8.

Princeton Survey Research Associates survey. 2001. September 13–17.

Putnam, Robert D. 2000. *Bowling Alone: The Collapse and Revival of American Community*. New York: Simon and Schuster.

Reagan, Ronald. 1983. Remarks at the annual convention of the national association of evangelicals, Orlando, Fla., March 8.

Rutenberg, Jim. 2001. "MTV, Turning Serious, Helps Its Generation Cope." *New York Times*, October 2.

Saad, Lydia. 2001. "Americans Anxious, but Holding Their Heads High." Gallup press release, October 1.

St. George, Donna. 2001. "After a Death, a New Way of Life." *Washington Post*, October 28.

Segal, David. 2001. "All Together Now." *Washington Post*, September 24, C-1.

Simpson, Jeffrey. 1986. "Living Beside a Cultural and Economic Colossus." *New York Times*, August 24, E3.

Strauss, Neil. 2001. "After the Horror, Radio Stations Pull Some Songs." *New York Times*, September 19.

Stuever, Hank. 2001a. "Miss America the Beautiful." *Washington Post*, September 22, C-1.

Stuever, Hank. 2001b. "The Bomb with a Loaded Message." *Washington Post*, October 27, C-1.

Sullivan, Robert. 2001. "New York's New 'Normal.'" *Time*, October 2.

Time. 1986. "Pop Goes the Culture." June 16, 73.

Time. 1992. "The Incredible Shrinking President," June 29.

Time/CNN/Harris Interactive poll. 2001. December 19–20.

Time/CNN/Harris Interactive poll. 2002. October 23–24.

USA Today. 2001. "USA Today Snapshots." October 19, 1-A.

Washington Post. 2001. "Text of Bin Laden Remarks." October 8, A-12.

Washington Post poll. 2002. September 3–6.

White, John Kenneth. 1998. *Still Seeing Red: How the Cold War Shapes the New American Politics*. Boulder, Colo.: Westview.

White, John Kenneth. 2002. *The Values Divide: American Politics and Culture in Transition*. New York: Chatham House.

Wilgoren, Jodi. 2001. "A Terrorist Profile Emerges That Confounds the Experts." *New York Times*, September 16, A4.

Wiltz, Teresa. 2001. "Playing in the Shadows." *Washington Post*, November 19, C-1.

Wirthlin Report. 2001. "America Responds." September 2–3.

Wirthlin Worldwide poll. 2001. October 5–8.

Wolfe, Alan. 1998. *One Nation, after All*. New York: Viking Press.

Wolfe, Alan. 2001. *Moral Freedom: The Impossible Idea That Defines the Way We Live Now*. New York: W. W. Norton.

Woodward, Bob. 2001. "A Test of Government's Trustworthiness." *Washington Post*, October 25, A-31.

Woodward, Kenneth. 2001. "A Peaceful Faith, a Fanatic Few." *Newsweek*, September 24, 68.

World Book Encyclopedia. 1964. Chicago: Field Enterprises Education Corporation.

Zogby, James J. 2001. "Arab-Americans Are Defended." *Washington Watch*, October 1.

Zogby International survey. 2001a. September 17–18.

Zogby Internation tracking date. 2001b. September 23.

Zogby International tracking poll. 2001c. October 5-7.

Zogby International poll. 2001d. October 8–10.

Zogby International survey. 2001e. October 12–15.

Zogby International tracking poll. 2001f. October 24.

Zogby International tracking poll. 2001g. November 3.

The War on Terrorism and the New Patriotism

These are the times that try men's souls: The summer soldier and the sunshine pa-
triot will, in this crisis, shrink from the service of his country; but he that stands it
NOW deserves the love and thanks of man and woman. . . . the harder the conflict,
the more glorious the triumph. What we obtain too cheap, we esteem too lightly.

—THOMAS PAINE, "The American Crisis, No 1" (1776)

Thomas Paine, a revolutionary pamphleteer, saw the "times that try men's souls" in the dark days in 1776 after the defeat of American forces in New York and New Jersey. Yet for him the crisis was more than military. It was a question of morale, and a test of whether Americans could become worthy of freedom through their sacrifices. "Heaven knows how to set a proper price upon its goods," wrote Paine, and he warned that God will not grant enduring liberty to a people who try to win it with cheap victories or empty gestures of "sunshine patriotism" (Paine 1995 [1776]).

If Paine worried about sunshine patriots, Karl Popper, a philosopher of science and another powerful defender of the open society, once observed that leaders in a national crisis are too often tempted to "appeal to our tribal instincts, to passion and to prejudice and to our nostalgic desire to be relieved of the strain of individual responsibility" (Popper 1966, 49). Now we face a new crisis. After the horrific terrorist attacks of 9/11, what kind of sacrifices and what sort of patriotism are necessary to defend liberty? Not since 1942 has there been such an opportunity for—or danger of—a massive civil mobilization of the U.S. population on the basis of American national identity. Government authorities after 9/11, facing an uncertain war with terrorism, attempted to protect the open society with a balance of calmness and vigilance, volunteer action with acceptance of greater police powers, civic sacrifice with more consumerism. In the end, the nation's leaders avoided both extreme xenophobia and the "sunshine patriotism" condemned by Tom Paine. But the result was a thin and "partly cloudy" patriotism that showed only the smallest regard for the kinds of sacrifices the president's policies might eventually extract from most citizens.

Others in this volume note how the horrific terrorist attacks of 9/11 have prompted patriotic reactions. An ocean of flags signify a powerful sense of unity and pride of country. Seeing a chance to build a new civic consciousness characterized by faith in government and volunteerism, Americans lined up to give blood, help others, and make even greater sacrifices if asked.

It is ironic that citizens were intent on connecting with government and public life, but the government told them to go shopping instead. This essay places the new patriotism in historical context and argues that mobilizing the U.S. population on the basis of American national identity for the war on terrorism opens up a political debate about the definition of sacrifice and about the character of those populations whose interests might be sacrificed. It opens a process in which claimed sacrifices and contributions can be parlayed into political advantage or into efforts to shift the war burden to others (Leff 1991, 1298).

Paine understood the "gravitating power" of shocking events, which temporarily strengthen "duty and attachment to each other" among atomistic individuals (Paine 1995). Personal trauma tends to distinguish and estrange the sufferer from the rest of society, while collective trauma like 9/11 pulls people together (Bellelli and Amatulli 1997; Neal 1998). In an attempt to get a handle on the crisis, they look for guidance from past experiences as interpreted by national myths and collective memories. When those narratives do not fit the new situation, it is a challenge and an opportunity for leaders to reinterpret them. We suspend our routines, gather in groups to reflect on the disaster, and begin to repair the social damage together. For most people, 9/11 was not a life-transforming personal trauma but a collective trauma—an assault on this society's way of life and expectations, exposing national vulnerability and leading individuals to reflect upon their identities as "American citizens."

After the terrorist attacks, Robert Putnam found "unmistakable evidence of change" in Americans' engagement with civic life (Putnam 2002, 20). He reported that trust in government, trust in the police, and interest in politics were all significantly higher than they were before 9/11. There were similar findings from other sources. A Gallup poll found in the week after the attack that over 80 percent of Americans displayed an American flag, 60 percent attended memorial services, almost 75 percent prayed, and an equal number said they were showing greater affection than usual for loved ones (Gallup 2001b). A *Washington Post*/ABC News poll (2001) found soon after the attacks that nearly three-quarters of the public described themselves as "strongly patriotic"—a level not recorded since the middle of the 1991 Gulf War (1991a). In addition, Major League baseball instituted the singing of "God Bless America" in the seventh-inning stretch.

The patriotic reaction had some features of a revival. Certainly, government had a window of opportunity to call for greater sacrifices and to begin institutionalizing greater cooperation between the federal government and the groups and institutions of "civil society." Shock and grief for the victims and anger at the terrorists gave way to inspiration as the stories of heroic airline passengers and selfless rescue workers became known. Inspirational images and patriotic attitudes during a crisis make for only brief surges in civic involvement, however. "Though the crisis replenished the wells of solidarity in American communities," Robert Putnam (2000, 22) has remarked "those wells so far remain untapped."

FOUNDATIONS OF AMERICAN PATRIOTISM

The problem of defining patriotism and civic obligation is not a new one. The idea of patriotism is ancient, rooted in the citizen's love of homeland and political institutions. It has been expressed in loyalty to regimes ranging from city-states to multinational empires. Nationalism, by contrast, is the effort to marshal allegiance in a population based on their belief that they share common and particular ethnic features (Connor 1994, xi; Barrington 1997, 712). Despite these conceptual distinctions, Popper would not have seen much practical distinction between patriotism and nationalism. In practice, ethnic nationalism and patriotism have been intertwined at least since the nineteenth century. Patriots are not immune to the temptation to call upon ethnic sentiments and xenophobia, and ethnic leaders have tried to build movements by attempting to make the ethnic nation the object of the patriot's devotion by using the language of patriotism (Viroli 1995). For much of our political identity, we are indebted to facts of cultural origin— such as place, language, history, and ancestry. For patriotism, however, these are not the ultimate objects of loyalty or identity. Unlike ethnic nationalism, patriotism requires us to look beyond unalterable ties of blood origins for our ultimate loyalties, and to recognize that we are political animals whose identity is constituted by the laws and institutions of a particular polity (Deneen 2002, Nielsen 1999).

The American founders in the eighteenth century faced a dilemma not encountered by European states, which built allegiance by identifying themselves with their particular national cultures. The constitutional framers instead had to construct a national identity to fit a newly established regime of vast continental scale based on an individualistic philosophy (Hayes 1928). They began their philosophy of patriotism with the idea that humans are naturally free and isolated individuals who construct government and agree to obey it in order to better serve their private purposes, mainly the security of their persons and property. They realized that state governments and local culture held a more powerful sway on the affections and loyalties of citizens than the new federal government. The prevailing conception of patriotism, held mainly by their opponents, was based on the belief that active citizenship is the expression of one's identification with local community (Dietz 1986, 270; Viroli 1995, 63). A government of the scale envisioned by the framers would inevitably be more impersonal and require more compromises than smaller and more intimate communities are accustomed to make. Their solution to this dilemma lay not in constructing a federal government with the ability to force states to comply with national policies. Instead, the framers argued that loyalty to large-scale organizations depends on their ability to act effectively in the lives of individuals. As Alexander Hamilton defended his idea of national government in the 27th *Federalist Paper* (1787), stable and "energetic" administration against "internal and external danger" over time will "touch the most sensible cords and put into motion the active springs of the human heart" and "conciliate the respect and attachment of the community" (Hamilton, Madison, and Jay 1982, 133).

Hamilton and the other founders were by no means confident that the federal government would become the supreme object of national loyalty. Rather, they hoped that as citizens became accustomed to consistent and energetic federal administration over the parts of their lives in which they took the most interest, the government would in time be able to make a claim on their loyalties at least as strong as their attachments to civic groups, locality, or family. They envisioned that people would come to see their self-interest coincide with the stability and strength of the federal government and its ability to defend the nation's security.

This variation on the social contract theory had its limits. The framers doubted that enlightened self-interest was sufficient to motivate citizens to risk or sacrifice their lives for the nation-state. They hoped instead that citizens would learn the ability to see themselves as *more than* self-interested individuals, to feel obligations beyond the self and immediate family. For the most part, though, leaders in that system would be required to appeal to private interests in their calls for public sacrifices.

Alexis de Tocqueville, a young French aristocrat touring America in 1830, recognized this dilemma when he said that the "instinctive patriotism" of the old monarchy, based on "a reverence for traditions of the past," incited "great transient exertions, but no continuity of effort" (Tocqueville 1990, 1: 242). In modernity, instinctive patriotism is gone, and "the country assumes a dim and dubious shape in the eyes of citizens" (Tocqueville 1990, 1: 241). The risk was that instinctive patriotism would be replaced by a chauvinistic nationalist pride that "resorts to a thousand artifices and descends to all the petty tricks of personal vanity" (Tocqueville 1990, 1: 244). In its sentimental guise, patriotism becomes more an expression of veneration for the state, scarcely able to steer a course toward a life of civic involvement and service.

He thought that the only alternative was for the United States to develop a "more rational" patriotism based on active participation in civic life. It was a patriotism "less generous and perhaps less ardent," but "more creative and more lasting" than instinctive patriotism. "It is nurtured by the laws; it grows by the exercise of civil rights; and in the end, it is confounded with the personal interests of the citizen" (Tocqueville 1990, 1: 242). Civic attachment would have to be forged in the small sacrifices of time and energy citizens make in their active involvement in churches, town meetings, social clubs, and political parties. Patriotism in a modern democracy, at its best, would be something more than unenlightened egoism and something less than unreflective identification with the nation. Tocqueville saw that there were some advantages of this union of patriotism and self-interest, but he worried that Americans would mistakenly see even their noblest, most generous, and self-sacrificing instincts as merely a product of self-interest:

"They are more anxious to do honor to their philosophy than to themselves" (Tocqueville 1990, 2: 122). He believed it was true that participation would likely begin in calculations of self-interest, but over time "men attend to the interests of the public, first by necessity, afterwards by choice; what was intentional becomes an instinct, and by dint of working for the good of one's fellow citizens, the habit and the taste for serving them are at length acquired" (Tocqueville 1990, 2: 105).

The links between local civic activity and national patriotic sentiment grew increasingly difficult to sustain as America entered its industrial phase, and government became ever more bureaucratic and distant from citizen control in the twentieth century. The older U.S. patriotism has been visible at times. In a national crisis, one's identity as a "patriotic citizen" may temporarily trump other identities, and public interest might trump private concerns. But in the long run, willingness to make even small sacrifices must be reinforced by popular culture and sustained by governmental institutions that will channel people's energies into public life. Even then, the content of that identity and the ways in which the burdens of patriotism are to be distributed depend on what historian Mark Leff calls "the politics of sacrifice" (Leff 1991). In a national crisis, the mystique of home front sacrifice can permeate the political landscape. But, Leff argues, these changes in the vocabulary of political obligation and membership do not imply open-ended commitments to civic life or erasure of private life and personal interests. Even though sacrifice is based on underlying conceptions of patriotism, it is nevertheless malleable to the interplay of prevailing interests (Leff 1991, 1318). Particular circumstances can "tip the scales" toward certain conceptions of patriotism and distributions of "sacrifice," and the post-9/11 political environment is no exception.

THE POLITICS OF SACRIFICE, 1941–2001

The terrorist attacks of 9/11 constituted a traumatic national incident most often compared to the attack on Pearl Harbor in 1941, which ushered in a time of major civic as well as military mobilization. Americans in 1941 were called to leave simple patriotic veneration behind, to redefine the nature of loyalty and affiliation. Sixteen million men and women served in the armed forces and millions more made lesser sorts of sacrifice. Historians of the

U.S. home front in World War II have shown, however, that sacrifice and solidarity here was a very different nationalism than that seen in Japan, Germany, or even Great Britain (Leff 1991; Bodnar 1996).

The 1942 "call to sacrifice" speech by President Franklin D. Roosevelt (FDR) admonished Americans to ration gasoline and meat, and to accept wage and price controls. Children collected grease and tin cans for the war effort. The president spoke of shared economic sacrifices:

> There is one front and one battle where everyone in the United States—every man, woman and child—is in action. . . . Here at home everyone will have the privilege of making whatever self-denial is necessary, not only to supply our fighting men, but to keep the economic structure of our country fortified and secure during the war and after the war. This will require, of course, the abandonment not only of luxuries but of many other creature comforts. (Roosevelt 1942)

FDR noted that "sacrifice" is not the "proper word with which to describe this program of denial. . . . The price is not too high. If you doubt it, ask the millions who live today under the tyranny of Hitlerism" (Roosevelt 1942).

Contrary to popular mythology, sacrifice on the home front was not a simple thing to do or define in World War II. While 68 percent indicated that they made "real sacrifices" in the war in 1943, by 1944 only 31 percent said so (Gallup 1943; Gallup 1944). Of those few who believed that they had made real sacrifices in 1944, 39 percent said a loved one had been killed in the fighting, 37 percent commented that the sacrifice was of a "financial nature" (the purchase of war bonds), and 19 percent noted that they had made sacrifices of a "material nature" in the form of higher prices, shortages, and rationing (Gallup 1944). After all, "real sacrifice" was what boys on the front line made. In fact, during the war years, about half of Americans felt that people were not "taking the war seriously enough" (Cantril 1951, 483).

At the time, staff in the American mobilization agencies commonly complained of the difficulties of transforming people's "willingness" to sacrifice into "action," and of cracking the "shell of half-hearted sacrifice" and unwillingness to forgo the ordinary pleasures and comforts of life. President Roosevelt attempted to scold the public into greater cooperation but expressed his disgust at the "whining demands of pressure groups" that continued to seek government support of their interests during the crisis (Leff 1991, 1297).

The rhetoric of shared sacrifices concealed a political battle to decide which labor and business groups would shoulder the greater burden of the war. In the end, "sacrifice" on the home front came to be defined as limitation of substantial gains, rather than the deprivation or destruction suffered by citizens of other countries. By 1944, government-led mobilization had sputtered to a stop. Instead, Roosevelt's administration enlisted the aid of the War Advertising Council to coordinate a vast private advertising campaign supporting wartime programs and propaganda themes. Privately donated advertising adopted the imagery of sacrifice, but it also allowed certain groups—industrial interests in particular—to get the upper hand in defining "sacrifice" in terms that over the long haul reinforced their own interests and political claims (Leff 1991, 1298).

After the New Deal and World War II, the U.S. government emerged as a vast welfare state with the largest and most powerful military in the world as well as a new adversary. President Harry Truman's speech to the nation introducing a national goal of containing communism set the stage for this new period. McCarthyism and the effort to root out "un-American" citizens is a chilling chapter in the history of American patriotism. But a key counterpoint was President John F. Kennedy's effort to reconstruct the ideal of patriotic sacrifice by combining cold war anticommunism with the hopeful progressive idealism of the New Frontier. "Now the trumpet summons us again—not as a call to bear arms, though arms we need; not as a call to battle, though embattled we are—but a call to bear the burden of a long twilight struggle year in and year out," Kennedy said in his 1961 inaugural address (Suriano 1993, 219). "Ask not what your country can do for you, ask what you can do for your country." The Vietnam War broke the Kennedy spell; patriotism became less a concept of national unity and more a flash point for political controversy between "hawks" and "doves." As John Schaar explained at the time, "if some people favor patriotism, largely for the wrong reasons, and if some oppose it, largely for the wrong reasons, others hardly think about it at all" (Schaar 1973, 60).

President Ronald Reagan attempted to revive patriotic language in a renewed cold war in ways that would have repercussions in post-9/11 politics (Turner and Ladd 1986; McLean 1999). Reagan's opportunity came with the

Iran hostage crisis in December 1979 and the Soviet invasion of Afghanistan in January 1980. Roper's poll in February 1980 found 43 percent of the public feeling more patriotic as a result of the hostage crisis (Roper Organization 1980). President Jimmy Carter's failed rescue attempt in March 1980 and the boycott of the 1980 Moscow Olympics after the Soviet invasion of Afghanistan allowed candidate Reagan to vow he would stand up to the Russians and Islamic fundamentalists. As president, Reagan's language of "standing tall" against the "evil empire" led to further evaporation of U.S.–Soviet détente and a seeming revival of cold war patriotism.

Yet 1980s patriotism was different in character. Popular memory today recalls that talk of patriotism by government leaders blossomed in the 1980s, thanks to Reagan and the new cold war. Indeed, a survey done in his first year in office found 32 percent saying they were prouder to be Americans than they were in 1971 (Merit Methodology 1981). Tables 1 and 2 reveal this rise in patriotic sentiments in the early Reagan years. Yet his rhetorical appeal to patriotism and old communal values must be viewed in the context of his language and policies based on individualism. Patriotism easily became a kind of ritualistic and amorphous sentiment of standing up to the Soviets, that lacks precise connections to citizen action or sacrifice. In Wilson Carey McWilliams's words, "Neither Ronald Reagan nor George Bush [had] been willing to ask Americans for sacrifice, and where their policies have imposed burdens, they have almost universally fallen on the less fortunate" (McWilliams 2000, 67). This is exemplified in a survey that found 61 percent agreeing with the idea that one does not have to do anything except feel love for the country in order to be patriotic. When the same poll went on to ask the respondents specifically which of their activities express(es) their patriotism, almost a quarter could not characterize any of their activities as patriotic, though when prompted, 17 percent could cite military service, 11 percent mentioned voting and displaying the flag, and 7 percent mentioned community volunteering (*New York Times* 1983a, 1983b).

After Reagan's reelection, trust in government reached its highest point since President Richard Nixon's resignation. In assessing the forms of patriotic sentiment of the Reagan years, we should bear in mind how little the military victories of the period cost in blood and treasure, and how even Reagan's most daring cold war ventures, such as the Iran-contra deal, were orchestrated in secret. In that episode, the administration violated its own policy against negotiation with terrorists in its covert plan to leverage the

TABLE 1. **Percentage of Americans Who Feel "Very Patriotic"**

Year	%
2001	72*
1999	49
1997	38
1994	51
1992	52
1991	55*
1990	48
1989	51
1988	51
1987	43
1985	56*
1983	52*

SOURCE: Pew Research Center and CBS News/*New York Times* (denoted by *). Data provided by the Roper Center for Public Opinion Research, University of Connecticut.

QUESTION: "Do you consider yourself very patriotic, somewhat patriotic, or not very patriotic?"

release of hostages by selling arms to Iran. Then, Colonel Oliver North, a National Security Council staff member, schemed to use the profits of the Iranian arms sale for military aid to the anti-communist *contra* rebels in Nicaragua without congressional knowledge or approval. Superpatriot North's eventual congressional testimony justifying clandestine deals with Teheran and *contra* rebels served to remind the nation of Vietnam, Watergate, and Iran hostages at the same time.

The Iran-contra affair revealed the weaknesses of Reagan-era patriotism. As table 1 shows, Americans who said they were "very patriotic" plummeted from 56 percent in 1985 to 43 percent in 1987. Reagan suffered a 20-point drop in job approval as the Iran-contra affair unraveled, and trust in government began a decline that did not reverse until 1994 (Brace and Hinkley 1992, 40). In fact, trust in government never returned to 1984 levels until 2000 (American National Election Studies 1958–2000).

By 1989, patriotic sentiments were recovering from the Iran-contra disgrace, but the imminent collapse of the Soviet Union led to a period of patriotism without a cold war threat. In the 1991 Gulf War, President George H. W. Bush's portrayal of President Saddam Hussein of Iraq as "Hitler revisited" harkened back to an earlier era, but in reality the war opened a new chapter in the politics of sacrifice. As table 4 shows, the percentage who agreed with the idea that we should all be willing to fight for our country whether it is right or wrong was low in 1987 but peaked during the first Gulf

TABLE 2. American Pride, 1981–2002: "Very Proud to Be American"

Year	% Very Proud
1981	78
1986	89
1990	74
1991	77
2000	73
2001	87[a] (January)
2002	90[a]

SOURCE: Gallup poll. Data provided by the Roper Center for Public Opinion Research, University of Connecticut.

a. Percentages combine those for "extremely proud" and "very proud." Gallup changed question wording in January 2001 to include "extremely proud" and "very proud."

TABLE 3. "Extremely Proud to Be American"

Date	%	Polling Organization
Nov. 1981	81	Roper
Nov. 1988	67	National Election Study
June 1991	87	AP poll
Jan. 1994	47	General Social Survey
Jan. 2001	55	Gallup
March 2002	74	Gallup
June 2002	65	Gallup
Sept. 2002	69	Gallup

SOURCE: Data provided by the Roper Center for Public Opinion Research, University of Connecticut.

QUESTION: "How proud are you to be an American—extremely proud, very proud, moderately proud, only a little proud, or not at all proud?"

War, returning the next year to close to historical norms. The display of yellow ribbons and the apparently apolitical call to "support the troops" undercut the antiwar groups, but it was not exactly a ringing endorsement of the war. Opposition to the war was diminished not so much by hyperpatriotism but by the international sanctioning of war by the United Nations (UN), and most Americans were relieved by the president's decision to adhere to the UN resolutions and not to advance to Baghdad.

This public ambivalence about the Gulf War is evident in the erratic readings on patriotic sentiments at various times and in various polls in 1991. According to John Mueller (1994, 94), the percentage saying they were proud to be American was actually lower than it had been in 1986 and no

TABLE 4. "We Should All Be Willing to Fight for Our Country, Whether It Is Right or Wrong"

Year	% Completely Agree
1999	21
1997	21
1994	25
1993	21
1992	24
1991	30
1990	22
1989	22
1988	23
1987	17

SOURCE: Times Mirror. Data provided by the Roper Center for Public Opinion Research, University of Connecticut.

higher than in 1981; his argument posits that concerns about the faltering economy in 1991 counteracted jubilation after the Gulf War.

On February 27, 1991, the day President George H. W. Bush announced the cease-fire in the Persian Gulf, a poll found 70 percent saying they were "strongly patriotic"; at the end of May, the number had dropped slightly, to 65 percent (*Washington Post*/ABC News 1991a, 1991b). A week later, a different poll found only 55 percent describing themselves as "very patriotic" (CBS News/*New York Times* 1991). Pride in country bounced back again in June 1991, reaching a record-high 87 percent during the week of New York City's triumphal military parade (Associated Press 1991). In November, another survey found 58 percent feeling "very patriotic," but that height would not be reached again until after the 9/11 attacks (*Times Mirror* 1991).

In another 1991 survey, 30 percent ranked the victory in the Gulf War as the event in their lifetime that made them most proud to be American— twice the percentage that ranked victory in World War II, the *Apollo 11* moon landing, and Martin Luther King Jr.'s leadership in the civil rights movement as the proudest moment (NBC News/*Wall Street Journal* 1991). The significance of Gulf War patriotism shifted as the 1992 presidential elections neared. When the same question was asked again in 1992, only 20 percent mentioned the Gulf War, while mentions of World War II increased to 25 percent (NBC News/*Wall Street Journal* 1992).

As voter cynicism and apathy grew, leaders began to ask what problems or goals might stir the next generation. The uneasy legacy of the Gulf War and the collapse of the Soviet Union left the United States supreme at what Francis Fukuyama prematurely called the "end of history," but without a strong political or ideological adversary. The only clear foreign policy goal after the cold war was the expansion of world trade. The novel *Generation X* raised doubts about the future (Coupland 1992), and Brokaw's nonfiction work *The Greatest Generation* helped to spawn a cottage industry celebrating the civic-minded older generation. Movies such as *Apollo 13, Saving Private Ryan, Pearl Harbor,* and *Thirteen Days* were cinematic reflections of Brokaw's book. However, what each film seemed to offer to Generation X and baby boomers was vicarious patriotism for mass consumption rather than lessons in courage for the next century.

Of course, anxiety about the patriotism and leadership qualities of the younger generation is as old as politics itself, and so is remembering the past as a more patriotic time. A poll in the late 1980s found that 65 percent thought teenagers were more patriotic "twenty years ago" (Gallup 1989). The *Washington Post* (1989) also found slightly more Americans believing the country was more patriotic "during the late 1960s" than in the present. Over two-thirds in a poll a decade later perceived that Americans were more patriotic "25 years ago" (Opinion Dynamics/Fox News 1998). Perhaps many respondents forgot momentarily the longhaired youth protesting war and burning their draft cards in 1969, or the slightly later malaise in the wake of Vietnam and Watergate in 1973. Whatever the cause, the polls revealed symptoms of growing anxiety about national purposes after the cold war.

Confronting these generational worries was the challenge for baby boomer Bill Clinton, first as a presidential candidate and then as president, and he attempted a post–cold war redefinition of patriotism. It was also a political necessity, as he was forced to respond to revelations that he not only avoided the Vietnam War draft but also demonstrated against the war while a Rhodes scholar at Oxford. By the end of the campaigns of 1992 and 1996, the public readily agreed that President George H. W. Bush and Senator Robert Dole (a presidential hopeful) were more patriotic than Clinton. Nevertheless, most Americans did not see patriotism as the defining quality for a president (McLean 1999).

But Clinton also hoped to change the American tradition of patriotism, by associating with community service the ideals of sacrifice and obligation common in American thinking about military service. Whether it was statesmanship, a campaign gimmick, or a way to resolve his own youthful ambivalence during the Vietnam War, Clinton in 1991 proposed the creation of a national youth service corps, what he called "a domestic G.I. Bill." The National Service Bill proposed to offer college students extra financial aid or assistance on college loans in return for a year of voluntary community service. The proposal stemmed in part from Clinton's own recognition that volunteerism tends to be sporadic, a kind of individualized and informal public service suitable for busy schedules, and tends to do more good for the volunteer than the community being served (Waldman 1995, 11). A service corps would offer young people a chance to directly and pragmatically deal with society's problems and work toward improving the urban and rural infrastructure, while also building civic character and bridges across socioeconomic divides.

Congress radically scaled back the Clinton service initiative when the members discovered how much it could cost taxpayers and the kinds of cuts that might be required in other programs (Rimmerman 2001, 112; Waldman 1995). This initiative and an array of similar efforts to boost citizenship through community service had mixed success in the later 1990s. In one study, researchers found that there were steady increases in the number of volunteers between 1995 and 1999 but also that the overall amount of time volunteered had declined. Moreover, the average volunteer in 1995 put in nearly four and a half hours of service for the year, but by 1999 it had decreased to three and a half hours (Steindorf 1999).

Volunteerism, as Robert Bellah has argued, is based on a view of the public good as a spontaneous consensus among the like-minded; the tension-filled process of dealing with the deeper issues and interests at the root of social maladies is seen as pointless or even illegitimate (Bellah et al. 1985). In times of national crisis, leaders often have to ask for sacrifices that are costly or painful; they call us to reshape our routines and challenge us to see ourselves more as citizens than as private individuals. Volunteerism in such times can be a powerful momentary catalyst for invigorating public life. Absent a crisis, though, volunteerism tends to celebrate a private willingness to engage in occasional altruistic service to relieve immediate suffering and "make a difference," but sees deeper commitments and political collaboration as a "hassle." Despite its noncontroversial appeal (or, rather, because of it), volunteerism remains a weak post–cold war substitute for patriotism.

This brief history of patriotism in politics from World War II to the Clinton era is intended to demonstrate how patriotic sentiment came to be considered a private feeling of pride and compassion, celebrated in public rituals and commemorated in popular culture. Leaders and citizens became increasingly uncertain how to connect these individual passions to any meaningful civic action, public service, or economic sacrifice for the wider community. The problem is rooted in the American founding, developed with the welfare state and cold war, and flourished after the terror attacks of 9/11.

THE WAR ON TERRORISM

Volunteerism and community service merged with patriotic symbolism in the first months after the 9/11 attacks. More Americans reported cooperating with neighbors to solve problems. Even church attendance saw a 7 percent spike, though it soon returned to its previous level (Gallup 2001d, 2001e). Emergency blood donations and even enlistment in AmeriCorps all increased dramatically (Copeland 2001). Volunteering increased, though only on an "occasional" basis (Putnam 2000). The *L.A. Times* in November 2001 found 20 percent saying they were spending more time involved in the community, though 35 percent of these people said their community involvement returned to previous levels after one month (*Los Angeles Times* 2001).

President George W. Bush seemed to understand the uncertainty of the post-9/11 period as an opportunity to revise the cold war version of patriotism. On the National Day of Prayer—September 14, 2001—he stressed that the United States was attacked for its responsible pursuit of liberty and democracy, and not for its selfishness, materialism, or capitalist economy. Moreover, the terrorists only succeeded in reminding Americans of the open and civic nature of their national identity:

> In this trial, we have been reminded, and the world has seen, that our fellow Americans are generous and kind, resourceful and brave. We see our national character in rescuers working past exhaustion; in long lines of blood donors; in thousands of citizens who have asked to work and serve in any way possible. And we have seen our national character in eloquent acts of sacrifice. (Bush 2001a)

In a sense a dilemma emerged from the president's initial impulse to call for a "war" on terrorism and his attempt to rally the population out of its complacency for a great national crusade. Terrorism could be considered an act of war or a crime, of course, but the idea of a "war" on terrorism suggests that sacrifices will be necessary in order to conquer the enemy. The appeal to patriotism succeeded in the short term but created long-term problems for American leadership. Terrorism is not a nation or even an "axis." It fits better into the vocabulary of "crime." Yet to treat it as crime suggests that it has violated domestic and international law, and the administration has made it clear that such norms should not constrain unilateral action by the United States. Wars can end, but crimes and terrorism continue even when military objectives have been achieved. Like crime, terrorism cannot be "defeated" militarily, only reduced in frequency (Mueller 2002).

Immediately following 9/11, there were some signs that the patriotic surge might jeopardize the open society. The week after the attacks, about half of Americans favored the idea that Arabs, even those who are U.S. citizens, should be required to carry special identification papers (Gallup 2001c). There was an immediate increase of hate crimes against Muslims, and on the September 13 airing of *The 700 Club,* the Reverend Jerry Falwell blamed the attacks on abortionists, feminists, gays, lesbians, and the American Civil Liberties Union (ACLU)—all "who have tried to secularize America" and turn the nation away from God (People for the American Way 2001). The Justice Department rounded up hundreds of foreign nationals (and some U.S. citizens) without filing charges, and many are still imprisoned as of this writing. Ten days after the attacks, one survey found Americans willing to give more power to the police—even if it means that "they might tap my phone, open my mail, or read my personal e-mail" (Ipsos-Reid 2001). In November 2001, according to the one poll, 58 percent of the public favored giving police the power to search "anyone who fits the general description of suspected terrorists," and a year later, the same polling organization showed that support had actually increased slightly (Fox News 2001, 2002). Another poll found almost half the public in favor of requiring all Arab-American citizens to carry a special identification card at all times (*Time*/CNN 2001). Captured Al Qaeda fighters were sent to prison camps in Cuba without the legal protections of either criminals or prisoners of war. President Bush's plans to hold secret military trials for suspected enemies came to be limited significantly thanks to public pressure. Congress and citizen groups pressured Attorney General John Ashcroft to withdraw his initiative that would have encouraged people to spy on neighbors.

Soon, though, most signs of xenophobia faded. Despite the arrest of Arab suspects, nothing on the scale of Roosevelt's internment of Japanese-Americans in World War II is likely to occur. Bush's rhetorical moves attempted to introduce a new moral balance in patriotism, calling for vigilance, compassion, and unity while discouraging xenophobic paranoia. To the president's credit, he was careful to stress in speeches and a visit to a mosque that peaceful and loyal Muslim Americans were not terrorists. His efforts to avoid demonizing all Arabs and immigrants may have made a difference in public attitudes. Two months after the attack, a poll found that 59 percent of the public had a more favorable view of Muslim Americans—almost 15 percent more favorable than in March 2001. The percentage dropped only slightly, to 54 percent, six months after the attack (Pew Research Center 2001, 2002). Opinions on immigration have also moved toward more openness. Immediately after the attacks, another polling organization found 17 percent more Americans favoring a decrease in immigration, but the percentage in favor of increased immigration had returned to pre-9/11 levels by September 2002 (Gallup 2001a, 2002).

In stressing tolerance and advising the nation to overcome panic, the president was hesitant to call for further sacrifice or to commit government to leading a full-scale mobilization of the civil society. In his speech to Congress and the nation on September 20, 2001, the president called on Americans to confound the terrorists with a patriotic equanimity, to "live your lives, and hug your children. I know many citizens have fears tonight and I ask you to be calm and resolute even in the face of continuing threat" (Bush 2001b). When asked in a news conference on October 11, 2001, why he had not called for sacrifice, Bush stated that Americans were sacrificing by having to endure longer waits in line at airports.

It was in his State of the Union message in 2002 that Bush began to articulate his vision. He underlined his view that patriotic sacrifices involved acting out of feelings of compassion for individuals in need and taking responsibility for helping others.

None of us would ever wish the evil that was done on September the 11th. Yet after America was attacked, it was as if our entire country looked into a mirror and saw our better selves. We were reminded that we are citizens, with obligations to each other, to our country, and to history. We began to think less of the goods we can accumulate, and more about the good we can do. For too long our culture has said, "If it feels good, do it." Now America is embracing a new ethic and a new creed: "Let's roll."

He lauded the heroism and compassion of firefighters, soldiers, police, and citizens during the crisis and said that they offered a glimpse of an emerging "culture of responsibility" (Bush 2002).

The president did hark back to the traditional ideal of community service, but in a limited sense. He called every American to volunteer a minimum of four thousand hours (two years) in community service over a lifetime. Government-sponsored service organizations like the Peace Corps and AmeriCorps would be expanded, and colleges would be required to place more students in community organizations in order to get federal funds. Finally, Bush has also created USA Freedom Corps, which will assist with homeland security and emergency efforts. Despite these initiatives, donating so many hours of service seems overwhelming, even to those accustomed to volunteering. If the president had asked for eight hours per month over a forty-year span, it may have seemed less daunting. Still, eight hours per month is a heavy service load even for the most involved Americans. In any case, government would mostly play the role of cheerleader—not leader—in community service opportunities. Bush's idea of citizenship reflected in the speech was one where individuals regard themselves as private persons with primary obligations to family and profession. Aiding those in need during a crisis is a compassionate reaction of a good individual, but not the common responsibility of a good citizenry.

One reason the president was unwilling to take the idea of service further is that volunteer labor is not free, from a government perspective; in fact massive mobilization of citizen volunteers is very expensive and would therefore open the door to a wider debate on the sacrifices needed to maintain it. A study by Jean Baldwin Grossman estimated that the additional 100 million Americans called for volunteer service would require management costs of around $30 billion (Krueger 2002). Screening, training, and monitoring volunteers, especially for the technical tasks of wartime mobilization and security, is costly, whether participants volunteer for government or for community organizations. To pay for volunteers, government would have to raise taxes or ask multimillionaires and corporations to fund service organizations. It is no wonder that Thomas Ridge, the director of the Office of Homeland Security (created in response to 9/11), seemed at a loss to explain what to do with volunteers—the day after Bush outlined his community service initiative. Ridge called for retired engineers, police officers, and health care professionals, instead of ordinary citizens, as the prime targets for volunteer recruitment (Mitchell 2001). Since Bush has vowed never to repeal the income tax cut, it seems that the administration will continue as long as possible to mobilize the citizenry on the cheap.

Whereas Clinton had hoped for government to create community service opportunities that would teach a public-oriented responsibility toward others, Bush considers compassion a fundamentally private concern that springs spontaneously first for immediate family and later for other citizens. In his view, government's role is to encourage the private feelings of compassion (at the lowest possible financial cost) in hopes that they can develop into personal and public responsibility. Bush's plea for compassion and volunteerism still left out a deeper conception of a widely shared duty to civic sacrifice. Without a serious public philosophy of shared sacrifice to use as a compass after the immediate crisis subsided, rival groups were able to claim that their own sacrifices justified shifting their burdens to others who have not made as many sacrifices. The new politics of sacrifice would soon emerge in three policy issues: compensation to 9/11 survivors, the growing budget deficit, and the cost of a war and occupation of Iraq.

Sacrifice obviously plays a role in the 9/11 Victim Compensation Fund. On September 21, 2001, the Air Transportation Safety Act was passed by the House and Senate. It was proposed three days earlier with the intention of protecting airlines from lawsuits by 9/11 victims' families and offered $15 billion to bail out airlines on the verge of bankruptcy. Democrats demanded that the act include a $6 billion Victim Compensation Fund to make up for damages they might have won from airlines in court (Belkin 2002). Never before has government made such payments to victims of an attack, not even as a result the Pearl Harbor or the Oklahoma City bombings, or in cases of natural disasters. The funds are not considered humanitarian aid to struggling families but compensation for their sacrifice; 9/11 victims have used the language of sacrifice to become a potent lobbying force, helping pressure Bush to create a 9/11 investigative commission. What will happen if there are more terrorist attacks? Will there be compensation if deaths do not involve an industry the government feels compelled to protect? Will other industries demand protection? Whose "sacrifice" counts more? Who will pay to compensate the "sacrifices" of favored groups or industries?

Another potential area of conflict in the debate about sacrifice is taxes and the growing budget deficit. The president vowed not to repeal the generous tax reduction passed early in his administration and aimed at relieving the tax burden on the wealthiest Americans; indeed, in 2003 he insisted that Congress make the tax cut permanent and find additional ways to cut taxes. The "war on terrorism" would be the first in American history in which taxes were not increased. Instead, sacrifices would be made elsewhere, mainly by the least advantaged. In order to maintain federal support for social services, states would be required to cut their welfare rolls even further by pushing more welfare clients into the workforce. Faith-based organizations would be allowed grants to pick up the slack in social services.

The bipartisan consensus after 9/11 gradually eroded as midterm elections approached. The Homeland Security Bill stalled in Congress as Democrats sought to preserve government employee job protections in the proposed new Homeland Security Agency. On September 23, 2002, at a rally in New Jersey, the president commented that "the Senate is more interested in special interests in Washington and not interested in the security of the American people" (Welch 2002). It was a shot across the Democrats' bow, just before the debate on congressional authorization for the president to use force against Iraq. Rather than meeting the patriotism question head-on, Democrats tried to change the subject to health care and the sluggish economy. It turned out to be a poor strategy, as the president used his political capital to help Republican candidates in key elections and to keep the focus on foreign policy. As a result, the Republicans expanded their majority in the House and regained control of the Senate, only the third time in history that a president's party gained seats during a midterm election.

President Bush and the Republicans controlled the agenda as the nation moved closer to war with Iraq. The cost of such a war was downplayed in the Senate debates about granting the president the authority to engage in a preventive war. But a second Gulf War will necessarily have far greater costs than the first. The Congressional Budget Office concluded that even a short, decisive war involving 250,000 U.S. troops could cost between $40 billion and $60 billion (Dobbs 2002). The first Gulf War cost nearly $80 billion in 2002 dollars, but 88 percent of the cost was picked up by America's allies.

Kuwait and Saudi Arabia, for example, paid for over half of the first Gulf War. This time, however, the Saudis refused to support a war against Iraq or foot the bill. Moreover, in contrast to the quick exit of U.S. troops from Kuwait in 1991, a large military presence will be necessary in Iraq to keep order and support a new government, at an additional cost of $15 billion to $20 billion per year for several years. In the end, according to Michael O'Hanlon of the Brookings Institution, the United States will have to pay $100 billion to $200 billion, even assuming "the coalition of the willing" or the United Nations shares the cost burden (Dobbs 2002). This is in line with an upper-bracket estimate by White House economics adviser Lawrence Lindsay, which the White House subsequently downplayed and which led to Lindsay's forced resignation in December 2002 (Dobbs 2002). Even a $200 billion price tag is only about 2 percent of gross domestic product (GDP) now (Dobbs 2002). The problem is that this amount is about 10 percent of a federal budget currently facing out-of-control deficits. If postwar budget deficits grow, new taxes will be necessary. Will the burden be shouldered by the top-bracket taxpayers or by those in the middle brackets? If taxes are cut, as President Bush intends, what indirect impact will rising national debt have on Social Security and private consumer finances?

As the costs of war mount, the politics of sacrifice will loom larger. While it is true that the cost of a second war with Iraq will cost less in relation to GDP than the 1991 war, it will drain an additional 5 to 10 percent from the federal budget in a time of decreased revenues due to the large tax cut of 2001—creating far more political battles about how to pay for the war over a longer period of time than the first Gulf War did.

Throughout the period between 9/11 and the war with Iraq in 2003, the public has struggled to determine what patriotism means in a war on terrorism. This task is particularly difficult when leaders of policy institutions seem determined to focus more on fighting the war than on posing hard problems in a national debate about the future of America in an interdependent world. In view of the aims of the terrorists to disrupt the normal patterns of an open society, it makes sense that government calls for moderation and tolerance. Patriotism can be costly. Yet there is also a political and civic price to be paid by not articulating the nature of the sacrifices needed in the war and by not calling on Americans to subordinate part of their personal and group interests to the national interest.

CONCLUSION

During the years following Vietnam and Watergate, the United States experienced a decline of civic involvement and trust in government; community spirit was replaced with rampant individualism, ethnic bitterness, and social isolation (Putnam 2000, McLean, Schultz, and Steger 2002). The public response to the 9/11 terrorist attacks represented a reversal of these trends, at least momentarily. Citizens rallied behind the president and waited for his signal regarding the burdens and sacrifices they would be expected to bear in the war on terrorism. So far, the new patriotism remains shapeless and "partly cloudy," and the window of civic opportunity is now closing. Trust in government skyrocketed from 31 percent in January 2001 to 55 percent in October, but by January 2002 it had crept down to 46 percent and returned to a steady 33 percent in July 2002. A survey in August 2002 showed that only 25 percent had gotten more involved in volunteer community service since the 9/11 attacks. One poll in September 2002 found 74 percent saying that patriotism and neighborliness had faded (Fox News 2002; CBS News/ *New York Times* 2001, 2001a, 2002). Likewise, President Bush's job approval rating, while still very high by historical standards, has begun a gradual decline.

Roosevelt's call to economic sacrifice in World War II demanded a national mobilization and widespread sacrifices as part of a winning strategy. Though only some make the ultimate sacrifice in modern warfare, there are small sacrifices such as taxes, inconvenience, and shortages of consumer goods that can be broadly acknowledged and shared. However, a Rooseveltian call for sacrifice in 2001 would be out of tune in a globalizing U.S. economy dependent on high levels of consumption and credit. Perhaps the best response to the terror attacks really is to buy more cars and homes, but it is hard to see it as a "sacrifice." Notwithstanding the very real need for bravery and sacrifice on the part of twenty-first-century soldiers, war and defense against stealthy attacks in our time have been represented as low-cost, antiseptic, and remote-controlled by experts in electronic surveillance and elite groups of soldier-technicians. Citizens can safely observe the combat round the clock live on cable television news networks.

The foundations of American political institutions and public philosophy embody formidable obstacles to reconstructing the language and practices of civic obligation. New national challenges can prompt individuals to realize their community sentiments in energetic participatory citizenship, if only momentarily. Still, the burst of civic activity after 9/11 showed that the ancient ideal of patriotism is not beyond the grasp of most Americans. While it would be wrong to describe such moments as "rebirths" of patriotism, they are opportunities for recasting the meaning of political obligation and for mobilizing citizens around competing symbols of sacrifice. Which symbols of sacrifice will prevail, whose interests they will serve, and who will make the sacrifices are sure to be matters of political process and influence, not destiny.

REFERENCES

American National Election Studies. Institute for Social Research, University of Michigan. 1958–2000. Telephone surveys with randomly selected national adults over period cited. Question: "How much of the time do you think you can trust government to do what is right—just about always, most of the time, or only some of the time?"

Associated Press Poll. 1991. Telephone interviews with 1,004 randomly selected U.S. adults, June 12–16. Question: "Generally speaking, how proud are you to be an American?" Extremely proud: 87%; somewhat proud: 11%; not proud at all: 1%; don't know: 1%.

Barrington, Lowell. 1997. "'Nation' and 'Nationalism': The Misuse of Key Concepts in Political Science." *PS: Political Science and Politics* 30 (December): 712–16.

Belkin, Lisa. 2002. "Just Money." *New York Times Magazine,* December 8, 92–97.

Bellah, Robert N., et al. 1985. *Habits of the Heart: Individualism and Commitment in American Life.* Berkeley: University of California Press.

Bellelli, Guglielmo, and Mirella Amatulli. 1997. "Nostalgia, Immigration, and Collective Memory." In *Collective Memory of Political Events,* ed. James W. Pennebaker, Dario Paez, and Bernard Rime. Mahwah, N.J.: Lawrence Erlbaum Associates.

Bodnar, John. 1992. *Remaking America: Public Memory, Commemoration and Patriotism.* Princeton: Princeton University Press.

Bodnar, John, ed. 1996. *Bonds of Affection: Americans Define Their Patriotism.* Princeton: Princeton University Press.

Brace, Paul, and Barbara Hinkley. 1992. *Follow the Leader: Opinion Polls and the Modern Presidents.* New York: Basic Books.

Brokaw, Tom. 1998. *The Greatest Generation.* New York: Random House.

Bush, George W. 2001a. President's remarks on National Day of Prayer and Remembrance, September 14. On-line at http://www.whitehouse.gov/news/releases/2001/09/20010914-2.html, accessed May 20, 2003.

Bush, George W. 2001b. Address to joint session of Congress, September 20. On-line at http://www.whitehouse.gov/news/releases/2001/09/20010920-8.html, accessed May 20, 2003.

Bush, George W. 2002. State of the Union message to Congress, January 29. On-line at http://www.whitehouse.gov/news/releases/2002/01/20020129-11.html, accessed May 20, 2003.

Cantril, Hadley, ed. 1951. *Public Opinion, 1935–1946.* Princeton: Princeton University Press.

CBS News/*New York Times* Poll. 1991. Telephone interviews of 1,424 randomly selected U.S. adults, June 3–6. Question: "There's been a lot of talk in the last few years about patriotism in America. Do you consider yourself very patriotic, somewhat patriotic, or not very patriotic?" Very patriotic: 55%; somewhat patriotic: 37%; not very patriotic: 5%; don't know/no answer: 3%.

Connor, Walker. 1994. *Ethnonationalism: The Quest for Understanding.* Princeton: Princeton University Press.

Copeland, Larry. 2001. "Volunteering Up since September 11." *USA Today,* November 23–25, 1A.

Coupland, Douglas. 1992. *Generation X: Tales for an Accelerated Culture.* New York: St. Martin's Press.

Deneen, Patrick. 2002. "Patriotic Vision: At Home in a World Made Strange." *Intercollegiate Review* 37 (spring): 33–40.

Dietz, Mary. 1986. "Populism, Patriotism, and the Need for Roots." In *The New Populism: The Politics of Empowerment,* ed. Harry C. Boyte and Frank Riessman. Philadelphia: Temple University Press.

Dobbs, Michael. 2002. "The Cost of War: In Iraq the U.S. Would Pick Up a Bigger Tab." *Washington Post,* national weekly edition, December 9–15, 6.

Fox News Poll. 2001. Telephone interviews with 900 randomly selected U.S. registered voters, September 8–9. Question: "Please tell me if you favor or oppose each of the following possible solutions that have been proposed as ways of dealing with terrorism. . . . Allowing police to stop and search anyone who fits the general description of suspected terrorists." Favor: 58%; oppose 36%; don't know: 6%.

Fox News Poll. 2002. Telephone interviews with 900 randomly selected U.S. registered voters, September 8–9. Question: "Please tell me if you favor or oppose each of the following possible solutions that have been proposed as ways of dealing with terrorism. . . . Allowing police to stop and search anyone who fits the general description of suspected terrorists." Favor: 62%; oppose 31%; don't know: 7%.

Gallup Poll. 1943. Open-ended, personal interviews of 1,500 randomly selected U.S. adults. Respondents could give more than one response. The questions were asked of those who said they have had to make sacrifices for the war (68%), August 26–September 2. Question: "What [real sacrifices for the war have you had to make]?" Son, husband, relative in service, self in service: 32%; no gasoline, tires, walk long distances to work: gas rationing, gave up automobile: 8%; less fuel oil, coal, etc., fuel rationing: 1%; less money, decreased income: 5%; paying more taxes:

8%; increased cost of living: 6%; less food, poorer quality and less variety of food—food rationing: 12%; loss of business or job (business sacrifices): 3%; loss of help and machinery (family workers in armed forces): 6%; taken war job (gave up job for this, moved from home state, frozen in present job): 6%; vague—way of life, doing without things we used to have: 9%; buying war bonds: 15%; volunteer work (air wardens, civilian defense, Red Cross, etc.): 2%; rationing in general: 1%; miscellaneous: less than 1%; no answer: 19%.

Gallup Poll. 1944. Open-ended, personal interviews of 1,500 randomly selected U.S. adults. Respondents could give more than one response. Asked of those who said they have had to make sacrifices for the war (31%), January 20–26. Question: "What [sacrifice have you had to make for the war]?" Son, husband, relative, self in service: 39%; sacrifices of financial nature—buying war bonds: 20%; sacrifices of financial nature (various answers) 17%; sacrifices due to material shortages (various answers): 19%; sacrifices of a business nature (various answers): 16%; sacrifices of time/volunteerism: 3%; less traveling: 1%; miscellaneous: 3%.

Gallup Poll. 1989. Telephone survey of 1,249 randomly selected U.S. adults, June 15–18. Question: "Does the following word apply more to young people in their teens and 20s today or young people in that same age group 20 years ago . . . patriotic." Today: 24%; 20 years ago: 65%; both: 4%; neither: 2%; don't know: 5%.

Gallup Poll. 2001a. Telephone survey of 1,004 randomly selected U.S. adults, including oversamples of blacks and Hispanics, June 11–June 17. Question: "In your view, should immigration be kept at its present level, increased or decreased?" Present level: 42%; increased: 14%; decreased: 41%; no opinion: 3%.

Gallup Poll. 2001b. Telephone survey of 1,032 randomly selected U.S. adults, September 14–15. Question: "As a result of the terrorist attacks this past Tuesday, have you, personally, done or plan to do any of the following?" Display American flag: yes: 82%; no: 18%. Attend memorial service: yes: 60%; no: 39%. Pray more than you usually do: yes: 74%; no: 25%. Show more affection for loved ones than you usually do: yes: 77%; no: 22%.

Gallup Poll. 2001c. Telephone survey of 1,032 randomly selected U.S. adults, September 14–15. Question: "I'd like to ask you a few questions about the events [terrorist attacks] that occurred this past Tuesday (September 11, 2001) in New York City and Washington, D.C. . . . . Please tell me if you would favor or oppose each of the following as a means of preventing terrorist attacks in the United States. How about . . . requiring Arabs, including those who are U.S. citizens, to carry a special ID?" Favor: 49%; oppose: 49%; no opinion: 2%.

Gallup Poll. 2001d. Telephone survey of 1,005 randomly selected U.S. adults, September 21–22. Question: "Did you yourself happen to attend church or synagogue in the last seven days, or not?" Yes: 47%; no: 53%.

Gallup Poll. 2001e. Telephone survey of 1,019 randomly selected U.S. adults, December 14–16. Question: "Did you yourself happen to attend church or synagogue in the last seven days, or not?" Yes: 41%; no: 59%.

Gallup Poll. 2002. Telephone survey of 1,003 randomly selected U.S. adults, September 2–4. Question: "In your view, should immigration be kept at its present level, increased or decreased?" Present level: 26%; increased: 17%; decreased: 54%; no opinion: 3%.

Hamilton, Alexander, James Madison, and John Jay. 1982 [1787]. *The Federalist Papers.* New York: Bantam Books.

Hayes, Carlton J. H. 1928. "Two Varieties of Nationalism: Original and Derived." Proceedings of the Association of History Teachers of the Middle States and Maryland 28: 71–83.

Ipsos-Reid Poll. 2001. Telephone interviews of 1,000 randomly selected U.S. adults, September 21–23. Question: "I'm now going to read you some statements about the terrorist attacks [on the World Trade Center and the Pentagon, September 11, 2001] and the United States' declaration of war on terrorism. For each one, I'd like you to tell me if you strongly agree, somewhat agree, somewhat disagree, or strongly disagree. . . . I'd be prepared to see our police and security services get more power to fight terrorism even if it means that they might tap my phone, open my mail, or read my personal e-mail." Strongly agree: 23%; somewhat agree: 26%; somewhat disagree: 17%; strongly disagree: 33%; not sure: 1%.

Krueger, Alan B. 2002. "Economic Scene: The President Wants Americans to Volunteer to Pick Up the Slack in Social Services. But Will That Be Enough?" *New York Times,* February 7, C2.

Leff, Mark H. 1991. "The Politics of Sacrifice on the American Home Front in World War II." *Journal of American History* (March): 1296–1318.

Los Angeles Times Poll. 2001. Telephone interviews of 1,995 U.S. adults, November 10–13. Question: "Thinking now about the community where you live . . . Some people say they feel like spending more time in their community since the September 11th [2001] attack [on the World Trade Center and the Pentagon], while others do not. By this I mean joining clubs or teams, or doing volunteer work, or going to church or synagogue or some other way of spending time in your community. How about you? Which of the following best describes how you have been spending your time since September 11th? . . . I have been spending more time in my community since September 11th. I spent more time in my community at first, but now I spend about the same amount of time in my community as I did before September 11th. I spent less time in my community at first, but now I spend about the same amount of time in my community as I did before September 11th. I am spending less time in my community since September 11th. There has been no change in the amount of time I spend in my community since September 11th." Spend more time: 13%; spend more time at first but not now: 7%; spend less time at first but not now: 2%; spend less time: 2%; no change: 76%.

McLean, Scott L. 1999. "Land That I Love: Feelings toward Country at Century's End." *Public Perspective* 10 (April/May): 21–25.

McLean, Scott L., David A. Schultz, and Manfred B. Steger, eds. 2002. *Social Capital: Critical Perspectives on Community and "Bowling Alone."* New York: New York University Press.

McWilliams, Wilson Carey. 2000. *Beyond the Politics of Disappointment? American Elections, 1980–1998.* New York: Chatham House.

Merit Methodology Poll. 1981. Telephone interviews of 1,200 randomly selected U.S. adults, October 19–24. Question: "Are you more or less proud to be an American today than you were 10 (ten) years ago, or haven't your feelings changed?" More proud: 32%; less proud: 5%; no change 60%; no opinion: 3%.

Mitchell, Alison. 2001. "After Asking for Volunteers, Government Tries to Determine What They Will Do." *New York Times,* November 10, B7.

Mueller, John. 1994. *Policy and Opinion in the Gulf War.* Chicago: University of Chicago Press.

Mueller, John. 2002. "Harbinger or Aberration? A 9/11 Provocation." *The National Interest* 69 (fall): 45–50.

NBC News/*Wall Street Journal* Poll. 1991. Telephone survey of 1,505 randomly selected U.S. adults, March 15–19. Question: "During your lifetime, which of the following events made you most proud to be an American?" John F. Kennedy's leadership as president: 12%; winning the war with Iraq: 30%; Martin Luther King's leadership on civil rights: 16%; Ronald Reagan's leadership as president: 4%; Americans landing on the moon: 15%; winning World War II: 14%; winning the 1984 Summer Olympics in Los Angeles: 2%; other/not sure/none: 7%.

NBC News/*Wall Street Journal* Poll. 1992. Telephone survey of 1,004 randomly selected U.S. adults, March 15–19. Question: "During your lifetime, which of the following events made you most proud to be an American?" John F. Kennedy's leadership as president: 13%; winning the war with Iraq: 20%; Martin Luther King's leadership on civil rights: 15%; Ronald Reagan's leadership as president: 3%; Americans landing on the moon: 16%; winning World War II: 25%; winning the 1984 Summer Olympics in Los Angeles: 2%; other/not sure/none: 2%.

Neal, Arthur. 1998. *National Trauma and Collective Memory.* Armonk, N.Y.: M. E. Sharpe.

New York Times Poll. 1983a. Telephone survey of 1,145 randomly selected U.S. adults, June 13–16. Question: "Does someone actually have to do something to be patriotic—or is it enough to love your country?" Have to do something: 33%; enough to love: 61 percent; don't know/no answer: 7%.

New York Times Poll. 1983b. Telephone survey of 1,145 randomly selected U.S. adults, June 13–16. Question: "There are many ways that people express love for their country. Everybody has their own way of expressing patriotism. Can you tell us some of the things you have done that you consider patriotic?" Fly American flag: 11%; obey laws: 3%; pay taxes: 3%; civic work/volunteer: 7%; served in armed forces: 17%; political/gov't work: 4%; way of life/raising children: 5%; vote/jury duty: 11%; observe holidays: 2%; speak well of country: 2%; other: 11%; don't know/no answer: 24%.

Nielsen, Kai. 1999. "Cultural Nationalism, Neither Ethnic nor Civic." In *Theorizing Nationalism,* ed. Ronald Beiner. Albany: State University of New York Press.

Opinion Dynamics/Fox News Poll. 1998. Telephone survey of 907 randomly selected

U.S. adults, June 3–4. Question: "Do you think average Americans are more or less patriotic than they were 25 years ago?" More 18%; less: 68%; same: 9%; not sure: 5%.

Paine, Thomas. 1995 [1776]. "The American Crisis, Number 1." In *Collected Writings.* New York: Penguin Books Library of America.

People for the American Way. 2001. "PFAW President Ralph Neas Addresses Divisive Comments by Religious Leaders." September 13. On-line at http://www.pfaw.org/ pfaw/general/default.x?oid-1817, accessed May 20, 2003.

Pew Research Center Poll. 2001. Telephone survey of 2,041 randomly selected U.S. adults, with an oversample of 197 African Americans, March 5–18. Question: "I'd like your views on some groups and organizations. As I read from a list, please tell me which category best describes your overall opinion of what I name. Would you say your overall opinion of . . . Muslim Americans . . . is very favorable, mostly favorable, mostly unfavorable, or very unfavorable?" Very favorable: 7%; mostly favorable: 38%; mostly unfavorable: 16%; very unfavorable: 8%; never heard of (volunteered): 4%; cannot rate: 27%.

Pew Research Center Poll. 2002. Telephone survey of 2,002 randomly selected U.S. adults, February 25–March 10. Question: "Now thinking about some specific religious groups, is your overall opinion of Muslim Americans very favorable, mostly favorable, mostly unfavorable, or very unfavorable?" Very favorable: 8%; mostly favorable: 46%; mostly unfavorable: 14%; mostly unfavorable or very unfavorable: 8%; never heard of (volunteered): 2%; cannot rate: 22%.

Popper, Karl R. 1966. *The Open Society and Its Enemies.* Vol. 1. Princeton: Princeton University Press.

Putnam, Robert D. 2000. *Bowling Alone: The Decline and Revival of American Community.* New York: Simon and Schuster.

Rimmerman, Craig A. 2001. *The New Citizenship.* 2d ed. Boulder: Westview Press.

Roosevelt, Franklin D. 1942. "A Call to Sacrifice," April 28. On-line at http:// www.fordham.edu/halsall/mod/1942roosevelt-sacrifice.html, accessed May 20, 2003.

Roper Organization Poll. 1980. Personal interviews of 2,005 randomly selected U.S. adults, January 5–18. Question: "Now I'm going to ask you a series of questions about the effect the [hostage] crisis in Iran has had on your opinions about important issues facing the United States. . . . Has the crisis made you feel more patriotic, less patriotic, or hasn't changed your patriotic feelings one way or another?" More: 43%; less: 3%; no change: 51%; don't know/no answer: 2%.

Schaar, John H. 1973. "The Case for Patriotism." *American Review,* May, 59–99.

Steindorf, Sara. 1999. "With Less Time to Give Time, Volunteers Seek Flexibility." *Christian Science Monitor,* December 6, 20.

Suriano, Gregory R. 1993. *Great American Speeches.* Avenel, N.J.: Gramercy Books.

Time/CNN Poll. 2001. Telephone interviews with 1,055 randomly selected U.S. adults, September 27. Question: "Please tell me if you would favor or oppose the government doing each of the following as a way to prevent terrorist attacks in the United

States. . . . require U.S. (United States) citizens of Arab descent to carry an identification card issued by the federal government." Favor: 49%; oppose 49%; not sure 2%.

Times Mirror Poll. 1991. Telephone interviews with 2,020 randomly selected U.S. adults, October 31–November 10. Question: "I am going to read you a series of statements that will help us understand how you feel about a number of things. For each statement, please tell me whether you completely agree with it, mostly agree with it, mostly disagree with it or completely disagree with it. . . . I am very patriotic." Completely agree: 58%; mostly agree: 33%; mostly disagree: 5%; completely disagree: 2%; don't know: 2%.

Tocqueville, Alexis de. 1990. *Democracy in America.* Ed. Phillips Bradley, trans. Henry Reeve. 2 vols. New York: Vintage Classics.

Turner, Frederick C., and Everett C. Ladd. 1986. "Nationalism, Leadership, and the American Creed." *Canadian Review of Studies in Nationalism* 13.2, 185–198.

Viroli, Maurizio. 1995. *For Love of Country: An Essay on Patriotism and Nationalism.* Oxford: Clarendon Press.

Waldman, Steven. 1995. *The Bill: How Legislation Really Becomes Law: A Case Study of the National Service Bill.* New York: Penguin Books.

Washington Post Poll. 1989. Telephone survey of 1,015 randomly selected U.S. adults, June 16–20. Question: "Do you think that the country is more patriotic, less patriotic, or about the same as it was in the late 1960's?" More: 32%; less: 39%; same: 22%; don't know: 6%.

Washington Post/ABC News Poll. 1991a. Telephone survey of 778 randomly selected U.S. adults, February 27. Question: "Do you consider yourself strongly patriotic, somewhat patriotic, or not very patriotic at all?" Strongly patriotic: 70%; somewhat patriotic: 26%; not very patriotic: 4%.

Washington Post/ABC News Poll. 1991b. Telephone survey of 1,511 randomly selected U.S. adults, May 30–June 2. Question: "Do you consider yourself strongly patriotic, somewhat patriotic, or not very patriotic at all?" Strongly patriotic: 65%; somewhat patriotic: 29%; not very patriotic: 5%.

Washington Post/ABC News Poll. 2001. Telephone survey of 1,215 randomly selected U.S. adults, September 25–27. Question: "Do you consider yourself strongly patriotic, somewhat patriotic, or not very patriotic at all?" Strongly patriotic: 73%; somewhat patriotic: 24%; not very patriotic: 2%.

Welch, William M. 2002. "Frayed Tempers Snap over Politics, Patriotism." *USA Today,* September 26, 6A.

PART THREE

Civil Liberties

JEROME M. MILEUR & RONALD STORY

America's Wartime Presidents: Politics, National Security, and Civil Liberties

All of America's wartime presidents, at least since Abraham Lincoln, have had to balance the interests of national security with the liberties of the people. The nature of the several wars, the politics of their times, and the personal predilections of the presidents have influenced the extent to which political dissent flourished or was stifled in these wartime administrations. By examining those times, we hope to shed light on our own—our "war against terrorism"—especially in the areas of rights, liberties, and dissent. Our examination includes the presidencies of Lincoln, Woodrow Wilson, Franklin D. Roosevelt, Harry Truman, and Lyndon Johnson before turning to that of George W. Bush. Some early presidents are discussed more than is Bush, largely because scholars know more about Lincoln and the rest than about Bush. We can be more sure about the earlier presidents than about the incumbent because we know how these stories developed and how they ended. There is no such certainty about our current crisis, which President Bush says might indeed never end.

LINCOLN AND THE CIVIL WAR

With the shelling of Fort Sumter in 1861 and the secession of the eleven Confederate states, the administration of Lincoln decided at the outset of the Civil War to take measures to keep the nation from collapsing. Many of these steps were extraordinary in their time: the raising of immense, extended-duty armed forces, partly through conscription; the equipping of these forces with unprecedented quantities of mass-produced war matériel; and the raising of vast revenues through bond issues and a broad array of taxes—from higher tariffs to income, estate, and value-added taxes, as well as stiff excises on, in James McPherson's words, "everything from tobacco and liquor to yachts and billiard tables," with license and stamp taxes thrown in (McPherson 2001, 225; see Beckert 2001). There was no formal rationing, but the other sinews of modern war—taxation, conscription, industrial contracts—were all present.

With these measures came the tightening of internal security. Initially, this was the responsibility of Secretary of State William H. Seward, a New York politician and erstwhile rival of Lincoln. Seward moved quickly to set up a secret service to protect government officials, especially Lincoln, from assault or assassination, a legitimate preoccupation throughout the war. He also established a network of informants to alert him to treasonous statements and behavior as well as personal threats, and he added dozens of men to the ranks of the U.S. marshals, the federal government's chief peace-keeping arm at that time (McPherson 2001, 317–18; see Neely 1991).

In the midwestern border states of Missouri and Kentucky and the southern reaches of Illinois, Indiana, and Ohio, which remained loyal to the North but harbored numerous individuals who sympathized with the South, U.S. marshals arrested hundreds of people for obstructing Union war measures and uttering "treasonous" remarks. Most were detained without trial. Strong tactics were also used in Maryland, a slave state that remained loyal to the United States but included Confederate sympathizers in its population. When some threatened to seize Washington, D.C., or at least prevent reinforcements from reaching it, U.S. soldiers imprisoned the mayor and police chief of Baltimore, where mobs had attacked volunteer units traveling through the city to reach the capital. A Maryland judge and several state legislators who swore enmity to the United States were also arrested, and Lincoln imposed martial law in the area. As fighting broke out across the Upper South—in Virginia and Tennessee as well as Missouri and Kentucky—army commanders assumed responsibility for dealing with treasonous behavior in their own districts, arresting hundreds of spies, saboteurs, and irregular guerrilla fighters. In early 1862, Lincoln shifted responsibility for internal security from Seward to Secretary of War Edwin Stanton, a starchy, combative antislavery man from Ohio. Stanton reduced the number of arrests and organized a commission to examine individual cases. Most detainees, including those in Maryland, were released after they took an oath of loyalty to the United States (McPherson 2001, 317).[1]

During the "Peninsula" offensive in spring and summer 1862, as Union General George McClellan moved toward Richmond, Virginia, arrests fell further. But when McClellan's campaign faltered and Union forces had to withdraw, arrests shot up, driven by Union anxieties as well as aggressive agitation against Lincoln's war policy by the Democratic Party and "copperheads" (Northerners who sympathized with the South). In September 1862, following the repulse of Confederate General Robert E. Lee at Antietam, Maryland, Lincoln issued two edicts. The first was the Emancipation Proclamation, which changed the purpose of the war and transformed the course of American history. The second, two days later, suspended habeas corpus and ordered military trials for "all Rebels and Insurgents [and] their aiders and abettors within the United States" charged with discouraging volunteer enlistments or resisting militia drafts or found guilty of "any disloyal practice" (McPherson 2001, 318–19).

These two measures went more or less together. The Emancipation Proclamation generated truly venomous criticism of Lincoln, who was—beyond compare—the most vilified of American presidents. Democrats looking to the November congressional elections castigated him as a race-mixing, mongrelizing African-lover, a fomenter of race war, a betrayer of the white race, a subverter of a Constitution that gave the president no authority to interfere with the rights of individual states or to seize personal property such as slaves. Moreover, Lincoln's critics now had the growing lists of Union dead and wounded to wield as political weapons. "He is killing your sons and brothers and husbands," they cried in effect, "for the benefit of the black man." Critics increasingly called for draft resistance, tax resistance, desertion, and replacing the Republican administration with Democrats more favorable to compromise with the South.

The suspension of habeas corpus and a more aggressive policy regarding treason gave Lincoln's opponents all the more ammunition. They now accused him of tyranny as well as race mixing. In the 1862 midterm elections, the Democrats gained thirty-two seats in the House of Representatives. But this was fewer than in any other off-year election in twenty years, and most of the gains were in either border areas or Catholic wards of northern cities, not the North as a whole. In the Senate, the Republicans actually gained two seats. The president's party was still solidly in control of Congress (McPherson 2001, 320; see McPherson 1988, 500 ff.; Oates 1998, 238 ff.). The congressional election of 1862 stands out for two reasons. First, it not only took place but was hotly contested even amid the throes of vast civil strife—testimony to the resilience of the nation's political order and to the fundamental commitment of its leaders to political competition and dissent. Second, the Republicans retained control of Congress, easing their anxiety about a settlement that would somehow sanction secession and jeopardize the existence of the nation.

Even so, as the war moved deeper into the rebel territory of the South— Louisiana, Arkansas, and Mississippi as well as Virginia and Tennessee— Union army commanders assumed greater authority over internal security. Increasingly, this included control of information, which was made much easier by the advent of modern means of communication, especially railroads, telegraph lines, and rotary printing presses. The army controlled telegraph lines in order to regulate the dispatches of news reporters. Generals sometimes barred certain newspapers from their areas so as to prevent military disclosures, and the War Department closed several newspapers briefly. "Treasonable" papers were occasionally barred from the mails, chiefly because they published military information (McPherson 2001, 317–18).

In 1863 and 1864, mobs of Northerners, goaded by Republican rhetoric against possible traitors, smashed the facilities of copperhead newspapers. Some mobs included U.S. soldiers, who often went unpunished. Democratic rioters in some northern cities targeted draft offices, Republican party headquarters, and African-Americans. A large-scale riot in New York City was suppressed only by calling in soldiers from Gettysburg. The federal government also arrested a leading copperhead politician and member of Congress, Clement Vallandigham of Ohio, who was convicted of treason by a military tribunal and then exiled to the South.

Much of the antiadministration agitation in 1864 was in anticipation of that fall's presidential election, when Confederate sympathizers, supported by money and organizational assistance from the South, hoped to capitalize on antidraft, antitax, anticarnage sentiment and replace Lincoln with Democrat George McClellan. This did not happen. Union General William T. Sherman captured Atlanta, and Union soldiers, like most Northerners, voted overwhelmingly for their president. By now the days of detainments were largely over, and even the Confederates stopped agitating, except for the occasional assassination plot—one of which, alas, succeeded (McPherson 2001, 388–89; see McPherson 1988, 596–97, 764–83).[2]

Overall, Lincoln's record on rights and liberties was not too bad, considering that he faced what William Earl Weeks calls the "largest mass act of treason in American history" (Chambers 1999, 733). Fifteen thousand people were detained, with the majority in the occupied South or in pro-Confederate border states. Most detainees were well treated, at least compared to prisoners of war, and were soon released unless proven to be actual spies or saboteurs. Military tribunals were seldom used outside actual war zones. The harsher detainments touched only such obviously treasonous leaders as Vallandigham, who had urged desertion and draft resistance and apparently took Confederate money. Military control of the news was almost exclusively a combat measure. Spontaneous anti-Democratic mobs were a problem, but not a widespread one. Political competition and criticism continued throughout the war everywhere in the North and in large areas of the occupied South. That Lincoln's party lost seats in 1862 and expected to lose more in 1864 speaks with some eloquence to the preservation of political criticism, dissent, and competition.

Indeed, the question arises why there was not an even greater suppression of liberty, as the government was facing so massive an armed insurrection. One reason is surely Lincoln's own long-standing commitment to civil rights and liberties and to constitutionalism, despite his various emergency war measures. He had opposed the antiforeign, anti-Catholic agitation of the "Know-Nothing" Party and defended the right of northern states to keep slave catchers at bay through personal liberty laws. His policies for suppressing secession were couched in scrupulously constitutional terms: no interference with southern states unless they opened hostilities first; no interference with slavery except as a war measure; no detainment or censorship except to protect war operations or the existence of the government itself. He suspended habeas corpus on the grounds of Article 1, section 9, of the Constitution, which forbids suspension "unless when in Cases of Rebellion or Invasion the public Safety may require it." This surely was applicable to these circumstances (Hall 1992, 357). As James G. Randall (1951, 520) has written, "Freedom of speech was preserved to the point of permitting the most disloyal utterances."

The nature of the enemy may have helped. The slave states had a wretched record on civil liberties, which most in the North, and certainly its

Republican majority, knew well: the seizure of antislavery literature; the dismissal of ministers and professors who questioned slavery; night-riding slave patrols; the employment of runaway-slave catchers; the arrest, following John Brown's raid in 1859, of every Northerner anywhere in the area; and more (see Eaton 1946).[3] Lincoln's America, facing an authoritarian undemocratic enemy, held fast to its liberal democratic principles. Anticipating the task of reabsorbing the rebel South, Lincoln did not magnify these differences. But people knew about them.

Yet there were detainments and censorship in the North, and one may wonder why there was no greater outcry. Three reasons besides the nature of the enemy suggest themselves. First, the outcry that did arise focused primarily on Lincoln's domestic policies—especially conscription, taxation, and emancipation—and not on detainments and censorship. The latter became more familiar as the war progressed and more accepted as essential to the victory that was eventually won.

Second, there was as yet no body of judicial opinion addressing the nature and limit of wartime civil liberties. This was partly because southern constitutional writers since John C. Calhoun and even Thomas Jefferson had construed liberty and the guarantee of individual rights as largely a local or state matter and not a federal question. The most relevant decision may have been *Dred Scott* in 1857, which seemed to undermine personal liberty (and even the doctrine of states' rights itself) (Fehrenbacher 1978). What was lacking at the time was a set of judicial pronouncements with which to frame a critique of Lincoln's policies. Decisions of this sort would prove vital in the development of later rights consciousness.

Last, the conflict was always presumed to have a visible end. At some point, either the South would surrender or the North would relinquish its claim to the breakaway states, and the country would return to an approximation of prewar America—no conscription or war taxes, no detainments or censorship, and a resolution of the slavery question one way or another. People could live with personal constraints if they could anticipate an end to them with an end to the conflict.

WILSON AND WORLD WAR I

World War I was a different experience for the United States, which had never been engaged in a ground war in Europe. Indeed, all the nation's wars had been fought in the northern half of the Western Hemisphere, save for the 1898 battle of Manila Bay in the Philippines in the Spanish-American War. A war in Europe meant involvement in the enmities of the Old World against the advice of generations of American statesmen. It also meant brutal fighting against imperial Germany, an enemy that seemed to pose no immediate danger to the U.S. mainland and whose behavior seemed little different from that of imperial Britain or colonial France. The necessity of war was therefore not absolutely clear, a fact that would drive President Wilson to extremes of salesmanship and opinion control; lacking a sufficiently appalling or threatening enemy, he had to manufacture one.

Equally important, America's entry came after decades of heavy European immigration had infused its population with large ethnic minorities. This had two serious consequences. First, U.S. entry into the war as an ally of Great Britain and a foe of Germany was unpopular with two large and politically important groups—Irish- and German-Americans—many of whom opposed Wilson's war policy and thus attracted suspicion to themselves. Second, the country had experienced a lengthy period of labor and socialist activism that seemed rooted partly in the huge new immigrant populations from eastern and southern Europe. The Bolshevik Revolution in Russia made these immigrants appear even more ominous than they would have seemed anyway (see Kennedy 1980).

Finally, this was a "total" war requiring massive troop mobilization, immense industrial production, and stringent economic incentives and controls ranging from huge contracts to heavy taxation to formal rationing. Congress authorized the president to control prices in critical industries, seize and run war-related plants, and operate water and rail transport. It drew upon the new progressive income tax and imposed "excess" profit and other taxes. These measures went far beyond those of a half century earlier and moved the country in a new direction—toward the militarized condition of the European states. Only the German collapse in 1918, not long after the Americans began to fight, arrested this drift (see Williams 1981, 383–98; Chambers 1987).

All these factors played a role in the Wilson administration's posture regarding dissent. Of equal significance was the attitude of key members of the administration. While much of the expansion of presidential power that irked laissez-faire conservatives lay in the mobilization of manpower and the economy, much also centered on the desire to portray a villainous enemy, to prevent disruption of the military buildup, and to deal with aliens and political radicals who seemed disloyal to the country or, more narrowly, to its dominant interests, including Wilson. A "progressive" reformer, Wilson sometimes urged tolerance but proved erratic at best in following through. Members of Wilson's administration, moreover, had divergent views on civil liberties in wartime. Some, like Secretary of War Newton Baker and Commissioner of Immigration Frederick Howe, were, in the words of Donald Johnson, "generous and tolerant," seeking to correct violations when they found them, following the model of Edwin Stanton. Others, like Postmaster Albert Burleson, Attorney General Thomas Gregory, and especially Gregory's successor, A. Mitchell Palmer, were "narrow, legalistic, and antisocialist" in their views and frequently indifferent to abuses of civil liberties (Johnson 1963, 53).

The Wilson administration thus came to pose a serious threat to dissent. "The story of freedom of speech during the World War I period," according to Paul L. Murphy (1972a, 22), "is a dreary and depressing tale of repression, 'witch-hunting,' and steady violation of individual liberties. Freedom of expression was one of the early casualties of the war." The Espionage Act of 1917, passed at Wilson's behest, forbade efforts to interfere with the prosecution of the war, in particular the publication or transmission of information that might help the enemy. These restrictions targeted conscientious objectors especially, requiring those drafted to choose noncombatant roles or serve in wholly separate units. The army subjected many of the latter to prosecution in apparent violation of orders from Secretary of War Baker and gave long sentences to more than five hundred who were convicted. The censorship provisions were abused extensively by Postmaster General Burleson, who directed local postmasters to confiscate publications containing matter that would cause "insubordination, disloyalty, mutiny, or refusal of duty . . . or otherwise embarrass or hamper the Government in conducting the war" (Johnson 1963, 55–56). In the first month after passage of the Espionage Act, Burleson banned fifteen publications from the mails, most of them socialist (Ferrell 1985, 208).[4]

The Sedition Act of 1918 was even broader and more threatening. It sought to outlaw any "disloyal, profane, scurrilous, or abusive language" about the federal government, the Constitution, the armed forces, the uniform, or the flag (Johnson 1963, 69). Responsibility for its enforcement fell to Attorney General Gregory, who created a special Bureau of Investigation (later the FBI) to investigate subversive activities. He also gave support to a quasi-vigilante group, the American Protective League, whose members were authorized to snoop on their fellow citizens. Aliens, radicals, and militant pacifists and their organizations—the Socialist Party, the International Workers of the World, the Nonpartisan League—became targets of Justice Department prosecutions. Not since the Alien and Sedition Acts of 1798 "had the federal government launched so vigorous a campaign to curtail dissent and attack critics of wartime government" (Murphy 1972b, 22).[5]

The Trading with the Enemy Act of 1917 authorized the government to confiscate and hold enemy property in the United States; regulate the conduct of enemy aliens resident in the country; censor communications by mail, cable, radio, or otherwise with foreign countries; and regulate the nation's foreign language press, a provision falling heavily on Yiddish and German papers in particular. The Alien Act of 1918 permitted the deportation of alien anarchists, those who believed in the violent overthrow of the government, or advocates of assassination of public officials (Ferrell 1985, 207–8). It was the Alien Act that led to the imprisonment of Eugene V. Debs, a former Socialist Party presidential candidate and a committed internationalist, and Victor Berger, the German-born mayor of Milwaukee, and also to the deportation of the Eastern European Jewish anarchists Emma Goldman and Alexander Berkman. The Wilson administration even had its own internal security program. One day after declaring war on Germany, the president ordered the heads of departments and independent offices to remove any employee whose behavior provided "ground for believing" that his retention was "inimical to the public welfare" (Corwin 1957, 101–385; Murphy 1972b, 2).

Finally, the Wilson administration, needing to justify its war policy to a skeptical citizenry, created the Committee on Public Information under George Creel. This became a clearinghouse for information about wartime rules, regulations, proclamations, and orders regarding the conduct of the war. It also mounted propaganda efforts for the president. Indeed, as Arthur Link reports, Creel "organized what was up to that time probably the most gigantic propaganda effort in history to convert (and coerce) the antiwar minority." Creel used motion pictures as well as print media, recruited scholars and some seventy-five thousand "Four Minute Men" as speakers on behalf of the war effort, and targeted grade and high schools. Link adds that Creel "portrayed the alleged German menace in lurid colors" that "encouraged a hatred of everything German and a war hysteria that needed no stimulation to run to awful excess" (Link 1963, 117–18).[6] One result was the virtual obliteration of the hitherto rich and autonomous German-American culture, which vanished so completely from American consciousness that few noticed when a German-American became supreme commander of Allied troops in the next war against Germany. Just as the various sedition measures can be explained partly by the existence of resistant ethnic and political groups in a country undergoing complete mobilization, so the Creel committee can be understood partly by the need for a properly evil and fearsome enemy.

American politics in the Wilson years was in partisan disarray. The GOP split in 1912 enabled Wilson to win the presidency with just 41 percent of the popular vote. In his first two years, Wilson won enactment of his New Freedom program, but the growing possibility of American involvement in the European war made "preparedness" an issue of increasing importance. The Republicans adopted a vigorous preparedness platform but nominated the moderate Charles Evans Hughes for president in 1916. The Democrats renominated Wilson on a platform that called for neutrality and reasonable preparedness, then rode to victory on the slogan "He kept us out of war." In Congress, resistance to the war cut across party lines. Many Democrats opposed conscription, and Wilson could find no one in his party's leadership who would introduce a draft bill even after war was declared in April 1917. He finally turned to a Republican (Mayer 1967, 349–50; see also Ferrell 1985, 16 ff.). Indeed, with Democrats continuing to resist their president, it was the Republicans who often rescued him. Despite their irritation over rising taxes, the GOP lent critical support to the Espionage and Sedition Acts as well as other wartime measures.

Unlike Lincoln after the departure of the secessionist Democrats, Wilson never enjoyed comfortable political majorities on the war, a situation that may have fed his turn to suppression and propaganda. In 1918, with the approach of midterm elections, he called for a moratorium on politics until the end of the war, and the congressional races that year focused mainly on nonwar issues, though the GOP did fault the administration for excessive partisanship in its war-related policies. When Democrats claimed that a Republican victory would be a rejection of Wilson's leadership and a comfort to the enemy, Republicans were annoyed—the more so because George Creel's propaganda operation already came close to branding any criticism of administration policies as unpatriotic. After Germany sued for peace in late September, Wilson broke his moratorium on politics. He charged that the Republicans, while prowar, had been anti-administration, and he called for the election of a Democratic Congress so that he might "continue to be your unembarrassed spokesman in affairs at home and abroad" (Mayer 1967, 350 ff.; Farrell 1985, 164).

Republicans reacted angrily to this "betrayal" by the president. They were quick to point out their support for the administration's war effort. Some charged that Wilson wanted to be a dictator, reflecting in part their fears that the presidency had been made too powerful as a consequence of the war, an accusation reminiscent of charges made against Lincoln and later to be made against Roosevelt. The Republicans won control of both houses of Congress by narrow margins; with the November 11 armistice, the anger generated in the last days of the campaign spilled over into the next Congress, ending the spirit of bipartisanship and frustrating Wilson's postwar plans, including entry into the League of Nations.[7]

"Security eclipsed liberty" in the aftermath of the war; ordinary Americans accepted "massive violations" of civil liberties with "equanimity" (Murphy 1972a, 22).[8] Several factors contributed to this. One was undoubtedly the successful demonizing of Germany, which made it appear the very incarnation of autocracy and militarism. Another was the need, whatever the war's cause or merit, to protect and support American troops abroad, a recurring leitmotiv in twentieth-century wars. A third was the growing acceptance of the essentials of modern war, with its mass mobilization of people, matériel, and revenues. If you were going to fight, this is the way you had to do it; interference with the war effort was unacceptable. Indeed, in sustaining wartime convictions, the Supreme Court almost always cited the danger of interference with mobilization. In addition, Wilson won over potential naysayers with various favors that Ronald Schaffer (1991) has termed "war welfare": women's organizations, through support for their suffrage; labor unions, through appointments to war boards and limited bargaining rights; and business, through contracts and managerial autonomy. With an uncertain majority in Congress, a war president bought support where he could.

Unlike the end of the Civil War in the 1860s, the end of World War I was accompanied by growing public anxieties about threats to the nation and especially its economic order. These fears were fed by members of the Wilson administration, principally Attorney General Palmer, for whom the domestic threat became not draft resisters and pacifists but revolutionaries, Bolsheviks, and foreign-born agitators. The explosion of a bomb at his home (he believed it the work of an anarchist) led Mitchell to establish a General Intelligence Division within the Justice Department to pursue radicals. A police strike in Boston, a huge steel strike in the Midwest, and a general strike in Seattle fed the paranoia. There ensued a Palmer-engineered "Red Scare" (in which the young J. Edgar Hoover, later head of the Federal Bureau of Investigation, played a part) and government retaliation: raids against labor radicals, anarchists, and communists; widespread beatings; thousands of arrests; and hundreds of deportations. Louis Post, assistant secretary of labor and a strong civil libertarian, canceled some of the deportations, but many of those arrested were held for long periods in crowded cells before their eventual release (Johnson 1963, 119, 139; Murphy 1972b, 5).[9]

The draconian Palmer raids did eventually sour public opinion. A far-reaching peacetime sedition bill, initially popular in Congress, languished and was buried. When the Republicans regained the presidency in 1920 behind Warren Harding, the new postmaster general, Will Hays, repudiated the practices of his predecessor. The Supreme Court witnessed its first significant dissent as Justices Oliver Wendell Holmes and Louis Brandeis elaborated their "clear and present danger" and "marketplace of ideas" doctrines that opened the door to future safeguards (see Hall 1992, 409; Menand 2001, 49–70).

ROOSEVELT AND WORLD WAR II

Like Lincoln, Franklin D. Roosevelt (FDR) was disposed to free expression but was nevertheless moved during World War II in 1940, following the fall of France and the British struggle for survival, to revive the World War I Sedition Act permitting the investigation of subversive activity, particularly among aliens. "Of course we have got this 5th column thing," he remarked, "which is altogether too widespread through the country. In the bringing in of new people we have got to be pretty darned careful" (Polenberg 1968a, 176; see O'Neill 1993, 226–28).[10] Over the next year, Roosevelt approved Secretary of State Cordell Hull's recommendation that aliens applying for visitor visas be fingerprinted; signed the Smith Act obliging aliens to register; and authorized wiretaps against "anyone suggested of subversive activities." The wiretaps were to be used, in FDR's words, against "those persons, not citizens of the U.S., and those few citizens who are traitors to their country, who today are engaged in espionage or sabotage" (Polenberg 2000, 26–27).

After the Japanese attack on Pearl Harbor, Roosevelt argued that "some degree of censorship" was essential in wartime to secure information such as troop movements, ship landings, and battle casualties. Reminiscent of Lincoln's early dark days, FDR also leaned toward censorship of "criticism of the government beyond reason," but he never acted on this inclination. In 1942 he directed J. Edgar Hoover, head of the FBI, to investigate profascist publications such as *Social Justice*—Father Charles Coughlin's influential, bitterly anti-Semitic, vituperatively anti-Roosevelt paper—which FDR eventually silenced through pressure on a reluctant Catholic hierarchy. He also urged Hoover to watch the isolationist *Chicago Tribune*, whose columns sometimes leaked government secrets and assailed American war aims. That same year Attorney General Francis Biddle indicted twenty-eight "native fascists" under the Espionage Act for inciting insubordination in the military. Taking advantage of the Sedition and Espionage Acts, Biddle, by the end of 1943, had brought indictments for improper exercise of free speech against some one hundred persons—a significant number, though fewer than in World War I or the Civil War (Polenberg 2000, 28).

Like Wilson, Roosevelt made some effort to manage the news, not only through control of war reporting but also by setting up the Office of War Information, which produced, among other things, the famous "Why We Fight" documentaries that were shown to every serviceman. FDR also urged Hollywood to produce "war morale" films such as *Mission to Moscow* and *The Moon Is Down* (about Nazi-occupied Norway). Government sponsorship, though large by comparison with the 1860s, was modest compared to that of other countries, including Britain, primarily because it was unnecessary. Roosevelt enjoyed, as Wilson had not, the support of a more or less united country, at least after the Battle of Britain and Pearl Harbor. The fact that Russia was an ally largely precluded serious left-wing opposition to the war. Admiration for Great Britain kept the "Solid South" in line. The attack on the nation's flag fleet, the nature of the Nazi dictatorship, and the ominous successes of German and Japanese mechanized and aerial campaigns combined to make the Axis threat palpable and immediate in a dramatic way.[11]

There were also differences in the treatment of ethnic groups. In February 1942, Roosevelt issued an executive order permitting Secretary of War

Henry Stimson to "prescribe military areas in such places and of such extent . . . from which any or all persons may be excluded." This neutral sounding order served, as everyone knew it would, to banish 110,000 West Coast Japanese to inland detention camps on the grounds that they were committing sabotage and espionage. This occurred at the height of national anxiety, following the attack on Pearl Harbor and before the battles at Midway and Guadalcanal had halted the Japanese advance thousands of miles across the Pacific (see Daniels 1993). As with prosecutions for seditious speech, attitudes shifted some with military success. Roosevelt eventually authorized army enlistments from among the American-born Japanese men in the camps and allowed his own Justice Department to challenge the constitutionality of the detentions (the challenge failed). But he refused to close the camps and let the detainees go home, and most lost nearly all their property and means of livelihood despite the actual paucity of evidence of espionage.

German-Americans and Italian-Americans, far more numerous and therefore more important both politically and as potential soldiers, were also more dispersed geographically, making it harder to round them up without massive disruptions. They were also more thoroughly assimilated, thanks largely to the double impact of the World War I crusade against things German and the Immigrant Act of 1924, which cut Italian immigration sharply. Although German and Italian aliens had to register as aliens of "enemy nationality," potential problems with Italian-American soldiers in the Mediterranean theater were avoided by government production of numerous films showing Marconi, Toscanini, and others as good anti-Fascists. Despite lingering traces of Mussolini's popularity, Italian aliens no longer were required to register by 1943 (see Polenberg 2000, 27–29).

World War II proved the apotheosis of mass warfare. Huge war contracts revitalized the economy. Taxes rose sharply. Rationing became commonplace, as did wage and price controls. Most important, the United States conscripted some ten million soldiers, and another six million volunteered. The administration therefore looked askance at efforts to impede mobilization. Given Roosevelt's "arsenal of democracy" policy of maximum output, deferments for work in war industries and agriculture were plentiful. Even so, over the course of the war, the Justice Department investigated 373,000 cases of draft evasion and won 16,000 convictions. Largely to keep industrial production and the draft at a high pitch, military surveillance expanded, in partial competition with the Federal Bureau of Investigation

(FBI). A new army Counter Intelligence Corps deployed civilian agents to report on minority or political dissidents; G-2, the military intelligence branch, was active in defense plants (Chambers 1999, 701, 181). With minor exceptions, the Supreme Court generally upheld the administration's control measures, including its decision to try eight captured Nazi saboteurs before a secret military commission rather than a civilian court. With regard to religious groups, local draft boards generally exempted Jehovah's Witnesses from the draft, although the antiwar propaganda of the Witnesses earned them resentment and some went to prison. But prison treatment of conscientious objectors was deemed "good" at the time by the American Civil Liberties Union (ACLU). The United States also adhered to the Geneva conventions in its treatment of enemy POWs on American soil (Polenberg 1968b, 91–94; see also Hall 1992, 944–45).

With the glaring exception of the interned Japanese-Americans, some manipulation of the mass media, and an all-out effort to sustain the mass mobilization required by modern warfare, Roosevelt's record on civil liberties in World War II looks comparatively mild, given the magnitude of the war and the profound terrors of the early years. There was no suppression of political criticism, which gathered itself chiefly around FDR's "socialistic" domestic policies. Roosevelt suffered defeats in the 1942 congressional elections comparable to those of Lincoln in 1862, and he won reelection by his smallest margin in 1944, when the United States became the sole combatant nation in the world to conduct an election.

Roosevelt's own liberal predilections probably played a role in sustaining this atmosphere of tolerance, as did those of his attorney general, Francis Biddle, a constitutionally more scrupulous man than Wilson's A. Mitchell Palmer (O'Neill 1993, 232–35; Polenberg 2000, 26–27; Roeder 1993, 99). But circumstances also helped. Unlike the situation during the Civil War in the 1860s, World War II pitted foreign powers against the United States, creating a feeling of national unity and a sense of the enemy as "out there" rather than "in here." As the war began to go better, domestic espionage and sedition seemed less threatening. In addition, even with the advent of long-distance air and naval power in the 1940s, the war was fought at a distance (as was the Civil War, for Northerners, after 1863); the country seldom felt subject to direct attack and was therefore perhaps less susceptible to suspicion and hysteria. There was also relatively little of the vigilante activity of the Civil War and World War I variety, partly because of national unity but also because the government in the 1940s had extensive surveillance and investigative agencies, especially the FBI, to do the snooping and punishing. You could "drop a dime" on a suspect rather than attack him yourself. Social tensions, when they surfaced, did so in the form of race riots.

While there was no great outcry against FDR's stifling of dissent in the interests of security (the ACLU seldom challenged the president's actions during the war), there was political opposition among Republicans and southern Democrats to Roosevelt's domestic programs: his "socialist scheming" and his support for high taxes, welfare programs, organized labor, and minority rights. Just as criticism of Lincoln centered on emancipation, FDR's domestic policies bothered his opponents more than his occasional manipulation of the media and surveillance of dissenters. Even his sweeping war measures—taxation, wage and price controls, and rationing—aroused hostility only to the extent that they seemed rooted in a New Deal agenda rather than in actual war needs. The Office of War Information stirred Republican ire not for promoting the war, but for promoting it on behalf of the Soviet Union and trade unionism. This opposition, by its strength, may have held the government's media controls and surveillance in check (see Dear and Fast 1995, 1188–89; Milkis and Mileur 2002, 281–82).

Finally, Roosevelt, like Lincoln but unlike Wilson, had a manifestly oppressive enemy, Nazi Germany, which destroyed all political, religious, intellectual, and labor rights wherever it seized power and therefore formed a real and powerful threat to American political values. With so malevolent an enemy, the nation, for all its hesitancy in the 1930s about another European war, rallied almost instinctively to guard its own liberties. In many ways, this made the job of providing home front security easier for Roosevelt's wartime administration than it had been for either Lincoln or Wilson.

TRUMAN AND KOREA

The Korean War differed from the Civil War and the two world wars in important ways. First, it was fought in a small, distant, nonindustrial country for the purpose of containing the ideological and military influence of two large neighboring Communist powers, the USSR and China, with whom the United States was locked in a cold war to prevent the spread of such regimes. There was no obvious military threat to America proper from Communist North Korea. Instead, the United States argued that if South Korea came to be dominated by the North, there would be a "domino effect"—with one country after another across Asia "going Communist," as China had in 1949. Second, there was no serious threat of domestic espionage or subversion from the North Koreans, or from the Chinese after they entered the fray. The espionage threats came instead from the international Communist ringleader, the Soviet Union, and its sympathizers, operating in part through front groups and in part through undetectable agents, a situation more like that faced by Lincoln than by Wilson or Roosevelt.

The war was psychologically and geographically distant, and it did not engage Americans' emotions at the same level as previous big wars. It was fought under United Nations (UN) auspices, mainly by South Korean troops, with U.S. forces reinforcing; there was no formal declaration of war and only modest live media coverage. President Harry Truman initially downplayed it as a "police action," although the administration, having earlier cut the military budget, had to take immediate and familiar steps to rebuild its capacity: conscription, higher taxes, industrial regulation, plant and rail takeovers. Congressional Republicans opposed many of these measures as "socialistic," and while there were no draft riots, some sixty-five thousand selective service registrants did seek conscientious objector status (see Patterson 1996, 207–42).

Korea was the first hot war of the nuclear age. Both the Soviet Union, North Korea's sponsor, and the United States possessed deliverable atomic weapons. American use of its most powerful weapon would risk Soviet retaliation against the continental United States, as would any military action in which U.S. troops appeared to threaten either China or Russia. The president was thus faced with having to fight a limited war, which became a source of immense and unprecedented national frustration. When General Douglas MacArthur, supreme commander of the UN forces, openly rejected this new kind of warfare, Truman relieved him, triggering a firestorm of outrage, especially among congressional Republicans (see Caro 2002, 367–72).

The June 1950 invasion of South Korea by forces from the North took place against the backdrop of World War II, the start of the cold war, the fall of China, and the perjury conviction of a former high-ranking state department official, Alger Hiss, for lying to Congress. A national security state, left over from World War II, was still largely in place, including the Central Intelligence Agency (CIA), an expanded FBI, and the Smith Act of 1940, which required the annual registration of aliens and prohibited advocacy of the violent overthrow of the government. Truman had also established a loyalty program for federal employees, mainly as a defense against Republican charges in the 1948 election that federal agencies were filled with communists.[12] The bloody fighting, which produced 4 million casualties, nearly 150,000 of them American, underscored "the existence of a Communist threat to America" and gave both Senator Joseph McCarthy and McCarthyism "a new lease on life" (Hamby 1973, 409).

Throughout his second term, Truman was under continuous attack from an increasingly conservative Republican Party, which had found anticommunism a powerful political weapon. The ambiguities of the Korean War helped Republican objections to Truman's presidency to become campaign attacks on Democrats during the midterm elections. Republicans gained twenty-eight seats in the House and five in the Senate, where Democratic losses included the party's majority leader, its whip, and its most outspoken critic of McCarthy. The election thus not only provided reinforcements for conservative Republicans but also forced President Truman to embrace a conservative South in order to secure his hold on the reduced party majorities on Capitol Hill, a situation reminiscent of Wilson's after 1918. The hearings of the House Un-American Activities Committee (HUAC) dovetailed with the attacks by McCarthy to cast suspicion on all dissent and to intimidate critics in the private as well as the public sector. "McCarthyism" became "the dominant force in American politics" (Hamby 1973, 415).[13]

Rhetorically, President Truman was a champion of civil liberties. He asserted in August 1950, "Extreme and arbitrary security measures strike at the very heart of our free society. . . . we must be eternally vigilant against those who would undermine freedom in the name of security" (Hamby 1973, 410). Yet his administration had a mixed record, owing partly to the Republican-centered conservatism of the times but also to the conservatism of his attorneys general. He had inherited the liberal Francis Biddle from Roosevelt, but Truman soon replaced him with a conservative Texan, Tom Clark, who was subsequently named to the Supreme Court, where he joined the majority in upholding the constitutionality of the Smith Act, the principal legal weapon against domestic communism.[14]

Clark's successor as attorney general was J. Howard McGrath, a conservative who had been chair of the Democratic National Committee. Under his aegis, the Justice Department became more aggressive in enforcing the administration's internal security program, which included a new standard for the dismissal of federal employees. The old standard had required "reasonable grounds" for thinking a person disloyal; the new standard permitted dismissal if "reasonable doubt" existed about a person's loyalty, which shifted the burden of proof toward the accused. Truman's final attorney general, James McGranery, was a staunch anticommunist close to both J. Edgar Hoover and leaders of the Catholic Church. McGranery enlarged the internal security section of the Justice Department to ferret out communists and hired Roy Cohn from McCarthy's staff as a special assistant. In the final year of his presidency, the Truman administration pursued communists "to a degree that bore little relevance to national security" (Hamby 1995, 567).

In his final two years, especially after firing General Douglas MacArthur, Truman was constantly assailed by Republicans for his "softness" on communism and his "socialistic" domestic schemes, much as copperhead Democrats had assailed Lincoln over emancipation. But, ironically, the most repressive legislation came from congressional Democrats. When Republican Richard Nixon, at that time a senator, filed an antisubversion bill, Patrick McCarran, Democratic chair of the Senate Judiciary Committee, reacted by authoring a substitute that increased the categories of subversive activities, targeted labor unions, strengthened immigration requirements and the Espionage and Sedition Acts, and created a Subversive Activities Control Board to police the new law. Truman vetoed the bill, but only ten senators and forty-eight representatives voted to sustain his veto. Many states and some private associations adopted similar measures that were sometimes enforced more aggressively than the federal statute.

In 1951, trying to blunt congressional action that would impinge on civil liberties, Truman created a President's Commission on Internal Security and Individual Rights and charged it with recommending ways to strengthen the laws against treason, espionage, and sabotage. But McCarran's Senate Judiciary Committee saw the initiative as a threat, scuttled it, and instead established an Internal Security Subcommittee (chaired by McCarran himself), which became the Senate counterpart to HUAC. McCarran won passage of an Immigration and Nationality Act in 1952 that restricted the immigration and naturalization of communists or anyone advocating the violent overthrow of the government, prevented such persons already here from being naturalized, and allowed the revocation of the citizenship of naturalized persons who joined the Communist Party or refused to testify before congressional committees investigating subversive activities (Hamby 1995, 569).[15]

There was little immediate change after Dwight Eisenhower regained the White House for the Republicans in 1952. He replaced Truman's internal security program with one that broadened the definition of "disloyalty" and put the onus clearly on federal employees to prove their innocence. HUAC vied with the Senate's Internal Security Subcommittee and Permanent Investigations Committee for anticommunist headlines. McCarthy led off by charging that the Truman administration had been "crawling with communists." The Communist Control Act of 1954 denied legal status to the Communist Party and subjected its members to the Internal Control Act. McCarthy meanwhile launched hearings on the Communist influence in the army.

But Eisenhower, the war hero, managed two things that Truman could not. First, he concluded the Korean War with an acceptable truce. Although leaving American troops in South Korea, this action reduced a key source of anticommunist fervor and permitted the overall reduction of armed forces. In turn, this move reduced the need for both conscript soldiers and higher war taxes, which further lowered tensions. Second, by his very presence, he helped the army to withstand McCarthy's attacks and ultimately bring an end to the Wisconsin senator's career and reputation. Despite Republican cries of "twenty years of treason," the Democrats regained control of Congress in the 1954 fall elections. Several Supreme Court decisions, building upon the Holmes and Brandeis dissents in the 1920s, narrowed the application of the Smith and Internal Control Acts. The Hungarian uprising in 1956 returned the political focus of Washington to Europe. Slowly, the flames of repression burned themselves out, as they had after Wilson, and the country lapsed into a kind of peace, punctuated by the emergence of the civil rights movement and a burgeoning nuclear arms race, until the shocks of the 1960s.[16]

JOHNSON AND VIETNAM

Vietnam was in many ways an extension of the "hot war" against communism that began with Korea. U.S. involvement began in the early 1950s, as French forces withdrew from the region, and was grounded in the same policy of preventing the spread of communism in Asia that lay behind the defense of South Korea. John F. Kennedy (JFK), who had regained the White House for the Democrats in 1961, also stressed U.S. prestige in the world: a loss to the communists anywhere would erode respect for America everywhere. In this view, the aborted Bay of Pigs invasion was a loss, the Cuban missile crisis a win when the USSR withdrew the weapons, and the building of the Berlin Wall a standoff. Inevitably, given this mind-set, rising communist activity in South Vietnam and the weakness of the government of President Ngo Dinh Diem there led to a deeper U.S. commitment, including more advisers, Green Beret forces, helicopters and other advanced American arms for the South Vietnamese, and finally endorsement of the overthrow of the Diem regime in favor of a string of military governments (see Patterson 1996, 486–523).

The war in Vietnam resembled the Korean conflict. Like Korea, Vietnam was a small, poor, distant, agrarian nation that posed no threat to the United States proper, only to American "interests"; the fear of the "domino effect" returned. There was no serious threat of espionage or subversion from the North Vietnamese, as the Soviet Union remained the real threat in this regard. Similarly, there was no declaration of war and no early declaration of emergency requiring maximum national commitment in war taxes, rationing, or an expanded draft. Because U.S. and Soviet nuclear arsenals were much more deadly than a decade earlier, greater care had to be taken to avoid a nuclear exchange, rendering America's main weaponry again unusable. Given the nuclear stalemate, Vietnam, like Korea, became a limited war of containment rather than a full-fledged fight to final victory of the type that MacArthur had demanded and many Americans still desired (Weigley 1973, 444 ff.).[17]

Following Kennedy's assassination in 1963, Lyndon B. Johnson (LBJ) came to the presidency sharing JFK's cold war philosophy and with greater experience in the bitter domestic anticommunism of the late forties and early fifties. In his first year, Johnson was preoccupied with the orderly assumption of power, a civil rights bill, and his own election as president in 1964. He also harbored ambitious plans for a broad-ranging domestic program. Johnson steadily escalated U.S. involvement in Vietnam as the situation there deteriorated and as he was regularly reminded, by Republicans such as Senator Everett Dirksen, that if Vietnam went "down the drain, it could conceivably cost us all of Southeast Asia" (Hulsey 2000, 198; see Patterson 1996, 524–61). In early 1964, he increased the U.S. military commitment, expanded covert raids on North Vietnam, and blanketed the whole area with U.S. air reconnaissance. The Republican nomination of the hawkish anticommunist Barry Goldwater for president only confirmed LBJ in this policy, which Congress overwhelmingly licensed through the so-called Gulf of Tonkin Resolution authorizing "all necessary measures" to defend American troops and deter North Vietnamese aggression. Running as the "peace" candidate, Johnson crushed Goldwater in November. But the escalation continued, to the cheers of Republicans, including Eisenhower and Dirksen, who insisted that efforts to end the war through negotiations would be "appeasement." At the end of 1965, there were 184,000 Americans in South Vietnam; three years later there were 543,000. U.S. aircraft flew 25,000 sorties against North Vietnam in 1965; they flew 108,000 in 1967 and dropped a quarter million tons of bombs (Hulsey 2000, 204–5).[18]

Johnson's attention, however, was centered mainly on the passage of his Great Society program of domestic reform, not on Vietnam. He therefore downplayed any talk of a military crisis even as he escalated the war effort. Gradually, he expanded conscription, but until 1968, his last year as president, he refused to press Congress to raise taxes. Brian Hulsey (2000, 214) observes: "While Johnson wanted to protect the Great Society, Dirksen and his Republican colleagues hoped that the bipartisan agreement to escalate the Vietnam War would adversely affect the White House's ambitious domestic agenda." GOP support in Congress for Johnson's Vietnam policies meant that, insofar as there was any criticism from the opposition, it was either perfunctory or urged even greater effort.

Partly for this reason and partly from the waning of McCarthyism, the LBJ era saw nothing comparable to the legislative threat to civil liberties that characterized the decade after World War II. Most congressional attention focused not on the subversive activities of communists or their sympathizers, but on antiwar and particularly antidraft protests, which began to mount dramatically in 1965. These protests resulted from increased news coverage of the war and rising conscription. Television cameras were everywhere and brought into the nation's living rooms images of the bloody fighting in rice paddies abroad, as well as the militant antiwar protests in the streets at home, to a degree unique in the history of war. This would make Vietnam far more "real"—and more difficult to accept—than was ever the case with Korea. In addition, while Johnson sought to deter the North Vietnamese through airpower, he had to deploy hundreds of thousands of ground troops to shore up a crumbling South Vietnamese army. By 1966, monthly draft calls were at thirty-five thousand; by 1967, draftees comprised half the army riflemen in Vietnam. Conscription always falls on the young, and in this case it fell on a huge "baby boom" bulge in the population, many of them in college. Colleges thus became centers of draft resistance in the same way German-American communities had under Wilson and copperhead counties under Lincoln. Nearly six hundred thousand youth became draft offenders in this war. Nearly two hundred thousand more became conscientious objectors (Patterson 1996, 598–99; Chambers 1999, 763–65).

The government tended to focus on this vexing problem of raising a mass army and maintaining its loyalty. It became a crime to knowingly destroy or mutilate a draft card, or to mutilate, deface, burn, or otherwise desecrate the flag in public. In 1967, Congress did revive the Subversive Activities Control Board (SACB), but a renewed hunt for communists did not appear to be the goal; rather, the board's resurrection seems to have been more an effort by the president to give some political cover to Senate Minority Leader Dirksen, under fire within his party for supporting the administration on civil rights and in other ways (Hulsey 2000, 214). The House Un-American Activities Committee continued its investigations, but it was concerned mainly with antiwar demonstrators. The Supreme Court meanwhile, with a liberal majority, found much of the Internal Control Act of 1950 to be unconstitutional. HUAC itself came under increasing criticism, including calls for its abolition (achieved finally in 1975).[19]

However upset Johnson may have been with the antiwar protests, the White House was not going to take repressive actions against them that would compete with its otherwise liberal domestic program. Moreover, there was no hint of an administration security program of the type developed by Truman or by Johnson's successor as president, Richard Nixon. LBJ's three attorneys general—Robert F. Kennedy, Nicholas deB. Katzenbach, and Ramsey Clark—were among the most liberal ever to occupy the office. Indeed, in the case of Clark, Johnson had to direct him to refer cases to the SACB in order to appease Everett Dirksen. Military surveillance did expand. In 1965, a new command center in Maryland began coordinating the work of counterintelligence agents at G-2 offices in the United States and preparing daily reports on right-wing, radical, and antiwar dissidents. By 1968, more than a thousand army plainclothes agents were monitoring civil rights and antiwar groups, infiltrating radical organizations such as Students for a Democratic Society (SDS), and sometimes discrediting them through provocative and illegal acts. This activity expanded under President Nixon (Pyle 1986).

Bipartisan support for Johnson's war policies was eroded significantly by the results of the 1966 midterm elections. The Republicans made major gains in Congress—forty-seven seats in the House, three in the Senate—though the Democrats retained control of both branches. More important, a new generation of GOP senators came to Washington—Charles Percy, Edward Brooke, Mark Hatfield, Howard Baker—all of whom had campaigned in some way against the war. They joined other Republicans in the Senate to urge an end to the war through negotiations, breaking with those in their party who saw negotiations as appeasement. A number of Democrats, including Majority Leader Mike Mansfield, joined them in a bipartisan coalition critical of administration policies and seeking an end to the fighting.

Johnson's presidency effectively came to an end with his 1968 announcement that he would not accept the Democratic Party nomination for president. The election year itself was the most turbulent in the nation's history, marked by the assassinations of Martin Luther King Jr. and Robert Kennedy and a tumultuous Democratic convention in Chicago that included massive street demonstrations against the war and a brutal police response. Yet the election year moved forward more or less normally as the political process weathered these upheavals, ending with the election of Richard Nixon and an orderly transition of power (Patterson 1996, 678–709).

BUSH AND THE WAR ON TERROR

Our current ordeal began with the unexpected and devastating attacks of 9/11, which in damage and loss of life proved similar to the Japanese bombing of Pearl Harbor but seemed worse because civilians were targeted on the U.S. mainland. The attacks were the work of Al Qaeda, a global network of Islamic extremists led by a wealthy Saudi named Osama bin Laden. Al Qaeda had previously been responsible for attacks on U.S. embassies and ships as well as an earlier bombing of the World Trade Center in New York. With Afghanistan as a command and training base, Al Qaeda had cells in dozens of countries from Western Europe to the Philippines. There was no "return address" on this attack; no nation was responsible, so there was none on which to declare war. President George W. Bush made this clear in a radio message shortly after the attacks, asserting that "this is a conflict without battlefields or beachheads," against opponents "who believe they are invisible." Victory, said the president, would come in a series of actions against terrorist organizations "and those who harbor and support them." The United States would mount a "broad and sustained campaign to secure our country and eradicate the evil of terrorism" (Sciolino 2001; Bush 2001).

In declaring a "war on terrorism," Bush took a number of steps that resembled those of other wartime presidents but also reflected the peculiar aspects of this situation. First, he sought congressional authority to use "all necessary and appropriate force against those nations, organizations or persons [the president] determines planned, authorized, committed or aided the terrorist attacks." He obtained permission to do so by a joint resolution that was passed unanimously in the Senate and with only one dissenting vote in the House within a matter of days (Pomper 2001, 2118). Bush quickly mobilized U.S. military strength and deployed it successfully against the ruling Taliban regime in Afghanistan—a radical Islamic theocracy that provided training and staging areas for Al Qaeda. American special forces and airpower, supported by dissident Afghan warlords, overthrew the Taliban in a matter of weeks and restored a more sympathetic government in the capital of Kabul.

Second, in late September 2001, by executive order, President Bush created a new Office of Homeland Security to "coordinate activities to make sure that anybody who wants to harm America will have a hard time doing so [and] to make sure our resources are deployed effectively." Thomas Ridge, governor of Pennsylvania, was named to head the new agency (Bettelheim 2001, 2253). The move anticipated a government reorganization that would either transfer federal agencies with security-related responsibilities to the Office of Homeland Security or, as in the case of the FBI and CIA, require them to share intelligence and coordinate operations with it. This launched a year-long debate in Congress over the Constitution and powers of the new agency, which was not resolved until after the 2002 midterm elections (with the president's signing of the Homeland Security Act on November 26, creating a new cabinet-level department).

Third, Attorney General John Ashcroft asked Congress for new powers that would give law enforcement agencies the tools with which to combat terrorism, including the authority to eavesdrop on suspects, conduct searches, and track Internet communications without the usual court permissions. The appointment of Ashcroft, known to his former Senate colleagues as a "stalwart conservative" and "something of a loner," to head the Justice Department had already prompted opposition from civil rights groups and civil libertarians. They were quick to express opposition to some aspects of his request, especially provision for so-called black-bag or sneak-and-peek searches of a suspect's home without having to notify the suspect immediately. Laura Murphy, head of the Washington office of the American Civil Liberties Union (ACLU), worried that "the courts may give more of a wink and nod" to the bill's provisions, adding that "the courts historically have given greater deference to Congress when we've been involved in war" (Palmer 2001, 2535). The USA Patriot Act ("Uniting and Strengthening America by Providing Appropriate Tools Required to Intercept and Obstruct Terrorism") passed the Congress in late November 2001. A year later, after more than a thousand people had been arrested, members of Congress concluded that the legislation had enabled authorities to make more effective use of intelligence data and to hold suspected terrorists for questioning, but they expressed frustration in efforts to oversee administration of the law because the Justice Department was reluctant to share even general information about how it was being used (Koszczuk 2002, 2284–88).

Bush's objective to "eradicate the evil of terrorism" meant that the conflict did not end with the Afghan campaign, for neither Al Qaeda nor bin Laden's forces had been entirely eliminated. There were other Islamic militants in Lebanon, Palestine, Chechnya, Indonesia, Pakistan, and elsewhere who posed threats to the United States and its interests. Bush specifically denounced three other countries—Iran, Iraq, and North Korea—as an "axis of evil" that harbored terrorists or presented other threats to the United States. Iraq became a particular focus of administration enmity. A nation against which his father had waged a limited war a decade earlier, Iraq was accused by President Bush of having weapons of mass destruction—biological, chemical, and nuclear—in violation of a United Nations directive. He demanded their destruction and threatened American military intervention if Iraq failed to do so, suggesting that the United States would go it alone if necessary (Erlanger 2002; Broad 2002; Bumiller 2002).

The threat of a first strike was a break with American diplomatic tradition, and it provoked bipartisan criticism coupled with calls for military coalition building and taking the U.S. case to the UN. The administration moved diplomatically in these directions, yet at the same time the White House maintained a determined public posture toward Iraq. In September 2002, Bush enunciated a new foreign policy doctrine, framed by the war on terror but with broader significance. This "Bush Doctrine" stressed the U.S. commitment to human rights and free trade as well as an implacable opposition to terrorism. The assertion of a right to strike preemptively against "rogue states and their terrorist clients before they are able to threaten or use weapons of mass destruction" was a claim that no previous administration had made. It committed the United States to building a military force that no potential adversary could hope to equal, a decision that abandoned the "sufficiency" or "parity" doctrines that had long guided American military policy (see Schribman 2002).

The Bush doctrine, which grew out of the threat of terrorism, was nonetheless made possible by advances in military technology (see Associated Press 2002 for full text). The commitment to a first-strike capability required a military buildup beyond that needed for Afghanistan, and accordingly the Bush White House proposed hefty increases in the military budget. Unlike previous war administrations, this new spending was not for increases in military personnel, but rather for high-tech weaponry capable of vanquishing "rogue" nations without deploying the mass armies required in previous wars.[20] The decision was significant politically in two ways. First, it largely precluded the need for conscription and reduced the risk of casualties, both of which had been causes of public controversy in other war administrations. Second, while costs would be substantial, it was possible that they would be less than required for a mass army, thereby reducing the immediate need for higher taxes.

Like Truman and Johnson but unlike the wartime presidents who preceded them, Bush sought to downplay the immediate impact of the war on the American people. There would be no military draft or higher taxes. Indeed, Bush won enactment of a massive, long-term tax reduction early in his administration, and his efforts since had been to make these cuts permanent. There was also no talk of rationing. Instead, the president urged Americans to be even more active consumers. Almost a year after the initial attack, Bob Herbert, a *New York Times* columnist, observed, "Not only are Americans not making any extraordinary effort to join in this fight for the defense of our country, we're not even being asked to contribute to the war effort by making any real sacrifices" (Herbert 2002, A19). Similarly, according to David Gergen (2002), a presidential adviser for Democrats and Republicans alike, "this is the first major war since the United States–Mexico war of 1846 that America has fought without having a draft or a tax increase."

With the approach of the November 2002 midterm elections, President Bush escalated his war rhetoric but also reversed course to seek a UN resolution demanding inspections of Iraqi weapons. He asked Congress to support his new doctrine and urged action to create a cabinet-level Department of Homeland Security, also a reversal of his earlier position. The Congress had never before been asked to endorse a possible preemptive strike against a sovereign nation, yet Bush, with control of Congress hanging in the balance, pressed hard for this authority (Riehl 2002, 2679). The resolution in Congress passed the House 2–1 and the Senate 3–1. The president then launched a vigorous personal campaign to secure GOP control of the Congress, attacking Democrats who had not voted for the resolution and blaming Senate Democrats for the failure of Congress to act on legislation to authorize a Department of Homeland Security. After the November elections, in which the GOP gained majorities in both houses of Congress, many agreed with Republican Senator Lincoln Chaffee's assessment that "Republicans picked up key states with this issue. We get what we want, or we use it as a bludgeon in the campaigns" (Dalrymple 2002, 3007).

The postelection Congress acted quickly to create the new department. In the largest government reorganization in a half century, twenty-two existing federal agencies were brought together in the new Department of Homeland Security, among them the Immigration and Naturalization Service, the Customs Service, the Secret Service, and the Coast Guard, as well as a number of science and technology, information and infrastructure, and emergency preparedness and response agencies. The bill provided a framework for the new department but left many questions undecided, including how Congress would oversee or fund it. For the most part, debate over the bill centered on denial of civil service and union protections to department employees, on limits to corporate liability for products related to homeland security, and on removal of the ban on federal contracts to companies that move offshore to avoid U.S. taxes.

There was much less discussion of civil liberties. The ACLU worried that the bill's provisions for intelligence sharing between the new department, FBI, and CIA could "usher in a wave of civil liberties violations." In addition, Jerry Berman of the Center for Democracy and Technology voiced concerns that, in creating the new department, "neither the President nor the Congress have answered any of the fundamental questions, including how this is going to work, what are the checks and balances, how will we know if it is effective, what data will be collected, and who will have access to it" (see Cohn 2002, 3073). More generally, Democrat Robert Byrd warned his Senate colleagues: "It is dangerous when a president believes that he supposes the people's consent to freely tamper with their rights and their liberties. It is even worse when we not only fail to impose restraint, but actually aid and abet the executive in a brazen power grab" (Dalrymple 2002, 3002).

But Bush, like the war presidents before him, argued that the threat of terrorism redressed the balance between the need for surveillance and the guarantee of civil liberties. In a dramatic policy statement of September 20, 2002, President Bush had asserted:

> We must strengthen intelligence warning and analysis to provide integrated threat assessments for national and homeland security. Since the threats inspired by foreign governments and groups may be conducted inside the United States, we must also ensure the proper fusion of information between intelligence and law enforcement. (Associated Press 2002)

To these ends, he ordered the Justice Department to detain individuals suspected of a connection with the 9/11 or future attacks, to withhold their names from the public, to try them by military tribunal as well as civil court, and to eavesdrop on their legal conversations. The president also proposed a return to the World War II/Korean War informant system via a Citizen Corps that would recruit Americans to report "suspicious activity" to police or the FBI. He pushed federal agents to monitor electronic messages and financial transactions more thoroughly, used army as well as Immigration and Naturalization Service personnel to watch our borders, and cracked down on visa violators. The administration has considered captured Afghan soldiers as criminal prisoners, not prisoners of war, and in some cases has handed the captives over to the intelligence services of other countries less inhibited by strictures against torture. And it chose to try an American captured among Afghan forces as a traitor rather than a POW, thus bypassing the Geneva conventions (Seelye 2002a, 2002b; Editorial Desk 2002).[21]

As with Lincoln and FDR, Bush has undertaken only a modest propaganda campaign. His administration has not pressed aggressively for media control, in part because most newspapers and television outlets are already broadly supportive; some, including major daily newspapers, numerous talk radio shows, and the Fox News and Christian Coalition–type cable networks, are clear partisans of the war on terrorism. In addition, the Ad Council, established in 1942 to rally support for World War II, has developed advertisements to do the same for President Bush's war on terrorism. There is, on the other hand, tight control within the government of information about the war, one reason for the reluctance to release the names of suspects or bring them to civil trial (Miller 2002; Levere 2002; Krugman 2002a; Daniels 2002).[22]

At the same time, however, surveillance has increased in many ways. The CIA, contrary to its original charter, has been given new powers to gather intelligence within the United States; at the administration's behest, Congress has given the FBI what the *New York Times* calls "nearly unbridled power to poke into the affairs of anyone in the United States, even when there is no evidence of illegal activities, including the right to search Web sites, chat rooms, and houses of worship." FBI agents now work on virtually every major university campus and may question anyone accused, even anonymously, of "disloyal" utterances. High schools must provide information on juniors and seniors to military recruiters, and college librarians must provide information about materials checked out by students and faculty (McAuliffe 2003). In addition, the Pentagon plans a computer system, "Total Information Awareness," that will survey personal bank records, phone logs, Internet mail, and credit card transactions without a search warrant, then cross-check these records and store them permanently in the Office of Information Awareness at the Defense Advanced Research Projects Agency. The Homeland Security Department will join in the collection and sharing of information at home and abroad, and a new military formation, the U.S. Northern Command in Colorado, is seeking—with the apparent support of the administration—to allow military personnel to engage in domestic law enforcement and intelligence gathering.[23]

There has been criticism of the "surveillance state." Libertarian conservative William Safire has condemned both the expansion of FBI powers to conduct investigations *"with not a scintilla of evidence of a crime being committed* [emphasis added]" and the plans for electronic tracking:

Consider the new reach of federal power: the income-tax return you provided your mortgage lender; your academic scores and personnel ratings, credit card purchases and E-Z pass movements; your political and charitable contributions, charge account at your pharmacist and insurance records; your subscription to non-mainstream publications like *The Nation* or *Human Events*, every visit to every Web site and comment to every chat room, and every book or movie you bought or even considered on Amazon.com—all newly combined with the tickets, arrests, press clips, full field investigations and raw allegations of angry neighbors or rejected lovers that flow into the F.B.I. (Safire 2002)

He also notes that prior safeguards have been swept away by executive fiat, with no public discussion, judicial guidance, or congressional action (Safire 2002).

Lincoln, Roosevelt, and Johnson withstood criticism of their wartime controls and surveillance in part because they were committed to the protection of individual liberty and appointed attorneys general—Stanton, Biddle, Ramsey Clark—who shared this commitment. Wilson and Truman, while rhetorically supportive of civil liberties, named attorneys general—Palmer, Clark, McGrath, and especially McGranery—who were political conservatives. The wartime administration of President Bush, however, is the first in the nation's history in which both the chief executive and the attorney general have been political conservatives. When he was a member of the Senate, Bush Attorney General John Ashcroft's voting record received consistently high marks from conservative groups and low scores from liberal groups.[24] A Christian fundamentalist who admires the Confederacy, opposes abortion and gay rights, and supports the death penalty, Ashcroft has been described by a British journal as "Cromwellian" (Dowd 2001).[25] Already, the attorney general's shifting of resources in the Justice Department away from organized crime and civil rights and toward the war on terrorism has had the effect of "utterly reshaping the department's mission." According to one writer, "For Ashcroft, the issue every day is terrorism" (Washington 2002). Other Bush appointees raise similar concerns, among them John Poindexter, the new head of the Total Information Awareness project, who was convicted in 1990 of conspiracy and lying to Congress about the illegal sale of arms to Iran in order to finance a covert war in Central America. Bush himself has shown a pronounced "bent for secrecy," ordering federal agencies to resist all Freedom of Information requests not clearly mandated by law, refusing to give documents to Congress relating to economic dealings of senior officials, and also battling to keep records from his Texas governorship secret (Cohen 2002).

It is premature to evaluate the Bush administration's attention to civil liberties. For now, criticism of the administration has centered on domestic policy—excessive and unfair tax cuts, unwise deregulation, corporate favoritism ("crony capitalism," as it has been called), much as criticism of Lincoln, Roosevelt, and Truman focused not on their surveillance and controls but on such issues as the emancipation of slaves and "socialistic" reforms said to have been taken under cover of war. The wave of corporate scandals and all that it suggests about Republican free-market capitalism should keep the political fires stoked and thereby provide some protection against invasions of freedom. Moreover, the brutal Taliban of Afghanistan, like the Iraqi regime of Saddam Hussein, provides a powerful negative reference for liberty lovers, as did repression in the post-secession South and in Nazi Germany. An oppressive enemy can lead to greater concern for civil liberties at home. Moreover, there have been no further attacks on U.S. soil, and the initial military operations have had a measure of success. Success at home and abroad can also breed tolerance toward government actions. Detentions declined in 2002 after the capture of Kabul, just as they did in 1864 after the fall of Atlanta and in 1943 after the victories at Midway, North Africa, and Stalingrad.

Surveillance and questioning, on the other hand, have accelerated, which is cause for concern; should surveillance be seen as the reason that attacks have not recurred, the public might become inured to being watched and questioned. There is the further difficulty that we are engaged in a "war" with terrorism and not with another nation. Because it was so destructive, 9/11 felt like an act of war. But a terrorist attack is a political crime, not an act of war. Our response—the assault on those who harbor, abet, hide, or support terrorists—although heavily militarized, is closer to the "war" against drugs than to our response to Pearl Harbor or Fort Sumter. We are thus using our armed forces for a kind aggressive police work, targeting particular territories and maintaining high vigilance, a practice we have previously used only in the drug war.

This approach has consequences. Wars between countries have ends, even if only armistices and truces, as with World War I and Korea. A war against terrorism that could last forever, as the president has repeatedly suggested, has no clear end, and if there is no end to the war, there can be no end to the deployment of forces and homeland defense. Lincoln and Roosevelt could say and believe that wartime measures—surveillance, mobilization, controls—would end with the war itself. Americans could tolerate them as short-term intrusions into their lives. But this does not appear to be the case today. To have a war that could last forever is to be in a situation—with respect to dissent, surveillance, and civil liberties—in which we have never before found ourselves. Thus, Paul Krugman (2002b) warns that if "our new, threatened condition isn't temporary" and "we're in this for the long haul," then "any measures we take to fight terrorism had better be measures that we are prepared to live with indefinitely."

Wars also require war measures. Historically, this has meant some combination of higher taxes, military conscription, and consumer rationing. The Bush administration has proposed none of these and, given its conservative political base, seems unlikely to do so in the foreseeable future. This may not, however, be good news for civil libertarians; a major source of public resistance to extended war has typically been opposition to these kinds of war measures. If President Bush can avoid taking the steps usually demanded by war, he might avoid the public criticism that has often provided a powerful political impetus to get the thing over with, and this, in turn, could be bad for dissent and for the preservation of civil liberties.

NOTES

1. For a brief summary of the Maryland crisis, see Gienapp 2002, 83–85.
2. On John Wilkes Booth and the Confederacy, see Starkey 1976.
3. We are indebted to Professor Gerald McFarland, University of Massachusetts—Amherst, for apprising us of the sweeping nature of the post-Brown raids and arrests.
4. Ferrell quotes Burleson's solicitor as giving this explanation of post office policies: "You know, I am not working in the dark on this censorship thing. I know exactly what I am after. I am after three things and only three things—pro-Germanism, pacifism, and 'high-browism.'"
5. State governments, responding to public clamor about traitors and spies, enacted statutes similar to the federal laws, and local district attorneys prosecuted cases and won convictions under both federal and state laws, as juries showed little concern for the civil liberties of the accused.

6. Donald Johnson (1963, 62) reports that George Creel said, "The President was against free speech in the height of the war. He said there could be no such thing—that it was insanity, and that men could, by their actions in America, stab our soldiers in the back."

7. On fifty-one roll calls in the House of Representatives between April 1917 and May 1918 that dealt with war measures, the average Republican support for the president was 72 percent, while the average for Democrats was 67 percent. See Moos 1956, 306.

8. Robert Ferrell (1985, 201) questions whether "the Progressive movement had accustomed Americans to government intervention in their lives, and made interference with civil liberties and civil rights easier to accept."

9. Only after the resignation of the liberal Frederick Howe as commissioner of immigration did Palmer begin his deportation proceedings.

10. On the German-American Bund, see Herzstein 1989, 121–213, which makes clear that anxieties about espionage and subversion, at least early on, were not wholly imaginary. For the text of the 1924 Immigration Act, with commentary, see Boller and Story, 1996, 75–78.

11. On government-sponsored and other forays into informing and persuading the public, much of it privately initiated without government pressure, see Roeder 1993, chs. 1–2. For the reality of the German threat, see Herzstein 1989, xiii–xix, and Weinberg 1994, 154, 175–76, 178.

12. This action was denounced by Arthur Garfield Hays, a leader of the ACLU, as "the most outrageous, undemocratic measure that could possibly be conceived" (McAuliffe 1976).

13. On McCarthy, national security, and civil liberties, see McAuliffe 1976, chs. 6 and 7.

14. See *Dennis* v. *U.S.*, 341 U.S. 496, in which the Court upheld the convictions of eleven Communist Party officials prosecuted under the Smith Act. It led Truman to lament that he had put Clark, that "damn fool from Texas" (McCullough 1992, 901), on the bench.

15. On the Truman security program, see McCullough 1992, 550 ff. In 1950, the regents of the University of California voted to discharge 157 members of the university staff for failing to declare that they were not members of the Communist Party, and the National Association for the Advancement of Colored People (NAACP) voted to expel any branch that was communist-dominated (Donovan 1982, 188).

16. For a summary of federal internal security and civil liberties actions in the decade after World War II, see *Congress and the Nation, 1945–1964*, vol. 1: esp. 1645–66. On Eisenhower and the Army-McCarthy hearings, see Wills 1970, 115–38. McCarthyism remained a political force through the 1950s. A year after censuring McCarthy, the Senate felt it necessary to adopt a resolution asserting that their action against him did not lessen their determination to investigate subversive activities.

17. During the Vietnam escalation, Robert McNamara, secretary of defense under Kennedy and Johnson, developed the concept of "Mutually Assured Destruction," an

acknowledgment of the nonutility of nuclear weapons. McNamara seems to have spent as much time dealing with the nuclear arms race as with Vietnam. See Dupuy and Dupuy 1984, 635 ff.

18. Some years later, it became clear that the attack on the destroyers *Maddox* and *C. Turner Joy,* which led to the Gulf of Tonkin Resolution, came after American maneuvering aimed at provoking a response from the North. For a text of the resolution with commentary, see Boller and Story 1996, 225–29.

19. For a summary of civil liberties and internal security legislation and court cases during the mid-1960s, see *Congress and the Nation: 1965–1968,* vol. 2: 409–19.

20. The weapons sought or in production were an impressive array of robotic vehicles and aircraft, satellite- and laser-guided bombs, high-intensity shoulder weapons controlled by hand-held computers, devices to "see" underground and through walls, and more. See Shanker and Schmitt 2002. See also Weinbert 2002. To other nations, the Bush Doctrine and the new American weaponry have a sinister appearance. See Gorce 2002, 10–11. In this view, not uncommon among Europeans, the wars in Afghanistan and Iraq are tests and demonstrations of America's capacity to dominate the earth.

21. On the reliance on countries that use torture as an interrogation technique, see Kuttner 2001.

22. The administration has, in fact, enlisted U.S. writers to give talks around the world on U.S. cultural virtues and plans to distribute booklets and other materials. See Wize 2002. For the sweep of media voices, see Krugman 2002a.

23. *New York Times* editorial, May 3, 2002. On the new role of the CIA, see Jackson 2002; Weiner 2002. On the Pentagon, see Firestone and Bumiller 2002. On the FBI, see Shenon and Johnston 2002. And on the Homeland Security Department and military surveillance, see Bumiller 2002.

24. In his final years, for example, Ashcroft's voting record received 100 percent scores from the Christian Coalition and the American Conservative Union, while getting 5% from the Americans for Democratic Action and 0 percent from the American Federation of State, County, and Municipal Workers union. See Barone and Ujifusa 1999, 929.

25. The "Cromwellian" epithet is from the *Economist,* as quoted in Dowd 2001. See also Dowd 2002 and Jackson 2002.

REFERENCES

Associated Press. 2002. "To Promote a Balance of Power That Favors Freedom." *Boston Globe,* September 21, A12.

Barone, Michael, and Grant Ujifusa. 1999. *The Almanac of American Politics 2000.* Washington, D.C.: *National Journal.*

Beckert, Sven. 2001. *The Monied Metropolis: New York City and the Consolidation of the American Bourgeoisie, 1850–1896.* Cambridge: Cambridge University Press.

Bettelheim, Adriel. 2001. "Tom Ridge." *CQ Weekly Report,* September 29, 2253.

Boller, Paul F., Jr., and Ronald Story. 1996. *A More Perfect Union: Documents in U.S. History.* 4th ed. Boston: Houghton Mifflin.

Broad, William J. 2002. "Threats and Responses: Inspection." *New York Times,* November 19, A20.

Bumiller, Elizabeth. 2002. "In Blunt Words, Bush Threatens Hussein Again." *New York Times.* November 21, A1, A22.

Bush, George W. 2001. "President Bush's Address on Terrorism Before a Joint Meeting of Congress" (transcript of speech). *New York Times,* September 21, B5.

Caro, Robert. 2002. *Master of the Senate.* New York: Alfred A. Knopf.

Chambers, John Whiteclay, ed. 1999. *The Oxford Companion to American Military History.* New York: Oxford University Press.

Cohn, Peter. 2002. "New Privacy Concerns." *CQ Weekly Report.* November 23, 3073.

Congress and the Nation: A Review of Government and Politics 1945–1964. Vol. 1. Washington, D.C.: Congressional Quarterly Service.

Congress and the Nation: A Review of Government and Politics 1965–1968. Vol. 2. Washington, D.C., Congressional Quarterly Service.

Corwin, Edward S. 1957. *The President: Office and Powers, 1787–1957.* 4th ed. New York: New York University Press.

Dalrymple, Mary. 2002. "Homeland Security Department Another Victory for Administration." *CQ Weekly Report.* November 16, 3002.

Daniels, Robert. 2002. "Detaining Minority Citizens, Then and Now." *Chronicle of Higher Education,* February 15, B11.

Daniels, Roger. 1993. *Prisoners without Trial: Japanese Americans in World War II.* New York: Hill and Wang.

Dear, I. C. B., and M. R. D. Fast, eds. 1995. *The Oxford Companion to World War II.* Oxford: Oxford University Press.

Donovan, Robert J. 1982. *Tumultuous Years: The Presidency of Harry S Truman: 1949–1953.* New York: W. W. Norton.

Dowd, Maureen. 2001. "Liberties; Uncivil Liberties?" *New York Times,* November 25, Sec. 4, p. 11.

Dowd, Maureen. 2002. "The Axis of No Access." *New York Times,* February 13, A31.

Dupuy, R. Ernest, and Trever N. Dupuy. 1984. *Military Heritage of America.* Rev. ed. Fairfax, Va.: Hero Books.

Eaton, Clement. 1946. *The Freedom-of-Thought Struggle in the Old South.* Rev. ed. New York: Harper and Row.

Editorial Desk. 2002. "Fair Trials in Security Cases." *Boston Globe,* October 28, A24.

Erlanger, Steven. 2002. "U.S. Officials Try to Assure Europeans on NATO." *New York Times,* February 3, A7.

Fehrenbacher, Don. 1978. *The Dred Scott Case: Its Significance in American Law and Politics.* New York: Oxford University Press.

Ferrell, Robert. 1985. *Woodrow Wilson and World War I: 1917–1921.* New York: Harper and Row.

Firestone, David, and Elizabeth Bumiller. 2002. "Stalemate Ends in Bush Victory on Terror Bill." *New York Times,* November 13, A1.

Gergen, David. 2002. "A Nation in Search of Its Mission." *New York Times,* June 17, A17.

Gienapp, William E. 2002. *Abraham Lincoln and Civil War America.* New York: Oxford University Press.

Gorce, Paul-Marie de la. 2002. "Bombardière pour controller, Washington a defini sa stratégie." *Le Monde Diplomatique,* March.

Hall, Kermit, ed. 1992. *The Oxford Companion to the Supreme Court of the United States.* New York: Oxford University Press.

Hamby, Alonzo L. 1973. *Beyond the New Deal: Harry S. Truman and American Liberalism.* New York: Columbia University.

Hamby, Alonzo L. 1995. *Man of the People: The Life of Harry S. Truman.* New York: Oxford University Press.

Herbert, Bob. 2002. "Stepping Up to the Plate." *New York Times,* July 8, A19.

Herzstein, Robert E. 1989. *Roosevelt and Hitler: Prelude to War.* New York: Paragon House.

Hulsey, Byron C. 2000. *Everett Dirksen and His Presidents.* Lawrence: University Press of Kansas.

Jackson, Derrick Z. 2002. "Who's Watching the Watchers?" *Boston Globe,* November 22, A25.

Johnson, Donald. 1963. *The Challenge to American Freedoms: World War I and the Rise of the American Civil Liberties Union.* Lexington: For the Mississippi Valley Historical Association, University of Kentucky Press.

Kennedy, David. 1980. *Over Here: The First World War and American Society.* New York: Oxford University Press.

Koszczuk, Jackie. 2002. "Lawmakers Struggle to Keep an Eye on Patriot Act." *CQ Weekly Report,* September 7, 2284–88.

Krugman, Paul. 2002a. "The Bully's Pulpit.." *New York Times,* September 6, A23.

Krugman, Paul. 2002b. "The Long Haul." *New York Times,* September 10, A25.

Kuttner, Robert. 2001. "No Ordinary Time." *American Prospect,* November 5, 2.

Levere, Jane. 2002. "The Media Business: Advertising. An Ad Council Campaign Sells Freedom, but Some Call It Propaganda." *New York Times,* July 1, C8.

Link, Arthur. 1963. *Woodrow Wilson.* New York: World Publishing.

Mayer, George H. 1967. *The Republican Party: 1854–1966.* New York: Oxford University Press,

McAuliffe, Mary Sperling. 1976. *Crisis on the Left: Cold War Politics and American Liberals, 1947–1954.* Amherst: University of Massachusetts Press.

McAuliffe, Michael. 2003. "Patriot Act Fuels Ire of Book-Lovers." *Springfield (Mass.) Sunday Republican.* January 12, 1.

McCullough, David G. 1992. *Truman.* New York: Simon and Schuster.

McPherson, James M. 1988. *Battle Cry of Freedom: The Civil War Era.* New York: Oxford University Press.

McPherson, James M. 2001. *Ordeal by Fire: The Civil War and Reconstruction.* 3rd ed. New York: Alfred A. Knopf.

Menand, Louis. 2001. *The Metaphysical Club: A Story of Ideas in America.* New York: Farrar, Straus and Giroux.

Milkis, Sidney, and Jerome M. Mileur, eds. 2002. *The New Deal and the Triumph of Liberalism.* Amherst: University of Massachusetts Press.

Miller, Judith. 2002. "U.S. Plans to Act More Rigorously in Hostage Cases." *New York Times,* February 18, A1.

Moos, Malcolm. 1956. *The Republicans: A History of Their Party.* New York: Random House.

Murphy, Paul L. 1972a. *The Constitution in Crisis Times.* New York: Harper and Row.

Murphy, Paul L. 1972b. *The Meaning of Freedom of Speech: First Amendment Freedoms from Wilson to FDR.* Westport, Conn.: Greenwood.

Neely, Mark E, Jr. 1991. *The Fate of Liberty: Abraham Lincoln and Civil Liberties.* New York: Oxford University Press.

Oates, Stephen B. 1998. *The Whirlwind of War: Voices of the Storm, 1861–1865.* New York: HarperCollins.

O'Neill, William L. 1993. *A Democracy at War: America's Fight at Home and Abroad in World War II.* New York: Free Press.

Palmer, Elizabeth A. 2001. "Terrorism Bill's Sparse Paper Trail May Cause Legal Vulnerabilities." *CQ Weekly Report,* October 27, 2535.

Patterson, James T. 1996. *Grand Expectations: The United States, 1945–1974.* New York: Oxford University Press.

Polenberg, Richard. 1968a. *America at War: The Home Front, 1941–1945.* Englewood Cliffs, N.J.: Prentice-Hall.

Polenberg, Richard. 1968b. "The Era of Franklin D. Roosevelt and Civil Liberties: The Case of the Dies Committee." *Historian* (February).

Polenberg, Richard. 2000. *The Era of Franklin D. Roosevelt, 1933–1945: A Brief History with Documents.* Boston: Bedford/St. Martin's Press.

Pomper, Miles A. 2001. "In for the Long Haul." *CQ Weekly Report,* September 15, 2118.

Riehl, Jonathan. 2002. "Broad Resolution Allows Bush to Set Terms of War without Revision." *CQ Weekly Report,* October 12, 2769.

Roeder, George H. 1993. *The Censored War: American Visual Experience during World War II.* New Haven: Yale University Press.

Safire, William. 2002. "J. Edgar Mueller." *New York Times,* June 3, A15.

Schaffer, Ronald. 1991. *America in the Great War: The Rise of the War Welfare State.* New York: Oxford University Press.

Sciolino, Elaine. 2001. "Long Battle Seen." *New York Times,* September 16, A1.

Seelye, Katherine Q. 2002a. "Powell Asks Bush to Review Stand on War Captives." *New York Times,* January 27, A1.

Seelye, Katherine Q. 2002b. "Threats and Responses: The Detainee." *New York Times,* October 28, A13.

Shanker, Thom, and Eric Schmitt. 2002. "Threats and Responses: Mobilization; Reserve Call-Up for an Iraq War May Equal 1991's." *New York Times*, October 28, A1.

Shenon, Philip, and David Johnston. 2002. "Seeking Terrorist Plots, the FBI Is Tracking Hundreds of Muslims." *New York Times*, October 6, A1.

Shribman, David M. 2002. "Bush Doctrine Slipping under Political Radar." *Boston Globe*, December 24, A3.

Starkey, Larry. 1976. *Wilkes Booth Came to Washington.* New York: Random House.

Washington, Wayne. 2002. "A Change in Mission for Ashcroft." *Boston Sunday Globe*, December 8, A6.

Weigley, Russell F. 1973. *The American Way of War.* New York: Macmillan.

Weinberg, Gerhard. 1994. *A World at Arms: A Global History of World War II.* Cambridge: Cambridge University Press.

Weinbert, Steven. 2002. "The Growing Nuclear Danger." *New York Review*, July 18.

Weiner, Tim. 2002. "The C.I.A. Widens Its Domestic Reach." *New York Times*, January 20, sec. 4, p. 1.

White, John Kenneth. 1998. *Still Seeing Red.* Boulder, Colo.: Westview.

Williams, T. Harry. 1981. *The History of American Wars.* New York: Alfred A. Knopf.

Wills, Garry. 1970. *Nixon Agonistes: The Crisis of a Self-Made Man.* Boston: Houghton Mifflin.

Wize, Michael Z. 2002. "Writers Do Cultural Battle around the Globe" *New York Times*, December 7, B7.

DANIEL KRISLOV

Civil Liberties and the Judiciary in the Aftermath of 9/11

How will the U.S. judiciary respond to the measures taken by the other branches of government to control terrorism? As of this writing there has been little time for post-9/11 cases to work their way through the judiciary system; much of what I state here will be speculation based upon what I consider the relevant considerations. An exploration of basic considerations precedes a discussion of probable responses by the federal courts.

First, we need to consider those characteristics of courts that might cause them to take a different approach to the issues from that taken by the other branches. The most obvious of these is the judges' relative insulation from electoral politics. Federal judges have lifetime tenure—they can leave office only through voluntary retirement or resignation, death, or impeachment and conviction by the Congress (an extremely rare occurrence). This means that judges generally do not have to worry about losing office if they issue unpopular decisions. This does not, of course, mean that the judicial branch is completely insulated from the effects of elections. The appointment process involves nomination by the president and confirmation by the Senate, and these elected actors can therefore affect the composition of the judiciary over time. On the other hand, a single unpopular decision is not likely to have any great consequences for the judicial branch in the short run, as the incumbents on the judiciary will be insulated from direct negative impacts on their careers.[1]

In theory, then, the courts have a special role to play in times of national crisis. If elected officials are overly likely to take ill-considered measures that violate civil liberties as a result of political pressures to "do something" about the crisis, the courts should be able to function as the prevailing "cooler heads." In other words, the courts should be in a better position to protect the rights of individuals from the effects of panic and fear on the majority. The courts are seen, in this view, as an institution better suited to striking a fair balance between the needs of the society as a whole and individuals' rights. There are, however, limitations on the ability of the courts to stand indefinitely in the face of intense majority opposition. For example, the Supreme Court has for the past few decades engaged in a long, partial retreat from some of its criminal procedure holdings of the 1960s and 1970s as a result of deliberate choices by the elective branches of government in the intervening years to pick judges who were "tougher on criminals." No doubt these personnel changes will have great effect in determining the outcome of the issues involving increased antiterrorism security. Nonetheless, the recent recommitment of the Court to the *Miranda* decision and some interesting stands taken in search-and-seizure cases seem to indicate that this Court may react differently from the elected branches to civil liberties issues.[2]

Predicting where the federal courts will stand on many of the legal issues involved in the "war on terrorism" is very difficult. The first reason is that many decades have passed since the nation faced a domestic threat of this magnitude; one has to go back to the years of World War II (Slackman 1990) and the early cold war (inclusively, an era from 1942 to about 1953) to find a period in which the government has been so active in attempting to increase security domestically. The era in which those measures were taken was, in many ways, very different from the present. The courts of that period were perhaps far less comfortable using their power than are courts today. Still somewhat cowed by the political rebuff to the Supreme Court's anti–New Deal stance, the courts of the 1940s appeared less likely to seek out confrontation with the elective branches of government. Further, it is fair to say that the *Brown* v. *Board of Education* case (1954), in addition to its landmark legal significance as a decisive stand against segregation in schools, was a transformative event in how the courts were perceived. Regardless of whether they are liberal or conservative, today's judges and justices seem more likely to view the courts as the proper place for resolving many of the nation's major political issues, and more willing to counter the decisions of the elective branches.[3] Thus, the precedents of that earlier era do not provide us with much foundation for determining how the current courts will decide similar cases.

The second reason for difficulty in predicting how current judges will respond to issues involved in the control of terrorism is that the relationship between security and liberty, often posited as if they were inevitably opposed, is enormously complicated. It is not as simple as civil libertarians would often have it, that one must sacrifice liberty in order to promote security. Rather, the absence of security can itself pose an awful danger to liberty. The place of terrorism in this conundrum is equally hard to discern.

An uncontested definition of terrorism has so far proven elusive. It does, however, seem to have some defining characteristics—i.e., the surprise use of deadly force against noncombatant targets for the purpose of furthering a political goal or set of goals (Schweitzer and Schweitzer 2002; Schmid 1993). The noncombatant targets themselves can be political or governmental figures (e.g., Israel's prime minister, Yitzhak Rabin) (Peri 2000), or they may be random targets chosen for their nationality or country of residence (e.g., those people who happened to be in the World Trade Center towers at the time of the attack). This does not mean, however, that any use of potential terror by the state or people is equivalent and should be labeled terrorism, as some postmodernists argue. Rather, it is to argue that the use of force is unjustified if it occurs in the absence of wrongdoing on the part of its objects or in the absence of prior notification that a particular area is to be targeted for the use of force to achieve political ends.

Efforts to control terrorism through the use of force, confinement, and surveillance are nearly automatically deemed threats to liberty and democracy by civil libertarians, yet the relationship between terror and democracy is far more complex than that. In the next section, I will attempt to systematically discuss the relationship between the control of terrorism and the preservation of democracy.

PART 1: TERRORISM AND THE STATE

In the United States, much political rhetoric and the constitution of our political institutions assume that the biggest threat to liberty of the individual and the democratic control of society is the potential abuse of power by the government. After the twentieth century, it is hard to argue that this is an unreasonable view. After all, the world's greatest human-created disasters during that century were largely caused by the overreaching of modern totalitarian states. Much of the repressive terror imposed by those states was rhetorically justified by pointing to supposed external and internal threats ("counterrevolutionaries" in the cases of the Soviet Union [USSR] and China, a "worldwide Jewish conspiracy" in the case of Nazi Germany) (Getty and Naumov 1999; Gonan 2000), so it is clear that the civil libertarian reaction to the citation of threats as a justification for increasing governmental security measures is not mere paranoia. Indeed, the threat of communism and Japanese espionage/sabotage domestically have been used as justification for some of the worst human rights violations perpetrated by the United States in the twentieth century, albeit nowhere near the extent carried out by the totalitarian regimes.

Less familiar to the American experience is the situation of inadequate government to prevent terrorism. The aphorism that "government governs best that governs least" may be appealing, but the reality is that it can be true only to a certain extent. At some point, government is necessary to check the violent tendencies of its most ruthless citizens. To give but one concrete twentieth-century example, the Kuomintang (KMT) government of China in the era prior to World War II was virtually powerless to govern anywhere. As a result, warlordism flourished, leaving the citizens of China prey to the depredations of tyrants. This situation deteriorated to the extent that the government was unable to effectively resist the Japanese incursions on the Chinese mainland; even after the defeat of the Japanese, the KMT fell in 1949 to the repressive Maoist regime (Bianco 1971).

All of this suggests a continuum, with five points identified:

Govt. by terror	Nonlegal govt./ Govt. encouraged terror	Legal govt./ Containment of terror	Legal govt./ Ineffective containment	Ineffective govt./ Competing terror
1	2	3	4	5

All of these points represent ideal types; it may be difficult to find "pure" examples of each of the types, but I believe it is useful to talk about the five different conditions described by the points.

Point 1 represents a government regime based upon a monopoly of the use of terror. In order to succeed, such a regime probably needs to dominate virtually all sources of power within that society; thus, this arrangement is most likely found in totalitarian regimes (Buchheim 1968). The government in this situation is able to use force upon the citizenry as it sees fit. No reason or justification need be offered, and even to ask for one might invite the use of force on the person(s) asking. As an unpredictable phenomenon, the use of force may have behind it no other reason than to demonstrate that the government has such power, thus deterring all opposition. In a totalitarian society, the only limitation on use of force is that of the resources available to the whole society, as all such resources can be commandeered by the all-controlling regime.

Point 2 indicates a situation more typical of authoritarian regimes. Again, the government is not likely to be constrained by legal norms, but in this situation the government does not have a monopoly on sources of power. Thus, such a government may arrange deals with other powerful actors in order to maintain its own power. For example, the regime might allow private landowners to use repressive measures of force against labor organizers as long as the landowners also use force to suppress opposition to the governmental regime. In this situation, the lines between official and unofficial violence become blurry. A private citizen probably feels equally terrorized by totalitarian and authoritarian regimes, as violence is unpredictable and pervasive. The major limitation on the use of force to further governmental ends in this second type of regime is the government's access to goods needed to maintain the loyalty of the private "contractors" of violence. As will be discussed in the next section of this essay, I believe that the American South prior to the victories of the civil rights movements may best be described as this sort of regime.

Points 3 and 4 designate perhaps the most difficult types of government to explain. Point 3 is an ideal "balancing point," where the government must comply with legal formalities before it can apply force, yet it retains enough effectiveness in its use of force that it can protect citizens from the depredations of terrorism. Governmental authority derives in this situation from legal authority. When the government lacks the legal authority to act, it cannot act—for example, this sort of state cannot arrest someone unless there is proof that the person has committed some sort of predefined criminal offense. If a state were to achieve this balancing point, there would be an optimal balance between civil liberties and the effectiveness of enforcement measures. Of course, defining the proper balance will always be a fundamentally contested normative question, but one of the attributes of a state approaching this balance is the opportunity for all to debate when this balance is achieved.

Point 4 represents a situation in which the government is attempting to comply with legal norms but has not been able to maintain adequate security against terrorism for whatever reason. In this situation, citizens may find that the biggest threat to the exercise of civil liberties derives from the actions of nongovernmental actors. A person may be attacked physically, for example, for asserting the right to practice his or her religion or to participate in economic activities. Even if the government formally states that such a right is protected, that guarantee may be meaningless if the government lacks the means to provide appropriate protection. Such a situation arose in post–World War II Sicily, when the Mafia used terror as a tool for dominating the governance of the island (McCarthy 2000).

The fifth point on the continuum represents a situation in which the government's ability to protect people from terrorism does not exist. For all practical purposes, this government has ceased to be (or failed to become) *the* government in the society. This can occur for any number of reasons. The government may simply lack the resources necessary to maintain order, or internal corruption within the government may have progressed to the point that officials are generally up for "hire" by the highest bidder. (In the latter situation, there may be similarities to point 2 on the continuum.) In such a society, people are subject to the will of the actor best able to apply force to control them. In its extreme form, the society may be ruled by a number of warlords, constantly engaged in territorial struggles among themselves. In this context, the notion of protected civil liberties becomes meaningless; rights, like power, flow from the end of a gun when there are no limitations on the private use of force.

The formal analysis in this section is designed to underscore a point. It suggests that there is a narrow band of arrangements of power in which participatory government can occur. An unconstrained government prevents the participation of citizens if that participation poses a threat to the governing power or even if the government just wants to target people randomly in order to terrorize other members of society. On the other end of the continuum, a government that is incapable of constraining the use of violence by other actors in a society is also incapable of protecting the rights of individuals within that society. Given these observations I will next discuss the complex relationship between governmental power and individual liberties in the United States.

PART 2: CIVIL LIBERTIES AND THE CONTROL OF TERROR IN THE UNITED STATES

As mentioned in the previous section, there is a general assumption in American political thought that the biggest threat to liberty is that posed by a too-powerful government. I have discussed the idea that this focus on one sort of threat to liberty is overly narrow. I now turn to a prime example of a situation in which American governments did not control terrorism but actually encouraged and profited from that terror. I speak of the American South during a period comprising roughly two-thirds of a century (approximately 1890–1965).

Following the collapse of the Reconstruction era in the late nineteenth century, the federal government and courts largely took a hands-off approach to dealing with issues of race and civil rights. This era is often typified by the *Plessy* v. *Ferguson* decision (1896), in which the U.S. Supreme Court held that the states were free to require segregation in public facilities as long as the accommodations were "separate but equal." This case put the federal courts' stamp of approval on "Jim Crow" laws, which imposed all sorts of social disabilities on black people throughout the South. During this era, all of the state governments in the Deep South—and several outside it—established segregation as their official policy (Packard 2002).

Left to themselves, these state governments quickly deteriorated into a "tyranny of the majority." The Jim Crow laws made it easier to isolate the black minority physically, economically, and politically, thus enabling the states to begin the illegal process of disenfranchising blacks systematically (Parker 1990). Polling places could be made inaccessible to blacks, and poll tax laws and literacy tests could be administered selectively so as to prevent blacks from voting. If all else failed, there was a semiofficial system of terror in place to prevent voting and other aspects of overt political activism by blacks. "Private" organizations (e.g., the Ku Klux Klan) dedicated themselves to suppression of black activism through the use of terrorist methods such as beatings, assassination, and lynching (George and Wilcox 1992).

Government officials were often a part of such activities or turned a blind eye to them. As a result, many of the disadvantages of slavery were reimposed during this period; for example, sharecropping did not involve direct ownership of the servant, but the constant state of indebtedness of the sharecropper to his landlord had largely the same effect (Royce 1993). To escape this pattern, the sharecropper would essentially have to exit to an entirely different region. As the economy of the South began to industrialize, blacks were relegated to the most menial and ill-paid jobs in the factories. Working conditions were largely unregulated and awful. Blacks were also systematically excluded from educational systems adequate to provide them with the social mobility necessary to escape this situation.

Serious improvement did not occur until the 1960s, when a largely peaceful grassroots movement among blacks in the South spurred the federal government to significant intervention on behalf of civil rights. The federal government had experienced impressive growth in power during the crises of the Great Depression and World War II; even in the early postwar period, however, the federal government did not become engaged in the struggle. Simply put, the federal government lacked the will or desire to do anything constructive in this area. Antiterrorism laws on the federal books went largely unenforced, as they were ignored by government's primary law enforcement agency, the Federal Bureau of Investigation (FBI), because of Director J. Edgar Hoover's hostility toward the civil rights movement. In addition, the passage of any meaningful civil rights legislation was blocked by the domination of senators from the South in terms of seniority and their use of filibusters (Ward 2001, 16–17). Essentially, then, the oppression of blacks was shielded from federal intervention.

This changed as a result of several factors. First, and most important, the Southern reaction to the grassroots movement among blacks in the South served to draw national and international attention to the brutal terror used for keeping the Jim Crow system in place. Scenes of peaceful protesters being beaten, knocked down by high-pressure fire hoses, teargassed, and attacked by police dogs appeared on national television, making clear the reality of oppression imposed upon people merely trying to exercise their civil liberties (Ward 2001, 20–21). In addition, "private" acts of terrorism, such as the murders of civil rights workers and church bombings went largely unchecked by local law enforcement and the local courts (Belknap 1987, 53). These highly visible acts of injustice in turn led to pressure on the federal government to get involved in the enforcement of civil liberties and civil rights. In essence, the federal government became an antiterrorist force, protecting protesters from direct onslaught and providing law enforcement protection when the local authorities were directly complicit in the violence or merely refused to stop it. The federal government had to resort to the very sort of tactics decried so vehemently by civil libertarians—the use of armed forces against civilians, infiltration of private organizations, and surveillance of various kinds. In addition, the practice of retrying before federal courts the same white terrorists who had been acquitted in state courts due to jury nullification weakened the extent of protection against double jeopardy.

I am not arguing against the use of those methods in the South in that context. Instead, I am suggesting that the events of the early 1960s demonstrate an important principle—that a government serious about protecting the rights of citizens must effectively employ force against those people who are themselves intent on using force to suppress the rights of citizens. There is no doubt that the protection of civil rights and liberties improved overall in the United States as a result of these actions. The rub here is that this principle can quickly degenerate into an "ends justify the means" rationale, so an important corollary to this principle is that such force must be measured, selectively targeted, and bound by legal norms whenever possible.

The use of force by government, then, is not an evil in itself that must be avoided at all costs, but rather a tool that can be used for good or bad. It is a special tool, in that its use is likely to entail hardship, pain, and even death. Therefore, from a utilitarian standpoint, its use should be minimized to the extent possible; from a Kantian individualist standpoint, its use should be limited to preventing and punishing the evil acts of wrongdoers (Kant 1887). A liberal government must constantly attempt to approximate a balance that minimizes the use of force while ensuring that the rights of members of society are protected from the depredations of other members of society or rogue elements of government within the society. Where this balance lies will always be fundamentally contested, and thus it is very difficult to predict how individual actors within government will define it.

PART 3: THE COURTS AND THE CURRENT CRISIS

As the terrible 9/11 events unfolded, it became quite clear that a terrorist organization had managed to carry out a well-coordinated and devastating attack within the confines of the United States. It was later confirmed that

this attack was realized by infiltrating dozens (or more) of Al Qaeda opera-
tives into the United States. Some of them had been resident within the
United States for over a year, and they acquired many of the skills needed to
accomplish the attacks from commercial sources within the country
(Gutman, Klaidman, and Tuttle 2001).

This event was quite unlike any that Americans had experienced in their
lifetimes. The previous half century had seen incidents of terror, but most of
them had domestic origins and were generally quite small in scale. The largest of these attacks had been the 1995 bombing of the Murrah Federal
Building in Oklahoma City, which killed 168 people. That event had been
dramatic, but without inspiring nearly as much fear as the 9/11 attacks. The
reasons are many. First of all, the Oklahoma City bombing does not appear
to have been the work of a large network of well-organized foreign terrorists,
but rather the action of a very small number of domestic terrorists acting on
their own. Second, the number of people killed in Oklahoma City was much
smaller than on 9/11. Third, the target of the Oklahoma City attack was not
familiar to most Americans, while the 9/11 attacks were aimed at two of the
most famous and important buildings in the nation. In short, the attack in
Oklahoma City seemed more the act of a few "nuts" who managed to kill a
number of people than an attack on the nation as a whole.

The 9/11 attacks, however, seemed to be just that—an attack on the
United States. The destruction of the World Trade Center, the symbolic
capitol of capital, and the partial destruction of the Pentagon, the center of
military command, seemed to strike at the heart of the country. The use of
airliners and the resulting shutdown of virtually all air traffic was also an attack on a vital element of modern American society (Schaffer 2002). Add to
this that the brunt of the attack and the main bulk of casualties occurred in
the largest city in the nation and basically live on television, and one sees
that this attack was well designed to deliver maximal trauma to the nation
with the resources that the terrorists had available.

It is true that the Al Qaeda organization and its predecessors had struck at
U.S. interests before, but those attacks had either been largely unsuccessful
or aimed at U.S. assets overseas. The previous attack on the World Trade
Center, a bombing in 1993, had been successful only in the sense that the
bomb had gone off and caused major damage to the complex. On the other
hand, the building remained standing, the deaths were limited to six people,
and, most important, the perpetrators were quickly apprehended because of

the incompetence of those responsible for carrying out the bombing (Thomas 2001). These factors may have led to a false impression that the territorial United States was relatively immune to a well-organized attack.

There had not been a comparable shock to the sense of U.S. invulnerability since the Cuban missile crisis of 1962 (Nathan 1992), but the relatively quick resolution of that crisis and the appearance that American interests had prevailed did not lead to a sense that the United States had fallen to a new level of vulnerability. The possibility of nuclear annihilation was always present, but the outcome of the crisis suggested that both sides would try very hard to avoid nuclear strikes. In addition, the Cuban missile crisis did not lead to a belief that the United States faced any new threats within its own borders. The most recent close analogies to 9/11 would be the Japanese attack on Pearl Harbor in 1941 and the collective events of the year 1949— when the Soviet test of an atomic bomb, the Berlin Blockade, and the fall of China to Communists occurred in relatively quick succession. The courts' reactions to those crises might discourage one's belief in their abilities to check the overreaction of the elective branches.

A direct result of Pearl Harbor was the president's issuance of an executive order requiring the internment of Japanese resident aliens as well as first- and second-generation Japanese-Americans on the West Coast (but not, interestingly, in Hawaii) for the duration of World War II (Ng 2002). This draconian act was upheld by the U.S. Supreme Court in *Korematsu v. United States* (1945). Less controversially, in *Ex Parte Quirin* (1942), the Court also upheld the conviction and death sentence by a military tribunal of a German saboteur captured in the United States, despite the fact that the saboteur had never officially renounced his American citizenship. The Court decided that his actions as an "enemy belligerent" allowed the government to try him before a military tribunal.

In 1949, the end of the American nuclear monopoly and the successful Communist conquest of the world's most populous nation led to a deep fear that the tide of history might be against the United States, and to a great fear of communist infiltration and/or espionage. Indeed, the widespread belief that the USSR had "stolen the secrets" of the atom bomb created a fear that the United States was rife with spies, and there was also a belief that China had been lost due to communist infiltration of the State Department. The ensuing "Red Scare" led to legislative and executive actions aimed at suppressing the communist threat (Caute 1978). On the legislative side, congressional hearings were held, often with seemingly little purpose but to destroy the careers of people with current or past communist beliefs (Fried 1997). Few real spies were exposed, but many in the entertainment, academic, and governmental professions had their careers ruined. On the executive side, the era witnessed new prosecutions under the Smith Act, an existing federal law that made it a crime to belong to an organization that advocated the overthrow by force of the government of the United States. There were also successful prosecutions of several individuals for espionage or related charges. All of these actions were subsequently approved by the courts. Indeed, the courts committed excesses of their own—for example, the execution of Ethel Rosenberg (Sharlitt 1989).

These "precedents" for judicial behavior under pressure of national emergency may not, however, provide us with much of a basis for predicting what the courts will do during the current crisis. Several significant factors have changed in the half century since those decisions. First, the institutional prestige of the courts, particularly the Supreme Court, was perhaps at its lowest ebb of the twentieth century during the 1940s. The Court had been forced as an institution to back down from its 1930s opposition to New Deal programs—first by President Franklin Delano Roosevelt's threat to pack the Court, then by the personnel changes that FDR was able to achieve by outlasting his opponents in office. He had premised his judicial nominations on a belief that they would not be activist justices; thus, the members of the judiciary at this point probably did not feel that they were in a strong position to take on the elected branches of government during a time of national emergency. It is hard to know whether to attribute the outcomes of cases such as *Quirin* and *Korematsu* to the justices' own estimation of what was needed to meet the emergency or their fear of taking on unpopular causes during wartime.

This reluctance to take an active stance would soon change, however, in the aftermath of *Brown* v. *Board of Education* and later civil rights cases. President Dwight Eisenhower's appointment of Earl Warren as chief justice provided the Court with a leader who was interested in using it as a platform for advancing progressive policies. The courts came to be perceived, rightly or wrongly, as the only branch of government willing and able to deal with the problem of segregation with any efficacy during the 1950s. This more activist stance on the part of the Court, I would argue, has not been abandoned, despite a switch in the political direction of that activism. The Court is simply a stronger institution than it was in the 1940s, better equipped to resist the pressures imposed by popular reaction and the other parts of government.

The second factor of change in the courts in the past half century has been the development of skepticism on the part of judges and others as to the security claims made by presidents. It is tempting to view this skepticism as an effect of the Vietnam War, but it appears to go back further than that. In 1952, President Harry Truman seized the nation's steel mills during a strike. Because he had no statutory authority to do so, Truman claimed that he was empowered by his constitutional designation as commander in chief of the armed forces and that the action was necessary to national security because of the Korean War (Marcus 1977). An overwhelmingly Democratic Supreme Court rejected a Democratic president's claim that the action was justified by the needs of national security (*Youngstown Sheet & Tube Co.* v. *Sawyer* 1952).

Indeed, the same rejection of a national security claim can be seen in the *New York Times* v. *United States* (Pentagon Papers, 1971) case. President Richard Nixon attempted to order the *New York Times* and the *Washington Post* to refrain from publishing these classified documents, a politically embarrassing history of U.S. involvement in the Vietnam conflict, but they contained no information of current troop deployments that would have been directly useful to the North Vietnamese or the Vietcong forces. Finally, one can point to the *Clinton* v. *Jones* decision (1997) as a fairly recent example of the Court's skepticism toward national security claims. In that case, the Court rejected President Clinton's categorical claim that suits against him for actions taken before he was president must be delayed until after his term in office. In his opinion for the Court, Justice John Paul Stevens dismissed, almost in an offhand way, the president's contention that forcing a sitting president to give reasons for delaying the case would create a "danger that national security concerns might prevent the President from explaining a legitimate need for a continuance."

Although these cases are too few and far apart to indicate any sort of pattern, they do make it clear that the Court is capable of casting a critical eye at claims that an action is necessary due to needs of national security. This may have been especially true in the cold war era because the seemingly permanent state of semiemergency made it possible for the government to make security claims for virtually any action. If, for example, the Court had ruled the other way in the "steel seizure" case during Truman's presidency, the constant high state of military readiness needed during the cold war could have been used to justify virtually any executive branch intervention in production, since the military was in constant need of all sorts of goods. In that case, the Court correctly saw that the normal deference it gave the president as commander in chief of the armed forces could not be applied indiscriminately to everything that had some connection to military readiness without jeopardizing congressional power. Likewise, in the Pentagon Papers case, the Court correctly saw that allowing the government to prevent the publication of information that could embarrass it domestically and internationally during a time of war would essentially open the door to suppression of all sorts of politically sensitive information. In both cases, a majority of justices seemed determined that the need for the president's freedom of military action to cope with external threats not be used as an excuse for expanding the president's power to act unilaterally without limitation domestically.

The third, and final, factor that has changed in the past half century has been the lasting concern of the Court with civil liberties. The Warren Court's "Rights Revolution" has had greater staying power than most of its other innovations. The current Court still seems committed to maintaining a strong protection of speech rights (see, for example, the Court's unanimous rejection of St. Paul's anti–hate speech ordinance in *R.A.V.* v. *City of St. Paul* [1992]). In the area of criminal procedure, the Court's current jurisprudence can only be termed intricate and somewhat confusing. It is the sort of pattern one sees when the Court is struggling to reach compromises other than complete abandonment or wholesale approval of existing precedents. For example, the Court has recently ruled in *United States* v. *Drayton* (2002) that a search of a bus passenger is voluntary (not requiring a warrant) when he is asked to allow the search by one police officer and another is standing by the doorway of the bus. On the other hand, in *Ferguson* v. *City of Charleston* (2001) the same Court has also ruled that the results of drug tests obtained from mothers on a maternity ward cannot be used in evidence because this is not a voluntary search, despite the fact that the mothers turned over the specimens voluntarily to medical personnel and signed consent forms indicating that the results of their tests might be handed over to law enforcement officials. Likewise, in *Kyllo* v. *United States* (2001) the Court has ruled that police officers must obtain a search warrant before performing an infrared scan of a home, despite the fact that such a scan does not require the police to enter the premises. These cases, and the recent reaffirmation of the *Miranda* decision, make it clear that the Court is trying to strike a new balance on matters of criminal procedure rather than returning to the pre–Warren Court's low levels of protection. In essence, the Court may be conservative by recent standards, but it is far more liberal than it was in the 1940s and early 1950s.

In sum, the precedents of World War II and the early cold war do not help us to predict the actions of the judiciary in the current crisis because (a) the courts today are in a much stronger position institutionally, (b) there is generally a higher level of skepticism toward claims made by governments in the name of national security, and (c) the courts are generally far more committed to protection of individual rights than they were fifty years ago.

In addition to these factors, which concern the nature of the courts, there are also significant differences in the nature of conflicts then and now. In World War II, it was easy to identify the enemy, as it was a war between nation-states. It was also clear that World War II was a fight to preserve the nation from potential destruction. The Germans and the Japanese both achieved spectacular military success through much of 1942, and both seemed on the verge of knocking all of the Allies out of the war; in particular, both the USSR and the British seemed on the verge of final defeat throughout 1942, and the Chinese did not present a significant threat to the Japanese. If the Germans and the Japanese had succeeded in defeating the United States and its allies, they would have been in control of the bulk of the world's resources, and there was a strong possibility that they would have gone on to defeat the United States in a war of attrition.

Likewise, the cold war presented a strong threat to continued U.S. existence. After the revolution that created the People's Republic of China in 1949, the Communists had a significant advantage in terms of the size of their military forces, an advantage magnified by both the weakened state of U.S. allies and the unwillingness to allow the Japanese and Germans to rearm. The seemingly close alliance between the world's most populous nation and the largest geographic entity in the world, both led by militaristic Communist regimes, posted a vital threat to the United States and her allies. The confrontation over Berlin and the clear expansionist moves made by the communists in Europe and Asia appeared to indicate that the Soviet Union and China were bent on world domination. The main U.S. hope was to beat the communists through technological and economic superiority. The rapid loss of the nuclear monopoly and the stalemates in Korea and Berlin seemed to indicate the collapse of that strategy (Offner 2002). Internationally, it was generally easy to identify our enemies, although there was the constant threat and reality of domestic espionage.

In the current conflict, the threat may seem more immediate than World War II and the cold war because the first major strike occurred on live television within the most populous city in the nation. That threat is, in actuality, nowhere near the scale of the previous conflicts. Despite the suggestions of the most fervent rhetoric, the continued existence of the nation is not under threat. Large-scale damage may occur, but there are not many outside Al Qaeda who believe that that organization is capable of destroying American society or its government.

Most unlike the previous conflicts, the current crisis involves an enemy very difficult to identify. The perpetrators of the 9/11 attacks do not appear to have been sponsored by any state, but rather by an amorphous and mysterious terrorist organization. Bases in Afghanistan served as the only geographical association for Al Qaeda, and those have been overrun. The organization is now completely underground throughout the world. Paradoxically, this has had the effect of making the enemy less threatening but more terrifying: less threatening because of the lack of state resources but more terrifying because of stealth and unpredictability. During World War II and the cold war, there was always a possibility that agents of the enemy were "over here," but we know that they have been and probably still are in the current conflict. Security photos of two of the hijackers purchasing items at a Wal-Mart in Portland, Maine, on September 10, 2001, served to dramatize the fact that these terrorists had indeed been "walking among us" (Stein 2002).

These issues make prediction of judicial action very difficult. Judges are, after all, part of American society, and American society seems ambivalent about the nature of the threat. We are not living in fear that the terrorists may end our world, but we are waiting for the possibility that the "other shoe" may drop without warning. Without any knowledge of where the strike may originate or what it might be, it is hard to assess whether security measures are necessary or draconian.

On the one hand, the terrorists have made clear that they can successfully infiltrate American society and commit atrocities within the continental

United States. On the other hand, as the attacks of 9/11 become more distant over time, continued claims by the U.S. government regarding such threats begin to seem less credible. The judges, as a result, may become more skeptical of claims that increased security measures can be justified by necessity. In the next section of this essay, I will attempt to forecast how the courts will handle various issues that may arise.

The Military Order of November 13, 2001

On November 13, 2001, President Bush issued an executive order to the military.[4] Citing his constitutional authority as commander in chief of the armed forces and statutory authority, he ordered that any noncitizen who "is or was a member of the organization known as al Qaida" or "has engaged in, aided or abetted, or conspired to commit, acts of international terrorism, or acts in preparation therefor, that have caused, threaten to cause, or have as their aim to cause, injury to or adverse effects on the United States, its citizens, national security, foreign policy, or economy; or . . . has knowingly harbored one or more [such] individuals" may, if "it is in the interests of the United States," be tried by military tribunal. An individual satisfying the above criteria (to be determined by the president in writing) will remain within "the control of the Secretary of Defense" or, if the individual is "under the control of any other officer or agent of the United States or any State," will be turned over to the secretary of defense (as in virtually all federal laws, orders, and regulations, the "Secretary of Defense" really means some official under his command). Trial would be held before a military commission, and conviction and sentencing would require the concurrence of two-thirds of the members of the commission present. According to the order, the individual, if convicted by the military commission, "may be punished in accordance with the penalties provided under applicable law, including life imprisonment or death." The order further specifies that appellate review is vested with the president or "the Secretary of Defense if so designated by me for that purpose" (the order does not specify whether the secretary may, in turn, delegate that authority to a subordinate), and that the individual

> shall not be privileged to seek any remedy or maintain any proceeding, directly or indirectly, or to have any such remedy or proceeding sought on the

individual's behalf, in (i) any court in the United States, or any State thereof, (ii) any court of any foreign nation, or (iii) any international tribunal.

The scope of this order is simply astounding, especially when one considers that it was issued without consulting members of Congress. The order purports to give the president power to command states to turn over suspects within their custody to federal military authorities, to command civilian federal authorities to turn over suspects to military authorities, and to remove the authority of the civilian judiciary to enforce the rights of suspects. The order makes no distinctions between illegal aliens and legally resident aliens, civilians and combatants, or arrests made within the United States and those made overseas. As such, it seems to purport to suspend the right to petition for a writ of habeas corpus, a power reserved by the Constitution for the Congress.

In essence, the order seems to challenge previous Supreme Court holdings on the areas of due process,[5] separation of powers,[6] and federalism.[7] One is tempted to predict, therefore, that the Supreme Court would, if a challenge to this order would reach it, decide that the order is unconstitutional, at least for aliens legally resident within the United States. The actions of those in the Bush administration since the issuance of this order seem to indicate that they understand that the order is on shaky legal ground. As for aliens residing legally within the United States, witness the case of Zacharias Moussoaui, the "twentieth hijacker," who was arrested shortly before 9/11 and who is an admitted operative of Al Qaeda (Stein and Ragavan 2002). All legal proceedings against him have been in federal (civilian) courts, and there has been no attempt made to remove him to the custody of the Defense Department.[8] With regard to the administration's faith in the legality of the order, notice that Richard Reid (the "shoe bomber"), a British citizen detained outside the territorial United States, has been allowed to plead guilty in a federal civilian court, and there was no attempt to remove his case to a military tribunal.

Indeed, the handling of noncitizen prisoners taken in Afghanistan indicates doubts among administration officials as to the legality of the order even as it applies to noncitizens interned on U.S. soil but captured elsewhere. The choice of the U.S. naval base at Guantánamo Bay, Cuba, for holding prisoners seems quite revealing in this regard. It appears that the military authorities do not want to bring the prisoners into the United States, lest constitutional protections attach to them. Likewise, it is telling to note that as of this writing, there has yet to be a single military tribunal proceeding. The obvious impression is that the administration is not yet itching for a legal showdown over the order.

Although there is no proof, I suspect that the administration has far simpler tools to use against the bulk of Al Qaeda members captured overseas, and I will discuss this issue now. When an administration is pursuing a military campaign against an enemy as amorphous as Al Qaeda, it is impossible to say with any assurance when that war is over. There is no one on the other side of the conflict equipped to declare a cease-fire or surrender even if so inclined; thus, the rest of us must probably defer to the assertions of the president as to when the war is over. Accordingly, people captured in Afghanistan and elsewhere can probably be confined as prisoners of war indefinitely and without trials of any kind. This will be the case until the courts and/or Congress declare that the war is officially over—an action neither branch has ever taken in previous conflicts. In other words, the confinement of these prisoners could continue without any type of legal proceeding for decades or even for the entire life of the prisoner.

The executive order, it appears, is probably a tool that the administration intends to use sparingly. The Supreme Court may not get an opportunity to test the legality of the order as used against resident aliens in the near future because of the lack of cases, but if it does, it will almost certainly find the order unconstitutional in this context. The order is just too great a challenge to the powers of the civilian courts to be allowed to stand, and the Court would strike it down on Fifth and Sixth Amendment grounds.

Although it now seems unlikely that the orders will be used against legal resident aliens, the administration is quite possibly planning to use it against high-ranking members of Al Qaeda captured overseas or as illegal immigrants. However, the administration does not need to employ any type of legal procedure to keep such prisoners confined indefinitely, as we have seen. Unless the administration intends to execute prisoners, the need for this order is thus obviated. I would predict that the Supreme Court would probably defer to the administration in these cases, allowing the tribunals and subsequent executions to proceed. The reasons are twofold. First, the administration is on its strongest legal ground here. In essence, the military will be able to claim that the Al Qaeda leaders captured outside of the country are not protected by the U.S. Constitution but are protected only by the provisions of international law. As war criminals, they are subject to military justice. Concerning members of Al Qaeda illegally infiltrated into the United States, the administration can point quite plausibly to the *Quirin* decision, which held that spies infiltrated into the country did not acquire constitutional rights upon their infiltration. The Court can acquiesce in the administration's action here without appearing to surrender judicial power. The second reason for the Court's deference to the administration would be the unlikelihood of Supreme Court justices wanting to risk the prestige of the institution to protect this type of defendant. The Court would have little to gain and much to lose by defying the administration under these circumstances.

In sum, the Supreme Court is likely to strike down provisions of the president's order that make it applicable to citizens and legal residents of the United States, because acquiescing in this assertion of executive power domestically would represent a great surrender of judicial branch power. Anticipating this resistance, however, the administration is not expected to try citizens and legal aliens in this manner; thus, the issue may never be judicially determined. The use of this order against noncitizens captured outside of the United States or illegally within the country is likely to be upheld by the Court because it lacks an institutional stake in this issue that would make it decide otherwise.

The USA Patriot Act

In the weeks following the 9/11 attacks, the Congress worked with the Bush administration to quickly produce legislation intended to increase national security with regard to terrorism. The resulting legislation was the "Uniting and Strengthening America by Providing Appropriate Tools Required to Intercept and Obstruct Terrorism Act of 2001," better known by its acronym, the USA Patriot Act. This rambling bill contains measures for helping survivors of terror victims and relief workers, statements of sentiment, and a host of miscellaneous funding provisions. Most important for the purposes of this chapter, Title 2 of the act includes several provisions augmenting the power of surveillance agencies to intercept electronic communications, to acquire information from grand jury proceedings, to share information between agencies, and to infiltrate organizations.

Despite the haste with which this bill was produced, it seems to be fairly well tailored to prevent it from being significantly overturned by the courts. I do not predict that there will be much judicial overruling of the provisions of Title 2 for several reasons. First, many of the provisions that deal with the sharing of information are attempts to revere the traditional divide between domestic and foreign intelligence. To some extent, this division reflects old political compromises needed to create a foreign intelligence structure in the late 1940s—compromises that simply do not reflect the current political environment. In essence, these compromises were put in place in order to assuage fears that the new foreign intelligence agencies would become secret police forces operating both in and out of the United States. The response to these concerns was to clearly delineate authority—the FBI would continue to operate as the primary law enforcement arm of the federal government domestically, while the newly created Central Intelligence Agency (CIA) and National Security Agency (NSA) would operate strictly on matters external to the country's boundaries. In part, this decision must be understood as stemming from fear at that time that J. Edgar Hoover, the seemingly eternal director of the FBI, would expand his already enormous domestic influence into the area of foreign policy. The separation between foreign intelligence and domestic surveillance is a congressionally created boundary unlikely to attract judicial support upon its abandonment by Congress.

Likewise, the provision allowing the release of grand jury transcripts to investigative and intelligence agencies is not expected to be seriously attacked by the judiciary. First, the customary "confidentiality" of grand jury testimony has always been somewhat ambiguous. Although the formal purpose of grand jury testimony is to provide the jury with sufficient information to make decisions about whether or not to issue criminal indictments, one of its primary uses is to provide investigatory material to prosecutors through the use of compelled testimony by witnesses. The information in the testimony is often funneled to law enforcement agencies in order to further criminal investigations even if the testimony itself is not, and this has never proven to be a problem in court. All the Congress and the administration did in the USA Patriot Act is marginally expand the potential uses of this testimony, and the uses of grand jury testimony have been limited by statute, not constitutional law cases. Presumably, if Congress wants to weaken the protection afforded to grand jury testimony by statute, it is hard to believe that the courts will see fit to find such protection in the Constitution (Harding, Shatz, and Samuels 2002). Also, it is quite likely that the statements disclosed will be used against people other than those who gave it.[9] Because the use of illegally obtained evidence is generally excluded only against the person whose rights are violated, the use of this testimony against others would not be prevented even if the courts were to find some sort of constitutional bar to the sharing of grand jury testimony.

The most controversial part of the bill, the expansion of surveillance of electronic communications, will not pose much of a problem legally. The reason is that the drafters of the bill anticipated the primary objections that the courts might pose, and they required the obtaining of warrants and subpoenas to acquire the information. By doing so, the drafters recognized that the courts are likely to recognize a "reasonable expectation of privacy" in E-mail communications, cell phone calls, and other forms of electronic communications. Thus, the courts will probably be satisfied with what they see as a reasonable judicial check on law enforcement agencies. The only exception to the requirements to obtain subpoenas or warrants is one that allows "a provider of remote computing service or electronic communication service to the public . . . [to] divulge a record or other information pertaining to a subscriber to or customer of such service . . . if the provider reasonably believes that an emergency involving immediate danger of death or serious physical injury to any person requires disclosure of the information without delay." This is not very different than the sort of "exigent circumstances" exceptions to the warrant requirements in search-and-seizure cases, which allow for warrantless searches to proceed when the time needed to obtain the warrant would result in the loss of evidence, or in danger to the officer or others. The courts are quite likely to uphold this exception in the Patriot Act.

CONCLUSION

The above discussion suggests that the courts are not especially likely to be active in checking the surveillance activities of the government during the ongoing "war against terrorism." This should not, however, be mistaken for an assertion that the courts are ineffective in protecting civil liberties during times of crisis. Rather, I am arguing that the courts may have already had great impact by passively preventing the passage of much repressive legislation. Other actors within the government seem to have anticipated many of the likely reactions of the courts and tailored their legislation accordingly. For example, there have not been serious legislative proposals for large expansions of powers of warrantless surveillance and searches, nor have there been legislative attempts to use the current crisis to legislatively test the exclusionary rule. Most of the proposals contained within the USA Patriot Act seem tailored to survive judicial scrutiny. In addition, we have not seen attempts to pass legislation limiting "unpatriotic" or "subversive" expression, nor have we seen legislation marking particular ethnic groups for confinement or surveillance, as we have in earlier conflicts.

I am not asserting here, however, that the elected branches of government will refrain from overreaching in the current conflict or that the courts will fail to intervene if they do. I believe it is fairly clear that the courts will become involved if, for example, the administration attempts to apply the executive order of November 13, 2001, to legal resident aliens. What I am asserting is that the previous actions of courts have already had a large indirect impact on the ranges of proposals that will or will not be considered seriously as security measures by the other branches of government. Courts can operate as the "cooler heads" during times of crises, but their existence can also remind others not to lose their cool in the first place.

NOTES

1. The insulation of individual judges from electoral considerations is, of course, not complete. Judges at the district court and circuit court levels may wish to be nominated for higher judicial posts. In addition, judges may plan to seek elective office outside of the judicial branch. As such, they may have to consider the political effects of their decisions on career prospects.

2. In *Miranda* v. *Arizona*, 384 U.S. 436 (1966), the Supreme Court ruled 5 to 4 that police had to inform suspects in their custody of their right to remain silent, the right to an attorney during questioning, and that an attorney could be provided free of charge. If the police failed to inform the suspect of these rights, any incriminating statements made by the suspect are rendered inadmissible in court. This decision was one of the most controversial made by the Warren court in the 1960s, and the Court had created several exceptions to the rule in the following decades. In 1968 Congress enacted 18 USC 3501 to legislatively overrule the *Miranda* decision. This law went untested until the case of *Dickerson* v. *U.S.*, 530 U.S. 428 (2000). In that case, the Supreme Court held in a 7-to-2 decision that 18 USC 3501 was unconstitutional, stating that the *Miranda* warnings were mandated by the constitution.

3. Liberals' tendency to view the courts in this way is perhaps best exemplified by *Roe* v. *Wade*, 410 U.S. 113 (1973), in which the Supreme Court invalidated all state laws prohibiting abortions in the first two trimesters of pregnancy. The conservatives'

tendency is best exemplified by *Bush* v. *Gore*, 531 U.S. 98 (2000), in which the conservative majority on the Court ordered Florida to cease its manual recount of ballots in the 2000 presidential election, thus ensuring an Electoral College victory for George W. Bush.

4. Military Order of November 13, 2001, Detention, Treatment, and Trial of Certain Non-Citizens in the War against Terrorism (66 F.R. 57833).

5. As regards legally resident aliens, the order appears to be a clear violation of the Sixth Amendment right to jury trial in criminal cases.

6. The order appears to suspend habeas corpus (a congressional power) and to give the executive branch the judicial powers of trial and appeal over civilians.

7. The current Supreme Court has recently been ruling against similar law enforcement measures as violations of the Tenth Amendment: "The Powers not delegated to the United States by the Constitution, nor prohibited by it to the States, are reserved to the States respectively, or to the people." See, e.g., *Printz* v. *United States*, 521 U.S. 898 (1997), which struck down a federal law requiring that state and local law enforcement officials perform background checks on prospective gun purchasers.

8. According to at least one newspaper account, the Justice Department has considered trying Moussoaui before a military tribunal, but has rejected the option because it will cause other nations to refuse to extradite suspects to the United States (Locy 2003). According to this account, the move to a tribunal was considered in order to avoid the defendant's use of the subpoena power to allow him to question Ramzi Bin al-Shibh. Bin al-Shibh is an Al Qaeda operative captured in Pakistan, and currently in United States' custody overseas. In an unpublished opinion, the trial judge ruled that Moussoaui may question Bin al-Shibh, a decision that will be reviewed by the Fourth Circuit Court of Appeals.

9. The reasoning behind this statement is that an admission of criminal activity in grand jury would already be admissible in court against the witness unless the statement was made under the grant of some form of immunity. Thus, if the information incriminated the witness, there would probably be no need for further investigation.

REFERENCES

Adams, Henry H. 1967. *1942: The Year That Doomed the Axis.* New York: David McKay.

Belknap, Michael R. 1987. *Federal Law and the Southern Order.* Athens: University of Georgia Press.

Bianco, Lucien. 1971. *Origins of the Chinese Revolution.* Stanford, Calif.: Stanford University Press.

Buchheim, Hans. 1968. *Totalitarian Rule.* Middletown, Conn.: Wesleyan University Press.

Caute, David. 1978. *The Great Fear: The Anti-Communist Purge under Truman and Eisenhower.* New York: Simon & Schuster.

Fried, Albert. 1997. *McCarthyism: The Great American Red Scare*. New York: Oxford University Press.

George, John, and Laird Wilcox. 1992. *Nazis, Communists, Klansmen, and Others on the Fringe*. Buffalo, N.Y.: Prometheus Books.

Getty, J. Arch, and Oleg V. Naumov. 1999. *The Road to Terror: Stalin and the Self-Destruction of the Bolsheviks, 1932–1939*. New Haven, Conn.: Yale University Press.

Gonan, Jay K. 2000. *The Roots of Nazi Psychology: Hitler's Utopian Barbarism*. Lexington: University of Kentucky Press.

Gunaratna, Rohan. 2002. *Inside Al Qaeda: Global Network of Terror*. New York: Columbia University Press.

Gutman, Roy, Daniel Klaidman, and Steve Tuttle. 2001. "Bin Laden's Invisible Network," *Newsweek*, October 29, 42.

Harding, Amber, Tiffany Shatz, and Brad Samuels. 2002. "Procedural Issues." *American Criminal Law Review* 39, no. 2 (spring): 923.

Kant, Immanuel. 1887. *The Philosophy of Law: An Exposition of the Fundamental Principles of Jurisprudence as the Science of Right*. Trans. W. Hastie. Edinburgh: T & T Clark.

Locy, Toni. 2003. "Moussaoui Prosecutors Wary of Tribunal," *USA Today*, May 14, 4A.

Marcus, Maeva. 1977. *Truman and the Steel Seizure Case*. New York: Columbia University Press.

McCarthy, Patrick. 2000. *Italy since 1945*. New York: Oxford University Press.

Nathan, James A. 1992. *The Cuban Missile Crisis Revisited*. New York: St. Martin's Press.

Ng, Wendy. 2002. *Japanese American Internment during World War II*. Westport, Conn.: Greenwood Press.

Offner, Arnold A. 2002. *Another Such Victory: President Truman and the Cold War, 1945–1953*. Stanford, Calif.: Stanford University Press.

Packard, Jerold M. 2002. *American Nightmare: The History of Jim Crow*. New York: St. Martin's Press.

Parker, Frank R. 1990. *Black Votes Count*. Chapel Hill: University of North Carolina Press.

Peri, Yoram. 2000. *The Assassination of Yitzhak Rabin*. Stanford, Calif.: Stanford University Press.

Royce, Edward. 1993. *The Origins of Southern Sharecropping*. Philadelphia: Temple University Press.

Schaffer, Michael. 2002. "A Very Painful Anniversary." *U.S. News & World Report*, September 9, 26.

Schmid, Alex P. 1993. "The Response Problem as a Definition Problem." In *Western Responses to Terrorism*, ed. Schmid and Crelinstein. London: Frank Cass & Co.

Schweitzer, Glenn E., and Carole Dorsch Schweitzer. 2002. *A Faceless Enemy: The Origins of Modern Terrorism*. Cambridge, Mass.: Perseus Publishing.

Sharlitt, Joseph H. 1989. *Fatal Error: The Miscarriage of Justice That Sealed the Rosenbergs' Fate*. New York: Charles Scribner's Sons.

Slackman, Michael. 1990. *Target: Pearl Harbor.* Honolulu: University of Hawaii Press.

Stein, Lisa. 2002. "Private Eye." *U.S. News & World Report,* October 7, 14.

Stein, Lisa, and Chitra Ragavan. 2002. "The Strange Case of Mr. M." *U.S. News & World Report,* September 23, 18.

Thomas, Evan. 2001. "The Road to September 11." *Newsweek,* October 1, 38.

Ward, Brian. 2001. *Media, Culture, and the Modern African American Freedom Struggle.* Gainesville: University of Florida Press.

Security versus Liberty: 9/11 and the American Public

INTRODUCTION

This essay explores the challenges an open society faces as it confronts the value trade-off between liberty and security brought about by the 9/11 terrorist attacks. It details American support of newly formulated anti-terrorist policies. It specifically presents data collected from respondents in the small New England city, Portland, Maine, where terrorist attackers spent the night before they flew a plane into one of the World Trade Center's Twin Towers. The survey was conducted six months after the 9/11 terrorist attacks. It compares, when possible, the opinions of Portland residents to those found in national trend data. When possible, I have embedded Portland survey data within tables I created that display national trend data. Portland survey questions and responses not matching trend data are found in Appendix A. Nontrend survey responses are referenced in notes according to survey organization and date.

After a brief discussion of civil liberties and national security, the essay explores how the terrorist threat is viewed by the public, focusing on whether individuals have felt personally threatened by terrorism in their daily lives. It also reports the public's confidence in the government's ability to deal with the terrorist threat. The next section addresses the perceived trade-off between security and liberty, and reports on public support for several governmental initiatives designed to combat such terrorism. It concludes that the post-9/11 consensus on many policy issues has started to splinter and the dramatic support found for administrative policies in the direct aftermath of the attack has begun to fade.

CIVIL LIBERTIES AND NATIONAL SECURITY

A recent survey reports that although Americans may not know specifics about the Constitution, they have internalized the core democratic values of liberty and egalitarianism embedded within it (Wadsworth 2002). Most Americans believe, at an abstract level, in individual rights such as freedom of speech, press, religion and assembly, a right to privacy, and the right of due process (Almond and Verba 1963; Dahl 1971; McClosky and Zaller 1984). Although these rights have had a long history of public support in the United States, they often are in conflict with the situational imperative of security during times of national threat and crisis. As Herbert McClosky and John Zaller (1984, 39) note, "the degree of freedom an open society permits varies with the degree of danger the society faces."

Throughout U.S. history, there have been numerous examples to illustrate the trade-off between security and liberty, especially when the exercise of the liberty is perceived as threatening. Less than a decade after adopting the document that codified civil liberties (the Bill of Rights), the Congress responded to threats from France's revolutionary government by passing the Alien and Sedition Acts (1798), violating the newly formulated freedoms of speech and press. In an effort to silence antiwar protestors, the Espionage Act, formulating during World War I, banned statements that could "promote the success" of America's enemies. Consequently, many war objectors were imprisoned under the auspices of the law. Japanese and Japanese-Americans were monitored by the government during World War II, and 120,000 were placed in internment camps. The fear of communist subversion during the cold war led to pervasive and invasive governmental investigations. Congressional hearings at this time publicly denounced defendants and created an atmosphere of suspicion in which many supposed "Reds" lost their jobs. Overall, governmental practices criminalized communism, effectively curtailing Americans' right to association (Fried 1997). In a sobering reflection on the history of civil liberties and national security in the United States, current Supreme Court Chief Justice William Rehnquist (1998, 23) concluded, "It is neither desirable nor is it remotely likely that civil liberty will occupy as favored a position in wartime as it does in peacetime."

America now faced an unprecedented security threat on its soil. The terrorist enemy is hard to identify, and there are, in all likelihood, more terrorists living in the United States. Given the unique nature of the terrorist threat, it can be argued that the government needs new tools to use in the war on terrorism. President George W. Bush asked for these tools in "Uniting and Strengthening America by Providing Appropriate Tools Required to Intercept and Obstruct Terrorism," more commonly known as the USA Patriot Act (2001), which the Congress quickly passed without legislative hearing. The president signed the Patriot Act into law on October 26, 2001, a mere month and a half after the tragic attacks on the World Trade Center and the Pentagon.

The act grants the government many new powers. It facilitates the ability of the Federal Bureau of Investigation (FBI) to spy by allowing the use of roving wiretaps, by granting greater subpoena power on forms of communication, and by increasing access to medical, financial, business, and education records. As long as authorities certify that the information sought is "relevant to an ongoing criminal investigation," search warrants are quickly granted. Homes can be secretly searched without a demonstration of "probable cause" of a crime (commonly known as the "sneak and peek" provision). The FBI can now monitor public gatherings and place undercover agents in houses of worship without having evidence of criminal activity. Much judicial oversight, established in the 1970s, after revelations of abusive governmental spying practices during the McCarthy and Vietnam eras, has been eliminated. The Patriot Act effectively blurs the line between intelligence gathering to fight terrorism and gathering of evidence for criminal proceedings.

The act also permits the government to detain noncitizens without a criminal conviction if the attorney general "certifies" that he has "reasonable grounds to believe" that their release will endanger the national security of the United States (USA Patriot Act 2001). At no other time has the executive branch been granted such power. In addition, on November 13, 2001, President Bush signed an executive order that establishes military tribunals to try suspected terrorists. These tribunals are not open to the public, nor will they have a jury, and defendants have no right to appeal. Convictions can result in a death sentence (Bush 2001).

Supporters of the act point out that more latitude in intelligence gathering in a technologically advanced society is needed for effective antiterrorist policies. Terrorist suspects are especially dangerous and may have vital information for future investigations; thus, secret detentions are required. Civil rights advocates believe the Patriot Act violates the right to privacy and unfairly applies the right to due process of the law found in the Fifth, Sixth, and Fourteenth Amendments, since Supreme Court rulings have expanded coverage of these rights to noncitizens (American Civil Liberties Union 2002; Solomon 2002). Defenders of civil liberties see increased threat as an unavoidable risk attached to the preservation of such liberties. Members of the threatened population, however, may not share this view.

Prior to 9/11, scholars found substantial public support for antiterrorist policies that are perceived to decrease the public's vulnerability to terrorist attacks, even though these policies restrict individual civil liberties and expand federal law enforcement agencies' power (Kuzma 2000; Hewitt 1993; Weinberg and Davis 1989). Further, as perceptions of threat increase, individuals become more willing to suspend civil liberties in order to obtain security. Will the Portland and American publics accept restrictions on their civil liberties in order to fight the new terrorist threat?

THE TERRORIST THREAT ON THE HOME FRONT

To begin an assessment of public support for antiterrorist policies, one must first establish the degree of threat perceived by the populace. Scholars have found that threat levels affect support for public policy initiatives (Huddy et al. 2002). A vast majority of Portland respondents expressed some concern that there will be future terrorist violence in the United States. Responses fluctuated only between either "very" (46 percent) or "somewhat" (45 percent) concerned. This response pattern was evident in national opinion surveys as well. Most Americans have expressed concern about terrorism over the years when polls have asked them about the subject, with only 12 percent, on average, reporting that they were "not very concerned." Given the general consensus that terrorist violence is of at least some concern, one may be surprised that there is no indication of a marked increase in those concerned after a specific terrorist attack (table 1) (See Appendix B for a list of the abbreviations used in the tables.).

When Portland residents were asked about the likelihood of another ter-

TABLE 1. How concerned are you that there will be violence from international terrorists in the United States . . . are you very concerned, somewhat concerned, or not very concerned?

Date	Very Concerned (%)	Somewhat Concerned (%)	Not Very Concerned (%)	Don't Know/ No Answer (%)	Number Polled
9/86 HARRIS	43	39	17	1	1,248
10/86 CBS/NYT	54	33	12	1	1,525
1/89 NBC/WSJ	51	34	13	2	2,025
7/93[a] PRIN	48	43	9	0	725
6/95[a] HART	44	46	10	1	1,008
8/96 ABC	31	43	18	8	1,514
4–5/02[b] Portland	46	45	9	0	640

a. How concerned are you that terrorists will commit acts of violence in the United States—are you very concerned, somewhat concerned, or not concerned?

b. How concerned are you that there will be more violence from terrorists in the United States . . . are you very concerned, somewhat concerned, or not very concerned?

rorist attack in the United States, a substantially large majority (83 percent) believed that it was either "very" (21 percent) or "somewhat" (62 percent) likely in the next six months. Few (15 percent) indicated that an attack was "not at all likely." The general public's anticipation of another terrorist attack varied according to the time that had passed since the last attack (CBS News 2002a; Huddy et al. 2002). Not surprising, directly after both the Oklahoma City and 9/11 attacks, those who believed another attack was "very likely" doubled to around half (48 percent, Yank/*Time*/CNN, April 1995; 48 percent, CBS, October 8–9, 2001; 53 percent, CBS/NYT, October 25–28, 2001). Polls taken between two and twelve months after 9/11 show that, on average, only one in four believed another attack was "very likely" in the next few months, returning to pre–Oklahoma City percentages. During the last fourteen years, most Americans believed a terrorist attack was either "somewhat" or "very" likely (table 2). This indicates a highly anticipatory public.

TABLE 2. How likely do you think it is that there will be another terrorist attack on the United States within the next few months: very likely, somewhat likely, not very likely, not at all likely?

Date	Very Likely (%)	Somewhat Likely (%)	Not Very Likely (%)	Not at all Likely (%)	Don't Know/ No Answer (%)	Number Polled
7/88[a] ABC/WP	28	52	0	19	1	1,500
3/89[a] ABC/WP	26	54	0	19	1	1,525
1/91 CBS/NYT	23	50	0	21	6	1,348
Oklahoma City						
4/95[b] Yank/*Time*/CNN	48	38	8	3	3	600
9/11						
9/20–23/01 CBS/NYT	36	42	16	4	2	1,216
10/8–9/01 CBS	48	36	10	3	3	870
10/25–28/01 CBS/NYT	53	35	8	2	2	1,024
11/2–4/01 GALLUP/CNN/ USA	24	50	16	6	4	1,021
12/7–10/01 CBS/NYT	23	50	19	5	3	1,052
3 months later						
1/5–6/02 CBS/NYT	18	47	27	6	2	1,060
1/21–25/02 CBS/NYT	23	48	21	4	3	1,034
2/24–26/02 CBS	18	44	29	5	4	861
6 months later						
4–5/02[c] Portland	21	62	0	15	2	640
6/02 CBS/NYT	36	45	13	3	3	1,001
7/02 CBS/NYT	30	43	22	4	1	1,010

(Continued)

TABLE 2. (**Continued**)

Date	Very Likely (%)	Somewhat Likely (%)	Not Very Likely (%)	Not at all Likely (%)	Don't Know/ No Answer (%)	Number Polled
1 year later						
9/2–5/02 CBS/NYT	23	46	23	5	3	1,021
10/02 CBS/NYT	27	47	15	7	3	1,208

[a] How likely do you think it is that there will be another terrorist attack on the United States within the near future: very likely, somewhat likely, not very likely, not at all likely?

[b] How likely do you think it is that an act of terrorism will occur somewhere in the United States in the next twelve months?

[c] In your opinion, how likely is another major terrorist attack in the U.S. within the next six months? Would you say . . . very likely, somewhat likely, or not at all likely?

Compared to the national public, Portland respondents were not as worried about terrorist violence in their daily lives. When asked if they felt a personal sense of danger from terrorists where they lived or worked, a very large majority (85 percent) did not. Directly after 9/11, national polling data show that 32 to 36 percent of the respondents felt personally concerned about a terrorist attack in the area where they lived. Time lessened the concern a little. A year later, national concern levels fluctuated between 25 percent and 32 percent (table 3). One can infer that the reason for the difference between the Portland and national publics is location. Those living in areas of the country where terrorist targets are few, like Portland, worry much less about terrorist attacks than those who either lived in a place that experienced an attack or can conceive of their community as a terrorist target. Not surprisingly, surveys found that New York and Washington residents worry more about terrorist attacks than the national public and that proximity to the attacks had an effect on people's beliefs, emotions, and behaviors (CBS News 2002b; Pew Research Center 2002). There is also evidence that these sentiments are shared by residents of other large cities (Pew Research Center 2001).

Although Portland residents did not express a feeling of danger from terrorism in their communities, they were as moderately worried as the rest of the country that they or someone in their family would become a victim of a terrorist attack. In view of the fact that individuals are mobile and not necessarily tied to place, concern about family members who may live in another

TABLE 3. Do you personally feel any sense of danger from terrorist acts where you live and work or not?

Date	Yes/ Concerned (%)	No/ Not Concerned (%)	Don't Know/ No Answer (%)	Number Polled
3/93 ZOGBY	12	87	1	905
Oklahoma City				
4/95 GALLUP/CNN/USA	16	84	0	1,008
7/95 CBS/NYT	20	79	1	1,209
9/11				
9/11–12/01[a] CBS/NYT	36	62	2	1,041
9/13–14/01[a] CBS/NYT	39	59	2	959
9/20–23/01[a] CBS/NYT	32	66	2	1,216
10/8–9/01[a] CBS	30	68	2	870
4–5/02 Portland	14	85	1	641
6/18–20/02[a] CBS	29	70	1	892
1 year later				
9/2–5/02[a] CBS/NYT	25	74	1	937
10/27–31/02 CBS/NYT	32	67	1	1,018

[a] Would you say you personally are very concerned about a terrorist attack in the area where you live, or not?

state, or worry for oneself as one travels, is to be expected. About one-third (34 percent) were either "very" (7 percent) or "somewhat" (27 percent) worried that they or a family member would become a victim. A majority (66 percent) responded as either "not too worried" or "not worried at all." The figures mirror those reported by a national survey around the same time (Gallup, February 4–6, 2002). Trend data show a slight decline over the year in the number of those who are worried about becoming a victim. Directly after 9/11, a majority was either "very" (23 percent) or "somewhat" (35 percent) worried. One year later, however, this trend reversed, with a solid

TABLE 4.
TABLE 4. How worried are you that you or someone in your family will become a victim of a terrorist attack: very worried, somewhat worried, not very worried, not worried at all?

Date	Very Worried/ Great Deal (%)	Somewhat Worried (%)	Not Very Worried (%)	Not at All Worried (%)	Don't Know/ No Answer (%)	Number Polled
Oklahoma City						
4/95[a] HART	14	28	33	24	1	1,008
4/96[a] PRIN	13	22	33	32	0	1,010
7/96[a] GALLUP/ CNN/USA	13	26	35	27	0	1,010
8/96[a] ABC/WP	11	27	29	33	0	1,514
4/97[a] YANK/TIME/ CNN	10	26	32	31	1	1,040
8/98 GALLUP	10	22	38	29	1	600
4/00[a] GALLUP/ CNN/USA	4	20	41	34	1	1,006
5/01 AP/ICR	11	23	34	32	0	1,004
9/11						
9/11/01 GALLUP/ CNN/USA	23	35	24	16	1	619
9/14–15/01 GALLUP/ CNN/USA	18	33	35	13	1	1,032
9/21–22/01 GALLUP/ CNN/USA	14	35	32	18	1	1,005
10/10–14/01 PSRA/PEW	18	32	29	19	0	1,488
10/19–21/01 GALLUP/ CNN/USA	13	30	33	23	1	1,006
11/2–4/01[b] GALLUP/ CNN/USA	11	28	34	26	1	1,012

TABLE 4. (Continued)

Date	Very Worried/ Great Deal (%)	Somewhat Worried (%)	Not Very Worried (%)	Not at All Worried (%)	Don't Know/ No Answer (%)	Number Polled
11/26–27/01 GALLUP/ CNN/USA	8	27	34	30	1	1,025
1/9–13/02[c] PSRA/PEW	12	26	38	24	0	1,201
2/4–6/02 GALLUP	8	27	39	25	1	1,011
4–5/02 Portland	7	27	43	23	0	640
8/14–25/02[c] PRIN	12	28	35	24	1	1,001
1 year later						
9/2–4/02[b] GALLUP	8	30	37	25	0	1,003
9/6/02[c] WP	11	27	32	29	0	1,003
10/10/02[d] PRIN	16	27	35	21	1	1,000
11/7–8/02[d] PRIN	13	23	34	30	0	1,000

[a] How worried are you that you or someone in your family will become a victim of a terrorist attack similar to the bombing in Oklahoma City: very worried, somewhat worried, not too worried, or not worried at all?

[b] How worried are you that you or someone in your family will become a victim of terrorism: very worried, somewhat worried, not too worried, or not worried at all?

[c] How concerned are you that you personally might be the victim of a terrorist attack—does that worry you a great deal, somewhat, not too much, or not at all?

[d] All in all, how worried are you that you or someone in your family will become a victim of a terrorist attack? Would you say you are very worried, somewhat worried, not too worried, or not worried at all?

majority responding that they were either "not very" (37 percent) or "not worried at all" (25 percent) (table 4). Again, the public's worry is greater directly after a terrorist attack and lessens over time.

One of a terrorist's main goals is to demonstrate the government's inability to fulfill primary security functions, which include safety and order (Wardlaw 1989). Have the 9/11 attacks eroded the public's confidence in the U.S. government? The Portland and national publics exhibit only a moderate amount of confidence in the government's ability to prevent terrorist attacks, although confidence levels increased directly after 9/11. A decade ago, surveys indicated that about one-half to two-thirds of Americans (46 to 64 percent) had "a great deal" or "a good amount" of confidence that the government could prevent terrorist attacks. These percentages significantly

TABLE 5. Generally speaking, how much confidence do you have in the ability of the U.S. government to prevent terrorist attacks against Americans in this country: a great deal, a good amount, only a fair amount, none at all?

Date	A Great Deal (%)	A Good Amount (%)	Only a Fair Amount (%)	Not Very Much (%)	None at All (%)	Don't Know/ No Answer (%)	Number Polled
4/3/89 ABC/WP	16	30	38	0	16	0	1,525
6/28/93 PRIN	17	47	24	0	10	2	1,000
Oklahoma City							
4/20/95 ABC	13	24	51	0	11	1	545
5/14/95 ABC/WP	12	24	51	0	12	1	1,011
6/95 HART	12	24	51	0	12	1	1,008
8/96 HART	12	21	49	0	16	0	1,203
6/2/97 ABC/WP	10	26	52	0	10	3	514
9/11							
9/11/01[a] ABC/WP	35	31	30	0	2	1	608
9/25–27/01[a] WP	35	31	30	0	3	1	1,215
11/5–6/01[a] ABC/WP	17	35	40	0	7	1	756
11/27/01[a] ABC/WP	24	39	32	0	5	1	759
1/24–27/02[a] ABC/WP	18	40	37	0	6	1	1,507
3/7–10/02[a] ABC/WP	18	38	39	0	5	0	1,008
4–5/02[b] Portland	10	28	39	18[b]	4	1	641
5/19/02 ABC/WP	17	29	42	0	10	2	1,011
6/02 ABC/WP	14	30	44	0	11	0	1,002
7/15/02 ABC/WP	13	33	45	0	9	0	1,001

TABLE 5. (**Continued**)

Date	A Great Deal (%)	A Good Amount (%)	Only a Fair Amount (%)	Not Very Much (%)	None at All (%)	Don't Know/ No Answer (%)	Number Polled
1 year later							
9/6/02 WP	10	31	48	0	11	0	1,003
9/02 ABC/WP	12	38	43	0	6	0	1,001

[a] How much confidence do you have in the ability of the U.S. government to prevent terrorist attacks against Americans in this country: a great deal, a good amount, a fair amount, or none at all?

[b] How much confidence do you have in the ability of the U.S. government to prevent terrorist attacks against Americans in this country: a great deal, a good amount, a fair amount, not very much, or none at all?

decreased over the years after the 1995 Oklahoma City bombing to around one in four (table 5). After 9/11, confidence in the government, on average, increased to a strong majority (66 percent) having either "a great deal" (35 percent) or "a good amount" (31 percent) of confidence (table 5). The terrorist attack by foreigners produced a rally effect (Parker 1995), boosting the public's confidence in the government directly afterward. This effect dwindled over time, with confidence levels remaining strong for only a few months. On 9/11's first anniversary, the American public was almost equally split between whether they had (a) a "great deal" or "good amount" (50 percent) of confidence in their government or (b) only a "fair amount" or "none at all" (49 percent), returning to post–Oklahoma City levels.

These findings show that, overall, the Portland and national publics are very concerned about terrorism and anticipate another terrorist attack. Both are somewhat worried that they or someone in their family will become a victim. National trend data indicate that respondents are more anticipatory of other attacks and are more worried directly after terrorist attacks. Unlike the general public, however, a large majority of Portland residents did not express feelings of danger where they lived or worked. Survey data show that Portland and national publics have only a moderate amount of confidence in the government's ability to prevent terrorist attacks, although confidence levels did increase directly after 9/11. One can conclude that a majority of Americans perceive a significant threat from terrorism and feel rather vulnerable.

Since the 9/11 terrorist attacks, the government is charged with protecting the rights of the individual as well as ensuring our collective safety. The antiterrorist policies the government institutes will, by necessity, be more invasive. Given their judgment of whether they deem that rights violations are warranted, Americans may or may not accept these initiatives. Directly after 9/11, 74 to 79 percent of Americans (CBS/NYT, September 13–14 and September 20–23, 2001) believed that it was "necessary" for the average person to give up some civil liberties in order to curb terrorism. Time seems to have eased people's fear and their willingness to relinquish civil rights. Six months after 9/11, a slight majority of Portland residents (57 percent) believed it was "necessary." A year after the attacks, the number who believed they would have to give up civil liberties to fight terrorism returned to post–Oklahoma City levels at just less than a majority of Americans (47 percent, PRIN, August 28–29, 2002; 49 percent, LAT, August 22–25, 2002; Huddy et al. 2002) (table 6). Americans have moved past the shock and fear of the attacks and are reevaluating the balance between their desire to boost national security and their support of individual freedom. According to a majority, it is still necessary to give up liberties.

When Portland residents were asked specifically if the new antiterrorist legislation threatened their own personal rights and freedoms, only 27 percent believed that it did. Of those who thought it threatened their rights, only 35 percent said it was a major threat. Close to half (45 percent) thought the new legislation would increase their security; most of the rest (37 percent) believed it would have no impact. Seventy-two percent expressed some level of confidence in the U.S. government's ability to fairly administer the new antiterrorist legislation (see Appendix A). Apparently, the Portland public does not judge the Patriot Act to be a violation of their civil rights and trusts that the government will be fair in the execution of its expanded powers.

Portland is not alone in this assessment. A year after the terrorist attacks, an NBC poll asked Americans if they thought the U.S. government had violated the civil liberties and rights of people living in the United States in its war against terrorism. Two-thirds of the American public (67 percent) judged that it had not (NBC/WSJ, September 3–5, 2002). According to another poll, 80 percent of Americans claimed that that government's anti-

TABLE 6. **In order to curb terrorism in this country, do you think it will be necessary for the average person, such as yourself, to give up some civil liberties or not?**

Date	Necessary/ Yes (%)	Not Necessary/No/ Government Will Go Too Far (%)	Don't Know/ No Answer (%)	Number Polled
4/95 LAT	49	43	8	1,032
4/97 LAT	29	62	9	1,206
9/11				
9/13–14/01[a] CBS/NYT	74	21	5	959
9/13–14/01 LAT	61	33	6	1,561
9/13–17/01 PSRA/PEW	55	35	10	1,200
9/20–23/01[a] CBS/NYT	79	19	2	1,216[a]
10/8/01[a] CBS	79	17	4	436
11/12/01[b] NPR/Kaiser/Kennedy	51	46	3	1,010
1/02[c] GALLUP/CNN/USA	47	49	4	507
4–5/02 Portland	57	40	3	640
1 year later				
8/22–25/02[d] LAT	49	38	13	1,372
8/28–29/02 PRIN	47	47	6	1,005
9/2–4/02[c] GALLUP/CNN/USA	33	62	5	507

[a] Do you think Americans will have to give up some of their personal freedoms in order to make the country safe from terrorist attacks, or not?

[b] In order to curb terrorism in this country, do you think it will be necessary for the average person to give up some civil liberties, or do you think we can curb terrorism without the average person giving up rights and liberties?

[c] To prevent additional acts of terrorism, should the U.S. government take steps that would violate your civil liberties?

[d] Do you think it is necessary to give up some civil liberties in order to make the country safe from terrorism, or do you think some of the government's proposals will go too far in restricting the public's civil liberties?

terrorism efforts were not an intrusion on their own civil liberties (ABC, September 25–29, 2002). In fact, 70 percent believe that the government is doing enough to protect the rights of average Americans and close to that number (65 percent) believe the same in regard to Arab-Americans and Americans who are also Muslim (WP, September 3–6, 2002).

Generally, the American public shares the beliefs of Portland respondents that the current legislation does not violate liberties and trusts that the government will protect civil rights. It is likely, however, that public support will vary according to the type of proposed government action as well as the target of the action. The following section examines public support for specific antiterrorist policies.

National Threat and Freedom of Expression

The First Amendment right of freedom of expression is considered to be the cornerstone of all other individual rights. The ability to express oneself allows for the realization of one's character and potentialities as a human being. Discussion and debate are vital for democratic governance and citizen participation in the governmental process. Maybe most important, freedom of expression "provides a method by which conflicts in a society can be resolved without resort to force, thereby maintaining a healthy balance between stability and change" (Emerson 1982, 57). Political tolerance and the guarantee of freedom of speech and press may be casualties during the war on terrorism. As Page and Shapiro (1992, 93–94) note, "the most natural thing in the world is to want to silence people who are offensive, or dangerous, especially in times of peril."

Because terrorists are widely perceived as extremely dangerous, it should be no surprise that a majority of the Portland and national publics would like to silence those linked to terrorism. When asked if someone who expressed support for terrorists should be allowed to make a speech at a college, 61 percent of Americans believed they should not. When asked if that person should be allowed to teach in the public schools, a substantial majority (85 percent) said "no" (NPR/Kaiser/Kennedy, November 21, 2001). Close to half (46 percent) of those surveyed in Portland supported restricting speeches on TV or radio that may encourage acts of terrorism, and 65 percent supported banning materials that encourage political terrorism via the Internet (see Appendix A).

The overall mood is one of intolerance for any type of expression that may legitimate terrorist activities or increase Americans' vulnerability to a terrorist attack. The American public is quite willing to restrict freedom of expression. Other studies have also found that the public is least tolerant of disliked or threatening groups in times of national threat (Stouffer 1955; Davis 1975; Nunn, Crocket, and Williams 1978; Sullivan and Marcus 1982; McClosky and Brill 1983; McClosky and Zaller 1984). This pattern continues in the war against terrorism.

Intelligence Gathering and a Zone of Privacy

"The function of privacy in a democratic society is to protect the dignity and autonomy of the individual citizen in his or her relations with the collective" (Emerson 1982, 70). Supreme Court rulings have established that individuals have the right to be left alone, that a "zone of privacy" exists, and that the government or others should not intrude upon it. Yet, the imperatives of the war on terrorism require that the government increase its intelligence gathering and surveillance activities of those within U.S. borders.

When asked generally if the right to privacy was under threat in the United States, the research organization Public Agenda (2002) found that a sizable majority believed that it was either under "serious threat" (41 percent) or "already lost" (24 percent). More than half (57 percent), however, identified banks and credit card companies as the culprit, whereas only 29 percent claimed it was the federal government and less than one in ten (8 percent) believed the threat was law enforcement agencies. One reporter has noted, "The essential paradox in the post–Sept. 11 era is that people seem willing to accept government intrusions but not commercial ones, even though the government's power is enormous and often wielded in secret" (Liptak 2002). But how much governmental intrusion will the public accept?

Highest overall support was found for government monitoring of public events, where individuals did not have an expectation of privacy. Close to four out of five (78 percent) Portland respondents supported establishing security checkpoints in office buildings and implementing random police searches of people entering large public events (77 percent). The level of support dropped dramatically when the respondent was unsure of the venue for the government intrusion. Only 32 percent supported allowing police to randomly search people when no venue was mentioned (see Appendix A). This level of support mirrored that found in a national survey taken directly after 9/11 (Gallup/CNN/USA, September 9, 2001).

Public support of government surveillance activities depended upon the targets and whether they were suspects, although many supported most types of surveillance. A majority (53 percent) of Portland respondents supported increasing the surveillance of U.S. citizens. Levels of support increased significantly (69 percent) when the targets of the surveillance were citizens of other countries who were in the United States. Three-quarters (76 percent) supported giving the Federal Bureau of Investigation (FBI) power to infiltrate groups it suspects of planning terrorist acts, even if it doesn't have hard evidence. The Portland public's support dramatically decreased (20 percent) when the government's target involved religious groups that gather at mosques, churches, temples, or synagogues without evidence that someone in the group has broken the law (see Appendix A). A year after 9/11, a large majority (80 percent) of the national public still supported new laws that would make it easier for the FBI to investigate terrorist suspects (WP, September 3–6, 2002). Two-thirds (66 percent) also showed willingness to support monitoring of gatherings at mosques and other religious places, Internet sites, and political rallies, even when there is no evidence of wrongdoing (Fox News, June 4–5, 2002; ABC, June 7–9, 2002).

In general, the Portland public is supportive of increasing governmental authority in its information-gathering activities as is the national public, although support has decreased since 9/11. Three out of four (76 percent) Portland respondents supported making it easier for the FBI to get information from credit agencies, hotels, and airlines. This same support level was found in the general public two months after 9/11 (NPR, November 20–25, 2001), although support for this activity decreased to only 32 percent close to 9/11's first anniversary (table 7).

The Portland public does appear discerning when considering which type of communication it would support in government monitoring. More than half (56 percent) supported giving broader authority to law enforcement for intercepting E-mail; however, close to the same percentage (57 percent) expressed opposition when asked about ordinary mail (see Appendix A). Fear of or unfamiliarity with the Internet may have led more individuals to support government monitoring of electronic mail. Portland respondents were equally split when asked whether they would give broader authority to law enforcement for wiretapping phones (47 percent support; 50 percent oppose). Apparently, the nature of the communication medium matters; how-

TABLE 7. In order to reduce the threat of terrorism in the U.S., would you support or oppose giving law enforcement broader authority to do the following things: track credit card purchases?

Date	Favor/ Support (%)	Oppose (%)	Don't Know/ No Answer (%)	Number Polled
11/20–25/01 NPR/Kaiser/Kennedy	75	21	4	1,206
4–5/02[a] Portland	76	20	4	640
8/14–15/02[b] PSRA/PEW	32	63	5	1,001

[a] In order to reduce the threat of terrorism in the U.S., would you support or oppose giving law enforcement broader authority to make it easier for the FBI to get information from credit agencies, hotels, and airlines?

[b] Would you favor or oppose the following measures to curb terrorism: allowing the U.S. government to monitor credit card purchases?

ever, government monitoring of communications is moderately supported by the Portland public.

A year after 9/11, the national public appears to be less willing to support government intrusions into their personal communications. When asked if they favored making it easier for law enforcement agents to monitor people's private telephone conversations and E-mail, close to three out of five thought that this went "too far" (table 8). Other scholars have found that when the target of phone or E-mail surveillance was unspecified, public support increased. However, support dropped significantly when the target was an ordinary American or respondents themselves (Huddy et al. 2002, 419).

When asked if they would support or oppose "requiring everyone in the US to carry a national identification card issued by the federal government, containing, among other things, the person's picture and fingerprints," 60 percent of the Portland respondents supported this initiative. The residents of this city are not unique in their support for national identification cards. Numerous national surveys conducted since 9/11 found equally high levels of support for such a policy initiative. Although this support has been somewhat tempered, a year after the terrorist attacks a majority of Americans still support ID cards (table 9).

The lowest level of public support was in regard to the Patriot Act's

TABLE 8. We'd like your opinion of some things that have been done—or might be done—to improve security and protect against terrorism in the United States. For each one, tell me if you strongly favor it, are willing to accept it if necessary, or think it goes to far: What about making it easier for intelligence and law enforcement agents to monitor people's private telephone conversations and E-mail?

Date	Strongly Favor/ Favor (%)	Willing to Accept (%)	Goes Too Far/ Oppose (%)	Don't Know No Answer (%)	Number Polled
9/13–17/01 PSRA/PEW	26	—	70	—	1,000
6/27–28/02 Newsweek	12	28	57	3	1,000
8/14–25/02[a] PSRA/PEW	33	0	61	6	1,001
8/28–29/02 PRIN	11	25	62	2	1,005
9/8–9/02[b] OD/FOX	38	0	53	9	900

[a] Would you favor or oppose the following measures to curb terrorism: Allowing the U.S. government to monitor personal telephone calls and E-mails?

[b] Please tell me if you favor or oppose each of the following possible solutions that have been proposed as ways of dealing with terrorism: allowing the government to increase monitoring of private telephone and E-mail communications?

"sneak and peek" search warrant provision. When asked if they supported or opposed the part of the new antiterrorist legislation indicating that "police could enter someone's house or office and conduct a search without leaving any kind of notice," a large majority (81 percent) of Portland respondents specified "opposed" (see Appendix A). A national survey that asked the same question two months after 9/11 garnered more public support, with 40 percent supporting (NPR, November 12, 2001). This could indicate that the Portland public values the right of privacy in their own homes more than those in other parts of the country. A more plausible, alternative explanation is that the intervening four months between the national and Portland surveys have brought about less tolerance for privacy invasions, especially in regard to one's home.

In general, the American public is supportive of the government's increased intelligence-gathering activities; the reason is that the government is not seen as intrusive upon civil liberties. Support is highest when the venue is public and the target is not an average American. The least amount

TABLE 9. In order to reduce the threat of terrorism in the U.S., would you support or oppose giving law enforcement broader authority to do the following: requiring everyone in the U.S. to carry a national identification card issued by the federal government, containing, among other things, the person's picture and fingerprints?

Date	Support/Favor (%)	Oppose (%)	Don't Know/ No Answer (%)	Number Polled
9/13–17/01[a] PSRA/PEW	70	26	4	1,200
9/19–24/01[b] HARRIS	68	28	4	1,012
9/20–23/01[c] CBS/NYT	56	38	6	1,216
11/12/01[d] NPR/Kaiser/Kennedy	59	38	2	1,208
4–5/02 Portland	60	36	4	639
8/14–25/02[c] PSRA/PEW	59	38	3	500
9/20–22/02[e] GALLUP/CNN/USA	56	41	3	518

[a] Would you favor or oppose the following measures to curb terrorism: requiring that all citizens carry a national identity card at all times and to show to a police officer on request?

[b] Here are some increased powers of investigation that law enforcement agencies might use when dealing with people suspected of terrorist activity, which would also affect our civil liberties. For each, please say if you would favor or oppose it . . . adoption of a national ID system for all U.S. citizens.

[c] In order to reduce the threat of terrorism, would you be willing or not willing for the government to require everyone in the United States to carry a national electronic identification card, or "smart card," that would have detailed information about each person?

[d] Would you favor or oppose requiring everyone in the United States to carry an identification card issued by the federal government?

[e] As part of the effort to combat terrorism, would you support a law requiring all adults in the USA to carry a national ID card that includes a photograph and Social Security number?

of support was given when the invasion of privacy was the home. In all cases, public support for government monitoring and surveillance decreased over the year.

Right to Due Process

Profiling has been at the heart of many legal debates in the United States. Although a large majority of Americans have not supported racial profiling in the past (N. Davis 2001), it appears that since 9/11 this practice is now supported by a majority of Americans. A solid majority (59 percent) of the

TABLE 10. **In order to reduce the threat of terrorism in the U.S., would you support or oppose giving law enforcement broader authority to do the following things: stopping people who fit the profile of suspected terrorists?**

Date	Support/Approve/ Favor (%)	Oppose/ Disapprove (%)	Don't Know/ No Answer (%)	Number Polled
9/13–14/01[a] LAT	68	29	3	959
4–5/02 Portland	59	36	5	639
9/8–9/02[b] OD/FOX	62	31	7	900

[a] Some people say that in order to fight terrorism, law enforcement should be allowed to randomly stop people who may fit the profile of suspected terrorists. Would you approve or disapprove of such a move?

[b] Please tell me if you favor or oppose each of the following possible solutions that have been proposed as ways of dealing with terrorism: allowing police to stop and search anyone who fits the general description of suspected terrorists.

Portland public supported stopping people who fit the profile of suspected terrorists (table 10). A majority (68 percent) support was also found in a poll conducted directly after the 9/11 terrorist attacks (LAT, September 13, 2002). In other polls, a majority (58 percent) favored more intensive security checks for Arabs, and half approved of special identification cards for Arabs (50 percent) (ABC/WP, September 13, 2001). A year after 9/11, 62 percent of Americans still supported profiling. Given the trends discussed in other sections of this essay, it is not surprising that support for profiling remained strong.

Support for detentions varied according to the length of time of the detention and whether the target was a citizen of the United States. When asked if they would support detaining terrorist suspects who are not U.S. citizens for a week without charging them, the Portland public was split (50 percent support; 43 percent oppose). When asked if they would still support detention for suspects with U.S. citizenship, 61 percent favored it. Support levels dropped dramatically (19 percent) when the detention was indefinite. Asked if they would support indefinite detentions for U.S. citizens, 52 percent would (see Appendix A). National support for detentions followed the Portland pattern (table 11), although 37 percent supported indefinite detention (NPR, November 25, 2002) (tables 12 and 13).

TABLE 11. In order to reduce the threat of terrorism in the U.S., would you support or oppose giving the law enforcement broader authority to do the following things: would you support or oppose giving them broader authority to detain terrorist suspects for a week without charging them?

Date	Support (%)	Oppose (%)	Don't Know/ No Answer (%)	Number Polled
11/12/01 NPR/Kaiser/Kennedy	58	38	3	1,206
11/17/01 NPR Kaiser/Kennedy	51	45	4	1,200
4–5/02[a] Portland	50	43	7	634

[a] In order to reduce the threat of terrorism in the U.S., would you support or oppose giving law enforcement broader authority to detain terrorist suspects of Arab or Middle Eastern descent for a week without charging them?

CONCLUSION

The nation's willingness to restrict civil liberties in the name of security after the 9/11 terrorist attacks follows historic patterns (Clymer 2002). We find that the public will support substantial limits on civil liberties during periods of national security threats. Included are limits on freedom of expression, privacy, and the right to due process. Fearing disorder, threat, and instability, the public was willing to make sacrifices and grant the government more leeway directly after the 9/11 attacks. As time passed, people began wrestling with the conflicting values of liberty and security. A year later, the public expressed more doubts over this trade-off. Time to think and the absence of more terrorist attacks led to the reduction of support for antiterrorist policies that may infringe upon civil liberties. The public's support for curbs on their liberties declined as the terrorist threat receded.

However, most people are still supportive of many government initiatives. Policies that are highly supported involve costs that are low for average Americans. Studies have shown that Americans are highly supportive of democratic principles in the abstract, but they become very intolerant when asked to make judgments concerning policies about threatening situations or noxious groups. As McClosky and Zaller (1984, 39) note, "the degree of freedom an open society permits is bound to vary somewhat from one group or occasion to another, and from one people to another, depending on the es-

TABLE 12. In order to reduce the threat of terrorism in the U.S., would you support or oppose giving law enforcement broader authority to do the following things: Would you support or oppose giving them broader authority to detain terrorist suspects indefinitely without charging them?

Date	Support (%)	Oppose (%)	Don't Know/ No Answer (%)	Number Polled
11/12/01 NPR/Kaiser/Kennedy	48	48	4	1,206
11/17/01 NPR Kaiser/Kennedy	37	61	3	1,200
4–5/02[a] Portland	19	76	5	634

[a] In order to reduce the threat of terrorism in the U.S., would you support or oppose giving law enforcement broader authority to detain terrorist suspects of Arab or Middle Eastern descent indefinitely without charging them?

TABLE 13. We'd like your opinion of some things that have been done—or might be done—to improve security and protect against terrorism in the United States. For each one, tell me if you strongly favor it, are willing to accept it if necessary, or think it goes too far. What about giving government the power to detain legal immigrants suspected of crimes indefinitely without review by a judge?

Date	Strongly Favor (%)	Willing to Accept (%)	Goes Too Far (%)	Don't Know/ No Answer (%)	Number Polled
11/29–30/01 Newsweek	35	43	19	3	1,002
6/27–28/02 PRIN	25	31	39	5	1,000
8/27–28/02 PRIN	24	23	49	4	1,005

timates made by authorities, the elites and the general public about the degree of danger they face."

Will public support of antiterrorist policies continue to wane? Since the war on terrorism is ambiguous, it will be harder for the Bush administration to create and maintain a "war mentality" in the general public. The lack of a tangible enemy will make it difficult for the public to judge if the government is winning or losing the war. Without evidence of a foe, it will be harder for the president to defend policies that continue to be intrusive. As time goes on, with more Americans affected by the policies and cases brought before the judicial system, support for antiterrorist policies may decline further. However, if there are more terrorist attacks on U.S. soil, the pattern of public support discussed above may repeat itself.

APPENDIX A

"Security vs. Liberty: Abbreviated Public Opinion and Terrorism Survey in Portland, Maine"
(Words in capital letters were not read to respondent.)

I would like to begin the survey with some general questions concerning terrorism:

1. How concerned are you that there will be *more violence from terrorists* in the U.S.? Would you say . . .
   very concerned (45.6 percent), somewhat concerned (45.2 percent), or not very concerned (8.9 percent)? NOT SURE (0 percent), NO OPINION (0.3 percent)

2. In your opinion, how likely is another major terrorist attack in the U.S. *within the next six months?* Would you say . . .
   very likely (20.8 percent), somewhat likely (61.7 percent), or not at all likely (14.7 percent)? NOT SURE (1.6 percent), NO OPINION (1.3 percent).

3. These days, how much do you worry about terrorism when you are in public places . . .
   a great deal (3.7 percent), a good amount (10.9 percent), not too much (53.8 percent), or not at all (31 percent)? DON'T KNOW (0.3 percent), NO OPINION (0.2 percent)

4. How worried are you that you or someone in your family will become a victim of a terrorist attack . . .
   very worried (7.2 percent), somewhat worried (27 percent), not too worried (42.5 percent), or not worried at all (23.1 percent)? DON'T KNOW (0 percent), NO OPINION (0.02 percent)

5. Do you personally feel any sense of danger from terrorist acts where you live or work?
   YES (13.9 percent), NO (85.3 percent), NOT SURE (0.8 percent)

6. Now I would like to ask some questions concerning the government's response to terrorism: How much confidence do you have in the ability of the U.S. government to prevent terrorist attacks against Americans in this country?
   a great deal (10.5 percent), a good amount (28.1 percent), a fair amount (38.8 percent), not very much (18.3 percent), or none at all (3.6 percent)? DON'T KNOW (0.8 percent)

7. In order to curb terrorism in this country, do you think it will be necessary for a typical citizen, such as yourself, to give up some civil liberties?
   NECESSARY (56.7 percent), NOT NECESSARY (39.2 percent), DON'T KNOW (3.3 percent), NO OPINION (0.8 percent)

8. How much confidence do you have in the U.S. government to *fairly administer* the new anti-terrorist legislation . . .

a great deal (7.8 percent), a good amount (28.3 percent), a fair amount (38.8 percent), not very much (18.3 percent), or none at all (3.6 percent)? DON'T KNOW (0.8 percent)

9. From what you know about the new anti-terrorist legislation, do you think it threatens your own personal rights and freedoms or not?

YES (26.9 percent) (GO TO 9a), NO (62.3 percent) (GO TO 10), DON'T KNOW (9.2 percent) (GO TO 10), NO OPINION (1.6 percent) (GO TO 10)

9a. Is it a *major* threat or a *minor* threat?

MAJOR (35.3 percent), MINOR (59.5 percent), DON'T KNOW (4 percent), NO OPINION (1.2 percent)

10. Now, I would like to ask you your opinion about specific governmental policies to combat terrorism. We will first focus on domestic policies and then move to international policies.

In order to reduce the threat of terrorism in the U.S., would you support or oppose giving law enforcement broader authority to do the following things? First . . .

Wiretapping telephones . . . would you support or oppose this?
SUPPORT (46.9 percent), OPPOSE (49.5 percent), DON'T KNOW (2 percent) NO OPINION (1.6 percent)

11. Intercepting e-mail?
SUPPORT (56.1 percent), OPPOSE (38.8 percent), DON'T KNOW (3 percent), NO OPINION (2.2 percent)

12. Intercepting ordinary mail?
SUPPORT (39.2 percent), OPPOSE (57.5 percent), DON'T KNOW (2.2 percent) NO OPINION (1.1 percent)

13. Allowing police to randomly search people?
SUPPORT (32.2 percent), OPPOSE (64.2 percent), DON'T KNOW (1.9 percent) NO OPINION (1.6 percent)

14. Increasing the surveillance of U.S. citizens?
SUPPORT (53.1 percent), OPPOSE (41.6 percent), DON'T KNOW (3 percent), NO OPINION (2.3 percent)

15. Restricting speeches on TV or the radio that may encourage acts of terrorism?
SUPPORT (45.6 percent), OPPOSE (50.2 percent), DON'T KNOW (1.6 percent), NO OPINION (2.7 percent)

16. Expelling citizens of other countries who are suspected of planning a terrorist act even if they have committed no crime?
SUPPORT (63.6 percent), OPPOSE (30.2 percent), DON'T KNOW (3.4 percent), NO OPINION (2.8 percent)

17. Making it easier for the FBI to get information from credit agencies, hotels, and airlines?
SUPPORT (75.3 percent), OPPOSE (20.3 percent), DON'T KNOW (2.3 percent), NO OPINION (2 percent)

18. Establishing security checkpoints in most office buildings like those found in airports?
    SUPPORT (78.4 percent), OPPOSE (18.9 percent), NO OPINION (2.7 percent)

19. Implementing random police searches of people entering large public events?
    SUPPORT (77 percent), OPPOSE (21.4 percent), DON'T KNOW (1.1 percent), NO OPINION (0.5 percent)

20. Increasing surveillance of citizens of foreign countries who are in the U.S.?
    SUPPORT (68.8 percent), OPPOSE (25.2 percent), DON'T KNOW (3.1 percent), NO OPINION (3 percent)

21. Investigating religious groups that gather at mosques, churches, or synagogues without evidence that someone in the group has broken the law?
    SUPPORT (19.7 percent), OPPOSE (77.5 percent), DON'T KNOW (1.7 percent), NO OPINION (1.1 percent)

22. Making it easier for the FBI to trace telephone calls?
    SUPPORT (74.1 percent), OPPOSE (22.7 percent), DON'T KNOW (1.4 percent), NO OPINION (1.9 percent)

23. Banning materials that encourage political terrorism from the Internet?
    SUPPORT (64.7 percent), OPPOSE (30.5 percent), DON'T KNOW (2.8 percent), NO OPINION (2 percent)

24. Giving the FBI power to infiltrate groups it suspects of planning terrorism, even if it doesn't have hard evidence?
    SUPPORT (76.4 percent), OPPOSE (21.3 percent), DON'T KNOW (0.9 percent), NO OPINION (1.4 percent)

25. Requiring everyone in the U.S. to carry a national identification card issued by the federal government, containing, among other things, the person's picture and fingerprints?
    SUPPORT (60.6 percent), OPPOSE (35.5 percent), DON'T KNOW (2.7 percent), NO OPINION (1.3 percent)

26. Stopping people who fit the profile of suspected terrorists?
    SUPPORT (58.5 percent), OPPOSE (36.2 percent), DON'T KNOW (3.4 percent), NO OPINION (1.9 percent)

27. One part of the anti-terrorism legislation would make it easier for law enforcement to get what's called "sneak and peek" search warrants. Usually, police must notify people at the time of a search, or at least leave a note saying they had conducted the search. Under the new law, however, police could enter someone's house or office and conduct a search without leaving any kind of notice. Do you support or oppose this part of the law?
    SUPPORT (15.4 percent), OPPOSE (80.8 percent), DON'T KNOW (2.4 percent), NO OPINION (1.4 percent)

28. Detain terrorist suspects of Arab or Middle Eastern descent for a week without charging them?
    SUPPORT (GO TO 28a) (50.3 percent), OPPOSE (GO TO 29) (42.6 percent), DON'T KNOW (GO TO 29) (3 percent), NO OPINION (GO TO 29) (4.1 percent)

28a. Would you still support it if they were U.S. citizens, or would you now oppose it?

STILL SUPPORT (61.3 percent), NOW OPPOSE (36.2 percent), DON'T KNOW (1.3 percent), NO OPINION (1.3 percent)

29. Detain terrorist suspects of Arab or Middle East descent *indefinitely* without charging them?
SUPPORT (GO TO 29a) (18.5 percent), OPPOSE (75.6 percent), DON'T KNOW (2.4 percent), NO OPINION (3.6 percent)

29a. Would you still support it if they were U.S. citizens, or would you now oppose it?
YES, STILL SUPPORT (52.1 percent), NO, NOW OPPOSE (46.2 percent), NO OPINION (1.7 percent)

APPENDIX B

Abbreviations/Names for Polling Organizations

ABC: ABC News
ABC/WP: ABC News/*Washington Post*
AP: Associated Press
AP/ICR: Associated Press/International Communications Research
CBS: CBS News
CBS/NYT: CBS News/*New York Times*
GALLUP: Gallup polls
GALLUP/CNN/USA: Gallup for CNN/*USA Today*
HARRIS: Louis Harris & Associates
HART: Hart & Teeter
LAT: *Los Angeles Times*
Mart: Marttila and Kiley
MG: Market Strategies and Greenberg
NBC/WSJ: National Broadcasting Company/*Wall Street Journal*
Newsweek
NPR/Kaiser/Kennedy: National Public Radio/Henry J. Kaiser Family Foundation/ Harvard University's Kennedy School of Government
OD/FOX: Opinion Dynamics for Fox News
ORC: Opinion Research Corporation
PSRA/PEW: Princeton Survey Research Associates for Pew
PRIN: Princeton University Survey
ROPER: Roper Organization
WP: *Washington Post*
YANK: Yankelovich Partners Inc. Yank/*Time*/CNN: Yankelovich Partners Inc./*Time* Magazine/Cable News Network
YCS: Yankelovich Clancy Shuman
YSP: Yankelovich, Skelly, and White Inc.
ZOGBY: Zogby Group

NOTES

1. Portland is the largest city in Maine, with a population of 64,249 citizens. It is fairly homogeneous, with a majority (91 percent) identified as Caucasian. Other major groups include Asian (3%), African American (2.5%), and Native American (0.47%). The median age is thirty-six years and the median household income is $35,650.

2. A telephone survey was administered by the Muskie School of Public Service at the University of Southern Maine to a random sample of 643 residents of the Greater Portland area in April–May 2002.

REFERENCES

Almond, Gabriel, and Sidney Verba. 1963. *The Civic Culture*. Princeton, N.J.: Princeton University Press.

American Civil Liberties Union. 2002. "Keep America Safe and Free." On-line at http://www.aclu.org/SafeandFree/SafeandFreeMain.cfm, accessed May 12, 2003.

Bush, George W. 2001. "Military Order—Detention, Treatment, and Trial of Certain Non-Citizens in the War against Terrorism." Executive order dated November 13, 66 *Federal Register* 57833 (November 16, 2001).

CBS News. 2002a. "Poll: America, a Changed Country," September 7. On-line at http:www.cbsnews.com/stories/2002/09/07/september11/, accessed May 12, 2003.

CBS News. 2002b. "New York City: One Year Later." September 11. On-line at http:www. cbsnews.com/stories/2002/09/16/opinion/polls, accessed May 12, 2003.

Clymer, Adam. 2002. "US Attitudes Altered Little by Sept. 11, Pollsters Say." *New York Times*, May 20.

Dahl, Robert. 1971. *Polyarchy*. New Haven, Conn.: Yale University Press.

Davis, J. 1975. "Communism, Conformity, Cohorts, Categories: American Tolerance in 1954 and 1972–73." *American Journal of Sociology* 81: 491–513.

Davis, Nicole, 2001. "The Slippery Slope of Racial Porfiling." Online at http://www.arc.org/C_Lines/CLArchive/story2001_12_05.html, accessed August 18, 2003.

Emerson, Tom I. 1982. "The First Amendment in the Year 2000." In *The Future of Our Liberties: Perspectives on the Bill of Rights*, ed. Stephen C. Halpern. Westport, Conn.: Greenwood Press.

Fried, Albert. 1997. *McCarthyism: The Great American Red Scare*. New York: Oxford University Press.

Hewitt, Christopher. 1993. *Violence and Terrorism*. Guilford, Conn.: Dushkin Publishing Group.

Huddy, Leonie, et al. 2002. "The Consequences of Terrorism: Disentangling the Effects of Personal and National Threat." *Political Psychology* 23: 485–509.

Huddy, Leonie, Nádia Khatib, and Theresa Capelos. 2002. "The Polls—Trends: Reactions to September 11th." *Public Opinion Quarterly* 66: 418–33.

Huntington, Samuel P. 1981. *American Politics: The Promise of Disharmony.* Cambridge, Mass.: Harvard University Press.

Kuzma, Lynn. 2000. "The Polls—Trends: Terrorism in the United States." *Public Opinion Quarterly* 64.

Liptak, Neil. 2002. "Court Overturns Limits on Wiretaps to Combat Terror." *New York Times,* November 25.

Marcus, George E., et al. 1995. *With Malice toward Some: How People Make Civil Liberties Judgments.* Cambridge, Mass.: Harvard University Press.

McClosky, Herbert, and Aida Brill. 1983. *Dimensions of Tolerance: What Americans Believe about Civil Liberties.* New York: Russell Sage Foundation.

McClosky, Herbert, and John Zaller. 1984. *The American Ethos: Public Attitudes toward Capitalism and Democracy.* Cambridge, Mass.: Harvard University Press.

Nunn, Clyde S., Harry J. Crocket, and J. Allen Williams. 1978. *Tolerance for Nonconformity.* San Francisco: Jossey-Bass.

Page, Ben I., and Robert Y. Shapiro. 1992. *The Rational Public.* Chicago: University of Chicago Press.

Parker, Suzanne. 1995. "Toward an Understanding of 'Rally' Effects: Public Opinion in the Persian Gulf War." *Public Opinion Quarterly* 59 (winter): 541.

Pew Research Center for the People and the Press. 2001. "Worries about Terrorism Subside in Mid-America," November 8. On-line at http://people-press.org/reports/display.php3?ReportID=15, accessed May 12, 2003.

Pew Research Center for the People and the Press. 2002. "One Year Later: New Yorkers More Troubled, Washingtonians More on Edge," September 5. On-line at http://people-press.org/reports/display.php3?ReportID=160, accessed May 12, 2003.

Rehnquist, William. 1998. *All the Laws but One: Civil Liberties in Wartime.* New York: Alfred A. Knopf.

Solomon, Alisa. 2002. "Things We Lost in the Fire." *Village Voice,* September 11–17.

Stouffer, Samuel. 1955. *Communism, Conformity, and Civil Liberties.* New York: Doubleday.

Sullivan, John L., and George E. Marcus. 1982. *Political Tolerance and American Democracy.* Chicago: University of Chicago Press.

Uniting and Strengthening America by Providing Appropriate Tools Required to Intercept and Obstruct Terrorism Act. 2001. 107th Congress, 1st sess., H.R. 3162, October 24.

Wadsworth, Deborah. 2002. "Knowing It by Heart: Americans Consider the Constitution and Its Meaning," On-line at http://www.publicagenda.org/specials/constitution/constitution_afterword.htm, accessed May 12, 2003.

Wardlaw, Grant. 1989. *Political Terrorism: Theory, Tactics, and Counter-Measures.* 2d ed. New York: Cambridge University Press.

Weinberg, Leonard B., and Paul B. Davis. 1989. *Political Terrorism.* New York: McGraw-Hill.

PART FOUR

Institutions and Public Policy

WILLIAM CROTTY

On the Home Front: Institutional Mobilization to Fight the Threat of International Terrorism

INTRODUCTION: SETTING THE CONTEXT FOR A WAR ON TERRORISM

The 9/11 attack was a new kind of threat, and initially it drew an uncertain and confused response. President George W. Bush was in a schoolroom in Florida promoting his legislative agenda when notified. He was to fly from one air force base to another, removed from public sight, while Vice President Richard Cheney was to coordinate activities in Washington. Top administration officials and the members of Congress were taken to secret bomb shelters. The media continued to develop the story: the attack on the World Trade Center towers and the Pentagon by terrorists piloting commercial planes as well as the downing of another hijacked commercial aircraft potentially aimed at the White House or Capitol Hill; the human suffering brought about by the tragedies; and the dedication and commitment of the fire, police, medical, and emergency workers who attempted to deal with the carnage. Television coverage included repeated images of the planes slamming into the Twin Towers and the explosions that followed. It has provided a tragic before/after marker for many. Few understood why it had happened, and fewer yet knew what it meant for the future.

The terrorist leader Osama bin Laden and his network, Al Qaeda, were to become familiar topics of discussion and speculation. As the details of the plots and the source of the threats became better known, the administration regained its footing and its approach to a response would dominate post-

9/11 developments. On September 15, 2001, President George W. Bush described the attacks as "despicable acts" and declared that "this act will not stand; we will find those who did it; we will smoke them out of their holes; we will get them running and we'll bring them to justice. We will not only deal with those who dare attack America, we will deal with those who harbor them and feed them and house them. Make no mistake about it: underneath our tears is the strong determination of America to win this war. And we will win it" (Bush 2001b).

A war it would be.

As the president had promised, extensive military action was taken against Afghanistan, the home base of bin Laden and his terrorist network. The offensive proved successful in driving Al Qaeda out of that country, destroying its bases and much of its weaponry, and—although no one could be totally sure—curtailing its activities. Despite repeated public threats to inflict mass destruction, Al Qaeda eventually appeared to fade from the primary attention given it by the administration. Though no links were established between terrorist activities in Afghanistan and Iraq, the debate over a war against Iraq and Saddam Hussein was to take center stage.

Meanwhile, the United States and its allies were engrossed in "nation building" in Afghanistan, choosing its leadership and attempting to restructure its tribal, ethnic, and regional rivalries along more democratic and Western lines. When newly elected, President Bush had proclaimed that he would never engage in such nation building. Nevertheless, a program was put in place in Afghanistan and further held out as the promised objective for Iraq after the anticipated overthrow of Hussein.

There were contradictions—and just as many problems—to emerge from the early days of the new era. At the same time that the president voiced his indignation and declared a desire "to not seek only revenge, but to win a war against barbaric behavior" (Bush 2001b), he was counseling Americans to continue their normal pursuits, to consume goods and services much as they had before, and to act basically as though nothing had happened to disrupt their lives. Yet the extent of the new threat to American security and the efforts required to meet it would be nothing short of monumental.

Before examining the actions taken by the president, we need to understand how he perceived the tasks ahead. At a memorial service for the victims on September 14, 2001, President Bush declared that "the United States of America is fighting a war against terrorists of global reach." It would be an extended war, different from any in American history, one whose virtues—"some seen, some unseen"—would accumulate. He commended the success in Afghanistan against Al Qaeda, welcomed support from other nations, and referred to the upcoming "governmental reorganization, the largest since the Truman administration in the early days of the Cold War" (Bush 2001a).

He vowed that the United States would be relentless in its efforts to fight terrorism. At West Point in June 2002, Bush further developed his foreign policy agenda in what would be the most complete public statement of his objectives:

The United States must defend liberty and justice because these principles are right and true for all people everywhere. . . . America must stand firmly for the nonnegotiable demands of human dignity: the rule of law; limits on the absolute power of the state; free speech; freedom of worship; equal justice; respect for women; religious and ethnic tolerance; and respect for private property. . . . America is . . . threatened less by conquering states than we are by failing ones . . . menaced less by fleets and armies than by catastrophic technologies in the hands of the embittered few. We must defeat these threats to our nation, allies and friends. This is also a time of opportunity for America. We will work to translate this moment of influence into decades of peace, prosperity, and liberty. The U.S. national security strategy will be based on a distinctly American internationalism that reflects the union of our values and our national interests. The aim of this strategy is to help make the world not just safer but better. Our goals . . . are clear: political and economic freedom, peaceful relations with other states, and respect for human dignity. . . . To achieve these goals, the United States will: . . . prevent our enemies from threatening us, our allies and our friends, with weapons of mass destruction; ignite a new era of global economic growth through free markets and free trade; expand the circle of development by opening societies and building the infrastructure for democracy; develop agendas for cooperative action with other main centers of global power; and transform America's national security institutions to meet the challenges and opportunities of the 21st century. (Bush 2002a)

He went on to lay out his assumptions and their political and international consequences in a limited series of carefully planned speeches in this country and, on occasion, abroad. The intent was clear, as was the scope of the projected offensive.

From the president's initial address at the National Cathedral on September 14, 2001:

> We will disrupt and destroy terrorist organizations by: direct and continuous action using all the elements of national and international power. Our immediate focus will be those terrorist organizations of global reach and any terrorist or state sponsor of terrorism which attempts to gain or use weapons of mass destruction (WMD) or their precursors, defending the United States, the American people, and our interests at home and abroad by identifying and destroying the threat before it reaches our borders. While the United States will constantly strive to enlist the support of the international community, we will not hesitate to act alone, if necessary, to exercise our right of self-defense by acting preemptively against such terrorists, to prevent them from doing harm against our people and our country; and denying further sponsorship, support, and sanctuary to terrorists by convincing or compelling states to accept their sovereign responsibilities.
>
> We will also wage a war of ideas to win the battle against international terrorism. This includes: using the full influence of the United States, and working closely with allies and friends, to make clear that all acts of terrorism will be viewed in the same light as slavery, piracy, or genocide: behavior that no respectable government can condone or support and all must oppose; supporting moderate and modern government, especially in the Muslim world, to ensure that the conditions and ideologies that promote terrorism do not find fertile ground in any nation; diminishing the underlying conditions that spawn terrorism by enlisting the international community to focus its efforts and resources on areas most at risk; and using effective public diplomacy to promote the free flow of information and ideas to kindle the hopes and aspirations for freedom of those in societies ruled by the sponsors of global terrorism. (Bush 2001a)

The agenda put forward is enormous, almost overwhelming. Its major points were to be repeated over and over again; they were meant to be taken at face value, as later events were to show, and the U.S. commitment was not to be doubted.

On November 14, 2001, Bush signed an order authorizing military commissions to try and sentence terrorists; it allowed the indefinite detention and interrogation of suspected terrorists without any of the traditional guarantees of rights, a position already endorsed in the USA Patriot Act passed by the Congress (and discussed later in this chapter).

At West Point Bush addressed the issue that was to become the most controversial of the proposals; it would seemingly be a litmus test of America's patriotism and an indication of the willingness to fight terrorism at any cost. This was his proposed option of employing necessary "preemptive actions." The possibility was made starkly clear in the West Point address:

> The United States has long maintained the option of preemptive actions to counter a sufficient threat to our national security. The greater the threat, the greater is the risk of inaction—and the more compelling the case for taking anticipatory action to defend ourselves, even if uncertainty remains as to the time and place of the enemy's attack. To forestall or prevent such hostile acts by our adversaries, the United States will, if necessary, act preemptively. (Bush 2002a)

Many found it difficult to accept such a declaration of unilateral war, with its supporting assumptions relying on the judgment of one individual and the potential use of nuclear weapons. It was controversial, but eventually the Congress would address the issue and give its endorsement. This congressional outcome did not, however, put an end to the concern about the possible consequences.

THE CONGRESS POST–9/11

The Congress moved quickly—extraordinarily quickly for a deliberative body—to respond to the terrorist attacks. By October 25, 2001, the Congress had passed an omnibus USA Patriot Act—legislation that included new proposals conceived under intense pressure and a large number of older proposals—some of which had been around for years but never acted upon and some that had previously been rejected. The bill was far from a model of considered legislation. It is better understood as a hurried response to a situation no one fully comprehended or knew how to remedy. The time pressures were intense.

For better or worse, this would be the dominant pattern in future considerations. The Congress was alarmed but lacked direction; the public wanted action. Congressional response to 9/11 included the passage of the Patriot Act and the creation of a new cabinet-level Department of Homeland Security as well as less important decisions. Its role was decidedly secondary and acquiescent. The initiative had passed to the presidency, and there it would remain.

This is not to say that the Congress was mostly inert. If anything, it overreacted, debating an extensive series of legislative proposals and resolutions. Among the pieces of legislation considered or passed during this early period are the following: a bailout of the airline industry, intended to assist in instituting increased measures of security and to help compensate for the loss of passengers; a grant to the airlines of $500 million to modify airplanes to deny access to the cockpits; an initiative to set new standards (in consultation with the White House) for airport security; proposals to select and train airport screeners and security personnel, and to make these functions federal activities (they had been privatized to that point); authorization of benefits for public safety officers and their families, those who responded to the alarms or were killed in the 9/11 attacks; establishment of a fund to aid the victims of this terrorism and their families (both aspects turned out to be difficult to implement equitably and became increasingly controversial); an act designating September 11 as Patriot Day; increased budgetary authorizations for national defense, intelligence, aviation and transportation security, the Immigration and Naturalization Service, disaster relief, and funding for the New York City relief efforts; financial and other aid for Afghan women and children; extensions of unemployment compensation for those whose livelihoods were affected by the attacks; allowance of increased latitude to government agencies in dealing with bioterrorism and biological toxins; extended legal and economic tools permitted the administration in employing trade sanctions as found necessary in tracing the international flow of funds to terrorists; increased aid and military personnel for the Philippines to fight internal terrorism; authorizations for greater flexibility in the use of military force and in mobilizing the National Guard; fiscal relief for small business in the wake of 9/11; farm credit assistance for activated reservists; postterrorism improvements in mental health facilities and programs; reconstruction authorizations for Afghanistan; increased penalties for terrorist acts; permission for the U.S. Treasury to issue "War Bonds" to help finance the recovery from the World Trade Center and Pentagon attacks; increases in vocational rehabilitation for individuals with disabilities related to the attacks; amendments to the federal revenue code to provide tax relief for victims of the terrorism; authorization of the U.S. Postal Service to issue a "September 11th Heroes' Stamp," both to honor those who lost their lives and to provide financial assistance to the families of emergency relief personnel killed or disabled in the aftermath of the explosions; authorizations for a series of memorials, including one on the Capitol grounds, to honor the victims and the emergency relief workers; and recommendations that the president award a series of medals to the survivors, to the families of fire and police personnel, and, among others, "to the people aboard United Airlines flight 93 who helped resist the hijackers and cause the plane to crash prematurely" (in a Pennsylvania field). Add to these commendations for air traffic controllers, the Capitol Police, "the increased importance of the United States steel industry since the attacks," the "trained service dogs . . . with the rescue and recovery efforts in the aftermath of the terrorist attacks," the National Guard in the District of Columbia, the "entire" Department of Defense as well as the "entire" congressional community for their response to both the terrorism of 9/11 and the anthrax attacks via U.S. mail of October 2001, the ironworkers for their service in recovery efforts, and Mayor Rudolph Giuliani and the residents of New York for their courage. Condemnations of bigotry and violence directed against Sikh Americans, Muslims, or Arabs living in the United States were also endorsed.

The list is hardly complete. A frenzy of activity followed the reassembling of Congress after the attacks. A good deal of the legislation and resolutions passed were to honor those who had been victimized and to commend the bravery of those who assisted in the recovery. The most important of the legislative acts granted new and, as it would turn out, highly discretionary authority to the executive branch. The seeds of what was to come are found in House Joint Resolution 63: "Declaring that a state of war exists between the United States and any entity determined by the President to have planned, carried out, or otherwise supported the attacks against the United States on September 11, 2001, and authorizing the President to use the United States Armed Forces and all other necessary resources of the United States Government against any such entity in order to bring the conflict to a successful termination."

Most of the actions proposed or enacted were not critical in themselves. They did, however, serve a purpose. They recognized, symbolically or with material and real needs, the requisite codes and legislation to increase the ability of the government to meet the terrorist threat. Two interrelated acts were to prove extraordinarily important, both in ceding powers to the executive branch and in reconstructing the face of American government. The first (formally titled "Uniting and Strengthening America by Providing Appropriate Tools Required to Intercept and Obstruct Terrorism" and called the USA Patriot Act) passed on a vote of 98 to 1 in the Senate and 357 to 66 in the House. The second significant grant of power occurred later in the congressional vote in favor of the creation of the new superdepartment, the Department of Homeland Security, for inclusion in the Cabinet.

THE PATRIOT ACT

The Patriot Act, signed into law by the president on October 26, 2001, is difficult to evaluate in the context of the normal legislative process. A harried Congress, virtually panicked by events and believing themselves pressed to do something of consequence immediately to meet the challenge posed by terrorists, threw together a warehouse of previously rejected or unenacted programs, added new ones, put its stamp on them, and basically passed the buck to the executive branch. Its contribution to U.S. recovery from 9/11 was that it did what the president asked. Few in Congress argued for restraint, a reasoned approach, a better understanding of the threat to national security, or the most productive ways to handle such an uncertain venture. The county was in shock, the Congress felt it needed to demonstrate its resolve, and, in the early days, suffered from a leadership vacuum. The Patriot Act was to provide the key, the response lawmakers felt was called for by the times.

Few could have believed that this congressional action would prove to be anything beyond a symbolic and largely temporary fix. It could be seen, and possibly justified, as an ameliorative effort on the part of the Congress in a period of unusual crisis, a quick response to a national emergency with little thought given to its ultimate consequences. Action was needed; the Congress passed the Patriot Act.

Depending on how all of this plays out, most specifically in the future direction of actions taken by the president as a result of this legislation and the related potential for the weakening of individual judicial and procedural safeguards, the very nature of the political system could be brought into question. A hurried act by the Congress could have serious long-term consequences. It needs emphasis: the executive branch fought for such powers, but Congress in the aftermath of 9/11 and later—following the midterm election of 2002, with the impressive congressional gains made by the Republican Party—proved more than willing to cede a host of unprecedented powers to the president. While the impact on the democratic system has yet to be evaluated, politically the formalities were observed. The public and congressional debate on the issues involved and how best to deal with these was severely limited. Yet the process of power giving was politically legal and procedurally correct. In short, it was done willingly.

By any standard, the Patriot Act is a terrible piece of legislation. The bill was a cut-and-paste effort that resulted in an omnibus, catch-all piece of legislation. The proposals in the bill received little debate on the floor or in the public arena. It is fair to say that the consequences will take years to sort through. It is best understood as an all-purpose antiterrorist bill encapsulating a wide variety of issues, many with little relation to each other. It allows an override of normal judicial and legal constraints. There are few to no statutes of limitations placed on the grants of authority given to the executive branch in critical areas. The legislation further shifts the locus of political power to the presidency, lessens the restrictions on what is already the world's most powerful position, and brings into question the very nature of constraints and accountability within the American system. The Patriot Act permits an exercise of discretionary powers by the president that has few if any parallels in American history. Since this redistribution of power was not the product of a full and reasoned national debate, few understand its implications. The hope is that the powers will not be abused and the political system will revert to something close to the pre-9/11 balance of powers. The initial signs, such as the implementation of the new Homeland Security Office (see Appendix A) and the dismissal of some of the early challenges brought against provisions in the act, are not encouraging.

The act is extraordinary inclusive (see Appendix C). It touches on a variety of areas, including authorization of the following: presidential power to take title to the property of potential enemies; judicial use of classified information without announcing it publicly; increased funding for technical support centers; reimbursement of agencies for costs incurred in the war on terrorism; stiffening of penalties for chemical and bioterrorism acts; broader wiretap authority, covering everything from computer hacking to suspected enemies' communications, and permitting access to such information by police, defense, intelligence, and security officials; the sharing of grand jury testimony among government agencies, a practice previously prohibited; a grant of discretionary power to the government to search the offices of firms representing foreign countries for ninety days (extendable to one year); an expansion of the kinds of records that can be obtained from communication providers; disclosure of information by computer service agents to the government without informing consumers; a "delayed" notice of search warrants if they could have an "adverse effect" on an investigation; the ability to obtain business records, Internet messages, recorded telephone conversations as needed; a relaxing of surveillance standards and limitations; increased penalties for money laundering; a directive to the treasury secretary to require the disclosure by financial institutions of suspicious transactions, and a prohibition against notification of the individuals involved; an application of the preceding provisions to securities brokers and commodities traders; increases in the number of Border Patrol, Customs Service, and Immigration and Naturalization workers; greater funding for the protection of the nation's borders; a redefinition and strengthening of standards for admission to this country (including broadening definitions of terrorist activity to those who contribute, knowingly or unknowingly, to support for terrorism); an expansion in the monitoring of the activities of foreign students and their reasons for being in the United States; financial rewards for information on terrorism; the ability of the Federal Bureau of Investigation (FBI) and other security agencies to issue "National Security Letters" on their own initiative for telephone, financial, and other types of personal records; elimination of the cap on monies awarded victims of terrorism; increased payments to public security personnel; expansion of regional, federal, and state interagency and data bank sharing of information; trade sanctions against countries suspected of supporting or harboring terrorist organizations; increased prison terms for terrorist conspiracies and related acts; stronger criminal penalties for possession of biological toxins unless used for peaceful purposes; a limitation on access to and development of biological agents that could be used for illegal purposes; the Crime Identification Technology Act, to assist in locating potential terrorists; a "National Infrastructure Simulation and Analysis Center," to protect domestic targets from attack; and funds to be made available to federal agencies, states, and localities to begin to implement these programs.

This is only a partial list. It does suggest the extent of the Patriot Act and how many areas it touches on. Many such powers may well have been needed; what their limits are is yet to be decided. When one selects an individual area and investigates it in greater depth, the inclusiveness and potential expansions in governmental authority become clearer. For example, in relation to communications and technology, the emphasis of the act is primarily on control, criminalization, and expanded government power in obtaining once-protected information. It expands the obligations of providers to the government but does not require the identification of companies on any materials, thus protecting them from potential consumer suits. The act makes no new design mandates or technical upgrade demands on providers; it gives them immunity in exchange for their cooperation; and it does not require cable or other operations in the vast majority of cases to notify subscribers of the information on personal usage it has provided the government.

Surveillance authority was expanded, with taps on telephones and the use of "roving wiretaps" legalized; law enforcement agencies have powers to investigate remodeling the design of telephone networks to increase surveillance; secretive new and broader international surveillance techniques were removed from constitutional restrictions; the FBI was permitted the use of a new program (called "Carnivore") to intercept Internet communications; the Department of Justice was allowed to implement new and less restrictive rules for seizing information on computers in criminal cases; the seizure of decryption keys was legalized, a move earlier opposed by the Clinton administration; grand jury as well as wiretap information and oral communications were made accessible to a range of government, police, and intelligence agencies; the scope of subpoenas to be issued for providers' and subscribers' records for intercepting electronic messages was broadened; "emergency situations" were defined, in which personal data can be made immediately available to authorities; easier access was sanctioned for court orders involving taps and trace authority related to communication believed to be relevant to an ongoing investigation; the types of information and activities that can be subjected to subpoenas were extensively expanded; "sunset" provisions applicable to much of the surveillance power have been overlooked; federal courts have been allowed to issue wiretap authorizations and search warrants nationwide, rather than being confined to a specific court jurisdiction; the government is protected from legal action under "warrantless" searches and interceptions; civil lawsuits are prohibited against federal agencies or individuals for unauthorized interceptions or disclosures; government access to bank records is increased while bank officers are protected from legal liabilities; criminal penalties for computer fraud and hacking were expanded; compensation for private lawsuits claiming damage to computer systems was capped (with exceptions provided for official agencies, including those engaged in national security or administration of justice pursuits); the presentation of information and personal data by companies, government agencies, or providers of services is required if officially requested; and obstacles were increased for those attempting to make class action suits against computer hardware or software firms for alleged defects, abuse of service, or negligent design.

This information is included in one subsection of the Patriot Act. As can be seen, the range is broad, and the changes in fundamental access to all levels of private data and communications can be considered extensive. The rules have been rewritten. The results heavily favor the government and security agencies, in the name of fighting terrorism. But a balance is needed between individual rights and legitimate security needs; that balance has been shifted decisively in favor of the government.

Throughout the Patriot Act, special interest groups, or at least the most politically alert of these (the airlines and the communication industry, among them) managed to have inserted provisions—subsidizing grants, protections for financial liabilities—that either protected their interests or absolved them of legal penalties in answering government requests. In this regard, the act is close to a typical piece of legislation. In another and more important way, it is a powerful bill that redistributes power within the government and authorizes a series of actions—some needed, others pushing the boundaries of democratic restraint in a government's relationship with its citizenry—that will be forced (eventually) to meet the test of constitutional permissibility. The same may be said of the later bill to authorize the cabinet-level Department of Homeland Security.

A DEPARTMENT OF HOMELAND SECURITY FOR THE CABINET

On October 8, 2001, President Bush used his authority to establish by executive order an Office of Homeland Security to be part of the executive office and headed by an assistant to the president, chosen by him.

Later, Thomas Ridge, former governor of Pennsylvania, was appointed to the post.

The mandate was broad: "The mission of the office shall be to develop and coordinate the implementation of a comprehensive national strategy to secure the United States from terrorist threats or attacks." The office was authorized to do the following:

- develop, coordinate, and implement "a national strategy" to secure the United States from terrorist threats or attacks
- pursue a strategy to respond to and recover from such attacks
- coordinate the efforts of the executive branch, federal agencies, and state, local, and private entities
- collect and analyze all information in cooperation with other offices of government
- prioritize the collection of foreign intelligence in association with the Central Intelligence Agency (CIA)
- ensure that agencies and departments have the technological know-how sufficient to collect and process data and to respond to attacks
- detect and respond to biological, chemical, and radiological hazards
- coordinate and disseminate to all agencies relevant information relating to terrorism
- evaluate and reassess all federal emergency response plans
- coordinate training programs relative to terrorist acts among federal, state, and local agencies charged with responding to such attacks
- evaluate and coordinate public health capabilities, including vaccination policies and adequacy of vaccine and pharmaceutical stockpiles and hospital capacities
- assess and exchange information on policies relating to visas and shipments of cargoes and prevent the entrance of terrorist materials to the country, including chemical, biological, radiological, nuclear, and other explosive materials
- improve the security of U.S. borders, territorial waters, and airspace
- protect critical infrastructure from sabotage
- strengthen protection of energy production, utilities, transportation, telecommunications, and nuclear facilities
- protect special national events from attack
- protect livestock, agriculture, water, and food for consumption from terrorist attack

- ensure the rapid restoration of transportation systems, energy production, telecommunications, financial markets, and other critical infrastructure after disruption from terrorism
- reassess plans for the continuity of American government if attacked
- coordinate all government communications with the public, subject to direction by the White House, in a national emergency
- coordinate and assess budgetary, executive proposals, legal powers, and proposals to "detect, prepare for, prevent, protect against, and recover from" terrorist threats, and work with state, local, and private organizations in reviewing the adequacy of their approaches to such acts
- establish a "Homeland Security Council"—including the heads of virtually all of the relevant executive, military and security, economic and budgetary, and federal law enforcement agencies—to advise and assist the president in all aspects of homeland security
- provide the director of the Homeland Security Office with the power to classify materials as "top secret" (and therefore of restricted circulation) at his discretion

The office had an extraordinary charge, one meant to encompass as many conceivable terrorist issues as a bureaucratic agency could possibly handle or that its originators could imagine.

The mission of the new agency appeared clear enough. The presentation of what was expected and the indication of the power to be exercised by the new office were extensive, arguably well beyond what many believed could be accomplished by one agency. It was to be "the most extensive reorganization of the federal government in the past fifty years." By implicitly comparing the reorganization to the creation of the Department of Defense during the Truman administration in 1947 at the beginning of the cold war, the Bush administration was underlining how serious, long-term, and fundamental it saw the threat to American interests.

In its first year of operation, the new office appeared bogged down in intrabureaucratic politics. It lacked focus in meeting its extensive obligations and the resources and political will to achieve its very ambitious charge. So, in June 2002, the president decided to up the ante, declaring his intention to create a cabinet-level Department of Homeland Security. Some in the Congress had already been working on such a proposal. It would create a new federal bureaucracy of 170,000 people, take an estimated five to ten years to implement, and cost a projected $4.5 billion, according to the

General Accounting Office. The new department would affect in one form or another all agencies of the federal government. Although its mission was basically the same as in its incarnation as an executive office, the department was to be a monumental undertaking. The bill creating the new cabinet-level Department of Homeland Security would provide the administration with a mega-agency imbued with a list of new powers to fight the war on terrorism. The strongest argument for the agency was made by President Bush in transmitting the legislation to create the new department to the Congress. His words bear repeating at length:

> I propose the most extensive reorganization of the Federal Government since the 1940s by creating a new Department of Homeland Security. . . . by substantially transforming the current confusing patchwork of government activities into a single department whose primary mission is to secure our homeland. . .
>
> Today no Federal Government agency has homeland security as its primary mission. Responsibilities for homeland security are dispersed among more than 100 different entities of the Federal Government. America needs a unified homeland security structure that will improve protection against today's threats and be flexible enough to help meet the unknown threats of the future.

> The mission of the new Department would be to prevent terrorist attacks within the United States, to reduce America's vulnerability to terrorism, and to minimize the damage and recover from attacks that may occur. The Department of Homeland Security would mobilize and focus the resources of the Federal Government, State and local governments, the private sector, and the American people to accomplish its mission. . . .
>
> One department would secure our borders, transportation sector, ports, and critical infrastructure. . . . analyze homeland security intelligence from multiple sources, synthesize it with a comprehensive assessment of America's vulnerabilities, and take action to secure our highest risk facilities and systems. . . . coordinate communications with State and local governments, private industry, and the American people about threats and preparedness. . . . coordinate our efforts to secure the American people against bioterrorism and other weapons of mass destruction . . . help train and equip our first responders. . . . manage Federal emergency response activities.

Our goal is not to expand Government, but to create an agile organization that takes advantage of modern technology and management techniques to meet a new and constantly evolving threat. (Bush 2002b)

The new department would include four major divisions (although this did not begin to indicate the complexity of the new agency; see table 1):

 • Border and Transportation Security
 • Emergency Response and Preparedness
 • Chemical, Biological, and Nuclear Countermeasures
 • Information Analysis and Infrastructure Protection

Its "critical mission areas" included, in addition to the above, domestic counterterrorism, protection of critical domestic targets and key assets, defending against catastrophic threats, and intelligence gathering, assessment, and dissemination. In short, it was to protect the United States against all forms of terrorist activity.

To provide an idea of the complexity of this operation: the legislation would transfer to the new department the Coast Guard, the Customs Service, the Immigration and Naturalization Service, the Border Patrol, the Animal and Plant Inspection Service, the Transportation Security Administration, the Federal Emergency Management Agency, the Nuclear Emergency Search Team (from the Department of Energy), the National Pharmaceutical Stockpile, and the Secret Service. The following table only begins to indicate the scope of the executive branch's reorganization and the comprehensiveness of the new department's commitments.

Clearly a new superdepartment had been created. It would rank third in size among cabinet departments and fourth in budgetary appropriations. (The size of its projected budget was disputed, with critics arguing that the suggested figure was minimal for the job that needed to be done; see table 2.)

The new bill was not without controversy, although this focused more on subsidiary issues and proposals put into the bill, rather than on its mission. Whatever the objections and the reservations, the overwhelming majority of the Congress endorsed the legislation creating the new superdepartment for the Cabinet; the vote in the House was 295 to 132, in the Senate 90 to 9. On November 26, President Bush (2002c) signed the Homeland Security Act of 2002, referring to it as a "historic action to defend the United States and protect our citizens against the dangers of a new era."

TABLE 1. Organization of the Department of Homeland Security

Agency Transferred	From	Personnel	Budget
Border and Transportation Security			
INS/Border Patrol	Justice	39,459	$6.4 billion
Customs Service	Treasury	21,743	3.8 billion
Animal and Plant Health Inspection Service	Agriculture	8,620	1.1 billion
Transportation Security Agency	Transportation	41,300	4.8 billion
Coast Guard	Transportation	43,639	7.3 billion
FAA (some powers)	Transportation	TBD	TBD
Federal Protective Services	GSA	1,408	418 million
Secret Service	Treasury	6,111	1.2 billion
Emergency Preparedness and Response			
FEMA	Independent	5,135	6.2 billion
Chemical, biological, radiological, and nuclear response assets	HHS	150	2.1 billion
National Domestic Preparedness Office	FBI	15	2 million
Nuclear Incident Response	Energy	TBD	91 million
Chemical, Biological, and Nuclear Countermeasures			
Civilian Bio-Defense Research Programs	HHS	150	2 billion
Lawrence Livermore Lab	DOE	324	1.2 billion
National Biological Warfare Defense Analysis Center	New	TBD	420 million
Plum Island Center	USDA	124	25 million
Information Analysis and Infrastructure Protection			
Critical Infrastructure Assurance Office	Commerce	65	27 million
Federal Computer Incident Response Center	GSA	23	11 million
National Communications System	DoD	91	155 million
National Infrastructure Protection Center	FBI	795	151 million
National Infrastructure Simulation and Analysis Center	Energy	2	20 million

SOURCE: *CQ Weekly* 60, no. 23 (June 8, 2002): 1500–1502

TABLE 2. Homeland Security Department in Comparison with Existing Departments

Discretionary Budgets

Defense	$379.3 billion
HHS	65.3 billion
Education	50.3 billion
Homeland Security	37.5 billion
HUD	31.5 billion

Civilian Workforce

Defense	647,000
Veterans Affairs	226,000
Homeland Security	170,000
Treasury	148,000
HHS	134,000

SOURCE: *CQ Weekly* 60, no. 23 (June 8, 2002): 1503

There were objections to the bill raised by a small minority. Some felt the new department, in particular, and the overall approach taken by the Bush administration would be extraordinarily expensive and consequently add significantly to the national debt. Others thought the new bureaucracy much too large and unwieldy to the extent that it would actually pose a liability in achieving the ends sought.

The most fundamentally serious issue included in the new bill was the authorization of "preemptive attacks" by the United States against enemies to be identified at the discretion of the president. The rationale for such an approval was developed by Bush in a talk he delivered on June 1, 2002: "In the war against global terrorism, we will never forget that we are ultimately fighting for our democratic values and way of life. Freedom and fear are at war, and there will be no quick or easy end to this conflict. . . . we are forging new, productive international relationships and redefining existing ones in ways that meet the challenges of the twenty-first century" (Bush 2002c).

The president went on to say: "The United States has long maintained the option of preemptive actions to counter a sufficient threat to our national security. . . . the United States will, if necessary, act preemptively" (Bush 2002a).

However, it was not "preemptive" military strikes or major concerns with the nature, size, or mission of the new department that took center stage in the debate over its authorization. Rather, it was a series of last-minute proposals added to the bill establishing the department. House Republican leaders tacked on a provision establishing a research center for homeland security, with wording that indicated funds were essentially guaranteed to Texas A&M University, where the first George Bush's presidential library is located; an amendment allowing corporations using foreign tax shelters to contract with the new department; and another extending legal protections to companies developing faulty vaccines. When Senate Republicans and Democrats reacted strongly to these provisions, Trent Lott, Senate Republican minority leader at the time, posted a sign saying "Trust" and according to moderate Republicans offered an "ironclad promise" that these particular issues would be revisited after January 2003 (they were not). However, the House Republican leadership (Ohio's Tom DeLay, assistant majority leader, and Texas's Dick Armey, the retiring majority leader) indicated no such willingness to go along with the removal of these provisions.

Senator Olympia Snowe, a moderate Republican from Maine, attacked what she described as "eleventh-hour additions" put in by the House leadership "in the cloak of night." The "stealth provisions," she argued, prompted "considerable and justifiable alarm." These included removing liabilities from pharmaceutical companies for defective products, which would benefit Eli Lilly and other manufacturers of Thimerosal, used in children's vaccines to treat a range of illnesses from hepatitis B to diphtheria. Lilly and other manufacturers were charged in class action suits with exposing as many as thirty million children to mercury levels that far exceed those considered safe and that have allegedly caused autism in children; allegedly, these manufacturers knew of the potential risks as far back as the 1940s but did not stop including the preservative in its vaccines. These suits and the liabilities Lilly and other pharmaceuticals faced would be dismissed. The counterargument in favor of the provision indicated that it was intended to protect needed pharmaceutical research; it was inserted in the bill by the House leadership with the explanation that it was "something the White House wanted." Tellingly, representatives of the pharmaceutical industry served on Bush's staff and on the Homeland Security Council.

The limitation on corporations using offshore or foreign banks to avoid paying taxes resulting from government contracts was also rescinded by a "stealth provision." As Snowe said: "What kind of precedent does this set when just five months ago . . . we were working to crack down on the most egregious corporate perversions?" Nonetheless, citing pledges from party leaders to reconsider these issues, she voted in favor of the bill.

Representative Martin Frost, Democrat of Texas, the ranking member of the influential House Rules Committee and a member of the Select Committee on Homeland Security, also objected to a number of additions that he claimed had been "snuck into" the bill. These, he said, would actually "threaten the effectiveness" of the new department. Included in his list of concerns: civil service protections for employees of the new department would be eliminated, reinstituting a "spoils system" that permitted the appointment of ideological cronies to office; Freedom of Information Act guarantees would be weakened, a change administration had wanted even pre-9/11; labor unions were barred from representing department employees, an issue that raised strong objections among Democrats; and the careers of whistle-blowers reporting wrongdoing, operational failures, and corruption would be subject to the mercy of superiors. Frost, no doubt, knew that whistle-blowers already faced incredulity when exposing problems; they would now also face the loss of their jobs. And wrongdoers might actually be rewarded for poor performance. For example, Coleen Rowley of the FBI's Minneapolis office, was a whistle-blower who bucked authority in a futile attempt to alert the Washington headquarters to the pre-9/11 activities of one of the hijackers. Rowley was named one of three "persons of the year" (all whistle-blowers) by *Time* magazine in 2002; ironically, the FBI official who had blocked the investigation of Rowley's allegations about the terrorist later "received a special presidential award" (Krugman 2002).

The grand scale and power of the department were not the focal points of the congressional debate or the public reaction (to the extent that either existed). However, some legislators were outspoken in their opposition, including Congressman Peter Stark, Democrat of California. He referred to "the so-called anti-terror efforts" and warned against the "McCarthy-like hysteria spread by the administration." He questioned why a department of the size anticipated, one that Congress could not fully monitor, would be needed; he also wondered why the Bush administration initially opposed the idea of a new Cabinet department but then hastily announced its approval and pushed the bill through the Congress. Was this action "the product of political calculation rather than a legitimate, well-conceived strategy" and an effort "to create . . . [a] shadow government," an approach he found "unacceptable and inconsistent with the values upon which our nation was founded"? Stark concluded by saying he could not "support a bill that includes such attacks on our democratic system of government" (Stark 2002). It was one of the strongest attacks on the need for a new agency and on the intent and motivations of the Bush White House.

Finally, Senate Democratic Majority Leader Tom Daschle of South Dakota may well have been speaking for many when he addressed a press conference in the postelection Congress the day after the bill passed:

> If I could have voted 51–49 last night, I would have done so. There is . . . [a] compelling case to be made that we have to begin changing the infrastructure in our federal government to deal more effectively with the ominous threats that I think are very real. . . . we were put in a no-win situation. We had to make a choice between disastrous special interest legislation that had no business in the bill and a recognition that if we don't begin somehow, sometimes dealing effectively with the response organizationally to the threat, we'd deserve even more criticism. . . . So I, like many of my colleagues, made a decision. It wasn't one I felt good about, wasn't one I felt comfortable about. . . . But that's the fact. I mean, this is a lousy bill in so many respects. But at least it puts in place the foundation upon which I hope we can build a better governmental infrastructure to deal with the war on terror. (Daschle 2002)

COLLATERAL FALLOUT

A number of events were to take place after the signing of the Patriot Act and creation of the Department of Homeland Security—some directly associated, others indirectly. And various groups began to object to the developments.

For example, John Poindexter—the national security adviser to Ronald Reagan whose felony conviction in the Iran-contra affair was overturned by a federal appeals court—was appointed to a controversial position created in the Defense Department. According to the American Civil Liberties Union (ACLU):

> The program's new Office of Information Awareness is building a system called "Total Information Awareness" that would effectively provide government officials with immediate access to our personal information: all of our

communications (phone calls, emails and web searches), financial records, purchases, prescriptions, school records, medical records and travel history. Under this program, our entire lives would be catalogued and available to government officials. Leading this initiative is John Poindexter, the former Reagan era National Security Adviser who famously said it was his duty to withhold information from Congress. In his new post as Head of the Pentagon Office of Information Awareness, Poindexter has been quietly promoting the idea of creating "a virtual centralized database" that would have the "data-mining" power to pry into the most minute and intimate details of our private lives. . . . it is clear that this proposal goes too far. . . . the Defense Department program makes a mockery of . . . privacy protections and threatens to bulldoze the judicial and Congressional restraints that have protected the public against domestic spying. (American Civil Liberties Union 2002)

President Bush also authorized military tribunals for trials of terrorists. The trials could (and, in most cases, would) be conducted in secrecy. The administration also sanctioned the detention of alleged and suspected terrorists for indefinite periods, denied them access to lawyers or any legal protections, and relaxed rules of interrogations. Complaints about the potential violation of human rights began to be raised. The early court rulings supported administration policies with slight variations (some aliens were allowed by the courts to speak with a lawyer). The issues promised to be a judicial battleground far into the future.

The administration moved to increase the military's role in domestic security and law enforcement and to break down the barrier between international spying and domestic intelligence gathering (as permitted by the Congress), so that the rules regarding the latter became far more permissive. A series of distinctions in law that existed since the creation of the Department of Defense in 1947 basically were voided.

In November 2001, with strong bipartisan support, the Congress created the Terrorism Risk Protection Act, which provided for "a temporary industry risk spreading program to ensure the continued availability of commercial property and casualty insurance and reinsurance for terrorism-related risks to limit immediate market disruptions, encourage economic stabilization, and facilitate a transition to a viable market for private terrorism risk insurance" (H.R. 3210). Translated, this means that the federal government, rather than private insurance companies, would pay insurance claims up to

$100 billion annually for three years in response to terrorist attacks. President Bush pushed hard for the legislation, arguing that it would speed economic recovery.

A year later, in November 2002, his administration announced that it would privatize up to 850,000 jobs, approximately one-half of the federal workforce. Labor unions responded furiously, but the precedent and their inability to do much about it was contained in the Homeland Security Act.

Strains developed in U.S. ties with Saudi Arabia, which has been the principal source of our imported oil and allegedly supplied bases for attacking Iraq in the Persian Gulf War. The Americans claimed that the Saudis were now not doing enough to stem the flow of funds to Al Qaeda. It also was shown that a Saudi princess (and wife of the Saudi ambassador to the United States) had supplied funds, directly or indirectly, to organizations that reportedly had recruited for terrorist activities; her response was that "our religion tells us to donate to the needy." Bin Laden was a member of a Saudi royal family, and his fundamentalist movement began in Saudi Arabia; seventeen of the original nineteen hijackers had come from there. Members of the Saudi government and a wealthy elite of roughly 7,000 (in a population of 23 million, most mired in overwhelming poverty) contributed to Muslim fundamentalist schools and groups throughout the Middle East. The accusation was that such contributions were intended to buy off challengers to the Saudis' ruling monarchy; such schools taught only from the Koran and had been proven to be a recruiting ground for terrorists. A report by the Council on Foreign Relations gave substance to the charges. It concluded that the kingdom had "turned a blind eye" to such funding and, in fact, had given to "charities" that financed terrorist networks. The Saudis reacted by launching a public relations campaign, including press conferences, reports, and advertisements in the *New York Times* and *Washington Post* proclaiming their long friendship with and assistance to the United States; they promised to do more to crack down on terrorist activities and financing. As the Congress and the media became increasingly critical of the Saudis, the Bush administration chose not to be a part of the fight and was denounced for protecting them. Saudi officials in Riyadh were reportedly furious at the public attacks; its representative in Washington told the press: "At the end of the day we're [the United States and Saudi Arabia] not much different" (Magnus 2002; Dao 2002; Johnson and Rigen 2002).

Regarding other matters, attorneys began court battles over the legal rights of detainees held indefinitely without charges at Guantánamo Bay naval base in Cuba. The U.S. government claimed that the detention of six hundred individuals from forty countries was needed to keep the detainees away from the battlefield, to facilitate intelligence gathering, and to allow interrogations in an isolated setting. Since the prisoners were being held outside the United States, they did not fall under the jurisdiction of federal courts ("a foreign entity without property or presence in this country has no constitutional rights" [Lewis 2002]). Lawyers for those being held protested that "this is the first time we have sacrificed the rule of law." One of them elaborated: "The government says no court may hear from my clients. Guantánamo is unique? It is utterly outside the law. . . . The question is whether they must detain them consistent with the rule of law" (Lewis 2002). The early court decision showed an inclination to side with the government.

The Justice Department moved under its authority in the antiterrorism laws to break down the wall between law enforcement (considered a domestic area of concern) and intelligence gathering (an area considered to be international affairs) with regard to matters such as procedure, access, and interdepartmental use and proof. The rules regarding foreign intelligence are much less restrictive, offer significantly fewer safeguards to individuals, and place fewer restrictions on government activities than do domestic law enforcement prohibitions. Previously legal restrictions kept the two clearly separated. The Justice Department sought secret wiretaps, the exchange of information between prosecutors and foreign intelligence specialists, and the use of wiretaps and other information collected under the Foreign Surveillance Act. Again, the courts showed an early willingness to broadly interpret the laws in these areas (Liptak 2002; Denniston 2002; Lichtblau 2002).

Lending emphasis to a pattern of decisions that had become increasingly clear, Human Rights Watch issued a report detailing its reservations about U.S. actions taken in the months following the 9/11 attacks:

> Human Rights Watch is concerned about post–September 11 U.S. policy because it opposes military assistance to governments that have engaged in a pattern of gross violations of international human rights or humanitarian law. Several of the policy's potential beneficiaries have poor human rights records that include torture, political killings, illegal detentions, and religious

persecution, as well as histories of international humanitarian law violations, such as unlawful attacks on civilians. The modifications in the U.S. foreign military assistance program make it easier for known violators to acquire the tools of abuse, thus implicating the United States in abuses that result. The loosening of restrictions on military assistance also sets a dangerous example for arms exporting nations around the world. (Human Rights Watch 2002)

The U.S. assistance included "sales, financing, equipment grants . . . training . . . and covert assistance" (Human Rights Watch 2002).

Of most immediate significance, the "war on terrorism" morphed into plans for a war against Iraq. This was to become the main emphasis of the media and the preoccupation of the Bush administration. Saddam Hussein replaced Osama bin Laden as "International Enemy Number One." In fact, the war against Al Qaeda receded into the background as the president focused on replacing Hussein by military force—in concert with other countries under a United Nations mandate if possible, acting alone if necessary.

No one argued that Iraq or Hussein supported or supplied Al Qaeda. The two parties would be enemies, representing different interests—power, the state, repression, and authority against Islamic fundamentalism, jihad, and revolution—in any normal accounting. (Bin Laden would declare, however, that any U.S. attack against Iraq would constitute an assault on Islam in general, playing for advantage in the Arab world.) Hussein's brutality and ambitions had repeatedly been made clear, and the Persian Gulf War in the early 1990s had failed to displace him. Now the administration's talk was of removing Hussein through U.S. military actions and instituting democratic nation building in Iraq, the latter an approach that Bush had belittled as a UN responsibility (for any country) when first entering office. An Iraqi opposition put together by the administration was encouraged to develop plans for a postwar Iraq. The United Nations sent inspectors to Iraq to search for weapons of mass destruction, the administration's publicized basis for focusing on Iraq, and the U.S. military began to plan its campaign and develop a strategy for war.

The Defense Department announced it would need a budgetary supplement of $10 billion per year beyond current budget grants to prepare for a war against terrorism. The FBI, CIA, and other agencies indicated they would also need budget supplements for costs incurred in their war on terrorism. The second-ranking official in the Treasury Department estimated that a war against Iraq would cost $200 billion; he was later fired. The administration revised the cost estimate downward to a total estimated expenditure of $50 billion to $60 billion. The White House's policy was to de-emphasize and, to the extent possible, avoid any discussions of the war's costs. The economy was in a slump, the stock market hit lows not seen in decades, and unemployment was up. In effect, the economy was in trouble regardless of any additional funds needed for the antiterrorism campaign.

This was a sore point with the president. The conventional wisdom was that his father had lost a chance for a second term in 1992 immediately after the Gulf War (and despite strong personal ratings) for failing to pay attention to domestic issues and specifically an economy in trouble. When George W. Bush campaigned for candidates in the 2002 congressional elections, he emphasized national security issues and ignored economic conditions. It worked. The Democrats were unable to make domestic problems the center of the campaign but were promising to do so in the 2004 presidential election.

The White House was also aware of the Vietnam experience. When a political battle becomes a choice between "guns and butter"—that is, appropriations for war against funds for domestic concerns—clearly the military and security needs will win out. There are consequences, however. Budget deficits soar, social welfare policies and domestic commitments and priorities suffer, and public discontent rises. The administration of Lyndon Johnson faced these problems in the 1960s; combined with an unpopular and ineffective war, they were enough to keep the president from seeking a second full term. The Bush Administration was doing its best to avoid such choices and public debate.

Any estimates of the cost of a war on terrorism, however they are calculated, are likely to fall far short of the actual expenditures. These estimates do not include side payments to allied governments, warlords, and others in a position to make a contribution to the fight. The administration's approach in Afghanistan and its strategy in preparations for any war against Iraq involved ignoring such costs (Woodward 2002). In addition, there would be the delivery of military hardware and other material support as well as emergency aid to friendly nations and groups important to the war effort. Absent from the books or official estimates, for the most part, would be the negotiation of favorable trade and economic agreements and the forgiveness of debts in exchange for military bases, intelligence help, and back-channel support with Turkey, Pakistan, Afghanistan, Israel, Jordan, Algeria, and countries in the Middle East. The hidden costs would serve to push up actual expenditures for any war, and all would eventually have an impact on domestic policy and politics.

As attention turned to a potential war with Iraq, "an independent bipartisan group" was formed in the United States, under the White House's direction, to "engage in advocacy and educational efforts in the United States and Europe" aimed at "freeing the Iraqi people from tyranny" (Schmitt 2002). The group included a number of present and former members of Congress (for example, Senators John McCain and Joseph I. Lieberman, considered the architects of the new Department of Homeland Security; former Representative Newt Gingrich; and George P. Shultz, former secretary of state and presidential adviser). The membership of the group was considered to be "hawkish."

There was of course, much more happening post-9/11, most of it beneath the radar of the public's attention and its level of concern. The promise was of considerably more to come. The wars—that of Al Qaeda and generalized international terrorism threats, as well as the battle against Iraq—had just begun. Their full consequences were yet to be felt.

CONCLUSION

The "war on terrorism" has enormous implications for the practice of American democracy. An examination of the legislative grants of power contained in the Patriot Act and of the creation of a megadepartment in the cabinet to take the lead in the war on terrorism provides some idea as to what is at stake. The institutional structure of the government has been redrawn. Extraordinary powers have been given to the president and government officials to fight terrorism. The potential assault on the individual rights previously enjoyed by American citizens raises alarms. Constitutional issues that need clarification are involved; the civil, legal, and procedural guarantees under which the country has operated so far need protection. All serve to indicate how fundamental are the changes under way. The consequences of these actions can have broad implications for the future practice of democracy.

The mainstream press—the *New York Times* and the *Washington Post* can serve as examples—have done a good job in reporting these developments and providing at least some indication of their potential significance. The Internet offers access to all of the major published reports and the deliberations (such as they are) of the Congress. Few seem interested. There has been no broad public debate over policy, and no realistic alternatives to the administration's agenda have been proposed. National security is, in truth, a sensitive area; Americans clearly feel uncomfortable discussing the subject, and the strong tendency is to give discretion to the administration in power, following its lead. In an increasingly volatile and globalized time, this deference can be disastrous, and the ultimate impact within the American democratic system may well exceed anything yet envisaged.

REFERENCES

American Civil Liberties Union. 2002. "Stop the Government Plan to Mine Our Privacy," November 26. On-line at http://www.aclu.org/Privacy/Privacy.cfm?ID?113237C~ 130, accessed February 20, 2003.

Bush, George W. 2001a. *National Security Strategy.* "Address at the National Cathedral," September 14. On-line at http://www.whitehouse.gov/nsc/nss.html, accessed May 15, 2003.

Bush, George W. 2001b. "President Urges Readiness and Patience," September 15. Online at http://www.whitehouse.gov/news/releases/2001/09/print/20010915, accessed January 16, 2003.

Bush, George W. 2002a. *National Security Strategy.* "I. Overview of America's International Strategy," June 1. On-line at http://www.whitehouse.gov/nsc/nss.html, accessed May 15, 2003.

Bush, George W. 2002b. "Message to the Congress of the United States by President Bush," June 18. On-line at http://www.whitehouse.gov/news/releases/2002/06/20020618-5.html, accessed December 12, 2002.

Bush, George W. 2002c. "President Bush Signs Homeland Security Act," November 26. On-line at http://www.whitehouse.gov, accessed February 26, 2003.

Dao, James. 2002. "Saudis Brush Aside Criticism of Record against Terrorism." *New York Times,* November 27, A1.

Daschle, Thomas. 2002. "Majority Leader Daschle Holds Regular New Conference," November 25. On-line at http://democrats.senate.gov/~dpc/releases/2002B21706.html, accessed February 24, 2003.

Denniston, Luke. 2002. "Tribunal Expands Wiretap Authority." *Boston Globe,* November 19, A1.

Human Rights Watch. 2002. "United States: Dangerous Dealings" 14, no. 1 (G), February. On-line at http://www.hrw.org/reports/2002/usmil/USass0202.pdf, accessed January 14, 2003.

Johnson, David, and James Rigen. 2002. "9/11 Report Says Saudi Arabia Links Went Unexcused." *New York Times*, December 2, A18.

Krugman, Paul. 2002. "The Good Guys," December 24. On-line at http://NYTimes.com/2002/12/24/opinion/24krug.html, accessed December 25, 2002.

Lewis, Neal A. 2002. "Threats and Responses: Detainees; Guantanamo Prisoners Seek to See Families and Lawyers." *New York Times*, December 3, A22.

Lichtblau, Eric. 2002. "U.S. Acts to Use New Power to Spy on Possible Terrorists." *New York Times*, November 24, A1.

Liptak, Adam. 2002. "In the Name of Security, Privacy for Me, Not Thee." *New York Times*, November 24, sec. 4, p. 1.

Magnus, Christopher. 2002. "Saudi Tries to Calm U.S. Opinion." *New York Times*, December 4, A1.

Schmitt, Eric. 2002. "New Group Will Lobby for Change in Iraqi Rule," *New York Times*, November 15, A16.

Stark, Pete. 2002. "Opposing HR 5005, the Homeland Security Act of 2002," July 26. On-line at http://www.house.gov.stark/documents/107th/homesecr.html, accessed May 15, 2003.

U.S. Congress, House of Representatives. 2001a. House Joint Resolution 63, "Declaring a state of war exists between the United States and any entity . . . ," September 13. On-line at http://Thomas.loc.gov/home/terrorlegprev.htm, accessed June 2, 2003.

U.S. Congress, House of Representatives. 2001b. H.R. 3162, "Summary of USA PATRIOT ACT as passed in the U.S. House of Representatives," October 26. On-line at http://Thomas.loc.gov/cgi-bin/bdquery/z?d107:HR03162:@@@D&summ2=1&, accessed May 15, 2003.

U.S. Congress, House of Representatives. 2002. H.R. 3210. Terrorism Risk Protection Act, "To ensure the continued financial capacity of insurers to provide coverage for risks from terrorism," November 26. On-line at http://Thomas.loc.gov/hometerrorlog.htm, accessed June 2, 2003.

Woodward, Bob. 2002. *Bush at War*. New York: Simon and Schuster.

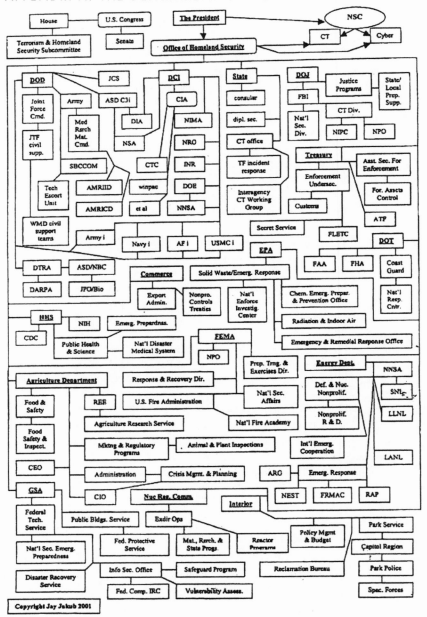

SOURCE: Office of Homeland Security.

APPENDIX B. ORGANIZATION OF THE DEPARTMENT OF HOMELAND SECURITY

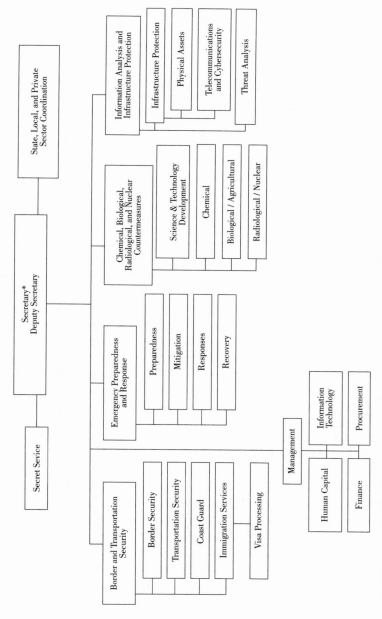

* Legal/Congressional/Public Affairs included in Office of the Secretary of Homeland Security.

APPENDIX C: SUMMARY OF USA PATRIOT ACT

SUMMARY AS OF: 10/24/2001—Passed House, without amendment.

Uniting and Strengthening America by Providing Appropriate Tools Required to Intercept and Obstruct Terrorism (USA PATRIOT ACT) Act of 2001—Title I: Enhancing Domestic Security Against Terrorism—Establishes in the Treasury the Counterterrorism Fund.

(Sec. 102) Expresses the sense of Congress that: (1) the civil rights and liberties of all Americans, including Arab Americans, must be protected, and that every effort must be taken to preserve their safety; (2) any acts of violence or discrimination against any Americans be condemned; and (3) the Nation is called upon to recognize the patriotism of fellow citizens from all ethnic, racial, and religious backgrounds.

(Sec. 103) Authorizes appropriations for the Federal Bureau of Investigation's (FBI) Technical Support Center.

(Sec. 104) Authorizes the Attorney General to request the Secretary of Defense to provide assistance in support of Department of Justice (DOJ) activities relating to the enforcement of Federal criminal code (code) provisions regarding the use of weapons of mass destruction during an emergency situation involving a weapon (currently, chemical weapon) of mass destruction.

(Sec. 105) Requires the Director of the U.S. Secret Service to take actions to develop a national network of electronic crime task forces throughout the United States to prevent, detect, and investigate various forms of electronic crimes, including potential terrorist attacks against critical infrastructure and financial payment systems.

(Sec. 106) Modifies provisions relating to presidential authority under the International Emergency Powers Act to: (1) authorize the President, when the United States is engaged in armed hostilities or has been attacked by a foreign country or foreign nationals, to confiscate any property subject to U.S. jurisdiction of a foreign person, organization, or country that he determines has planned, authorized, aided, or engaged in such hostilities or attacks (the rights to which shall vest in such agency or person as the President may designate); and (2) provide that, in any judicial review of a determination made under such provisions, if the determination was based on classified information such information may be submitted to the reviewing court ex parte and in camera.

Title II: Enhanced Surveillance Procedures—Amends the Federal criminal code to authorize the interception of wire, oral, and electronic communications for the production of evidence of: (1) specified chemical weapons or terrorism offenses; and (2) computer fraud and abuse.

(Sec. 203) Amends rule 6 of the Federal Rules of Criminal Procedure (FRCrP) to permit the sharing of grand jury information that involves foreign intelligence or counterintelligence with Federal law enforcement, intelligence, protective, immigration, national defense, or national security officials (such officials), subject to specified requirements.

Authorizes an investigative or law enforcement officer, or an attorney for the Government, who, by authorized means, has obtained knowledge of the contents of any wire, oral, or electronic communication or evidence derived therefrom to disclose such contents to such officials to the extent that such contents include foreign intelligence or counterintelligence.

Directs the Attorney General to establish procedures for the disclosure of information (pursuant to the code and the FRCrP) that identifies a United States person, as defined in the Foreign Intelligence Surveillance Act of 1978 (FISA).

Authorizes the disclosure of foreign intelligence or counterintelligence obtained as part of a criminal investigation to such officials.

(Sec. 204) Clarifies that nothing in code provisions regarding pen registers shall be deemed to affect the acquisition by the Government of specified foreign intelligence information, and that procedures under FISA shall be the exclusive means by which electronic surveillance and the interception of domestic wire and oral (current law) and electronic communications may be conducted.

(Sec. 205) Authorizes the Director of the FBI to expedite the employment of personnel as translators to support counter-terrorism investigations and operations without regard to applicable Federal personnel requirements. Requires: (1) the Director to establish such security requirements as necessary for such personnel; and (2) the Attorney General to report to the House and Senate Judiciary Committees regarding translators.

(Sec. 206) Grants roving surveillance authority under FISA after requiring a court order approving an electronic surveillance to direct any person to furnish necessary information, facilities, or technical assistance in circumstances where the Court finds that the actions of the surveillance target may have the effect of thwarting the identification of a specified person.

(Sec. 207) Increases the duration of FISA surveillance permitted for non-U.S. persons who are agents of a foreign power.

(Sec. 208) Increases (from seven to 11) the number of district court judges designated to hear applications for and grant orders approving electronic surveillance. Requires that no fewer than three reside within 20 miles of the District of Columbia.

(Sec. 209) Permits the seizure of voice-mail messages under a warrant.

(Sec. 210) Expands the scope of subpoenas for records of electronic communications to include the length and types of service utilized, temporarily assigned network addresses, and the means and source of payment (including any credit card or bank account number).

(Sec. 211) Amends the Communications Act of 1934 to permit specified disclosures to Government entities, except for records revealing cable subscriber selection of video programming from a cable operator.

(Sec. 212) Permits electronic communication and remote computing service providers to make emergency disclosures to a governmental entity of customer electronic communications to protect life and limb.

(Sec. 213) Authorizes Federal district courts to allow a delay of required notices of the execution of a warrant if immediate notice may have an adverse result and under other specified circumstances.

(Sec. 214) Prohibits use of a pen register or trap and trace devices in any investigation to protect against international terrorism or clandestine intelligence activities that is conducted solely on the basis of activities protected by the first amendment to the U.S. Constitution.

(Sec. 215) Authorizes the Director of the FBI (or designee) to apply for a court order requiring production of certain business records for foreign intelligence and international terrorism investigations. Requires the Attorney General to report to the House and Senate Intelligence and Judiciary Committees semi-annually.

(Sec. 216) Amends the code to: (1) require a trap and trace device to restrict recoding or decoding so as not to include the contents of a wire or electronic communication; (2) apply a court order for a pen register or trap and trace devices to any person or entity providing wire or electronic communication service in the United States whose assistance may facilitate execution of the order; (3) require specified records kept on any pen register or trap and trace device on a packet-switched data network of a provider of electronic communication service to the public; and (4) allow a trap and trace device to identify the source (but not the contents) of a wire or electronic communication.

(Sec. 217) Makes it lawful to intercept the wire or electronic communication of a computer trespasser in certain circumstances.

(Sec. 218) Amends FISA to require an application for an electronic surveillance order or search warrant to certify that a significant purpose (currently, the sole or main purpose) of the surveillance is to obtain foreign intelligence information.

(Sec. 219) Amends rule 41 of the FRCrP to permit Federal magistrate judges in any district in which terrorism-related activities may have occurred to issue search warrants for searches within or outside the district.

(Sec. 220) Provides for nationwide service of search warrants for electronic evidence.

(Sec. 221) Amends the Trade Sanctions Reform and Export Enhancement Act of 2000 to extend trade sanctions to the territory of Afghanistan controlled by the Taliban.

(Sec. 222) Specifies that: (1) nothing in this Act shall impose any additional technical obligation or requirement on a provider of a wire or electronic communication service or other person to furnish facilities or technical assistance; and (2) a provider of such service, and a landlord, custodian, or other person who furnishes such facilities or technical assistance, shall be reasonably compensated for such reasonable expenditures incurred in providing such facilities or assistance.

(Sec. 223) Amends the Federal criminal code to provide for administrative discipline of Federal officers or employees who violate prohibitions against unauthorized disclosures of information gathered under this Act. Provides for civil actions against the United States for damages by any person aggrieved by such violations.

(Sec. 224) Terminates this title on December 31, 2005, except with respect to any particular foreign intelligence investigation beginning before that date, or any particular offense or potential offense that began or occurred before it.

(Sec. 225) Amends the Foreign Intelligence Surveillance Act of 1978 to prohibit a cause of action in any court against a provider of a wire or electronic communication service, landlord, custodian, or any other person that furnishes any information, facilities, or technical assistance in accordance with a court order or request for emergency assistance under such Act (for example, with respect to a wiretap).

Title III: International Money Laundering Abatement and Anti-Terrorist Financing Act of 2001—International Money Laundering Abatement and Financial Anti-Terrorism Act of 2001—Sunsets this Act after the first day of FY 2005 if Congress enacts a specified joint resolution to that effect.

Subtitle A: International Counter Money Laundering and Related Measures—Amends Federal law governing monetary transactions to prescribe procedural guidelines under which the Secretary of the Treasury (the Secretary) may require domestic financial institutions and agencies to take specified measures if the Secretary finds that reasonable grounds exist for concluding that jurisdictions, financial institutions, types of accounts, or transactions operating outside or within the United States, are of primary money laundering concern. Includes mandatory disclosure of specified information relating to certain correspondent accounts.

(Sec. 312) Mandates establishment of due diligence mechanisms to detect and report money laundering transactions through private banking accounts and correspondent accounts.

(Sec. 313) Prohibits U.S. correspondent accounts with foreign shell banks.

(Sec. 314) Instructs the Secretary to adopt regulations to encourage further cooperation among financial institutions, their regulatory authorities, and law enforcement authorities, with the specific purpose of encouraging regulatory authorities and law enforcement authorities to share with financial institutions information regarding individuals, entities, and organizations engaged in or reasonably suspected (based on credible evidence) of engaging in terrorist acts or money laundering activities. Authorizes such regulations to create procedures for cooperation and information sharing on matters specifically related to the finances of terrorist groups as well as their relationships with international narcotics traffickers.

Requires the Secretary to distribute annually to financial institutions a detailed analysis identifying patterns of suspicious activity and other investigative insights derived from suspicious activity reports and investigations by Federal, State, and local law enforcement agencies.

(Sec. 315) Amends Federal criminal law to include foreign corruption offenses as money laundering crimes.

(Sec. 316) Establishes the right of property owners to contest confiscation of property under law relating to confiscation of assets of suspected terrorists.

(Sec. 317) Establishes Federal jurisdiction over: (1) foreign money launderers (including their assets held in the United States); and (2) money that is laundered through a foreign bank.

(Sec. 319) Authorizes the forfeiture of money laundering funds from interbank accounts. Requires a covered financial institution, upon request of the appropriate Federal banking agency, to make available within 120 hours all pertinent information related to anti-money laundering compliance by the institution or its customer. Grants the Secretary summons and subpoena powers over foreign banks that maintain a correspondent bank in the United States. Requires a covered financial institution to terminate within ten business days any correspondent relationship with a foreign bank after receipt of written notice that the foreign bank has failed to comply with certain judicial proceedings. Sets forth civil penalties for failure to terminate such relationship.

(Sec. 321) Subjects to record and report requirements for monetary instrument transactions: (1) any credit union; and (2) any futures commission merchant, commodity trading advisor, and commodity pool operator registered, or required to register, under the Commodity Exchange Act.

(Sec. 323) Authorizes Federal application for restraining orders to preserve the availability of property subject to a foreign forfeiture or confiscation judgment.

(Sec. 325) Authorizes the Secretary to issue regulations to ensure that concentration accounts of financial institutions are not used to prevent association of the identity of an individual customer with the movement of funds of which the customer is the direct or beneficial owner.

(Sec. 326) Directs the Secretary to issue regulations prescribing minimum standards for financial institutions regarding customer identity in connection with the opening of accounts.

Requires the Secretary to report to Congress on: (1) the most timely and effective way to require foreign nationals to provide domestic financial institutions and agencies with appropriate and accurate information; (2) whether to require foreign nationals to obtain an identification number (similar to a Social Security or tax identification number) before opening an account with a domestic financial institution; and (3) a system for domestic financial institutions and agencies to review Government agency information to verify the identities of such foreign nationals.

(Sec. 327) Amends the Bank Holding Company Act of 1956 and the Federal Deposit Insurance Act to require consideration of the effectiveness of a company or companies in combating money laundering during reviews of proposed bank shares acquisitions or mergers.

(Sec. 328) Directs the Secretary take reasonable steps to encourage foreign governments to require the inclusion of the name of the originator in wire transfer instructions sent to the United States and other countries, with the information to remain with the transfer from its origination until the point of disbursement. Requires annual progress reports to specified congressional committees.

(Sec. 329) Prescribes criminal penalties for Federal officials or employees who seek or accept bribes in connection with administration of this title.

(Sec. 330) Urges U.S. negotiations for international cooperation in investigations of money laundering, financial crimes, and the finances of terrorist groups, including record sharing by foreign banks with U.S. law enforcement officials and domestic financial institution supervisors.

Subtitle B: Bank Secrecy Act Amendments and Related Improvements—Amends Federal law known as the Bank Secrecy Act to revise requirements for civil liability immunity for voluntary financial institution disclosure of suspicious activities. Authorizes the inclusion of suspicions of illegal activity in written employment references.

(Sec. 352) Authorizes the Secretary to exempt from minimum standards for anti-money laundering programs any financial institution not subject to certain regulations governing financial recordkeeping and reporting of currency and foreign transactions.

(Sec. 353) Establishes civil penalties for violations of geographic targeting orders and structuring transactions to evade certain recordkeeping requirements. Lengthens the effective period of geographic targeting orders from 60 to 180 days.

(Sec. 355) Amends the Federal Deposit Insurance Act to permit written employment references to contain suspicions of involvement in illegal activity.

(Sec. 356) Instructs the Secretary to: (1) promulgate regulations requiring registered securities brokers and dealers, futures commission merchants, commodity trading advisors, and commodity pool operators, to file reports of suspicious financial transactions; (2) report to Congress on the role of the Internal Revenue Service in the administration of the Bank Secrecy Act; and (3) share monetary instruments transactions records upon request of a U.S. intelligence agency for use in the conduct of intelligence or counterintelligence activities, including analysis, to protect against international terrorism.

(Sec. 358) Amends the Right to Financial Privacy Act to permit the transfer of financial records to other agencies or departments upon certification that the records are relevant to intelligence or counterintelligence activities related to international terrorism.

Amends the Fair Credit Reporting Act to require a consumer reporting agency to furnish all information in a consumer's file to a government agency upon certification that the records are relevant to intelligence or counterintelligence activities related to international terrorism.

(Sec. 359) Subjects to mandatory records and reports on monetary instruments transactions any licensed sender of money or any other person who engages as a business in the transmission of funds, including through an informal value transfer banking system or network (e.g., hawala) of people facilitating the transfer of money domestically or internationally outside of the conventional financial institutions system.

(Sec. 360) Authorizes the Secretary to instruct the United States Executive Director of each international financial institution to use his or her voice and vote to: (1) support the use of funds for a country (and its institutions) which contributes to U.S. efforts against international terrorism; and (2) require an auditing of disbursements to ensure that no funds are paid to persons who commit or support terrorism.

(Sec. 361) Makes the existing Financial Crimes Enforcement Network a bureau in the Department of the Treasury.

(Sec. 362) Directs the Secretary to establish a highly secure network in the Network that allows financial institutions to file certain reports and receive alerts and other information regarding suspicious activities warranting immediate and enhanced scrutiny.

(Sec. 363) Increases to $1 million the maximum civil penalties (currently $10,000) and criminal fines (currently $250,000) for money laundering. Sets a minimum civil penalty and criminal fine of double the amount of the illegal transaction.

(Sec. 364) Amends the Federal Reserve Act to provide for uniform protection authority for Federal Reserve facilities, including law enforcement officers authorized to carry firearms and make warrantless arrests.

(Sec. 365) Amends Federal law to require reports relating to coins and currency of more than $10,000 received in a nonfinancial trade or business.

(Sec. 366) Directs the Secretary to study and report to Congress on: (1) the possible expansion of the currency transaction reporting requirements exemption system; and (2) methods for improving financial institution utilization of the system as a way of reducing the submission of currency transaction reports that have little or no value for law enforcement purposes.

Subtitle C: Currency Crimes—Establishes as a bulk cash smuggling felony the knowing concealment and attempted transport (or transfer) across U.S. borders of currency and monetary instruments in excess of $10,000, with intent to evade specified currency reporting requirements.

(Sec. 372) Changes from discretionary to mandatory a court's authority to order, as part of a criminal sentence, forfeiture of all property involved in certain currency reporting offenses. Leaves a court discretion to order civil forfeitures in money laundering cases.

(Sec. 373) Amends the Federal criminal code to revise the prohibition of unlicensed (currently, illegal) money transmitting businesses.

(Sec. 374) Increases the criminal penalties for counterfeiting domestic and foreign currency and obligations.

(Sec. 376) Amends the Federal criminal code to extend the prohibition against the laundering of money instruments to specified proceeds of terrorism.

(Sec. 377) Grants the United States extraterritorial jurisdiction where: (1) an offense committed outside the United States involves an access device issued, owned, managed, or controlled by a financial institution, account issuer, credit card system member, or other entity within U.S. jurisdiction; and (2) the person committing the offense transports, delivers, conveys, transfers to or through, or otherwise stores, secrets, or holds within U.S. jurisdiction any article used to assist in the commission of the offense or the proceeds of such offense or property derived from it.

Title IV: Protecting the Border—Subtitle A: Protecting the Northern Border—Authorizes the Attorney General to waive certain Immigration and Naturalization Service (INS) personnel caps with respect to ensuring security needs on the Northern border.

(Sec. 402) Authorizes appropriations to: (1) triple the number of Border Patrol, Customs Service, and INS personnel (and support facilities) at points of entry and along the Northern border; and (2) INS and Customs for related border monitoring technology and equipment.

(Sec. 403) Amends the Immigration and Nationality Act to require the Attorney General and the Federal Bureau of Investigation (FBI) to provide the Department of State and INS with access to specified criminal history extracts in order to determine whether or not a visa or admissions applicant has a criminal history. Directs the FBI to provide periodic extract updates. Provides for confidentiality.

Directs the Attorney General and the Secretary of State to develop a technology standard to identify visa and admissions applicants, which shall be the basis for an electronic system of law enforcement and intelligence sharing system available to consular, law enforcement, intelligence, and Federal border inspection personnel.

(Sec. 404) Amends the Department of Justice Appropriations Act, 2001 to eliminate certain INS overtime restrictions.

(Sec. 405) Directs the Attorney General to report on the feasibility of enhancing the Integrated Automated Fingerprint Identification System and other identification systems to better identify foreign individuals in connection with U.S. or foreign criminal investigations before issuance of a visa to, or permitting such person's entry or exit from, the United States. Authorizes appropriations.

Subtitle B: Enhanced Immigration Provisions—Amends the Immigration and Nationality Act to broaden the scope of aliens ineligible for admission or deportable due to terrorist activities to include an alien who: (1) is a representative of a political, social, or similar group whose political endorsement of terrorist acts undermines U.S. antiterrorist efforts; (2) has used a position of prominence to endorse terrorist activity, or to persuade others to support such activity in a way that undermines U.S. antiterrorist efforts (or the child or spouse of such an alien under specified circumstances); or (3) has been associated with a terrorist organization and intends to engage in threatening activities while in the United States.

(Sec. 411) Includes within the definition of "terrorist activity" the use of any weapon or dangerous device.

Redefines "engage in terrorist activity" to mean, in an individual capacity or as a member of an organization, to: (1) commit or to incite to commit, under circumstances indicating an intention to cause death or serious bodily injury, a terrorist activity; (2) prepare or plan a terrorist activity; (3) gather information on potential targets for terrorist activity; (4) solicit funds or other things of value for a terrorist activity or a terrorist organization (with an exception for lack of knowledge); (5) solicit any individual to engage in prohibited conduct or for terrorist organization membership (with an exception for lack of knowledge); or (6) commit an act that the actor knows, or reasonably should know, affords material support, including a safe house, transportation, communications, funds, transfer of funds or other material financial benefit, false documentation or identification, weapons (including chemical, biological, or radiological weapons), explosives, or training for the commission of a terrorist activity; to any individual who the actor knows or reasonably should know has committed or plans to commit a terrorist activity; or to a terrorist organization (with an exception for lack of knowledge).

Defines "terrorist organization" as a group: (1) designated under the Immigration and Nationality Act or by the Secretary of State; or (2) a group of two or more individuals, whether related or not, which engages in terrorist-related activities.

Provides for the retroactive application of amendments under this Act. Stipulates that an alien shall not be considered inadmissible or deportable because of a relationship to an organization that was not designated as a terrorist organization prior to enactment of this Act. States that the amendments under this section shall apply to all aliens in exclusion or deportation proceedings on or after the date of enactment of this Act.

Directs the Secretary of State to notify specified congressional leaders seven days prior to designating an organization as a terrorist organization. Provides for organization redesignation or revocation.

(Sec. 412) Provides for mandatory detention until removal from the United States (regardless of any relief from removal) of an alien certified by the Attorney General as a suspected terrorist or threat to national security. Requires release of such alien after seven days if removal proceedings have not commenced, or the alien has not been charged with a criminal offense. Authorizes detention for additional periods of up to six months of an alien not likely to be deported in the reasonably foreseeable future only if release will threaten U.S. national security or the safety of the community or any person. Limits judicial review to habeas corpus proceedings in the U.S. Supreme Court, the U.S. Court of Appeals for the District of Columbia, or any district court with jurisdiction to entertain a habeas corpus petition. Restricts to the U.S. Court of Appeals for the District of Columbia the right of appeal of any final order by a circuit or district judge.

(Sec. 413) Authorizes the Secretary of State, on a reciprocal basis, to share criminal- and terrorist-related visa lookout information with foreign governments.

(Sec. 414) Declares the sense of Congress that the Attorney General should: (1) fully implement the integrated entry and exit data system for airports, seaports, and land border ports of entry with all deliberate speed; and (2) begin immediately establishing the Integrated Entry and Exit Data System Task Force. Authorizes appropriations.

Requires the Attorney General and the Secretary of State, in developing the integrated entry and exit data system, to focus on the use of biometric technology and the development of tamper-resistant documents readable at ports of entry.

(Sec. 415) Amends the Immigration and Naturalization Service Data Management Improvement Act of 2000 to include the Office of Homeland Security in the Integrated Entry and Exit Data System Task Force.

(Sec. 416) Directs the Attorney General to implement fully and expand the foreign student monitoring program to include other approved educational institutions like air flight, language training, or vocational schools.

(Sec. 417) Requires audits and reports on implementation of the mandate for machine readable passports.

(Sec. 418) Directs the Secretary of State to: (1) review how consular officers issue visas to determine if consular shopping is a problem; and (2) if it is a problem, take steps to address it, and report on them to Congress.

Subtitle C: Preservation of Immigration Benefits for Victims of Terrorism—Authorizes the Attorney General to provide permanent resident status through the special immigrant program to an alien (and spouse, child, or grandparent under specified circumstances) who was the beneficiary of a petition filed on or before September 11, 2001, to grant the alien permanent residence as an employer-sponsored immigrant or of an application for labor certification if the petition or application was rendered null because of the disability of the beneficiary or loss of employment due to physical damage to, or destruction of, the business of the petitioner or applicant as a direct result of the terrorist attacks on September 11, 2001 (September attacks), or because of the death of the petitioner or applicant as a direct result of such attacks.

(Sec. 422) States that an alien who was legally in a nonimmigrant status and was disabled as a direct result of the September attacks may remain in the United States until his or her normal status termination date or September 11, 2002. Includes in such extension the spouse or child of such an alien or of an alien who was killed in such attacks. Authorizes employment during such period.

Extends specified immigration-related deadlines and other filing requirements for an alien (and spouse and child) who was directly prevented from meeting such requirements as a result of the September attacks respecting: (1) nonimmigrant status and status revision; (2) diversity immigrants; (3) immigrant visas; (4) parolees; and (5) voluntary departure.

(Sec. 423) Waives, under specified circumstances, the requirement that an alien spouse (and child) of a U.S. citizen must have been married for at least two years prior to such citizen's death in order to maintain immediate relative status if such citizen died as a direct result of the September attacks. Provides for: (1) continued family-sponsored immigrant eligibility for the spouse, child, or unmarried son or daughter of a permanent resident who died as a direct result of such attacks; and (2) continued eligibility for adjustment of status for the spouse and child of an employment-based immigrant who died similarly.

(Sec. 424) Amends the Immigration and Nationality Act to extend the visa categorization of "child" for aliens with petitions filed on or before September 11, 2001, for aliens whose 21st birthday is in September 2001 (90 days), or after September 2001 (45 days).

(Sec. 425) Authorizes the Attorney General to provide temporary administrative relief to an alien who, as of September 10, 2001, was lawfully in the United States and was the spouse, parent, or child of an individual who died or was disabled as a direct result of the September attacks.

(Sec. 426) Directs the Attorney General to establish evidentiary guidelines for death, disability, and loss of employment or destruction of business in connection with the provisions of this subtitle.

(Sec. 427) Prohibits benefits to terrorists or their family members.

Title V: Removing Obstacles to Investigating Terrorism—Authorizes the Attorney General to pay rewards from available funds pursuant to public advertisements for assistance to DOJ to combat terrorism and defend the Nation against terrorist acts, in accordance with procedures and regulations established or issued by the Attorney General, subject to specified conditions, including a prohibition against any such reward of $250,000 or more from being made or offered without the personal approval of either the Attorney General or the President.

(Sec. 502) Amends the State Department Basic Authorities Act of 1956 to modify the Department of State rewards program to authorize rewards for information leading to: (1) the dismantling of a terrorist organization in whole or significant part; and (2) the identification or location of an individual who holds a key leadership position in a terrorist organization. Raises the limit on rewards if the Secretary of State determines that a larger sum is necessary to combat terrorism or defend the Nation against terrorist acts.

(Sec. 503) Amends the DNA Analysis Backlog Elimination Act of 2000 to qualify a Federal terrorism offense for collection of DNA for identification.

(Sec. 504) Amends FISA to authorize consultation among Federal law enforcement officers regarding information acquired from an electronic surveillance or physical search in terrorism and related investigations or protective measures.

(Sec. 505) Allows the FBI to request telephone toll and transactional records, financial records, and consumer reports in any investigation to protect against international terrorism or clandestine intelligence activities only if the investigation is not conducted solely on the basis of activities protected by the first amendment to the U.S. Constitution.

(Sec. 506) Revises U.S. Secret Service jurisdiction with respect to fraud and related activity in connection with computers. Grants the FBI primary authority to investigate specified fraud and computer related activity for cases involving espionage, foreign counter-intelligence, information protected against unauthorized disclosure for reasons of national defense or foreign relations, or restricted data, except for offenses affecting Secret Service duties.

(Sec. 507) Amends the General Education Provisions Act and the National Education Statistics Act of 1994 to provide for disclosure of educational records to the Attorney General in a terrorism investigation or prosecution.

Title VI: Providing for Victims of Terrorism, Public Safety Officers, and Their Families —Subtitle A: Aid to Families of Public Safety Officers—Provides for expedited payments for: (1) public safety officers involved in the prevention, investigation, rescue, or recovery efforts related to a terrorist attack; and (2) heroic public safety officers. Increases Public Safety Officers Benefit Program payments.

Subtitle B: Amendments to the Victims of Crime Act of 1984—Amends the Victims of Crime Act of 1984 to: (1) revise provisions regarding the allocation of funds for compensation and assistance, location of compensable crime, and the relationship of crime victim compensation to means-tested Federal benefit programs and to the September 11th victim compensation fund; and (2) establish an antiterrorism emergency reserve in the Victims of Crime Fund.

Title VII: Increased Information Sharing for Critical Infrastructure Protection—Amends the Omnibus Crime Control and Safe Streets Act of 1968 to extend Bureau of Justice Assistance regional information sharing system grants to systems that enhance the investigation and prosecution abilities of participating Federal, State, and local law enforcement agencies in addressing multi-jurisdictional terrorist conspiracies and activities. Authorizes appropriations.

Title VIII: Strengthening the Criminal Laws Against Terrorism—Amends the Federal criminal code to prohibit specific terrorist acts or otherwise destructive, disruptive, or violent acts against mass transportation vehicles, ferries, providers, employees, passengers, or operating systems.

(Sec. 802) Amends the Federal criminal code to: (1) revise the definition of "international terrorism" to include activities that appear to be intended to affect the conduct of government by mass destruction; and (2) define "domestic terrorism" as activities that occur primarily within U.S. jurisdiction, that involve criminal acts dangerous to human life, and that appear to be intended to intimidate or coerce a civilian population, to influence government policy by intimidation or coercion, or to affect government conduct by mass destruction, assassination, or kidnapping.

(Sec. 803) Prohibits harboring any person knowing or having reasonable grounds to believe that such person has committed or to be about to commit a terrorism offense.

(Sec. 804) Establishes Federal jurisdiction over crimes committed at U.S. facilities abroad.

(Sec. 805) Applies the prohibitions against providing material support for terrorism to offenses outside of the United States.

(Sec. 806) Subjects to civil forfeiture all assets, foreign or domestic, of terrorist organizations.

(Sec. 808) Expands: (1) the offenses over which the Attorney General shall have primary investigative jurisdiction under provisions governing acts of terrorism transcending national boundaries; and (2) the offenses included within the definition of the Federal crime of terrorism.

(Sec. 809) Provides that there shall be no statute of limitations for certain terrorism offenses if the commission of such an offense resulted in, or created a foreseeable risk of, death or serious bodily injury to another person.

(Sec. 810) Provides for alternative maximum penalties for specified terrorism crimes.

(Sec. 811) Makes: (1) the penalties for attempts and conspiracies the same as those for terrorism offenses; (2) the supervised release terms for offenses with terrorism predicates any term of years or life; and (3) specified terrorism crimes Racketeer Influenced and Corrupt Organizations statute predicates.

(Sec. 814) Revises prohibitions and penalties regarding fraud and related activity in connection with computers to include specified cyber-terrorism offenses.

(Sec. 816) Directs the Attorney General to establish regional computer forensic laboratories, and to support existing laboratories, to develop specified cyber-security capabilities.

(Sec. 817) Prescribes penalties for knowing possession in certain circumstances of biological agents, toxins, or delivery systems, especially by certain restricted persons.

Title IX: Improved Intelligence—Amends the National Security Act of 1947 to require the Director of Central Intelligence (DCI) to establish requirements and priorities for foreign intelligence collected under the Foreign Intelligence Surveillance Act of 1978 and to provide assistance to the Attorney General (AG) to ensure that information derived from electronic surveillance or physical searches is disseminated for efficient and effective foreign intelligence purposes. Requires the inclusion of international terrorist activities within the scope of foreign intelligence under such Act.

(Sec. 903) Expresses the sense of Congress that officers and employees of the intelligence community should establish and maintain intelligence relationships to acquire information on terrorists and terrorist organizations.

(Sec. 904) Authorizes deferral of the submission to Congress of certain reports on intelligence and intelligence-related matters until: (1) February 1, 2002; or (2) a date after February 1, 2002, if the official involved certifies that preparation and submission on February 1, 2002, will impede the work of officers or employees engaged in counter-terrorism activities. Requires congressional notification of any such deferral.

(Sec. 905) Requires the AG or the head of any other Federal department or agency with law enforcement responsibilities to expeditiously disclose to the DCI any foreign intelligence acquired in the course of a criminal investigation.

(Sec. 906) Requires the AG, DCI, and Secretary of the Treasury to jointly report to Congress on the feasibility and desirability of reconfiguring the Foreign Asset Tracking Center and the Office of Foreign Assets Control to provide for the analysis and dissemination of foreign intelligence relating to the financial capabilities and resources of international terrorist organizations.

(Sec. 907) Requires the DCI to report to the appropriate congressional committees on the establishment and maintenance of the National Virtual Translation Center for timely and accurate translation of foreign intelligence for elements of the intelligence community.

(Sec. 908) Requires the AG to provide a program of training to Government officials regarding the identification and use of foreign intelligence.

Title X: Miscellaneous—Directs the Inspector General of the Department of Justice to designate one official to review allegations of abuse of civil rights, civil liberties, and racial and ethnic profiling by government employees and officials.

(Sec. 1002) Expresses the sense of Congress condemning acts of violence or discrimination against any American, including Sikh-Americans. Calls upon local and Federal law enforcement authorities to prosecute to the fullest extent of the law all those who commit crimes.

(Sec. 1004) Amends the Federal criminal code with respect to venue in money laundering cases to allow a prosecution for such an offense to be brought in: (1) any district in which the financial or monetary transaction is conducted; or (2) any district where a prosecution for the underlying specified unlawful activity could be brought, if the defendant participated in the transfer of the proceeds of the specified unlawful activity from that district to the district where the financial or monetary transaction is conducted.

States that: (1) a transfer of funds from one place to another, by wire or any other means, shall constitute a single, continuing transaction; and (2) any person who conducts any portion of the transaction may be charged in any district in which the transaction takes place.

Allows a prosecution for an attempt or conspiracy offense to be brought in the district where venue would lie for the completed offense, or in any other district where an act in furtherance of the attempt or conspiracy took place.

(Sec. 1005) First Responders Assistance Act—Directs the Attorney General to make grants to State and local governments to improve the ability of State and local law enforcement, fire department, and first responders to respond to and prevent acts of terrorism. Authorizes appropriations.

(Sec. 1006) Amends the Immigration and Nationality Act to make inadmissible into the United States any alien engaged in money laundering. Directs the Secretary of State to develop a money laundering watchlist which: (1) identifies individuals worldwide who are known or suspected of money laundering; and (2) is readily accessible to, and shall be checked by, a consular or other Federal official before the issuance of a visa or admission to the United States.

(Sec. 1007) Authorizes FY 2002 appropriations for regional antidrug training in Turkey by the Drug Enforcement Administration for police, as well as increased precursor chemical control efforts in South and Central Asia.

(Sec. 1008) Directs the Attorney General to conduct a feasibility study and report to Congress on the use of a biometric identifier scanning system with access to the FBI integrated automated fingerprint identification system at overseas consular posts and points of entry to the United States.

(Sec. 1009) Directs the FBI to study and report to Congress on the feasibility of providing to airlines access via computer to the names of passengers who are suspected of terrorist activity by Federal officials. Authorizes appropriations.

(Sec. 1010) Authorizes the use of Department of Defense funds to contract with local and State governments, during the period of Operation Enduring Freedom, for the performance of security functions at U.S. military installations.

(Sec. 1011) Crimes Against Charitable Americans Act of 2001—Amends the Telemarketing and Consumer Fraud and Abuse Prevention Act to cover fraudulent charitable solicitations. Requires any person engaged in telemarketing for the solicitation of charitable contributions, donations, or gifts to disclose promptly and clearly the purpose of the telephone call.

(Sec. 1012) Amends the Federal transportation code to prohibit States from licensing any individual to operate a motor vehicle transporting hazardous material unless the Secretary of Transportation determines that such individual does not pose a security risk warranting denial of the license. Requires background checks of such license applicants by the Attorney General upon State request.

(Sec. 1013) Expresses the sense of the Senate on substantial new U.S. investment in bioterrorism preparedness and response.

(Sec. 1014) Directs the Office for State and Local Domestic Preparedness Support of the Office of Justice Programs to make grants to enhance State and local capability to prepare for and respond to terrorist acts. Authorizes appropriations for FY 2002 through 2007.

(Sec. 1015) Amends the Crime Identification Technology Act of 1998 to extend it through FY 2007 and provide for antiterrorism grants to States and localities. Authorizes appropriations.

(Sec. 1016) Critical Infrastructures Protection Act of 2001—Declares it is U.S. policy: (1) that any physical or virtual disruption of the operation of the critical infrastructures of the United States be rare, brief, geographically limited in effect, manageable, and minimally detrimental to the economy, human and government services, and U.S. national security; (2) that actions necessary to achieve this policy be carried out in a public-private partnership involving corporate and non-governmental organizations; and (3) to have in place a comprehensive and effective program to ensure the continuity of essential Federal Government functions under all circumstances.

Establishes the National Infrastructure Simulation and Analysis Center to serve as a source of national competence to address critical infrastructure protection and continuity through support for activities related to counterterrorism, threat assessment, and risk mitigation.

Defines critical infrastructure as systems and assets, whether physical or virtual, so vital to the United States that their incapacity or destruction would have a debilitating impact on security, national economic security, national public health or safety, or any combination of those matters.

Authorizes appropriations.

SOURCE: http://thomas.loc.gov/cgi-bin/bdquery/z?d107:HR03162:@@@D&summ2=1&, accessed May 15, 2003.

Are We Safer Today?: Organizational Responses to Terrorism

The awful events of 9/11 have been used to explain, characterize, and justify a vast range of actions in the public and private sectors. A great deal of the analysis has focused on questions of war and peace, and has been dominated by the paradigms of military science or international relations. Perhaps more that anything else, however, 9/11 has been used to indicate the shortcomings of the public sector. Following those events, analysts have offered any number of explanations for the failure of government to detect the terrorist threats, and to prevent the attacks on New York and Washington. Politicians and many in the public accused American government of failing in one of its most basic duties—protecting the people.

A principal dimension of both blame and response has been organizational. At one level, individual organizations such as the Federal Bureau of Investigation (FBI) and the Central Intelligence Agency (CIA) have been considered culpable because of their own internal failings to provide adequate warning of the possible attacks. In particular, these organizations have been characterized as excessively bureaucratic, with internal cultures that suppressed information sharing and discussion (Henniger 2002). The failings of these organizations follow other disasters, such as the Aldrich Ames and Robert Hanssen spy scandals, to present an image of federal intelligence and law enforcement organizations that are incapable of performing their tasks in even a minimally acceptable manner.

In addition to problems within individual organizations, the failures of those organizations to communicate with one another and with other law enforcement agencies have played a major role in the success of the terrorist attacks, according to some critics (Mitchell 2002). A new cliché—that these organizations have not been able to "connect the dots"—was spawned: although each of them had a part of the picture, there was no ready mechanism for creating a more complete understanding of the threats facing the country while the attacks were being planned. Major reorganizations and reforms of the organizational structure of the federal government have been proposed by the Bush administration as components of the extensive set of remedies for the difficulties that were encountered, and many of these reforms are now in the process of implementation.

This essay will examine the claims of organizational failures as a major contributing factor in the success of the 9/11 attacks but will focus primarily on the organizational *responses* to those events. Coordination and the allied concept of policy coherence are philosophers' stones in the study of the public sector, pursued as the means to solve problems in the design and delivery of public programs (Jennings and Crane 1994; Peters 2002) for decades, if not for centuries. One assumption of the Bush administration in responding to 9/11 is that if government can be made to function in a more coherent manner, then it will be able to address the domestic security challenges faced by the United States more effectively. The question is whether this simple and often repeated assumption about governing is adequate to address the significant public problems of coping with terrorism. Further, if this strategy is successful, at what cost will it be successful?

ORGANIZATIONS AS SOLUTIONS AND PROBLEMS

Terrorism and the presence of threats to "homeland security" within the borders of the United States pose a series of organizational issues in government (Campbell Public Affairs Institute 2002), both within and among organizations. Although investigating operations in extremis may expose more readily the importance of organizations, this approach should be considered a general means of understanding policy making and behavior within government. Many aspects of governing organizations are the building blocks that shape behavior and define the nature of problems as well as the available solutions to those problems (Seidman 1998). Thus, understanding how policy will function requires an understanding of the collection of public organizations that surround that policy area, and the way in which they function individually and as a group.[1]

The problems encountered within the FBI itself and several other organizations were to a great extent those frequently encountered in failures of organizational intelligence and communication (Wilensky 1967; Stinchcombe 1990). The FBI very much depends on its field staff, as do most law enforcement organizations; the agents in charge of the various local offices have been characterized as the "barons" of this system. Despite that apparent decentralization, there was increased centralization of control, and the center of the organization appeared unwilling to accept the information generated by or the judgment of the field staff in the lead-up to 9/11 (Dorning 2002). This behavior at the FBI was an empirical example of the assessment of modern organizations made some years ago by Victor Thompson, who argued (1961) that modern organizations would be characterized by the concentration of information at the bottom of their hierarchies and the concentration of decision at the top of those structures.

As well as the simple failure of the organization to process information coming from below, the problems within the FBI demonstrated the difficulties that organizations often have in coping with novelty. Organizations have programmed responses to situations and tend to code any new situation into the categories already existing in their programs (Simon 1969). Somewhat paradoxically, the more successful an organization is in institutionalizing—and therefore in creating a common value system and perspective for its members—the greater the difficulties it may encounter when it is faced with either novelty or change (see March 1999). Over several decades the FBI was very successful internally and externally in creating such an organizational identity, albeit not always a positive one (Garrow 1981), and in inculcating a set of values into the members of the organization (Kessler 1993). That success made identifying and coping with new types of situations more difficult than would have been the case for less "successful" structures.

Another way of conceptualizing the failure to deal with novelty is to examine it through the lens of organizational learning. As the environment of organizations continues to change, organizations often do not learn or draw lessons from their own failures—and successes (Olsen and Peters 1996; Rose 1993). The clearest locus for learning with respect to 9/11 would have been the bombing of the Murrah Federal Building in Oklahoma City in 1995. This attack demonstrated the vulnerability of the United States to terrorism. There was some response from the FBI and other law enforcement organizations, albeit primarily in monitoring domestic right-wing organizations such as militias. There was less effort put into learning more broadly about domestic vulnerability or in conceptualizing the multiple possible sources of attacks against individuals and structures within the country itself. Further, the politicization of organizational issues as a result of terrorism, especially after 9/11, will make reflection and learning more difficult, given the immense pressures for an immediate reaction to the perceived threats (Senge 1990).

Organizational Culture

In addition to the familiar organizational problems that might be expected from any large organization, public or private, the particular value system of the FBI indicates yet another organizational basis for failures in coping with terrorism. The FBI is primarily a law enforcement organization, with procedures designed to identify crimes and to apprehend the perpetrators. As Benjamin and Simon (2002, 297) point out, "Deeply rooted habits came into play, leading the FBI to favor crime solving and not terrorism prevention." The internal culture and the basic mission of the FBI, therefore, emphasizes maintaining the chain of evidence more than it does detection and prevention.[2] For this organization to be successful in preventing terrorism, it would have had to become more concerned with prospective detection and then move toward a more active stance in prevention. Even after the Oklahoma City bombing, the organization does not appear to have been willing to make this change in the way that it approached its responsibilities.

These problems with communications and hierarchy within this single organization were important in understanding the failures of the FBI to make more effective use of the information that was available. The center of the organization apparently refused to accept the incoming information that did not fit its own gestalt, to the point of attempting to punish field agents who would not passively accept decisions at the center that disregarded what they considered to be serious threats. The FBI, and to some extent also the CIA, had suffered a number of organizational embarrassments in the months prior to 9/11. Some internal issues had begun to take the gloss off the organization, but the magnitude of the problems did not become clear until after the events.

Coordination and Coherence

As significant as the problems within individual organizations were in contributing to the failures of intelligence and response, the coordination problems were at least as significant and also involved a cultural element. The difficulties that these organizations encountered in working with each other should not have been unexpected. Rather, the findings from most studies of attempts to make policies and programs more coherent are that organizations in the public sector resist coordination (Bardach 1998; Considine 2002). Organizations find ways of resisting attempts from political and administrative leaders who want to create more efficient and effective services for the public. Even in the vitally important areas of defense and law enforcement, coordination appears difficult.[3]

Public organizations appear uncooperative and reluctant to engage in collaborative activities with other organizations for a number of reasons, including the perceived need to protect their "turf." Through those turf battles, organizations attempt to protect, or expand, their budget and to maintain their control of certain policy domains without interference from other public organizations (see Wilson 1989; Downs 1967). While turf battles are endemic in bureaucracies, they may be especially virulent when they involve the control of information. Public bureaucracies are predominantly information processing structures; any organization that possesses information has power over others that do not. Given that coordination preventing 9/11 would have involved sharing information, the cooperation problems—in hindsight—seem more readily predictable. Some analysts (Benjamin and Simon 2002) have argued that the FBI was almost obsessive about the protection of their information as a resource for maintaining its operational independence from other federal organizations and even from the Department of Justice, of which it has been at least nominally a component.

Several explanations exist for the behavior of organizations faced with the need to cooperate or the opportunity to cooperate. When organizations are attempting to protect their budgetary and policy positions, they often find it difficult to cooperate with organizations that are most similar to themselves. We might hypothesize that organizations with similar functions are those most likely to impinge upon each other's policy space and budgetary allocations (Downs 1967). Very dissimilar organizations may be less threatening, and greater cooperation may therefore be possible, with the goals and instruments used being more complementary than competitive. For instance, the FBI may find it easier to cooperate with the Centers for Disease Control (CDC) around the anthrax scare than to cooperate with other federal law enforcement organizations.

An alternative explanation for patterns of coordination would be that organizations with similar knowledge bases and similar methodologies for addressing issues would be more likely to cooperate than would organizations with more diverse values. For example, in studies of social policy, health organizations have been found to be more willing to cooperate with other health organizations than with different types of social programs, even though all the programs were involved in providing services to the same needy clients. In this model of cooperation, organizations find it easier to work with other members of their own "epistemic community" and to share information and clients within the context of their common value basis and a common paradigm of intervention.

Organizations may fail to cooperate with other organizations for less avaricious reasons. The members of most public organizations have a sincere belief in what they do and how they do it; not likely to be welcomed are any suggestions that they might achieve their own goals, and broader collective goals for the society, more readily through cooperation than through persisting with their own pattern of action. Perhaps even more basically, organizations have tunnel vision about what constitutes public problems and public goals. Organizations don blinders, constraining their capacity to recognize and cope with new challenges and opportunities.

The failures to cooperate among the intelligence organizations that might collectively have uncovered the plot to attack the World Trade Center and the Pentagon appear to have been the result of a number of factors. One of the most important was the clash of the distinctive cultures of the organizations that should have been involved at the federal level. As already noted, the FBI has a law enforcement culture and a "tough guy" image. The internal culture of the CIA, on the other hand, has been described as that of "loopy spy stories" (*Nation* 2002). Even if the two organizations had been successful on their own, they should not have been expected to work well together (Risen 2002).

In addition, each of these organizations simply did not seem to believe that the other was particularly relevant for dealing with the issue of terrorism. The FBI was interested primarily in collecting any domestic evidence that they could develop and may not have recognized the importance of the international contacts of the CIA. Similarly, the CIA is forbidden by its charter from being involved in domestic surveillance and may not have considered the importance of the information held by the FBI for understanding the full picture of terrorist threats to the United States. To "connect the dots," the participants in the process must first know of the existence of the dots and their potential impact.

While it is easy to focus any blame for the shortcomings of the intelligence and law enforcement organizations on those organizations themselves, there are also external factors involved in their failures. In order for any organization to perform its functions adequately, it must have the financial and personnel resources necessary to do that job. The evidence appears clear that this was not the case for the CIA and the National Security Agency (NSA) after the end of the cold war (Risen and Johnston 2002a). The number of agents, translators, and computers necessary may not have been available to the agencies. Their tasks were more difficult in many ways after the cold war, with the absence of a clear enemy that played the game of international politics and military action by relatively conventional rules. These agencies were no longer sure of the individuals and groups they should have been watching; they needed to be able to cast the net wider.

Perhaps the greatest failing of the intelligence and law enforcement communities around 9/11 was the failure of imagination. Given that no one had considered seriously the possibilities of the type of attack that occurred, the evidence that was available to analysts in the various law enforcement organizations did not telegraph the pattern that is now so obvious. Whether greater resources or better coordination of the agencies could have overcome that fundamental conceptual problem will never be known. It is clear, however, that the combination of inadequate resources, inadequate coordination, and failure of imagination made the attacks easier than anyone would have anticipated.

ORGANIZATIONAL ANSWERS

The question now is whether organizational reforms—individually and collectively—will be able to resolve the perceived problems in managing responses to terror. In any case of responding to a severe shock such as that already experienced, organizations have a tendency to learn lessons too well and to prepare for what has already happened. Generals frequently are accused of fighting the last war when they fail to take into account technological or strategic improvements in their prospective enemy, and the "generals" fighting the war on terror may face some of the same organizational problems. While there is a great deal that might be asked about reform of the individual organizations involved in providing improved protection, I will focus on the problems and prospects of coordination among the organizations and on the role of the new Department of Homeland Security as a coordinator.

Is coordination the answer to the questions that have been advanced about domestic terrorism? The above discussion focused on the problems of coordination between the FBI and the CIA. There are, however, broader issues concerning how best to organize the federal government to cope with problems of terrorism and homeland security. Those two organizations have very important roles to play in combating terrorism, but any number of other agencies and bureaus within the federal government can also contribute to that effort. Further, state and local law enforcement agencies are crucial actors, and they believe that their information and warnings were not adequately considered prior to September 11.

The Department of Homeland Security

The most obvious organizational response of the Bush administration has been to create first the Office and then the Department of Homeland Security (DHS). The legislation for this reorganization will produce the largest change in the federal bureaucracy since the National Security Act of 1947, which created the Department of Defense and much of the rest of the current national security apparatus in the United States. This new organizational creation represents one approach to achieving improved collaboration among the participants in the process. It assumes that if all the relevant actors are under one organizational roof, they will work well together and perform more effectively in achieving the goals of the organization—in this case, the dominant goal of improved protection against terrorism.

The Department of Homeland Security, as approved by Congress, draws upon several dozen preexisting organizations in the federal government, from eight cabinet departments and several independent executive organizations. The range of cabinet departments involved—from Agriculture to Treasury—will be reflected in equally diverse organizational and professional values as well as organizational cultures, and in differences in standard operating procedures. A move into the new department upsets established patterns of thought, not to mention established organizational communications, and challenges the "logics of appropriateness" (March and Olsen 1989) that had been created within the organizations over some period of time.

The problems of adapting to a new culture may be most marked for organizations with images of themselves as domestic and rather peaceable; they will now be directly involved in what is styled a "war" on terror in a department that has at least some trappings of a military style. Organizations such as the Coast Guard, which are multipurpose, will be asked to emphasize one of their several roles and to devalue the others. Even enforcement organizations such as the U.S. Customs Service that are being moved into this new structure may find that the strengthened emphasis on strict enforcement and the "war" aspects of their new mission will challenge the understandings that have built up within the organization.[4]

GENERAL CONCERNS

While this umbrella approach to coordination appears on its face plausible, it also raises a number of organizational and policy questions. This pattern is very much in the tradition of creating "super-ministries" that attempt to position all relevant activities under a single department roof and give power to one leader to achieve the desired results. This seems logical but also sets up the possibility of creating immense managerial problems. For example, Australia went through a major process of amalgamation of departments, and the Canadian government created Human Resources Canada in the mid-1990s in an attempt to put the full range of social services into one megadepartment, eliminating the redundancies and lacunae that appeared in the system prior to that time (Aucoin and Bakvis 1993). These were noble efforts, but they also created several administrative monsters that are difficult, if not impossible, for any one minister (or limited set of ministers) and the top civil servants to control effectively.

The U.S. creation of a megadepartment for security will also impose an immense transition cost on government and require some time to become effective. For example, the 1947 reforms creating the Department of Defense took years, perhaps decades, to create a smoothly performing defense structure.[5] The organizations comprising that department were all military and might have been expected to have a relatively easy time in harmonizing their activities. In addition to relatively similar values, these organizations were composed of people accustomed to following orders given by their hierarchical superiors. When they were told to cooperate, they might have been expected to do so, but in reality they often did not, at least not willingly.

Depending upon one's perspective on the politics of coordination, the homeland security task may be more or less daunting than the task facing the military managers over fifty years ago. The military services, natural competitors to some extent, continue to vie for funding and for the definition of priorities, so collaboration may have been difficult. On the other hand, coordination may be more difficult if components for a new entity are drawn from such a disparate set of policy areas as is the case with the new department.

Even if this transition for DHS should be smoother than that to the Department of Defense, it will still be difficult. From the simplest issues such as getting letterhead and phone lists to more complex issues of management and policy, creating a new organization is not easy. Indeed, it may be more difficult to merge organizations than to create a new organization from scratch. There is a need in a merger to resocialize individuals, many or most of whom may have been very happy doing things the way they had been done for some time. Any change is threatening, and organizational change is no different, so managers should expect resistance. Appeals to patriotism and national security will help, but no one should be so naive as to expect that these values will overcome resistance to change and some genuine commitment to the old ways of doing things.

In addition to the transitional issues of moving from a more decentralized and disaggregated system of delivering services, there are other organizational issues arising from the attempts to combat the terrorist threat. Any organizational structure in the public sector (and almost certainly in the private sector as well) is imperfect (Seidman 1998). The design of structures involves making trade-offs and choices about which values to attempt to maximize and which to assign lower priorities (see Goodin 1996; U.S. General Accounting Office 2002c). The issues that appear most relevant for consideration here are the following: What is in? What is out? What does it mean to the rest of government? The last question extends the discussion and asks what are the consequences of these reforms for the range of other services that the American people expect from the federal government.

The first question involves which organizations are included and why. Some of these entities were obvious candidates for inclusion in a new Department of Homeland Security. For example, the Federal Emergency Management Agency (FEMA) has obvious responsibilities for managing any domestic crisis, whether caused by nature or by human action. Likewise, the U.S. Customs Service has important roles in protecting the borders and interdicting any threats before problems are created within the national boundaries; the General Services Administration (GSA), through its protective services staff, has duties to protect federal buildings from possible attacks. These organizations were already performing important activities related to domestic security and law enforcement and would fit into DHS with little difficulty.

On the other hand, transferring a significant portion of the Animal and Plant Health Inspection Service (APHIS) from Agriculture to this new department appears to put this fish very much out of its water. The office being transferred has responsibilities for research and prevention for some diseases that could be instruments for bioterror, but it is not clear that the organizational style of this organization will fit well with Customs or with Immigration and Naturalization. The tasks that this organization has been performing have simply been unrelated to the overall mission and style of the cabinet-level structure being created. If the purpose is to create a common identity and a common commitment to the overall goal of security, bringing together such disparate structures may delay, rather than hasten, the creation of a more integrated approach to domestic security in the federal government.

The selection of organizations to be in this larger entity reflects one of the long-standing issues in the study of public organizations. Theorists going back at least to Gulick and Urwick (1937) have said that "like should go with like," but public organizations tend to have a number of different dimensions, and making the choice of what "like" is in these cases may not be obvious. The Coast Guard is perhaps the clearest case of a multipurpose organization, having some responsibilities in defense, environmental protection, maritime safety and regulation, interdiction of drugs and illegal immigrants, and aiding in collecting customs, among others. Putting this organization in any one of at least five possible cabinet-level departments will be correct in some ways but incorrect in others.

One major justification for government reorganization efforts, as Lester Salamon has pointed out (1981), is to alter the flow of communications coming to the organization that is being moved. For example, in the case of the Coast Guard, moving the organization out the Department of Transportation will mean that it will receive much less information about transportation safety but that it will receive more communications about domestic security and protecting the maritime borders of the United States. That shift in information flows will naturally affect the priorities that the organization assigns to various of its tasks (Wood 2002) and ultimately may affect the nature of the organization itself—e.g., potentially making the internal style of the Coast Guard more military and perhaps less "client friendly" when dealing with ordinary boaters and shippers.

WHAT IS OUT?

While the legislation creating the Department of Homeland Security did envision a sprawling and seemingly unwieldy structure, there are still some elements that appear left out of the mix. Given the initial discussion of the roots of 9/11 in this chapter, the most glaring possible omission is a significant intelligence function. This omission could leave the new DHS hanging around, waiting for something to happen, but better prepared to pick up the pieces. That is perhaps too negative a characterization of the prospective role of the department, since there are certainly a number of preventive elements included in its structure, but "working blind" may happen, without a strong intelligence function to identify the nature and source of threats. For example, the Customs Service has the task of interdicting dangerous cargoes, but it could do its job better if it can be sure of good intelligence about what may be on the way to the United States.

Although so much of the blame for 9/11 has been associated with intelligence lapses, the new department, somewhat paradoxically, does not contain any elements of intelligence collection or coordination. There is a good deal of discussion in Washington about the need to create a new "admiral of the fleet" who could bring together the FBI and the CIA, as well as discussion of removing the domestic intelligence function from the FBI entirely and creating a new domestic analogue to the CIA (Risen and Johnston 2002b). Should these changes be adopted, however, the result would still be intelligence collection performed independently of the organizations in Homeland Security, which nominally has responsibility for protecting the public. It is assumed that the prevailing ethos of a commonly fought war will facilitate the flow of information, but that assumption is perhaps too optimistic, given the cultures of most intelligence organizations, in which sharing information is considered anathema.

The choice of a coordinator of coordinators is indeed one of the problems often encountered in designing coordination systems or other systems of collaboration. We can design institutions that pull together a range of services and structures that should interact with one another, but that structure will inevitably leave out something—in this case, something potentially crucial to the success of the entire policy system. There is, of course, a certain logic to grouping the intelligence activities and in keeping them separate from organizations that are oriented more toward research, damage control, detection, and interdiction, but there is an equally powerful logic for greater integration of all these activities.

Several theories have been advanced about how to group government functions into departments or other larger organizations. Gulick (1937) argued that activities and organizations could be grouped by any one of four criteria: process, purpose, clientele, and area. The discussion above explored one set of organizations grouped by process (intelligence) and another grouped on the basis of purpose (homeland security). These are worthwhile methods for grouping organizations, and each makes sense for some aspects of the general mission regarding the safety of the population. Still, that does not answer the question of how to get the two resulting organizations to communicate effectively with one another. And neither set of coordinated organizations—or neither of the new organizations—may be able to do its own job effectively without the other.

WHAT DOES IT MEAN FOR THE REST OF GOVERNMENT?

The creation of the Department of Homeland Security may be able to maximize, or at least to enhance, the attainment of one important value for the federal government. It would be difficult to argue that protecting the public against terrorism is not an important value. On the other hand, it may be that the current obsession with this one value undermines other important values in government. If one viewed the issues posed by this reorganization simply in terms of human lives, it is clear that we have lost several thousand people from terrorism on American soil to date, but we lose many thousands from poverty or from inadequate health care for the poor every year. Is it therefore desirable or prudent, from a policy perspective, to reorder government so entirely in order to meet this one perceived threat?[6] Politically, of course, terrorism is perceived as the more potent threat, and therefore the president and his advisers are well advised to focus on that risk to the society.

The points to be made now have been foreshadowed by the discussion above. Few organizations in government perform a single function; locating an organization in one place or another will emphasize some values and minimize others. For example, the Coast Guard is a multipurpose organization that has moved among a number of cabinet departments in its history. The proposal to move it again will emphasize its role in protecting the country against certain types of threats carried on ships but may well de-emphasize issues such as marine safety.

The other aspect of the organizational dilemma arises when the decision is made to remove one specific element from a larger organization and transfer it into a new location in government. There are several such moves anticipated in the formation of the Department of Homeland Security. We have already mentioned the issues involved in moving part of APHIS out of the Department of Agriculture. The question becomes whether this organizational fragment will be able to perform its functions well if it is cut off from the range of information that would be coming to it as a part of APHIS and the rest of Agriculture (U.S. General Accounting Office 2002b). Of course, this part of the new organization can make efforts to maintain its contacts with its former home, but it will be more difficult to do so once it becomes a part of new lines of authority and information. The question becomes whether this is an agricultural organization that has some relevance for security, or whether it is a security organization that happens to be interested in agricultural issues.

CONCLUSION

Everyone in Washington, and in the country as a whole, agrees that the 9/11 disaster cannot be allowed to happen again. There is perhaps not much agreement on anything else about the response that should be made to the continuing threat of terror attacks. Congress was able to enact a bill creating the Department of Homeland Security, with Thomas Ridge, former governor of Pennsylvania, to serve as the first secretary. There is, however, no certainty that the structure created, or indeed any structure, can create a foolproof defense against possible terrorist attacks within the United States. There are many questions about the nature and components of the new department being created, and about the separation of that organization from most of the intelligence-gathering organizations that must provide DHS with warnings of impending attacks.

The government reaction to 9/11 and the ongoing planning for future defenses emphasizes the importance of organizational thinking for understanding how the public sector operates. It would be easy to become entangled in the law enforcement and military aspects of homeland defense without asking the seemingly simple questions about how to organize these activities. Organizational failures, individual and collective, were significant factors in the success of the terrorists in New York, Washington, and Pennsylvania; better organizational design must therefore be a part of the response. But there is unfortunately no certain technology for the design of effective organizations, whether in the public or private sectors. The Department of Homeland Security follows a well-worn path toward the creation of mega-departments, but there may be no reason to expect that the experience in this case will be any more positive than in previous efforts.

NOTES

1. In almost all cases it will be a collection of organizations, rather than the "single, lonely organization" that will be relevant for understanding. That characteristic at once complicates the problems of implementation and diffuses responsibility for the outcomes of the process.

2. The same issue arose with respect to the TWA flight 800 crash off the coast of Long Island. Consistent with its organizational ethos, the National Transportation Safety Agency wanted to retrieve the crash from the seafloor to determine the cause in order to prevent future accidents. The FBI, on the other hand, was keen to keep the wreckage there in order to maintain the chain of evidence.

3. For example, there have been numerous examples of the several branches of the armed forces being incapable of communicating with one another in the field, and of police forces in contiguous communities using totally incompatible communications protocols.

4. For example, increasing numbers of enforcement agencies find that negotiation and encouraging compliance have been more successful than strict enforcement, a style that does not appear compatible with the emerging department.

5. Some might argue that the service rivalries and simple misunderstandings persist, albeit in a somewhat improved fashion, after more than a half century.

6. It is important to note that the department is being created to meet the possibility of attacks similar to those occurring on 9/11. The actions of the Transportation Security Administration, for example, appear premised on an attack just like the last one. As

has already been noted, government and private organizations spend a good deal of their time preparing for the last threat rather than anticipating the next one. Without some careful attention to issues of foresight, the reaction to 9/11 may simply institutionalize a pattern of detection and response suitable for past, rather than future, threats.

REFERENCES

Aucoin, Peter, and Herman Bakvis. 1993. "Consolidating Cabinet Portfolios: Australian Lessons for Canada." Paper presented at annual meeting of the Canadian Political Science Association, Ottawa, Ontario.

Bardach, Eugene. 1998. *Getting Agencies to Work Together: The Art and Practice of Managerial Craftsmanship.* Washington, D.C.: Brookings Institution Press.

Benjamin, Daniel, and Steven Simon. 2002. *The Age of Sacred Terror.* New York: Random House.

Campbell Public Affairs Institute. 2002. *Governance and Public Security.* Syracuse: Campbell Institute.

Considine, Mark. 2002. "The End of the Line: Accountable Governance in an Age of Networks, Partnerships and Joined-Up Services." *Governance* 15: 21–40.

Dorning, Mike. 2002. "FBI Whistleblower Describes Organization's Bureaucracy as Stifling, Cumbersome." *Chicago Tribune,* June 6.

Downs, Anthony. 1967. *Inside Bureaucracy.* Boston: Little, Brown.

Garrow, David J. 1981. *The FBI and Martin Luther King, Jr.: From "Solo" to Memphis.* New York: W. W. Norton.

Goodin, Robert. 1996. *The Theory of Institutional Design.* Cambridge: Cambridge University Press.

Gulick, Luther. 1937. "Notes on the Theory of Organization." In *Papers on the Science of Administration,* ed. Luther Gulick and Lyndall Urwick. New York: Institute of Public Administration.

Gulick, Luther, and Lyndall Urwick, eds. 1937. *Papers on the Science of Administration.* New York: Institute of Public Administration.

Henniger, Daniel. 2002. "The FBI and CIA Are First of All Bureaucracies." *Wall Street Journal,* June 6.

Jennings, Edward T., and D. Crane. 1994. "Coordination and Welfare Reform: The Quest for the Philosopher's Stone." *Public Administration Review* 54: 341–48.

Kessler, Ronald. 1993. *The FBI: Inside the World's Most Powerful Law Enforcement Agency.* New York: Pocket Books.

Landau, Martin. 1969. "The Rationality of Redundancy." *Public Administration Review* 29: 346–58.

March, James G. 1999. "A Learning Approach to Network Dynamics of Institutional Integration." In *Organizing Political Institutions,* ed. Morten Egeberg and Per Laegreid. Oslo: Scandinavian University Press.

March, James G., and Johan P. Olsen. 1989. *Rediscovering Institutions*. New York: Free Press.

Mitchell, A. 2002. "C.I.A. and F.B.I. Faulted." *New York Times*, September 10.

Nation. 2002. "September 11 Questions," June 10, 3.

Olsen, Johan P., and B. Guy Peters. 1996. *Lessons from Experience: Experiential Learning in Administrative Reforms in Eight Democracies*. Oslo: Scandinavian University Press.

Peters, B. Guy. 2002. "The Politics of Horizontal Management." Unpublished paper, Department of Political Science, University of Pittsburgh.

Risen, James, 2002. "C.I.A. and F.B.I. Agree to Truce in a War Waged in Whispers." *New York Times*, June 14.

Risen, James, and David Johnston. 2002a. "F.B.I. Report Found Agency Not Ready to Counter Terror." *New York Times*, June 1.

Risen, James, and David Johnston. 2002b. "Lawmakers Want Cabinet Position for Intelligence." *New York Times*, December 8.

Rose, Richard. 1993. *Lesson-Drawing in Public Policy*. Chatham, N.J.: Chatham House.

Salamon, Lester M. 1981. "The Question of Goals." In *Federal Reorganization*, ed. Peter Szanton Chatham, N.J.: Chatham House.

Seidman, Harold. 1998. *Politics, Position, and Power: The Dynamics of Federal Organization*. 5th ed. New York: Oxford University Press.

Senge, Peter. 1990. *The Fifth Discipline: The Art and Practice of the Learning Organization*. New York: Doubleday.

Simon, Herbert A. 1969. *The Science of the Artificial*. Cambridge, Mass.: MIT Press.

Stinchcombe, Arthur L. 1990. *Information and Organizations*. Berkeley: University of California Press.

Thompson, Victor A. 1961. *Modern Organization*. New York: Alfred A. Knopf.

U.S. General Accounting Office. 2002a. *Strategy Needed for Setting and Monitoring Levels of Effort for All Missions*. Washington, D.C.: USGAO. GAO-03-155.

U.S. General Accounting Office. 2002b. *Homeland Security: New Department Could Improve Biomedical R and D Coordination but May Disrupt Dual Purpose Efforts*. Washington, D.C.: USGAO. July 9, GAO-02-924T.

U.S. General Accounting Office. 2002c. *Homeland Security: Management Challenges Facing Federal Leadership*. Washington, D.C.: USGAO. December, GAO-03-260.

Wilensky, Harold. 1967. *Organizational Intelligence*. New York: Basic Books.

Wilson, James Q. 1989. *Bureaucracy*. New York: Basic Books.

Wood, Daniel B. 2002. "Coast Guard Cuts New Path in Terror War." *Christian Science Monitor*, August 6.

The Presidency Responds: The Implications of 9/11 for the Bush Administration's Policy Agenda

INTRODUCTION

In the wake of the terrorist attacks of 9/11, there has been a great deal of discussion about the impact on the presidency, the current administration, and, indeed, President George W. Bush himself. Numerous commentators have suggested that the events of 9/11 caused the public to move beyond questions of Bush's presidential legitimacy, which stemmed from the unusual nature of the 2000 election. In the public's mind, the president seemed to grow in stature in the days and weeks following the attacks. Some have even argued that Bush himself changed. Fred Greenstein (2002), for one, has argued that Bush's leadership qualities and cognitive engagement grew substantially during the early weeks of the crisis.

I am less concerned in this discussion with the impact of 9/11 on George Bush the man, instead focusing on the impact of the terrorist attacks on the manner in which the Bush administration has interacted with the broader political environment. This distinction between the president and the presidency is surely one of the most entrenched dichotomies in the study of American political institutions. The trend in political science in recent years has clearly been toward increased attention on the institution of the presidency, with a marginalization of the individual qualities of presidents themselves. While not discounting the possibility for individual initiative in the presidency, scholars have found that the impact of individual presidents is secondary to institutional and situational factors in a wide range of areas such as legislative success with Congress (Bond and Fleisher 1990;

Edwards 1989, 1997; Peterson 1990), bureaucratic management (Moe 1993), and relations with the public (Hager and Sullivan 1994; Powell 1999). This is not to suggest that the preferences and actions of individual presidents are irrelevant. Certainly, presidents differ greatly in their leadership styles and the policies they pursue. In the end, it is the interaction of context and individual styles that determines presidential leadership success, especially during times of crisis.

I will argue that 9/11 did, in fact, have an impact on the Bush presidency and its place in the universe of American politics, but not necessarily in the way commonly believed. Many observers have argued that the 9/11 attacks had the effect of distracting Bush from his stated policy goals by shifting both the public agenda and the president's time away from his domestic priorities. However, as we will see, the terrorist attacks gave the Bush administration the opportunity to alter course from a political situation that was deteriorating for the president. He was able to shore up his political standing, at least in the short run, by moving to more favorable political terrain. This shift in focus can be best understood not only as a response to a legitimate national security threat, but also as a predictable response to changes that had been taking place in the domestic political environment.

Just as the post-9/11 Bush presidency represents a response to an external series of events, the pre-9/11 administration was largely shaped by external forces, albeit less tragic ones. Four distinct stages emerged over the course of the first sixteen months of the Bush presidency, each with a unique political dynamic. Interestingly, these phases seemed to unfold in roughly four- to five-month intervals. One significant theme stands out in his manner of relating to changing circumstances: Bush has been a very skilled leader when he has been able to behave proactively according to carefully constructed strategic plans. He has been much less successful, at least in the short run, when forced to respond to unexpected events.

During his first one hundred days in office, the president pursued a meticulously crafted legislative plan in a very disciplined manner. With few external distractions, he was extremely successful in controlling the public agenda, and his legislative priorities faired well in Congress. In the second one hundred days, a number of unexpected crises emerged, forcing Bush into a more reactive stance. As a result, he lost control of the public agenda, and his public approval ratings began to decline. The tragic events of 9/11 ushered in a new phase for the Bush presidency. In a time of crisis, the public expected strong presidential leadership in fighting the war on terrorism. Bush redefined the mission of his presidency in terms of this new conflict. In 2002, however, a fourth phase emerged as new issues—economic troubles, corporate scandals, and violence in the Middle East—moved to the public agenda alongside terrorism. As he had in his second one hundred days, Bush had difficulty defining his key priorities. Once again, questions about his leadership began to surface and his popularity declined.

I begin this essay by reviewing the political context encountered by the administration during the transition into the presidency and the first few months in office. I then examine the development of the Bush administration's policy agenda, its subsequent fate in Congress, and the effect of 9/11. The Bush agenda will be explored primarily through the president's attempt to shape the public agenda as measured through his speeches.[1] I argue that the administration's shift in focus after 9/11 not only was a reaction to the terrorist attacks but also represented a predictable response to other developments in the broader political environment. Finally, I conclude with some observations about the ways in which the terrorist attacks restructured the political landscape for Bush in the areas of domestic politics and foreign policy.

THE CONTEXT

As the first president since 1888 to win an election in the Electoral College but not the popular vote, George Bush entered office in a weaker political position than any of his recent predecessors. His situation was made even more precarious because of the highly unusual ballot-counting controversy that transpired in Florida in the thirty-six days following the 2000 election. According to Patricia Conley (2001), a new president can credibly claim a presidential mandate when he is perceived to have a high level of public support and/or his party dominates Congress. With a bitterly divided electorate and a nearly even split between the parties in Congress, Bush clearly lacked a political mandate to pursue sweeping changes in policy.

Although the Republicans won control of the presidency and both houses of Congress for the first time since the 1952 election, their razor-thin advantage gave Bush very little room to maneuver. In the Senate, the election resulted in an even fifty-fifty partisan split, with Republicans gaining the nominal edge because of the vice president's prerogative in casting tie-breaking votes. The situation in the House was not much different, with Republicans clinging to a nine-seat edge. This close partisan split was critical; prior research has demonstrated that the greatest predictors of presidential success in passing an agenda with Congress are not connected to the personal leadership qualities of individual presidents but instead emanate from the partisan and ideological composition of Congress (Bond and Fleisher 1990; Edwards 1989, 1997; Peterson 1990; Powell and Schloyer 2000). Moreover, as presidential coattails have diminished over time, presidents now have little influence over the composition of Congress (Campbell and Sumners 1990; Cohen, Krassa, and Hamman 1991). This was especially evident in Bush's case, where the Republicans actually lost seats in both houses in the 2000 elections. In short, presidents have been shown to have very limited ability to influence congressional votes either through direct intervention in policy debates or through attempts to alter the composition of Congress.

Because of these historically unusual factors, political pundits suggested that Bush would have to strike a conciliatory stance with the Democrats. Numerous observers, including Democratic leaders in Congress, pronounced the Bush campaign agenda "dead on arrival," counseling Bush to pursue bipartisan compromise and even appoint Democrats to high-level cabinet positions. Notably, Bush was publicly prodded to scale back his widely touted campaign proposal to cut taxes by $1.3 trillion.

One of the main themes of Bush's campaign, coming on the heels of the rancorous Clinton years, had been restoring a tone of civility to political debate in Washington. Upon entering office, Bush followed through quickly on this campaign promise, scheduling a series of highly publicized informal gatherings with congressional Democrats. He even invited Senator Edward Kennedy for an evening of movie watching in the White House theater. The president's first several weeks in office were filled with an ambitious schedule of courtesy calls and meetings with an unprecedented number of congressional Republicans and Democrats alike. In an extension of his governing style in Texas, the President assigned chummy nicknames to nearly every member of Congress he met.

Somewhat surprisingly, Bush's conciliatory tone did not extend to the substance of his policy proposals. Ignoring calls to scale back his ambitious agenda, he pushed aggressively for a large tax cut, education reforms, increased defense spending, and his faith-based initiative, as if he had won the preceding election in a landslide. While paying lip service to Democratic priorities like prescription drug benefits for seniors, a patient's bill of rights, and campaign finance reform, the Bush administration clearly viewed these as secondary to the president's announced priorities.

THE BUSH AGENDA

Although presidents are not able to routinely alter the outcome of congressional floor votes, they still have a great deal of influence over policy outcomes for a number of reasons, including their constitutional powers to veto legislation and to issue executive orders (Mayer 2001). Rhetorical leadership, one of the most significant presidential powers, is not found in the Constitution itself but has evolved through custom over the course of American history. Utilizing the bully pulpit, presidents are in a unique position to shape the public and, hence, the congressional agenda (Kernell 1986; Tulis 1987). While ultimate success is by no means certain, presidents have the ability to influence the topics receiving attention and frame policy debates (Cohen 1997; Edwards 2001; Light 1982). The power to shape the agenda is most significant for presidents who are newly inaugurated and enjoy high approval ratings (Page and Shapiro 1984). The Bush administration, in its early days, demonstrated a clear understanding of the importance of moving quickly.

There are few agreed-upon truths in political science, but scholars are nearly unanimous in their advice for newly elected presidents pursuing ambitious policy agendas. History has shown that the failure of presidents to pass their programs typically stems from a lack of swift action (Jimmy Carter, George H. W. Bush) and/or a lack of focus on a relatively small number of key agenda items (Carter, Bill Clinton). Presidents who win important first-year victories, such as Ronald Reagan in 1981, must demonstrate a significant amount of discipline to remain focused on their key priorities and resist external intrusions on the presidential agenda.

Because of the importance of swift, disciplined actions, the short transition period between Election Day and Inauguration Day has assumed a high degree of importance for modern presidents (Burke 2000; Jones 1998). During these brief weeks, presidents must make a dizzying array of personnel and management decisions while devising policy and political game plans for the first months of the new administration. Political scientists and close observers of the presidency generally counsel presidents to begin with key White House positions such as chief of staff, director of personnel, press secretary, and legal counsel before dealing with higher-profile cabinet positions (Kumar et al. 2000). In fact, presidents are under increasing pressure to decide on key staffing decisions, if only in private, long before Election Day.

Given the already difficult task facing presidents-elect during their transitions, one might expect that Bush's task was even more daunting because of the protracted battle over the outcome of the 2000 election. After all, Bush had to devote considerable attention and resources to the election conflict and saw the already short transition period cut in half. On the other hand, the election fight provided Bush with some unique opportunities. During the election battle in Florida, the nation's attention was riveted on the ballot recount controversy while the major news networks carried twenty-four-hour coverage of every twist and turn of the events. Normally, a president-elect is the focus of a great deal of media speculation over key appointments. However, in the weeks following the 2000 election, Bush was able to retire to his remote ranch in Crawford, Texas, where he worked on the possible transition in near anonymity with key advisers such as Richard Cheney, Andrew Card, Clay Johnson, and Karl Rove. Bush benefited immensely from the experience of these advisers, most of who had served in senior positions in prior Republican administrations. With the nation focused on Florida, they were able to deliberate on key decisions without the normal flood of press attention and speculation about the new administration. They assembled one of the most experienced administrations in modern American history.

Bush and his staff were highly attuned to the successes and failures of past administrations. Aided by his advisers and by a series of transition reports emanating from presidency scholars under the leadership of Martha Joynt Kumar, the Bush team carried out the most well calibrated transition since Reagan's in 1981. Indeed, it was the Reagan model, rather than that of Bush's father, that guided the new administration. The incoming president understood the need for quick high-profile victories, like Reagan's tax cuts, which would give needed political momentum to other priorities.

It was during this transition period that the Bush campaign agenda was skillfully translated into a strategy for governing. He and his staff demonstrated a mastery of several of the key lessons from past presidential transitions. For example, Bush's first actions were to settle on his key White

House positions rather than higher-profile cabinet posts. Andrew Card, a former aide to Bush's father and an experienced Washington insider, had been tagged as the new chief of staff prior to Election Day. Bush then entrusted his primary strategist, Karl Rove, with the task of developing a political strategy to build support for the new administration's policy agenda.

Bush ignored the advice of those counseling restraint and decided to pursue a two-pronged strategy. On the one hand, he would work to build goodwill with key constituencies, such as Congress and the public, while pursuing an ambitious policy agenda. During the transition, Rove assembled a minutely detailed legislative and public relations map of the first months of the Bush administration. This plan established a carefully orchestrated series of legislative proposals based on the administration's priorities, centered around weekly themes such as education reform and tax cuts. These proposals were then supported through high-profile presidential meetings with key constituent groups, trips, speeches, and public relations events. Bush signed off on the plan well before Inauguration Day and committed his administration to following its course.

The new administration was also the recipient of some unforeseen good fortune during the transition and its first weeks in office, as they were able to pursue their agenda with a minimum of press scrutiny. The press was instead focused on a series of missteps made by the outgoing Clinton administration in its final days, including pardon scandals, allegations that the Clintons had looted the White House by taking public property, and reports of vandalism involving White House offices and equipment. These stories also aided Bush in his attempt to strike a clear contrast to his predecessor on character issues.

One of George Bush's most vivid personality traits throughout his political career has been discipline (Greenstein 2002). While he had some well-publicized failures in his early adulthood, this streak of discipline can be seen at different stages of his life. As a new student at Yale, for example, Bush immediately worked to memorize the name of every member of his first-year class, while his fellow students could scarcely name several. As a politician, he has displayed an unusual ability to remain focused. As governor of Texas, Bush articulated a few clear goals and then pursued them with uncommon single-mindedness.

His political discipline had also been evident during the 2000 election campaign, when he rarely strayed off message. The Bush campaign had a clearly defined set of priorities that the candidate repeated daily. His critics saw this as evidence that he was dangerously ignorant when it came to key foreign and domestic policy issues, suggesting that he was unable to discuss specifics beyond a set of carefully chosen campaign themes such as taxes, education, missile defense, Social Security reform, and personal character. The outgoing president, Bill Clinton, had demonstrated a remarkable ability to speak articulately, about nearly any topic that was raised, usually in great detail. While this might make for exciting politics, Clinton had a very difficult time controlling the political agenda because of his lack of focus on priorities. For better or worse, Bush's leadership style proved to be very different.

THE FIRST ONE HUNDRED DAYS: A RHETORICAL EXAMINATION

During the first one hundred days in office, a traditional marker since President Franklin Roosevelt's early success in 1933, the Bush administration worked very hard in pushing a few key agenda items. Because speech-making offers the best opportunity to influence the agenda, the best way to examine an administration's priorities is through the president's public speeches. The most important opportunity for presidents to define their agendas is through their annual State of the Union addresses or, in the case of newly inaugurated presidents, prime-time addresses to special joint sessions of Congress. However, State of the Union addresses are just one weapon in the president's vast rhetorical arsenal. Increasingly important are the regular minor addresses that presidents deliver to specialized groups around the country. The ability to deliver these minor addresses has been facilitated by modern transportation, which enables presidents to deliver speeches in many different states on the same day and still return to the White House by evening.

Bush's address to a special joint session of Congress on February 27, 2001, provided a clear articulation of his administration's policy priorities and serves as a baseline for assessing Bush's efforts to influence the public and secure passage of his proposals in Congress. In his address to Congress, Bush laid out an ambitious agenda that focused on several key issues. His speech was especially notable because of its vivid contrast to those made by other recent presidents, who have used such occasions to present laundry lists of policy proposals. Clinton, for example, became known for speeches that lasted up to ninety minutes and contained scores of policy proposals. In contrast, Bush's first speech to Congress lasted only fifty minutes and focused primarily on his four highest priorities: tax cuts, education reform, national defense, and his faith-based initiative. He wisely avoided the temptation to expand his agenda.

Like most recent presidents, Bush also delivered prerecorded, weekly radio addresses each Saturday. These radio addresses are broadcast on a large network of radio stations around the country, but the primary benefit of them is garnering attention for the president through coverage on the weekend television news broadcasts. Since weekends are usually slow news periods, the president's address is typically given prominent attention. In their Saturday radio addresses, presidents typically attempt to highlight the part of their agenda they think is most important at the time. As such, the topic of the radio address provides a clear window on a president's priorities.

Table 1 displays the topics covered in each of President Bush's weekly radio addresses. In his February 27 address to Congress, he declared education to be his administration's highest priority. And, in fact, the president's first radio address focused on that issue. It is apparent, however, that Bush's focus on education as the top priority was a strategic decision designed to build goodwill with moderates so that his administration could turn its attention to its true highest priority, tax cuts. Tax cuts were the focus of the second week's address and were discussed by the president in seven of the first ten radio broadcasts. In contrast, education was discussed in only three addresses. The only other topics discussed by Bush in his first ten radio addresses were his faith-based initiative and national defense. Not until after the first ten broadcasts did he begin to focus on issues—such as energy, human values, and free trade—beyond his four main priorities.

Bush's focus on his key agenda items, particularly taxes and education, was in keeping with the original plan devised by Rove for the administration's first months in office. This discipline was evident in the president's daily speechmaking as well. In addition to rallying support for his policy agenda from the public and Congress, a more subtle aim of the administration was to buttress the president's public support in general and to increase the perception that Bush was a "legitimate" president, despite losing the popular vote to Al Gore. In looking at Bush's schedules for travel and speechmaking, these goals were apparent. First, he traveled and spoke at a

TABLE 1. President Bush's Weekly Radio Addresses

Date	Topic	Date	Topic
2001		Sept. 8	Education
Jan. 27	Education	Sept. 15	Terrorism—values
Feb. 3	Taxes	Sept. 22	Terrorism, economy
Feb. 10	Defense	Sept. 29	Terrorism
Feb. 17	Taxes	Oct. 6	Terrorism—Afghanistan
Feb. 24	Taxes, education	Oct. 13	Terrorism—Afghanistan
March 3	Taxes, budget	Oct. 20	Terrorism
March 10	Taxes	Oct. 27	Terrorism
March 17	Taxes	Nov. 3	Terrorism
March 24	Budget	Nov. 10	Terrorism
March 31	Education, taxes, faith-	Nov. 24	Terrorism
	based initiative	Dec. 1	Economy
April 7	Education, taxes	Dec. 8	Administration priorities,
April 14	Values		congressional agenda
April 21	Free trade	Dec. 15	Economy, taxes
April 28	Review of first 100 days	Dec. 22	Holiday greetings
May 5	Mexican relations	Dec. 29	Terrorism, education, taxes
May 12	Energy	**2002**	
May 19	Energy	Jan. 5	Economy
May 26	Memorial Day	Jan. 12	Economy, terrorism
June 2	Taxes	Jan. 19	MLK Jr., education,
June 9	Home ownership		disadvantaged children
June 16	Father's Day	Jan. 26	Terrorism, defense, economy
June 23	Patient's bill of rights	Feb. 2	401(K) plans
June 30	Defense	Feb. 9	MLK Jr., race
July 7	Education	Feb. 16	Asian affairs
July 14	Medicare	Feb. 23	Energy
July 21	International cooperation	March 2	Education
July 28	Americans with	March 16	Afghanistan
	Disabilities Act	March 23	Free trade
Aug. 4	Patient's bill of rights	March 30	Easter
Aug. 11	Stem cell research	April 6	Terrorism, Israel
Aug. 18	Compassion agenda	April 13	Taxes
Aug. 25	Government reform	April 20	Terrorism, Israel
Sept. 1	Education	April 27	Free trade

SOURCE: *Weekly Compilation of Presidential Documents*

dizzying pace, delivering more speeches in more places than any president in U.S. history. In the first hundred-day period of his presidency, he delivered nearly 150 speeches. Bill Clinton, the previous record holder in this regard, delivered only 90 speeches during the comparable period in his first term. The contrast with Clinton does not end there. As shown in figure 1, Bush traveled much more extensively than Clinton, visiting twenty-four states in twenty-six trips. In the same period, Clinton visited just eight states in seventeen trips. In fact, Clinton did not visit his twenty-fourth state until nearly a full year into his presidency.

Bush's selection of travel destinations also differed significantly from Clinton's, reflecting their very different political bases. The current president's visits tended to be in the South, Plains, and interior West. His most frequently visited state was Florida, owing to its pivotal role in his election and to the fact that his brother, John Ellis ("Jeb"), was the incumbent governor of the state. As part of his legislative strategy, George Bush took a considerable number of trips to states that he had won in the election but that were represented by Democratic senators. For example, South Dakota, the home state of Democratic leader Senator Tom Daschle, received particular attention from the president. Clinton, on the other hand, tended to visit large states that had voted Democratic in 1992, such as California, New York, and Illinois. On average, Clinton visited California at least once per month, sometimes spending several consecutive days in the state. Bush did not visit the largest state in the nation until late May, over four months into his presidency. He didn't travel to New York until the sixth month of his presidency.

Just as he had done in his weekly radio addresses, Bush demonstrated a significant degree of discipline in the topics he addressed in the first one hundred days. Over 50 percent of Bush's speeches focused solely on his four main priorities. This is particularly impressive in light of the incredible demands on presidents to speak on varied topics at numerous ceremonial functions. President Clinton, for example, spoke about a wide variety of topics in his first one hundred days—gays in the military, the economy, technology, health care, environmental issues, government reform, and education, just to name a few.

From the perspective of its own agenda, the Bush administration's first one hundred days were a success. Through a rigorous and disciplined public relations campaign, it managed to keep the nation's policy agenda focused on its main priorities, particularly education and taxes. By the end of this

FIGURE 1. Presidential Travel: Bush's and Clinton's First One Hundred Days

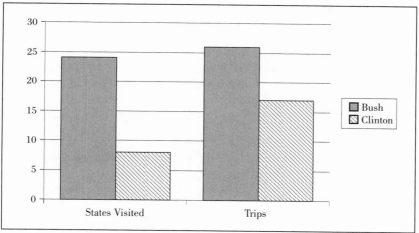

SOURCE: *Weekly Compilation of Presidential Documents*

period, Bush's tax and education plans were receiving a favorable reception from a majority in Congress, although the administration was forced into several considerable compromises. The administration avoided serious pitfalls and scandals, and the president's approval ratings remained respectable, in the high 50s to low 60s, about average for recent presidents.

As we will see in the next section, the administration's fortunes began to change for the worse during its second one hundred days, in part because of a lack of focus but also due to a series of unanticipated events.

THE SECOND ONE HUNDRED DAYS: BUSH LOSES CONTROL OF THE AGENDA

The Bush administration's success in controlling the policy agenda during its first one hundred days was primarily a result of the skillful planning and discipline displayed by the president and his staff. However, the administration also benefited from a paucity of surprises, allowing it to maintain a proactive stance.

Beginning in April 2001, the Bush administration found itself facing a whole series of unanticipated events that threatened to derail its carefully crafted plan. Bush faced his first international crisis on April 1, when a U.S. Navy spy plane was forced to make an emergency landing in China after a collision with a Chinese fighter jet. A tense standoff ensued over the next few weeks, during which time the Chinese government delayed the return of the American servicemen and the spy plane. The crisis threatened Sino-American relations at a fragile time, when Bush was attempting to deal with the controversial sale of an Aegis radar system to Taiwan. Complicating matters was the fact that Bush had also just recently scheduled his first trip to China for the coming October.

A domestic crisis of sorts had also arisen, with severe energy crises in California. Many areas of the state had begun experiencing blackouts due to insufficient power supplies and a complex pricing scheme that had evolved in the wake of energy deregulation. Bush was forced to spend an increasing amount of time on energy policy. The issue was potentially troublesome for him, since both he and Vice President Cheney had been energy industry executives in the past. Having to deal with the energy crisis also raised politically controversial questions about Bush's record on environmental matters. He and Gore had differed sharply on energy and the environment during the 2000 campaign, with Bush preferring to increase oil supplies through drilling in the Arctic National Wildlife Refuge (ANWR). Gore, on the other hand, supported aggressive government action to protect the environment through conservation and tax incentives to develop alternative energy sources.

As the energy crisis worsened, Bush used the opportunity to renew his call for ANWR drilling. A number of stories began to appear in the press that criticized the president's environmental record. This issue threatened to hurt Bush's standing with key suburban voters around the country, who tended to favor greater protection of the environment. The controversy over energy and the environment was exacerbated by the administration's decision to withdraw from the Kyoto Treaty, dealing with the emission of greenhouse gases. The Kyoto decision rankled American allies in Europe, who viewed the U.S. president as a dangerous unilateralist on this and other key issues such as missile defense, the Anti-Ballistic Missile (ABM) Treaty, and the international criminal court.

During the early months of the Bush presidency, it also became apparent that the United States was experiencing an economic downturn after many prosperous years. Although the downturn had begun in the final year of the Clinton presidency, it would be Bush's job to deal with the shaky economy. At first, he adeptly used the news as an argument for the necessity of enacting his tax cut proposals. As the administration entered its second one hundred days, Bush was forced to spend more time dealing with an economic recession.

The political situation in Washington, D.C., became more difficult for the president, as well. On May 24, Senator James Jeffords of Vermont announced his decision to leave the Republicans to become the Senate's only independent. Because the Senate had been divided fifty-fifty between the parties, the switch shifted control of the upper house of Congress to the Democrats. Of course, this had very little effect on roll-call votes in the Senate, but the Democrats acquired important powers over the scheduling of votes and, more important, took control of committee chairs. With Daschle elevated to Senate majority leader, Bush faced a much more difficult task in shepherding his program through Congress and gaining speedy approval for his executive and judicial branch nominees.

As the president was forced to become a much more reactive leader, he lost a great deal of his ability to control the policy agenda. As a result, a whole series of issues began to surface that were not among his administration's main priorities. The economy, prescription drug benefits for seniors, a patient's bill of rights, stem cell research, and the politically troublesome issue of Social Security reform were all pushed onto the public agenda by other political actors and events. These were issues that were much less advantageous for Bush, and they stole time and attention from his priorities.

Bush's public speaking and travel schedule during his second one hundred days in office (May–mid-August 2001) shows that indeed the president's attention was diverted away from his preferred priorities. He was not able to dedicate as much time to political travel, visiting only half as many states (twelve) as he had in the first one hundred days. His overall speech making dropped by nearly 20 percent.

The move toward a more reactive presidency was particularly apparent in Bush's choice of topics for his public addresses. As shown in table 1, the percentage of speeches dedicated to the administration's main priorities dropped from over 50 percent in the first one hundred days to less than 20 percent in the second one hundred days. For instance, Bush delivered as many speeches on the topic of energy as he did on either taxes or the environment. Across the board, he was forced to deal with a much wider range of issues.

The more difficult policy terrain for the president was also reflected in his approval ratings with the public. Bush's ratings gradually declined over the summer. His highest approval rating during this period, 57 percent, was 5 points lower than during the first one hundred days. In early August, Bush departed for a month-long vacation to his ranch in Crawford, Texas. When he returned to Washington in early September, his public standing had reached the lowest point of his presidency. On September 10, as he left for a trip to Florida, only 51 percent of Americans approved of Bush's handling of the presidency—a fall of 6 points in just a few weeks. The president's political position was deteriorating, and he faced what promised to be a difficult period of dealing with issues not among his main priorities. However, the tragic events of the next morning would remake the political landscape as no other sudden events had since the Japanese attack on Pearl Harbor in 1941.

PRESIDENTIAL LEADERSHIP IN THE WAKE OF 9/11

The attacks of 9/11 occurred at a time in which the Bush administration was struggling to find a new message while dealing with a web of difficult political developments. Bush's main priorities had either been accomplished or had been subverted by unexpected events. Although his highest priority, tax cuts, was signed into law on June 7 and his education plan looked to be headed for eventual passage, the president was spending an increasing amount of time reacting to unanticipated crises.

Immediately after the terrorist attacks, he and his advisers announced that henceforth the overriding goals of Bush's presidency would be the fight against terrorism and protecting homeland security. Of course, this was to be expected in light of the most horrific attack on American civilians in history. It also provided the opportunity for Bush to find a "new voice." On one level, this shift in focus seemed to be a response to the events of 9/11. But the scale of the tragedy obscures other factors contributing to Bush's change in priorities, such as the problematic political context of his presidency.

As observed by Steven Shull (1991), the American system of separation of powers creates structural incentives for presidents to gradually devote increasing amounts of attention to foreign policy concerns over the course of their administrations. The evolution of executive power under the U.S. Constitution has made it easier for presidents to exercise greater control over foreign policy than domestic policy. In most areas of domestic policy, presidents must gain Congress's approval for significant initiatives. Congress, while certainly given some influence over foreign affairs, has historically acceded to the president in this area. Thus, presidents typically tire of attempting to mobilize support in Congress for their domestic agendas and begin to spend more time on foreign affairs. The incentives for presidents to make this shift become greater when the legislative avenue is more difficult. Divided government, increasingly an institutionalized feature of American government, contributes to this shift.

For most presidents, this change in emphasis occurs gradually over a number of years. In Bush's case, however, there were at least four important reasons for it to occur earlier: his precarious electoral victory, the closely divided Congress (exacerbated by Vermont's Jim Jeffords's switch to independent status in the Senate), unforeseen domestic and foreign crises, and the attacks of 9/11. These factors dovetailed to prod the Bush administration into shifting its focus abruptly after 9/11 from its domestic priorities to the war on terrorism.

Without a doubt, Bush's refashioning of his agenda represents a sensible response to a serious national security threat. Protecting the nation from attack is certainly among the most central duties of any president. However, the policy agenda is ultimately a zero-sum game. A decision to move terrorism to the highest rung on the ladder of national priorities necessarily involves the sacrifice of other priorities. The simple act of putting off some of these other issues—the environment, Social Security reform, and health care, to name a few—has important long-term consequences. However, the public can focus its attention on only a small number of issues at one time.

It is tempting to conclude that the terrorist attacks of 9/11 alone sidetracked the Bush administration's policy agenda. In altering his administration's priorities, Bush clearly placed his key agenda items on the back burner. Indeed, Bush's public efforts to shape the agenda underwent a dramatic change after 9/11. A significant portion of his public addresses from that point onward focused on issues related to terrorism and homeland security. This interpretation, however, fails to take account of the fact that Bush's focus on his highest priorities had already decreased substantially in the months leading up to September 2001. The attacks presented an opportunity for Bush to reposition his administration's efforts on much more favorable political terrain.

To judge from the rallying effect during past national crises, the outpouring of support for the president in the days following 9/11 was to be ex-

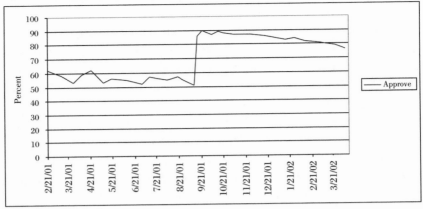

FIGURE 2. **President Bush's Public Approval Ratings, January 2001–April 2002**

SOURCE: Gallup poll

pected. Bush's approval ratings skyrocketed overnight from 51 to 86 percent (see figure 2). What was truly historic, however, was the duration of Bush's boost in popularity. Six months after the 9/11 attacks, his approval rating remained at 80 percent. In contrast, six months after the Persian Gulf War in 1991, his father's approval rating as president had receded to the high 60s. This prolonged period of popularity provided Bush with an opportunity for leadership that few presidents ever experience.

Many observers were concerned that Bush failed to inspire confidence in his early comments about the attacks. His public remarks on 9/11, including a national address in the evening, were not among his best performances. He was mildly criticized in the days following the attacks for referring to terrorists as "folks" and promising a "crusade" against terrorism. However, the president's rhetoric grew more confident over the next few days. The pivotal day for the Bush presidency was September 14, when he delivered an emotional speech during a service of remembrance at the National Cathedral and then traveled to New York City to visit the site of the World Trade Center ruins. For many Americans, Bush's stature grew immensely with his now-famous, spontaneous comments to rescue workers at the site. Later, his resolute national address to a joint session of Congress on September 20 was widely heralded as the strongest speech of his presidency up to that point. Three weeks later, in his first prime-time news conference, Bush showed that he was more engaged in complex policy questions than ever before.

Whereas Bush had been struggling to find a message throughout the summer months, examination of his post-9/11 speeches shows that his priorities became very clear. In the one hundred days following the terrorist attacks, the president's priorities clearly shifted away from his domestic policy goals toward fighting terrorism and homeland security. Terrorism accounted for 70 percent of his public addresses. Another 8 percent focused on topics related to human values and personal tributes. During this period, Bush did not deliver any speeches on his education plan, which was still under consideration in Congress. In fact, only 21 of his 120 addresses dealt with topics other than terrorism or human values. Because of time constraints and security concerns, Bush's travel schedule was curtailed dramatically; during the final three and a half months of 2001, he traveled only nineteen times, visiting just eight states.

Bush's speech and travel schedule began to return to a more normal routine in 2002. In the first one hundred days of 2002, he made fifty-nine trips, visiting a total of twenty-six states. This was a pace nearly equal to that of his first one hundred days in office. And Bush began to move away from topics related to terrorism in the early months of 2002. Bush halved his speeches on terrorism from the preceding period; only 32 percent focused on terrorism, 39 percent when including those on human values. However, as in the period immediately preceding the 9/11 attacks, Bush failed to articulate a clear set of priorities for his administration. After terrorism, education accounted for the greatest percentage of speeches on any single topic, representing just 7 percent of his rhetorical output. But most of those speeches were delivered after the signing of his education plan, as part of an attempt to highlight the administration's achievements.

Looking at the president's speeches made during this time, one finds that a substantial number essentially repeated the same message. Bush began this standard speech, delivered dozens of times, by making some general references to the war on terrorism; inserted several paragraphs on the theme of the day (corporate responsibility, energy, taxes, free trade, Social Security reform, etcetera), which was generally tailored for the specific audience; and then concluded with a call for Americans to become more involved in volunteerism. Besides this call for volunteerism, no significant theme emerged during this period.

Stepping back to look at the big picture, we see that Bush's commitment to a focused agenda ebbed and flowed in a pattern that repeated itself throughout his first sixteen months in office. He would dedicate himself to a clearly defined policy agenda, only to see his attention distracted over time. His presidential leadership became significantly less effective as he moved away from his chosen policy focus.

We see this pattern reemerging in the final three months of 2001, when Bush maintained a disciplined focus on issues related to terrorism. His commitment to his administration's agenda in his public speeches bore many similarities to his first one hundred days in office. However, just as Bush's focus had become distracted during his administration's second one hundred days, the onset of 2002 brought unexpected new events and crises. His attention to terrorism-related topics began to wane accordingly. Perhaps even more troubling for Bush, no clear priorities emerged to take their place; his rhetoric once again lost its focus.

POLICY LEADERSHIP OF THE BUSH ADMINISTRATION IN THE POST-9/11 ERA

Domestic Policy

As the midterm elections of 2002 moved nearer, the future course of the Bush administration seemed uncertain, much like the situation in his father's presidency in mid-1991. Moreover, key questions remained about the long-term implications of 9/11 for the policy leadership of George W. Bush. The president largely withdrew from the public debate about key domestic issues after 9/11. His popularity remained at unprecedented levels throughout the first half of 2002. The comparisons with his father, whose popularity soared as a result of the Persian Gulf War in the early 1990s, are impossible to ignore. George H. W. Bush squandered his popularity by failing to use it as a means of accomplishing other important policy goals, particularly in domestic affairs, and his son may have also missed a unique opportunity for presidential leadership. Scholarship on the presidency has demonstrated quite clearly that popularity is not something that can be preserved indefinitely. Popular presidents must find a way to translate their goodwill into support for their policy agenda before the opportunity passes. As the saying goes, "use it or lose it." This is a lesson that the first President Bush learned the hard way after losing reelection because of widespread concerns that he had failed to take action on the domestic front.

As I discussed above, the current President Bush seemingly learned from his father's mistakes in many areas, particularly in how to execute a well-disciplined transition and articulate a clear agenda in the first one hundred days of an administration. However, there has been no serious attempt up to this point to translate the president's sky-high popularity into support for his domestic initiatives. With a shaky economy and a rash of corporate scandals dominating the public's attention, Bush has run the risk of seeming unresponsive on domestic matters.

The debate over ANWR oil drilling was telling of Bush's lack of willingness to tap into his reserve of popularity for legislative purposes. The president has been a long-time supporter of increased oil exploration in ANWR as part of a plan to increase U.S. oil supplies, and his position on ANWR had been a point of contention in the 2000 campaign. In early 2002 the House voted to allow oil drilling in ANWR. As the closely divided Senate neared a vote on the matter, Bush chose not to initiate a public relations offensive in support of his position. This was particularly surprising because ANWR drilling was one of the cornerstones of Bush's energy policy.

The contrast between the way he approached the tax cut debate and the ANWR vote is particularly notable. In the 2000 campaign, Bush had championed tax cuts as an issue of fundamental fairness. As the economy worsened in late 2000 and early 2001, he continued to support substantial tax cuts but changed his rationale from one of fairness to the need for economic stimulus as a mitigating factor in the downturn. In doing so, Bush demonstrated the ability to adapt his political rhetoric to changing circumstances in support of his policy proposals. The ANWR debate provided Bush an ideal opportunity to replicate this strategy by arguing that drilling in ANWR would help the United States become less dependent on the strife-ridden Middle East. This argument could have been quite powerful, given the American public's concern at the time about frequent suicide attacks on Israeli civilians by Palestinian bombers, Israeli attacks on Palestinian-controlled areas, continuing tensions with Iraq, and terrorism in general. Although a great deal of research suggests that presidential influence over congressional votes is marginal, this is one instance where presidential efforts could have been a success, since forty-six senators were on record supporting ANWR drilling. In the end, the president decided to allow the vote to pass without delivering any major speeches on the topic.

Bush's refusal to use his reservoir of political capital for his domestic priorities extended to other areas as well, including campaign finance reform.

Throughout the 2000 campaign, in the primaries and general election, Bush expressed his clear opposition to reform of the campaign finance system along the lines of the McCain-Feingold and Shays-Meehan proposals. Depending upon the setting, Bush argued against such reforms because he said they (a) would curtail First Amendment freedoms, (b) did not include paycheck protection clauses allowing workers to prevent unions from using their dues for political purposes, and (c) would disproportionately hurt Republicans. Following the corporate scandals of late 2001 and early 2002 involving Enron, WorldCom, Tyco, and other major corporations, momentum began to build for passage of campaign finance reform. The president was largely absent from the debate, saying only that he had some reservations about the proposed reforms and that congressional opponents of the reforms should not count on him vetoing the bill if it passed. In the end, campaign finance reform was passed by Congress and signed by a clearly reluctant Bush. Once again, he agreed to go along with the wishes of Congress in an instance in which he most likely could have prevailed by making a clear case to the American public. Instead, the low-key signing ceremony for the bill on March 27, 2002, was the first time in his presidency that Bush delivered a significant address on the topic of campaign finance.

Foreign Policy

On the international front, the effects of 9/11 are as yet unclear, especially in terms of how the Bush administration views the place of the United States in the world community. Prior to 9/11 he became embroiled in a series of contentious international disagreements, especially with traditional American allies in Europe. Some of the distrust of Bush stemmed from the widespread perception that he was a neophyte on international affairs, but the most serious chasms occurred as a result of the perceived unilateralism of his administration. Upon taking office, Bush signaled a number of dramatic shifts in American foreign policy, which seemed to suggest that he was much less willing to cooperate with the international community than his predecessors had been. As has been previously mentioned, he withdrew the United States from environmental and chemical weapons treaties, kept the United States out of the international criminal court, announced he was considering withdrawal from the 1972 ABM treaty with Russia, and doggedly pursued a missile defense system over international objections.

The events of 9/11 clearly changed the manner in which the Bush administration interacted with foreign nations, at least in the short run. Bush took advantage of the outpouring of international outrage over the attacks to strengthen alliances with a number of countries. He built a limited international coalition with traditional allies to lead the fight against Taliban and Al Qaeda forces in Afghanistan and began friendlier negotiations with President Vladimir Putin of Russia on a range of issues.

Over time the Bush administration seemed to return to its unilateralist instincts. In the 2002 State of the Union address, he offended nations around the world in identifying what he termed an "axis of evil" consisting of Iran, Iraq, and North Korea. European allies who preferred negotiations with these nations instead of open conflict were particularly upset with Bush's characterization. They feared that the United States was looking to expand its use of military force in the effort against terrorism. This unilateralist inclination became even more apparent as the Bush team continued to openly discuss plans to attack Iraq in order to oust Saddam Hussein from power. American officials pledged to seek international support for such an action but made it clear they would act on a unilateral basis if necessary. A number of traditional allies, such as Canada, Germany, and France, openly declared their opposition to an attack on Iraq. That Bush would persevere in such war plans despite international opposition showed that strong unilateralist tendencies continued to exist in the administration even after 9/11.

As 2002 progressed, American unilateralism began to resurface in other ways, including the president's announcement in March of a series of sizable tariffs on foreign steel imports in an effort to protect U.S. steelmakers. This statement was widely denounced by nations around the world, who in turn threatened retaliation against U.S. agricultural exports and promised to take action against the United States with the World Trade Organization. Allies also expressed concern relating to the Geneva conventions over the treatment of Al Qaeda detainees in Guantánamo Bay, continued U.S. support for Israel, and the U.S. withdrawal from the enforcement protocol of the biological weapons convention.

This is not to suggest that there is something fundamentally wrong with the Bush administration's unilateralist agenda; that is a debate best left for another forum. There are some sensible reasons for him to pursue a more independent foreign policy, especially as it relates to domestic politics. While some Americans have expressed concern over Bush's foreign policy, the majority of Americans have been largely sympathetic to his unilateralism. Polls taken throughout the post-9/11 period consistently show that the public gave Bush higher marks in foreign policy and the war on terrorism than any other area. Most of this support plainly stemmed from the lasting impact of 9/11, but some of it certainly reflected a deeper reaction against Clinton's multilateralism on nearly all international fronts, which was not perceived by many Americans as in the best interests of the United States. Nevertheless, Bush's unilateralist stance has some very important implications for long-term U.S. interests around the world and may limit the range of options that are available in handling future international crises. In short, his administration has shown that it will adopt a multilateral stance when it is perceived to be in the short-run interests of the United States, but this seeming willingness is mitigated by strong countervailing instincts toward unilateral action.

CONCLUSION

President Bush clearly responded to the events of 9/11 in an aggressive fashion. However, his administration largely failed to articulate a post-9/11 agenda beyond terrorism-related issues. The reasons for this failure are not entirely due to the president's focus on fighting terrorism and preserving homeland security. Throughout 2002, terrorism had actually receded to the background in the president's public rhetoric, but no new message arose to fill the void. Like his father, Bush chose not to translate his public approval gained from international conflict into the arena of domestic policy.

I have argued that the administration's response to 9/11 and subsequent events was certainly a reflection of the seriousness of the terrorist threat to the United States. However, the form of the response was influenced by the external political environment. In most instances, the president responded in ways that did not involve significant legislative initiative, relying on areas traditionally reserved for executive power. This reaction represented the typical shift of presidents from domestic to foreign policy, but in a dramatically expedited fashion. The unusual nature of Bush's election to the presidency as well as the closely divided Congress contributed to this shift. These same instincts toward strong executive action were apparent on the world stage, as Bush made it clear that he would pursue unilateral action on a broad range of fronts if other countries refused to cooperate.

In looking at the president's public speeches, we have seen a pattern emerge in which Bush has engaged in carefully planned proactive planning, only to see his efforts undermined over time by unexpected events. During the first sixteen months of his presidency, Bush displayed two conflicting traits. On the one hand, when viewed from the vantage point of his own goals, he has been one of the most successful recent presidents in pursuing sweeping policy changes. Through his public speechmaking, Bush has been able to maintain a highly focused discipline when attempting to shape the political agenda. On the other hand, he has had a more difficult time in some situations that have called for dexterity in responding to unexpected events and crises—economic recession, Middle East violence, energy shortages, and corporate scandals. When faced with such events, Bush has been much less focused in his public rhetoric. His political leadership has been markedly less effective during these periods of uncertainty. A cycle has seemingly emerged in which the president is able to focus attention on a set of key issues, only to lose control of the agenda because of the administration's difficulty in fashioning a rhetorical response to emerging issues.

Over time we will gain a better understanding of Bush's leadership style and his administration's record in tackling difficult policy questions. However, we can expect that the remainder of the Bush presidency will largely center around tensions that have already emerged: his extraordinary discipline when acting proactively versus his tendency to lose focus when facing unexpected challenges; an "America first" unilateralist instinct in foreign affairs versus the need to forge international alliances; the desire for sweeping domestic policy changes versus the political difficulties in dealing with an intransigent Congress; and the war on terrorism and protecting homeland security versus other important long-term policy matters. It will be the interaction of President Bush's individual style, institutional realities, and the political context that will ultimately determine the the success or failure of his agenda.

NOTE

1. For this essay I examined the public speeches of President Bush in his first sixteen months in office (January 2001–April 2002) as an indicator of his administration's policy agenda. A full record of Bush's speeches can be found in the *Weekly Compilation of Presidential Documents*, later compiled into the *Public Papers of the Presidents*. I examined all public addresses by the president, omitting brief, passing remarks made to reporters.

REFERENCES

Bond, Jon, and Richard Fleisher. 1990. *The President in the Legislative Arena*. Chicago: University of Chicago Press.

Burke, John P. 2000. *Presidential Transitions: From Politics to Practice*. Boulder, Colo.: Lynne Rienner.

Campbell, James E., and Joe A. Sumners. 1990. "Presidential Coattails in Senate Elections." *American Political Science Review* 84 (June): 513–24.

Cohen, Jeffrey E. 1997. *Presidential Responsiveness and Public Policy-Making*. Ann Arbor: University of Michigan Press.

Cohen, Jeffrey E., Michael A. Krassa, and John A. Hamman. 1991. "The Impact of Presidential Campaigning on Midterm U.S. Senate Elections." *American Political Science Review* 85 (March): 165–78.

Conley, Patricia Heidotting. 2001. *Presidential Mandates: How Elections Shape the National Agenda*. Chicago: University of Chicago Press.

Edwards, George C., III. 1989. *At the Margins: Presidential Leadership of Congress*. New Haven, Conn.: Yale University Press.

Edwards, George C., III. 1997. "Aligning Tests with Theory: Presidential Approval as a Source of Influence with Congress." *Congress and the Presidency* 24 (autumn): 113–30.

Edwards, George C., III. 2001. "Can the President Focus the Public's Attention?" Paper presented at the Midwest Political Science Association meeting, Chicago, April 18–20.

Greenstein, Fred. 2002. "The Changing Leadership of George W. Bush: A Pre- and Post-9/11 Comparison." *Presidential Studies Quarterly* 32 (June).

Hager, Gregory L., and Terry Sullivan. 1994. "President-Centered and Presidency-Centered Explanations of Presidential Public Activity." *American Journal of Political Science* 38 (November): 1078–1103.

Jones, Charles O. 1998. *Passages to the Presidency: From Campaigning to Governing*. Washington, D.C.: Brookings Institution Press.

Kernell, Samuel. 1986. *Going Public: New Strategies of Presidential Leadership*. Washington, D.C.: CQ Press.

Kumar, Martha Joynt, et al. 2000. "The Contemporary Presidency: Meeting the Freight Train Head-On: Planning for the Transition to Power." *Presidential Studies Quarterly* (December).

Light, Paul C. 1982. *The President's Agenda*. Baltimore: Johns Hopkins University Press.

Mayer, Kenneth R. 2001. *With the Stroke of a Pen: Executive Orders and Presidential Power*. Princeton, N.J.: Princeton University Press.

Moe, Terry. 1993. "Presidents, Institutions, and Theory." In *Researching the Presidency*, ed. George C. Edwards III, John Kessell, and Bert Rockman. Pittsburgh: University of Pittsburgh Press.

Page, Benjamin I., and Robert Y. Shapiro. 1984. "Presidents as Opinion Leaders: Some New Evidence." *Policy Studies Journal* 12: 647–62.

Peterson, Mark. 1990. *Legislating Together.* Cambridge, Mass.: Harvard University Press.

Powell, Richard J. 1999. "'Going Public' Revisited: Presidential Speechmaking and the Bargaining Setting in Congress." *Congress and the Presidency* 26 (fall): 153–70.

Powell, Richard J., and Dean Schloyer. 2000. "Voting Scared: The Impact of Public Presidential Appeals on Electorally Vulnerable Members of Congress." Paper presented at the 2000 annual meeting of the American Political Science Association, Washington, D.C.

Shull, Steven. 1991. *The Two Presidencies: A Quarter-Century Assessment.* Chicago: Nelson Hall.

Tulis, Jeffrey K. 1987. *The Rhetorical Presidency.* Princeton, N.J.: Princeton University Press.

Conclusion: Terrorism, Security, and the American State

This volume raises many questions and offers few, if any, answers. Crises can lead to extraordinary actions, some positive, others less so. In the midst of the confusion, basic questions arise. What makes a democracy a democracy? What are the core values that form the essence of the American democratic system? What, in effect, is to be defended? There is much at stake in a fight against terrorism. The threat can seem all-encompassing. How far do you go? What additional powers are needed by the government to meet the test? What are the limits, if any, to be set on these powers? Do the contemporary (post-9/11) grants of power establish precedents for future government actions? The questions are significant. The stakes are very high.

A few final observations are offered here.

The security concerns and the country's needs are real. In testimony before a joint intelligence committee of the Congress by heads of the Central Intelligence Agency (CIA) and Federal Bureau of Investigation (FBI) a year after the attacks, CIA Director George Tenet warned that "the threat environment we find ourselves in today is as bad as it was . . . before 9/11." Despite the vast expansion in counterterrorism efforts, he went on, "It is serious, they've reconstituted, they are coming after us, they want to execute attacks" (Johnston 2002).

In a question-and-answer period, Tenet was clear about the limits these agencies faced:

> You can disseminate all the threat reportings you want. You can do the strategic analysis about airplanes. You can do the strategic analysis about

car bombs, truck bombs, assassination attempts, fast boats and everything else, and you can put all that out there to people. Unless somebody is thinking about the homeland from the perspective of buttoning it down to basically create a deterrence that may work, your assumption will be that the FBI and the CIA are going to be 100 percent flawless all the time, and it will never happen, notwithstanding all the improvements we have made with your help. It is not going to happen.

. . . one of the things that we have learned is in hindsight: the country's mindset has to be changed fundamentally. (Tenet 2002)

A panel of emergency experts, including those from government agencies such as the Federal Emergency Management Agency (FEMA), the FBI, and the Nuclear Regulatory Commission (NRC) as well as private groups (the American Red Cross among others), examined the need for a high-tech warning system for periods of national crisis. Regarding weapons of mass destruction, the chair of the panel reported that "if you can get to people right away and tell them to get out of harm's way, you can save thousands of lives. Our ability to do that at the moment is almost nonexistent" (Stenor 2002). In part, this was a criticism of the administration's color-coded alert system supplied to the media to indicate the level of seriousness of an anticipated threat. But the panel had something far more ambitious in mind: "Our version down the road is that every person at risk from natural disaster, an accident or terrorism would get a heads-up. . . . Every piece of electronics you own—be it a cellphone, a computer, a radio, a television—should have the ability of giving you that heads-up" (Stenor 2002).

In December 2002, a Senate panel released a limited report on intelligence capabilities as they related to the 9/11 attacks (a more comprehensive investigation would follow). The committee's recommendation of a cabinet-level director for national security (in addition to the cabinet position for the secretary of homeland security) received substantial attention. Unexpectedly for a negotiated document bridging both congressional parties and all legislative factions, the report's recommendations were highly critical of the American intelligence community, civilian and military, for not averting the attacks. It was particularly critical of the FBI and the CIA, and it recommended that the senior officials in these agencies be held accountable for their actions. The panel's investigation revealed a continuous series of "missed opportunities to disrupt the September 11 plot." Senator Richard Shelby, the ranking Republican on the committee, charged that the intelligence officials "failed in significant ways to ensure that this country was as prepared as it could have been." The report itself concluded:

> Neither the U.S. government as a whole nor the intelligence community had a comprehensive counterterrorist strategy for combating the threat posed by Osama bin Laden. The intelligence community was neither well organized nor equipped, and did not adequately adapt, to meet the challenge posed by global terrorists focused on targets within the domestic United States. (Risen 2002)

The committee's chairman, Senator Bob Graham of Florida, charged that Americans had been given an "incomplete and distorted picture" of the foreign assistance given to the hijackers; with Shelby, he accused the CIA and FBI in particular of failing to aggressively investigate the connection with Saudi Arabia. He pointed out that the funds from the Saudi royal family were placed in bank accounts used by two of the hijackers. Graham added that the internal terrorist threat continued: "It is equally believable that the infrastructure remains in place and is supporting the current generation of terrorists who are inside the United States, plotting the next attack against us" (Guggenheim 2002; Risen and Johnston 2002).

Chaired by two former members of the Senate, Gary Hart of Colorado and Warren Rudman of New Hampshire, a government-sponsored Commission of National Security for the Twenty-First Century had earlier studied the security threat to the United States; over a two-year period, it released three reports, the final one in February 2001. The reports anticipated coming events.

> The combination of unconventional weapons proliferation with the persistence of international terrorism will end the relative invulnerability of the U.S. homeland to catastrophic attack. A direct attack against American citizens *on American soil* is likely over the next quarter century. The risk is not only death and destruction but also a demoralization that could undermine U.S. global leadership. In the face of this threat, our nation has no coherent or integrated government structures. (Hart and Rudman 2001, viii)

The series of reports went on to recommend the following: redesigning key institutions in the executive branch; creating a National Homeland Security Agency; promoting interagency information sharing and cooperative response capabilities; significantly increasing the federal research and development budget; reorganizing Congress to accommodate the recommended bureaucratic realignment to fight terrorism (an issue yet to be addressed and one that relates to congressional oversight of impending threats and the administration's responses to these); increasing grants to aid in the development of technology; upgrading science education; and changing budgetary processes, among other things. Overall, it advocated that "strategy should once again drive the design and implementation of U.S. national security policies" and that "the President should personally guide a top-down strategic planning process and that process should be linked to the allocation of resources throughout the government" (Hart and Rudman 2001, 1).

In hindsight, the recommendations appear almost conventional. More alarming was the warning of domestic terrorist attacks to come. The report was basically ignored. The problem is not going to go away (as the directors of the CIA and FBI testified). Despite efforts at change to meet the new security threats, the country was as vulnerable a year after 9/11 as it had been a year earlier.

The loss of over three thousand lives at the World Trade Center, the Pentagon, and a rural field in Pennsylvania graphically illustrated the horrors of such a war and the essential vulnerability of an open society such as the United States to such attacks. The response to terrorism involves the following components: What should be done? When? What are the ultimate objectives? Which allies do we depend on? Europe? Central Asia? The Middle East? At what cost to us? How do we see the enemy? Why the hatred of the United States? How much of the effort is driven as much by politics as by security concerns (something Americans do not like to think about)? The questions involve such issues as foreign policy and international relations, protecting the public against domestic acts of terrorism, and safeguarding the freedoms that distinguish us as a democratic society.

Americans do not know or seem to care much about security or foreign policy in general. Notwithstanding the likely significant impact that these issues have on people's lives, they are willing to leave decision making to the political leadership. Public support for President George W. Bush ranged in the 90th percentile among the public following 9/11; support for his father as president during the Persian Gulf War of 1990–91 was also in the 90th percentile. As the first Bush's loss in the 1992 election shows, it is not the genius of the individual in the Oval Office or support for the president's policies that explains the virtually unquestioning support granted during a national ordeal invoking feelings of vulnerability. It is the need for decisive leadership, whatever the consequences, and a perception of the president as the embodiment of the country, acting in its best interests. In these regards, foreign policy is totally different from domestic policy. Regarding domestic issues, individuals have a clear idea of their interests; political parties divide along economic, class, and policy lines; and major proposals are doggedly fought out. The political approach is determinedly interventionist, and self-interests are clearly promoted. The process is understandably and totally political. Change is incremental. This is not true for foreign affairs. In the area of national security, the freedom and goodwill ceded the presidency is virtually open-ended. As it has been in the past, the ultimate result may be war.

This war on terrorism is different from battles of the past mostly, it would appear, in its unconventional nature. Previous patterns of public and congressional response are, however, likely to be repeated. Discussion is curtailed; individual freedoms are limited. The government assumes power it never could approach in peacetime. The country's energies and resources are devoted to the war effort. But, when the threat is long-term (as at present) rather than immediate (such as a Pearl harbor–type invasion), there *is* time for reflection and for a studied response to the threat. This presumes some type of national debate, open communication, and reasoned alternatives put forth by the administration, the opposition party, and national leaders. Such a debate did not happen in the aftermath of 9/11. The consequence was that the Bush administration defined the problem, set the policy agenda, established the options, and directed attention to the responses it believed most appropriate. In the process, it reaped political benefits, as in Republican successes during the off-year election of 2002 and in congressional acceptance of proposals labeled critical to the war effort (oil exploration in environmentally protected areas, a cutback in environmental standards, subsidies to the airlines and key industries, a revised tax code to benefit investment, and so on). Obviously, national security issues are not without political consequences.

George W. Bush relies on a small number of key advisers. Two (Vice President Richard Cheney and Secretary of Defense Donald Rumsfeld) are present and/or former secretaries of defense or White House chiefs of staff (both for the Ford administration). Another, George Tenet, is CIA director. Not so much policy makers as administrative organizers are Condoleezza Rice, the national security adviser, and Andrew Card, White House chief of staff. Bush's most intimate adviser, Karl Rove, came along from the Texas governor's office and embodies Hard Right conservatism (as does the administration in its policies). Rove understands domestic politics but has no foreign policy experience. His job has been to fashion the public's perceptions of administration policies and to maximize electoral support. In the 2002 elections, he and the administration excelled at marketing their policies, campaigning for their candidates, and, ultimately, increasing the margin of control in the House and winning control of the Senate. In view of the weakened economy and an incumbent president's usual losses in midterm elections, it was an impressive performance by any standard. Unlike his father, the president himself has little experience in national politics or in elective office at any level (outside of the Texas governorship) and no experience in foreign affairs.

The odd man out in this inner circle of decision makers is Secretary of State Colin Powell, chairman of the Joint Chiefs of Staff during the first Gulf War. Powell has argued for moderation, restraint, multinational commitment, and reliance on United Nations support and its inspection teams in approaching terrorism as well as in planning war with Iraq. It has been a hard sell. His ties to the president are not strong, and his policy positions the least appealing to the commander in chief. From day one, Bush wanted quick, decisive, and punitive retaliations. The preparatory period for air and ground strikes, ultimately quite successful in Afghanistan, tested his patience, and the time needed to build multinational coalitions for any involvement in Iraq went well beyond what he wanted. His instinct was for action. As a consequence, tensions existed among Bush's closest advisers and especially between Rumsfeld and Powell. Rumsfeld was interested in identifying military targets, the logistics of war, and setting a schedule for action. At different times, Powell was banned from giving television interviews and appearing on news programs because his opinions were so out of line with

Bush and the others in his immediate circle (Woodward 2002). Powell saw the administration's stance as one of a "willingness to toss 50 years of American commitment to collective security out of the window" (Powers 2002).

There seems little doubt that the United States will ultimately adjust to and contain the terrorist threat. Containing the terrorist threat is not the only issue here; also significant is the effect that the counterterrorism efforts will have within the United States and in this nation's international relations.

WHY DO THEY HATE US?

In a widely discussed book, *The Clash of Civilizations and the Remaking of World Order* (1996), Samuel Huntington makes a number of relevant points. Among these are the following:

1. A "civilization-based world order" is in the process of developing. Crossover from one "civilization" to another will not be successful (in fact, the "civilizations" will clash because of different values, goals, ethnic and religious identities, histories, etcetera).
2. The West has "universalist pretensions" that will, in effect, engender conflict.
3. Conflict is most likely to occur at critical "fault lines" of contesting societies. One example is the Muslim/non-Muslim divide.
4. Global society should be "multicivilizational," and world leaders should accept and pursue such ends.
5. *"The survival of the West depends on Americans reaffirming their Western identity and Westerners accepting their civilization as unique not universal and uniting to renew and preserve it against challenges from non-Western societies.* Avoidance of a global war of civilizations depends on world leaders accepting and cooperating to maintain the multicivilizational character of global politics" (Huntington 1996, 20–21, emphasis added).
6. The importance of the foregoing is that global relationships are largely being redefined along cultural fault lines. This is a departure from the past.
7. Newly independent nations (as well as those with significantly different histories and collective values) wish to free themselves from Western dominance.

8. The West, however, "is attempting . . . to sustain its preeminent position and defend its interests by defining those interests as the interests of the 'world community'" (Huntington 1996, 184).

9. The power of the Western nations in dominating world affairs is in decline.

10. The West is likely to have problematic ("antagonistic") relations with Muslim nations and with the emerging power in the Far East, China.

It is not a happy prognosis. Many would accept these views, and many would argue (as some have) that the attacks of 9/11 lend credibility to the argument advanced by Huntington.

Are there other reasons that the West, and particularly the United States, occupies such an uneasy position in the world? Clearly, the answer is yes. Israel is a problem for America. It has been at war with its Arab neighbors (and much of the Muslim world) since its inception. Its policies of retaliation, invasion, assassination, and torture in the war with the Palestinians have been relentless, as have those of its enemies. Saddam Hussein's missiles in the Gulf War targeted Israeli civilian populations. The casualties were not great, but the threat from Iraq or elsewhere is nevertheless frightening in the constant struggle for world peace.

Israel is considered a democracy, but there is a split between Jewish hardliner fundamentalists (who have dominated politically) and a more secular strain in the society; it is a nation of people arriving from different countries, some moderate, others not. The United States supports Israel unequivocally, a product of its perception that Israel is democratic and, more directly, a consequence of domestic political pressures. The United States supplies Israel with financial aid, preferential trade agreements, and military hardware. In fact, Israel is the chief recipient of U.S. foreign and military aid, amounting to 55 percent of the world total for U.S. foreign military financing in fiscal year 2001, at $1.9 trillion (Department of Defense 2002). The movements and countries that hate the Israelis have no doubt about its chief sponsor.

A second concern is religious fundamentalism versus secularism. The United States is seen as the embodiment of secularism—exploitative, money-driven, sex-mad, vulgar, and obscene. Religious justifications provide a useful tool for fundamentalists opposed to the West and its values. The split between Islam and Christendom goes back more than a millennium. The Koran in its various interpretations is used to justify action against people considered to be godless.

The Western way of life *does* provide many challenges to the Muslim faith. Syndicated columnist William Pfaff has commented:

> The power and material dynamism of the West seem inseparable from a value system that demands that Muslims give up their moral identity. . . . why should we blame Islam for trying to reject "Western technology, Western institutions, Western conceptions of religious freedom" when all of these "involve a rejection of the idea on which Islam is founded—the idea of God's immutable will, revealed once and for all to his prophet, in the form of an unbreachable and unchanging code of law."

Western nations, the United States included, have conceptions of the Muslim world that are far from favorable, as Pfaff has noted:

> The West takes for granted that the existing religious assumptions of Islamic society have to be overturned, not only because they don't suit the West but because the West believes that they are unsuitable for the Muslims themselves. There is constant Western pressure on Islamic governments to conform to Western conceptions of human rights and promote free, critical religious and political thought. In short, they are to become us. . . . Standard American discussions of American destiny and the "end of history" take for granted an eventual benevolent Americanization of global society. To the observant Muslim, that means apostasy, immorality, and God's condemnation. Westernization, to Westerners, means liberation. (Pfaff, 2002)

The message in Huntington's *Clash of Civilizations* reflects these concerns.

Fundamentalism and state-sponsored support for fundamentalists has been explained as a strategy for directing attention away from the inequalities in wealth in the Arab donor states. Such support includes Saudi Arabian aid for fundamentalist Islamic schools in the Middle East, a breeding ground for terrorist organizations, and grants to voluntary societies that fund Islamic terrorist movements, including Al Qaeda. Beyond Saudi Arabia, the poverty and imbalances in many nations could serve as grounds for directing hatred at the well-off Western countries, especially the United States. A perusal of the data can illustrate the argument (table 1).

TABLE 1. Social and Economic Indicators in Selected Countries

HDI Rank		Life expectancy at birth (years), 2000	Adult (15 and above) literacy rate, 2000	Combined primary, secondary, and tertiary gross enrollment ratio, 1999	GDP per capita (PPP US$), 2000	Life expectancy index	Education index	GDP index	Human development index (HDI) value	GDP per capita (PPP US$) rank minus HDI rank
	High-Income OECD[b]	78.2	99.0	94	27,639	0.89	0.97	0.94	0.932	
	Arab States	66.8	62.0	62	4,793	0.70	0.62	0.64	0.653	
6	United States	77.0	99.0	95	34,142	0.87	0.98	0.97	0.939	−4
22	Israel	78.7	94.6	83	20,131	0.90	0.91	0.89	0.896	1
39	Bahrain	73.3	87.6	80	15,084	0.81	0.85	0.84	0.831	−2
45	Kuwait	76.2	82.0	59	15,799	0.85	0.74	0.84	0.813	−10
46	United Arab Emirates	75.0	76.3	68	17,935	0.83	0.74	0.87	0.812	−19
51	Qatar	69.6	81.2	75	18,789	0.74	0.79	0.87	0.803	−25
64	Libyan Arab Jamahiriy	70.5	80.0	92	7,570	0.76	0.84	0.72	0.773	−2
71	Saudi Arabia	71.6	76.3	61	11,367	0.78	0.71	0.79	0.759	−26
75	Lebanon	73.1	86.0	78	4,308	0.80	0.83	0.63	0.755	20
78	Oman	71.0	71.7	58	13,356	0.77	0.67	0.82	0.751	−38
98	Islamic Rep. of Iran	68.9	76.3	73	5,884	0.73	0.75	0.68	0.721	−22
99	Jordan	70.3	89.7	55	3,966	0.76	0.78	0.61	0.717	−1
106	Algeria	69.6	66.7	72	5,308	0.74	0.69	0.66	0.697	−22
108	Syrian Arab Republic	71.2	74.4	63	3,556	0.77	0.71	0.60	0.691	−2
115	Egypt	67.3	55.3	76	3,635	0.70	0.62	0.60	0.642	−10
138	Pakistan	60.0	43.2	40	1,928	0.58	0.42	0.49	0.499	−7
144	Yemen	60.6	46.3	51	893	0.59	0.48	0.37	0.479	14
149	Djibouti	43.1	64.6	22	2,377	0.30	0.50	0.53	0.445	−28

a. PPP: Purchasing power parity, a normalizing measure that reflects the gross domestic product in a given country and allows for more accurate comparisons.
b. OECD: Organization for Economic Cooperation and Development.
SOURCE: United Nations Human Development Report 2002

On every major indicator—literacy, educational levels, life expectancy, and the UN human development index—the Arab countries are well behind the United States (and Israel, although this is not their reason for opposing the Israelis). On the basis of wealth alone, as measured by the gross domestic product (GDP), the United States is roughly six to seven times more prosperous than the combined measure for the Arab states. These countries are not unaware of the enormous discrepancies in resource allocations and living standards—a globalized communications and entertainment industry disseminates this information to even the most apolitical of people. Societies that culturally and religiously reject such wealth as well as the secularism and excesses accompanying it, feel justified in targeting the United States as oppressor and symbol of all that they oppose.

On one side is modernization and its attendant values, capitalism, a competitive ethos, meritocracy, democracy, advanced technology, high levels of education, and secularism. On the other is traditionalism, consensualism, ethnic identity, a status hierarchy, parochialism, a fixed sense of place, and the extended values of existing in a virtually static environment. Most critically, perhaps, many individuals in other societies may feel themselves unprepared for the demands being made upon them by what they would see as a new and alien world order. It is a challenge of basic proportions with no easy or clear resolution.

The discrepancies clearly are enormous. Yet they have had little role in the discussions of the "war on terrorism," the causes for the hatred directed against the United States, or the long-run consequences of the actions taken or contemplated.

Two commentaries are relevant. First is that of Thomas Powers (who has written on Al Qaeda, among other subjects), in reviewing Bob Woodward's *Bush at War:*

> To fight the war on terror, perhaps the most important parts of the debate were the things on which "the principals" in the war cabinet had little to say. . . . In the war on terror who, exactly, is the enemy? What is the source of the anger that prompted Al Qaeda to such bloody attacks? Why does the administration assume that "any serious, full-scale war against terrorism would have to make Iraq a target"? Will victory over the Taliban and Saddam Hussein be the end of it? What is going on in the collective mind of the Islamic world as it watches America crush one Muslim regime after an-

other? Answers to these questions would help us to understand where we can expect to find ourselves in 10 or 20 years' time, but about them . . . President Bush and his team rarely speak. (Powers 2002)

And second, syndicated columnist William Raspberry comments:

One of the key questions . . . is how those who make our policy see the role of the United States. Are we . . . the only ones with both the clarity of vision and the military wherewithal to undertake the unpleasant task of belling the aggressive cats of the world? Do they see us as Johnny Appleseeds of democracy, doing what we can to spread its joyous gospel? Or do they see us . . . as some sort of international Dirty Harry, packing lots of heat and requiring only the thinnest of pretexts (and little patience for procedural and evidentiary niceties) to rid the world of its scum? . . . do they think—does America think—that it's too late to work at peace, that it's wimpish to wonder why so much of the world dislikes us, that it's a form of appeasement to try to show the world our better nature? (Raspberry 2002)

Whether these questions will receive serious attention is also unknown.

THE IRAQI QUESTION

Punitive action directed against Iraq was considered an option from the beginning of the war on terrorism. There was no evidence to suggest Iraq was involved in the 9/11 attacks and none to suggest that Iraq and Saddam Hussein were associated with Al Qaeda or Osama bin Laden. In fact, they represent opposite ends of the political continuum; one a fundamentalist return to extreme religious orthodoxy, antisecularity, and tribalism; the other a secular authoritarian state built on military power and political repression. Nonetheless, Iraq and Saddam Hussein were in the crosshairs of the Bush administration from the first day of the 9/11 attacks.

The concern with Iraq might be seen as residual from the 1991 Persian Gulf War and the failure to unseat Saddam Hussein in what was an otherwise highly successful campaign. The first Bush administration sought to "defend democracy in Kuwait," the oil-rich sheikdom Hussein had invaded. A second war in the Persian Gulf could conceivably detract from the broader war against terrorism, a point Colin Powell has made repeatedly. George W.

Bush's justification for military action against Iraq is to eliminate "weapons of mass destruction." There was no question that Iraq had these in the earlier war and that it would use them to serve its own ends in attacking other countries if it chose to do so. Allegedly, Iraq has been attempting to increase its threat capabilities through the development of more powerful nuclear weapons and agents of germ warfare.

Colin Powell was joined by Hugh Shelton, chairman of the Joint Chiefs of Staff (whose term in office was soon to expire), in opposing the launch of a war against Iraq. Dick Cheney and Paul Wolfowitz, deputy secretary of defense, joined the president in favoring an aggressive military intervention. From the very beginning, the vice president argued that Iraq and Saddam Hussein were somehow implicated in the suicide bombings and should be dealt with directly.

It was felt that no response could equal the terror of the attacks. President Bush referred to the "barbarism" of the attacks. He and his advisers were angry and all options were on the table. The question was which type of response would be most appropriate—multilateral, military, or political.

A few among the public were skeptical. According to a report in the *New York Times:* "People said they hungered for a coherent explanation from the president—stripped of what one woman called his recent 'yippee-ki-yay' rhetoric—that laid out why Iraq was suddenly such a threat. There was also widespread apprehension about terrorist repercussions" (Harden and Kilborn 2002). But most people seemed to reflect Cheney's views that Iraq was involved in the Al Qaeda attacks of 9/11, and they appeared willing to support some kind of action directed against Saddam Hussein. Ostensibly, confusion and a desire for retaliation for the 9/11 bombings were the main reasons.

As the president described it:

> We haven't seen this kind of barbarism in a long period of time. . . . No one could have conceivably imagined suicide bombers burrowing into our society and then emerging all in the same day to fly their aircraft—fly U.S. aircraft—into buildings full of innocent people and show no remorse. . . . This crusade, this war on terrorism is going to take a while. (Woodward 2002, 94)

Woodward has depicted the tragedy:

September 11 was not only the deadliest attack on the American homeland, surpassing Pearl Harbor in body count, but the most photographed and filmed violent assault in history. Who could forget the crystal-clear video reruns of the gently banking United Airlines Flight 175 plowing into the 80th floor of the South Tower of the World Trade Center, depositing its lethal fireball and nearly emerging from the other side. Or the image of the smoking Twin Towers. Or the video of the collapsing towers, one then the other, and the cloud of debris and smoke suffocating Lower Manhattan. Or the pictures of the people jumping from the uppermost floors to their deaths to escape the unbearable heat inside. Or the despair on the faces of all Americans. (Woodward 2002, 94–95)

The argument for attacking Iraq (even in preference to Afghanistan) after 9/11 was probably best put by Wolfowitz, whose right-wing credentials as an ideologue have long been recognized. "Attacking Afghanistan would be uncertain. . . . about 100,000 American troops [could be] bogged down in mountain fighting in Afghanistan [in] six months. . . . In contrast, Iraq was a brittle, oppressive regime that might break easily. It was doable. [Wolfowitz] estimated that there was a 10 to 50 percent chance Saddam was involved in the September 11 terrorist attacks. The U.S. would have to go after Saddam at some time if the war on terrorism was to be taken seriously" (Woodward 2002, 83).

The argument against invading Iraq and concentrating on bin Laden was made at different points by Powell, who stated that roughly sixty nations had indicated they were sympathetic to a U.S. response focusing on Afghanistan, the haven for Al Qaeda, and Osama bin Laden. A handful indicated a willingness to help the United States in its military operations. To go after Iraq or every state that supported terrorism at once was a mistake. "All the states that supported terror, you can do at a time of your choosing . . . They are not going anywhere [a repetition of the words Bush had used the previous day in a memorial service at the National Cathedral]. Don't go with the Iraq option right away, or we'll lose the coalition we've been signing up. They'll view it as a bait and switch—it's not what they signed up to do" (Woodward 2002, 87).

The message: Keep the focus on Al Qaeda; attack its bases of operation in Afghanistan; destroy its sanctuaries and capabilities to the extent possible; set the time and circumstances for later campaigns; and develop and sustain a multinational commitment. There were many potential targets; the United States could not, and should not, take it all on at once or alone.

The decision was that the initial military campaign would be directed against Al Qaeda's bases in Afghanistan. However, with time, after the successful completion of the Afghanistan campaign (although not the dismantling of Al Qaeda) and the installation of a new Western-supported government there, principal attention turned to Saddam Hussein and Iraq. The reason, it was constantly argued by the Bush administration, was the necessity to neutralize "weapons of mass destruction." George W. Bush now wanted to finish the job his father started in the early 1990s—and drive Hussein from power.

OPENNESS, DEMOCRATIC PROCEDURES, AND CRISIS SITUATIONS

What qualifies a nation as democratic? How far do you go in defense of a nation-state? To what extent do you curtail civil liberties? The basic debate facing the United States today in its war on terrorism concerns the extent to which the rights and privileges enjoyed by citizens are restricted or eliminated in the name of national security. So far the debate has been one-sided. Or to be more blunt, it has yet to be engaged. Whatever the Bush administration has deemed has passed as acceptable, and opposition has been feeble to nonexistent. The public little understands the consequences of the actions being undertaken, nor does it appear to be very concerned. Congress has not offered a forum for the national debate on these issues that one might expect in a democratic society. The opposition party has chosen not to make this a point of contention. The media have little to say beyond reporting, in the way of news, the actions taken or anticipated.

The terrorist threat itself was clearly and drastically illustrated by the horrific 9/11 bombings of the World Trade Center towers and the Pentagon, as well as by the crash of another hijacked airplane in Pennsylvania that same day. It can be argued that the administration has done precisely what it should do in the face of such a crisis. It could also be argued that the Bush administration has chosen a potentially destructive path to fighting worldwide terrorism, one that brings into question the very nature of the American democratic system. And it has done so in something of a vacuum, with little overt opposition or discussion.

The Patriot Act and the Department of Homeland Security are cases in point; they could be (but have not been) a lightning rod for such concerns. Instead, the major objections to these initiatives have been the patronage power given the president, the relaxation or elimination of civil service guarantees in the name of national security, and Bush's successful efforts to nullify union prerogatives and controls over the workforce. A few isolated voices have raised questions about broader issues, such as the breach of civil rights protections for the public and the extraordinary power placed in the hands of one man, the president.

Most distressing is the fact that this power is being exercised by a presidency that has set new standards for secrecy. According to one noted historian: "The Bush Administration has put a much tighter lid than recent presidents on government proceedings and the public release of information, exhibiting a penchant for secrecy that has been striking to historians, legal experts and lawmakers of both parties." Further, his "instinct is to release nothing" (Clymer 2003). The process began prior to 9/11 and has only accelerated since. This history-making addiction to secrecy and other disturbing developments such as the weakening (and in some cases failure) of established legislative processes are not inclined to build confidence in this administration's commitment to the normal workings of a democracy.

THE WASHINGTON MIND AT WORK: THE VICTIMS' 9/11 INQUIRY COMMISSION

The White House, after a year of opposing it, agreed to the creation of an independent commission to investigate the terrorist attacks. It was the product of an intense campaign by the victims' families among the media and lawmakers. Senator John McCain, a proponent of the investigatory commission, described the compromise with the administration in these terms: "equal bipartisan membership, a broad mandate to review policies and responses to the range of government agencies, and subpoena power to dig deep to find out what went wrong and how we can make sure it never happens again." The hope was that this commission would lead to the most complete and authoritative assessment of how and why the attacks had occurred and how similar events could be avoided in the future. A leader of the family groups representing the victims of the tragedies, while indicating he was "optimistic," went on to say: "We're not crazy about the President appointing the chair" (Firestone 2002).

He (and the victims' families) had reason to be concerned. The chair Bush appointed to head the commission was Henry A. Kissinger. It was a controversial choice. A former national security adviser and secretary of state in the Nixon and Ford administrations, and an adviser to the Reagan administration, he was the perfect choice for many. According to the president, "his chairmanship would have provided the insight and analysis the government needs to understand threats we face" (Firestone 2002).

For others, Kissinger was the ultimate Washington insider, known for his "cynicism" and secrecy in dealing with the press and the public. While Kissinger is a Nobel Peace Prize laureate for his work in helping to end the Vietnam War, he has also been accused of committing war crimes. His record was not promising: he had business ties with Saudi Arabia; he had urged the Reagan administration to expand its military ties to El Salvador and the contras in Nicaragua in the 1980s; and he was a supporter of the overthrow (through assassination) of the democratically elected Salvador Allende in Chile, as well as a backer of the authoritarian and repressive Pinochet regime that followed. There had been calls for his trial in international courts for human rights abuses relating to his alleged role in civilian deaths in southeast Asia in the 1960s and in relationship to the Pinochet regime. He was a proponent of Operation Condor, an American-supported program to encourage "South American dictatorships to track and kill their opponents in exile," a policy resulting in the death by assassination in Washington, D.C., of an American and a former Chilean official who opposed the military junta that ruled that country. The *Boston Globe* called him a "poor choice" and elaborated thus: "Kissinger either devised or supported policies that resulted in the deaths of thousands of civilians in Indochina as the Vietnam War dragged on through the Nixon Administration. He also endorsed policies by Pakistan and Indonesia that resulted in the deaths of thousands of civilians in Bangladesh and East Timor" (*Boston Globe* 2002).

In November 2002, the *New York Times* editorialized:

> In naming Henry Kissinger to direct a comprehensive examination of the government's failure to prevent the Sept. 11 attacks, President Bush has selected a consummate Washington insider. Mr. Kissinger obviously has a

keen intellect and vast experience in national security matters. Unfortunately, his affinity for power and the commercial interests he has cultivated since leaving government may make him less than the staunchly independent figure that is needed for this critical post. . . . it is tempting to wonder if the choice of Mr. Kissinger is not a clever maneuver by the White House to contain an investigation it long opposed. It seems improbable to expect Mr. Kissinger to report unflinchingly on the conduct of the government, including that of Mr. Bush. He would have to challenge the established order and risk sundering old friendships and business relationships. (*New York Times* 2002)

An editorial a month later in the *Nation* added: "For many in the world, Kissinger is a symbol of U.S. arrogance and the misuse of American might." It was argued by some that his appointment to the commission undermined its moral authority and weakened the U.S. case against terrorism.

The Democrats had the power to select the vice chair of the committee. They chose George Mitchell, former Democratic majority leader in the Senate and chief author of the "Good Friday Agreement" in Northern Ireland, a plan laying the groundwork for an end to sectarian violence there. Mitchell resigned within a matter of days, saying it would take too much time from his law practice.

Kissinger resigned a few days later, after the Senate Ethics Committee had ruled, despite intense pressure from the White House to allow Kissinger an exception, that all members of the new commission would have to comply with congressional financial disclosure requirements. This meant that Kissinger would have to publicly reveal his list of clients. He refused. He wrote to the president: "It is clear that, although specific potential conflicts can be resolved in this manner, the controversy would quickly move to the consulting firm I have built and own. I have, therefore, concluded that I cannot accept the responsibility you proposed" (Fournier 2002).

The Democrats replaced Mitchell with Lee Hamilton, head of the Woodrow Wilson Center in Washington, a former congressperson from Indiana, and a former chair of the House Intelligence Committee. The Bush administration replaced Kissinger with Thomas Kean, the president of Drew University and a former governor of New Jersey. Kean, a Republican, was considered a moderate, liberal on social issues and conservative on economic policy; he had a reputation for being able to work with both Democrats and Republicans. Well respected, he had none of the political baggage of his predecessor.

With these changes, the committee was finally in a position to get on with its business. While signing the act establishing the commission, the president had declared that it "should carefully examine all the evidence and follow all the facts, wherever they lead" (Stevenson 2002). At the same time, the White House made it clear that the president did not intend to appear before the group, which had eighteen months to make its report.

The Kissinger controversy says a lot about Washington politics, even in the most trying of times. Politics usually comes first; the 9/11 commission was to prove no exception. Its eventual report was expected to be the most comprehensive evaluation as well as the fairest and most balanced of those to emerge from the tragedies. It would also be among the most influential in defining the administration's preparedness for such attacks and its actions in their aftermath. The commission's long-range significance was established before it even began its deliberations. The report is scheduled to appear in the middle of the 2004 presidential election year, making its political impact unavoidable.

The families of the victims who had campaigned hard for just such a commission wanted justice—this meant the best and most complete analysis possible. The television coverage of the utter horror of the World Trade Center explosions, in particular, and the buildings' collapse were powerful tools in their quest, as was emphasis on the heroism of the fire, police, and aid workers in the tragedy's aftermath. The victims' families organized, strategized, took their case to the public through the media, and lobbied Congress and the White House. They were not acquiescent, and they would not be bought off by partial explanations, flawed investigations, or the promise of financial aid. From the beginning, they saw the process as political. With growing organization, self-financing, and a more considered strategy, they stayed the course. Eventually they got what they sought.

Seldom does a grassroots effort build into a successful national campaign. The victims' families had a powerful case and an implicit nationwide constituency. They used these well. In this context, it is a classic example of a successful political movement.

Many in the Congress—some for personal reasons, some sensing political gain—agreed with the victims' families on the need for an independent investigation. Others hoped for an insight into the means of protecting the country from further assaults; their primary concern was national security.

The Bush administration did not want a commission in any form. Once forced to accept it, the White House wanted to set its course, control its deliberations, and come out with a report it could accept. Hence the appointment of Kissinger: a person of unsurpassed credentials, a sensitivity to the needs of those in power, and, as it turned out, a number of liabilities serious enough to force his resignation.

Bush's resistance and the perseverance of the victims' families set up a classic political battle. The consistent public attention to events more than likely proved decisive in the unusual outcome. The empowerment of an independent body in the hands of a respected leadership to investigate a highly charged political event is rare indeed.

The quest for justice, or security, or information, or useful prescriptions as to how to proceed in the future after the 9/11 attacks evolved into a classic test of political wills. The scope of the tragedy and the eventual resolution of the conflict about examining the disaster were anything but normal. Paradoxically, however, this was a case of Washington politics as usual.

THE DEMOCRATS AND TERRORISM

Post-9/11, the approach of the Democrats was essentially to agree with the president's policies on national security, attacking on a few peripheral issues but not challenging the administration or presenting reasonable alternatives to the major initiatives before the American people. The party's hope was that by agreeing with Bush on terrorism policies, the concern would be neutralized and Democratic candidates (as in the 2002 elections) could direct attention to a sour economy, an issue base that traditionally works to their benefit. The strategy did not work in the off-year elections in which Bush campaigned fiercely for his candidates; the Republican Party was able to mobilize its enormous resources and focus on the winnable races, and the campaign was conducted in a political environment debating the approach to and timing of a war against Iraq. The Republicans won big, taking seats in the House and taking the Senate 52 to 48, results that served to strengthen the president's hand.

It appeared that the Democratic Party had lost its sense of direction and suffered for it. Its message was unclear, its national leadership missing in action or nonexistent. It had no unified approach and attempted to override a debate on security issues by stressing local constituency concerns. It did not work. When Dick Gephardt, majority leader in the House and a candidate for his party's presidential nomination, resigned after the election, new stewardship came in the form of the first woman to hold the position of party leader, Nancy Pelosi of California.

A step toward Democratic renewal may have been made in Bill Clinton's speech to the Democratic Leadership Council, the group that had helped propel him to the presidency in the 1992 election. In a number of respects, Clinton chose to defend his administration's accomplishments while offering a contrast to those of George W. Bush's administration. In other respects, he put forth viable strategies for challenging the Bush agenda. He spoke of a slumping stock market, a bad economy, tax rates that benefited the rich, trade policies, income differentials, fiscal responsibility, a new energy policy, school programs, environmental protections, the plight of working people, Social Security, and debt relief for developing countries. He focused more on economic rather than on military alliances (referring to the former as "positive assistance"). These are all familiar Clinton themes and Democratic Party concerns.

An aggressively prepared and informed opposition party could initiate a nationwide assessment of the terrorist threat and the best ways to handle it. Clinton was blunt on this subject: "When people are feeling insecure, they'd rather have someone who is strong and wrong rather than someone who is weak and right" (Clinton 2002). Clinton proposed a Democratic program. "First, on national security, the facts are that the majority of the Democrats have been clear and virtually unanimous in the fight against terror, and in supporting defense increases, the majority of us stood up and said, yes, we do have to have unlimited and unambiguous inspections in Iraq and the ability to use force, if necessary, if those inspections and the mandate of the UN are not honored. . . . But it's not nearly enough" (Clinton 2002).

Having said that the Democrats supported the administration's defense initiatives and agreed that the party had pushed for many of these against Republican opposition, Clinton then questioned the very basis of the Bush administration's assumptions. "What should our security position be? First of all . . . Iraq is important but the terrorist network is more urgent in terms of its threat to our immediate security" (Clinton 2002). Further questions are obvious. Can or should the United States fight what amounts to two separate wars at the same time? Can they be fought with equal commitment and equal intensity? Which is the more important? The more challenging? The one demanding immediate attention? And the one involving the greatest immediate risk to America?

Clinton went on to argue for accountability in intelligence gathering, information sharing, in modernizing information technology, and developing sources of energy. He also focused on domestic policy:

> We ought to get to real homeland security, to matters more important than that department. The Democrats have a stronger position here than the Republicans. . . . You can reorganize all you want, but what are you doing to protect the tunnels, the bridges, the water systems, the utility systems, to provide for adequate first responders, police and fire and people to respond if there's an anthrax attack or a chemical release? The Democrats have pushed and pushed and pushed, against constant resistance from the Republicans, to provide adequate funding for these things. That's a national security issue, a homeland security issue that matters a lot more than where bureaucratic boxes are. We didn't say it in the last elections and if we had, it would have made a difference. . . . It's not important just for political reasons; it's important because people's lives are at stake here. (Clinton 2002)

This argument would be a launching point for a party and a spark for public debate on options and priorities essentially missing in the first year post-9/11.

CLOSING THOUGHTS

The terrorist threat, as seen in the shocking 9/11 attacks, is not to be taken lightly. It could be argued that the Bush administration has chosen an appropriate series of responses representing the best interests of the American public. It could also be argued that the administration has chosen a particularly repressive and potentially destructive path in fighting worldwide terrorism, one that could eventually bring into question the very nature of the American democratic system. And it has done this in something of a vacuum.

Jimmy Carter made a number of relevant points in accepting the 2002 Nobel Peace Prize. They are worth pondering. As he indicated, the United States is the world's only superpower. It is not discussed in these terms but its powers are overwhelming, historically without parallel. They need to be exercised wisely and with restraint. Carter commented, "For powerful countries to adopt a principle of preventive war may well set an example that can have catastrophic consequences." He developed the argument:

> There is only one superpower, with unprecedented military and economic strength. The . . . budget for American armaments will be greater than those of the next fifteen nations combined. . . . there are troops from the United States in many countries throughout the world. Our gross national economy exceeds that of the three countries that follow us, and our nation's voice most often prevails as decisions are made concerning trade, humanitarian assistance, and the allocation of global wealth. This dominant status is unlikely to change in our lifetimes.
>
> Great American power and responsibility are not unprecedented, and have been used with restraint and great benefit in the past. We have not assumed that super strength guarantees super wisdom, and we have consistently reached out to the international community to ensure that our own power and influence are tempered by the best common judgment. (Carter 2002)

The clear message was that the laudatory principles mentioned should guide Americans through a trying time. The hope is that the resilience of the nation's bedrock values and its historic democratic commitments will prove to be the ultimate triumph post-9/11.

REFERENCES

Boston Globe. 2002. Editorial, "Kissinger's Unfit Past," November 30, A14.
Carter, Jimmy. 2002. Nobel speech, December 10. On-line at www.pbs.org/newshour/updates/december02/carter_speech.html, accessed December 12, 2002.
Clinton, William. 2002. *Remarks by Former President William Clinton to the Democratic Leadership Council*, December 8. On-line at http://www.ndol.org, accessed December 12, 2003.

Clymer, Adam. 2003. "Government Openness at Issue as Bush Holds on to Records." *New York Times,* January 3, A1.

Department of Defense, Defense Security Cooperation Agency. 2002. *DSCA (Facts Book)—Foreign Military Sales, Foreign Military Construction Sales and Military Assistance Facts, September 26, 2002.* Set no. 3, Foreign Military Financing (FMF) Program. On-line at http://www.dsca.osd.mil/programs/Comptroller/2001_FACTS/default.htm, accessed January 14, 2003.

Federation of American Scientists Arms Sales Monitoring Project. 2002. *Database on U.S. Security Assistance FY 1990-2001.* On-line at http://www.fas.org/asmp/profiles/aid/aidindex.htm, accessed January 14, 2003.

Firestone, David. 2002a. "Kissinger Pulls Out as Chief of Inquiry into 9/11 Attacks." *New York Times,* November 14, A1.

Firestone, David. 2002b. "White House Yields on 9/11 Inquiry Backed by Congress." *New York Times,* November 15, A1.

Fournier, Ron. 2002. "Kissinger Quits as Chairman of 9/11 Panel." Associated Press, December 13. On-line at yahoo news.com, accessed January 15, 2003.

Guggenheim, Ken. 2002. "Lawmakers OK Report on Pre-9/11 Failures." *Boston Globe,* December 11, A33.

Harden, Blaine, and Peter Kilborn. 2002. "9/11 Looms in Nation's Debate on Iraq." *New York Times,* October 6, A1.

Hart, Gary, and Warren Rudman. 2001. "Road Map for National Security: Imperative for Change." In *The Phase III Report of the U.S. Commission on National Security/ 21st Century.* On-line at http://www.nssg.gov/Reports/reports.htm, accessed May 15, 2003.

Huntington, Samuel P. 1996. *The Clash of Civilizations and the Remaking of World Order.* New York: Simon and Schuster.

Johnston, David. 2002. "CIA Puts Risk of Terror Strike at 9/11 Levels." *New York Times,* October 18, A1.

Kranish, Michael. 2002. "Kissinger Resigns as Chairman of 9/11 Panel." *Boston Globe,* December 14, A1.

Nation. 2002. Editorial, "The Kissinger Deceit," December 23, 5.

New York Times. 2002. Editorial, "The Kissinger Commission," November 29, A32.

Pfaff, William. 2002. "A Conflict of US, Muslim Values." *Boston Globe,* December 16, A19.

Powers, Thomas. 2002. "The Commander in Chief." Book review of *Bush at War,* by Bob Woodward. *New York Times Book Review,* December 15, 11.

Raspberry, William. 2002. "Nagging Questions about the War with Iraq." *Boston Sunday Globe,* December 29, D11.

Risen, James. 2002. "Inquiry Is Sharply Critical of Intelligence Agencies for Failing to Prevent Attacks." *New York Times,* December 12, A22.

Risen, James, and Daniel Johnston. 2002. "Lawmakers Want Cabinet Position for Intelligence." *New York Times,* December 8, A1.

Stenor, Philip. 2002. "Panel Calls for High-Tech Warning System." *New York Times,* November 25, A15.

Stevenson, Richard W. 2002. "President Names Kissinger to Lead 9/11 Commission." *New York Times,* November 28, A1.

Tenet, George. 2002. "Excerpts from Testimony by Directors of the CIA and FBI on Sept. 11." *New York Times,* October 18, A12.

Woodward, Bob. 2002. *Bush at War.* New York: Simon and Schuster.

Contributors

William Crotty is the Thomas P. O'Neill Chair in Public Life and director of the Center for the Study of Democracy at Northeastern University. He is the author or coauthor of a number books about national and international politics and political development, including *Assassinations and the Political Order* and *The State of Democracy in America*, his latest published work. He has served as codirector of the Task Force on Political Assassinations of the National Commission on the Causes and Consequences of Violence, a presidentially appointed commission intended to assess the threat of political violence to American society. He has written and lectured on this subject and is the editor and coauthor of *Assassination and Political Violence*. Before arriving at Northeastern in 1995, he was a professor at Northwestern University in Chicago for nearly thirty years.

Daniel Krislov is assistant professor of political science at the University of New Hampshire. He has a Ph.D. in jurisprudence and social policy from the University of California at Berkeley and a J.D. from Stanford University. He has also served as a consultant for the RAND Corporation.

Lynn M. Kuzma is assistant professor of political science and director of international studies at the University of Southern Maine. She teaches classes on U.S. foreign policy, international relations, and international organizations. Her research interests focus on public opinion and terrorism. Since 9/11, she has given numerous presentations on the subject, and her work has recently appeared in *Public Opinion Quarterly*.

Scott L. McLean is associate professor of political science at Quinnipiac University and analyst in the Quinnipiac University Polling Institute. He specializes in political thought, U.S. elections, and public opinion, and is a frequent commentator in regional and national news media. He is coeditor of *Social Capital: Critical Perspectives on Community and "Bowling Alone."* McLean serves on the advisory boards for the Albert Schweitzer Institute and for civic education under the Connecticut secretary of state; he is also a member of the Quinnipiac University Committee on Service Learning. His most recent research focuses on civic education and American nationalism.

Jerome M. Mileur is professor of political science at the University of Massachusetts—Amherst. He is editor of *Liberalism in Crisis: American Politics in the Sixties* and coeditor of *Challenges to Party Government, Progressivism and the New Democracy,* and *The New Deal and the New Liberalism.* He also serves as coeditor of the University of Massachusetts Press series Political Development of the American Nation. He has published extensively and has presented papers on political terrorism, among other subjects, at professional meetings.

Stephen Nathanson is professor of philosophy at Northeastern University. He holds a B.A. from Swarthmore College and a Ph.D. from Johns Hopkins University and is the author of numerous books and articles on ethical aspects of legal and political issues. His books include *An Eye for an Eye? The Immorality of Punishing by Death; Should We Consent to be Governed? A Short Introduction to Political Philosophy; Patriotism, Morality, and Peace;* and *Economic Justice.*

B. Guy Peters is Maurice Falk Professor of American Government at the University of Pittsburgh, as well as honorary professor of public administration at the City University of Hong Kong and senior fellow of the Canadian Centre for Management Development. He has written or edited more than fifty books on comparative public administration and policy, comparative politics, and American government; he has also served as a consultant for a number of national and international government organizations. He is currently writing a book on the process of policy coordination.

Richard J. Powell is assistant professor of political science at the University of Maine. He holds a B.A. from Connecticut College as well as a master's degree and doctorate from Northwestern University. His research and teaching interests include the U.S. presidency, Congress, mass media, legislative elections, and research methodology. Professor Powell is currently finishing a book on the communications strategies employed by recent U.S. presidents. He is the author of journal articles on presidential-congressional relations, presidential communications, congressional elections, and the political ambition of state legislators.

Ronald Story is professor of history at the University of Massachusetts—Amherst. He is author of *The Forging of an Aristocracy: Harvard and the Boston Upper Class,* coauthor of *Generations of Americans: A History of the United States,* editor of *Five Colleges: Five Histories,* and author of numerous essays on American politics and culture.

John Kenneth White is professor of politics at the Catholic University of America. He has written extensively and is the author of several books on American politics, most notably *The New Politics of Old Values, Still Seeing Red: How the Cold War Shapes the New American Politics,* and *The Values Divide: American Politics and Culture in Transition.*

Index

Ames, Aldrich, 235
Animal and Plant Inspection Service, 206, 245, 248
Anthrax attack, 38, 58, 197, 240
Anti-Ballistic Missile Treaty, 264, 272
ANWR, 264, 271
APHIS, 206, 245, 248
Arab Americans, 57–59, 79–80, 174, 180, 197
Arabs, 51, 52, 285, 286–88. *See also* Islam; *specific Arabic countries and peoples*
Arrests. *See* Detention
Arthur Andersen scandal, 42
Ashcroft, John, 58, 80, 119–20, 125, 129n.24
Assassination (political): of Americans, 38, 39, 99, 118; by Israel, 285; justifications for, 14; Kissinger's support for, 294; as terrorism, 136
Attorneys general, 125. *See also specific attorneys general*
Authoritarianism, 138, 289, 294

Band of Brothers (television series), 40
Banks. *See* Financial transactions
Al-Banna, Hasum, 50
Barber, Benjamin, 52
Beamer, Lisa, 45
Beamer, Todd, 44, 45
Bellah, Robert, 77
"Bend over backward" rule, 30–31
Berlin (Germany), 115, 148–49
Biddle, Francis, 107, 109, 112, 125
Bin al-Shibh, Ramzi, 157n.8
Bin Laden, Osama: Afghanistan as base for, x, 118–20, 149, 192, 291; and gap between West and East, 48, 49; and GWB, 47, 215; as responsible for 9/11 bombings, x, 39, 46, 118, 120, 191, 192, 280; Saudi connections of, 213, 280. *See also* Al Qaeda; September 11, 2001, attack
Biological weapons, 38, 58, 120, 196, 197, 200, 206, 240, 245, 273, 290
Bombing: of buses, 11; with cars, 16–17, 21; of cities, 12–13, 23–27, 144; high altitude, 17, 29; in Oklahoma City, 82, 143, 164, 171, 237–38; of Palmer's

house, 106; of Pearl Harbor, 38, 69, 108, 118, 144, 291; of U.S. embassies and ships, 12, 118, 143. *See also* Airplanes; Civilians; Cluster bombs; Land mines; September 11, 2001, attack; *specific wars*
Border control, 200, 206
Brandeis, Louis, 106, 114
Britain, 23–24, 26, 27, 70, 101, 107, 148
Brown v. Board of Education, 135, 145
Budget (U.S.), 83–84, 121, 196, 239, 300. *See also* Costs; Taxation
Burleson, Albert, 102
Bush, George H. W., 53, 72, 73, 76, 209, 283; approval ratings of, in first Gulf War, 46, 268, 270–71, 282; domestic policy of, 256, 274; economic conditions under, 75, 216; presidency of, not model for GWB, 46, 257. *See also* Gulf War
Bush, George W. (GWB): advisers of, 257, 258, 260, 283–84, 289–91; approval ratings of, xii, 46, 85, 253–54, 263–68, 270, 271, 281–82; on "axis of evil," 120, 273; and citizenship, 81–82; discipline of, 253, 256, 258–60, 262, 263, 270, 275; domestic agenda of, 255–63, 269, 270–72; economy under, 216, 254, 264–65, 271, 283, 297, 298; foreign policy of, 120–21, 193–95, 266–67, 272–74, 282; handling of criticism by, 46; inequality of sacrifice under, 72, 83, 84, 86; legitimacy issues regarding presidency of, 252, 254–57, 260, 274; and nation building, 192, 215; and 9/11 investigation commission, 296, 297; 9/11's impact on, ix, xii–xiii, 191, 252–77; orders of, to shoot down planes, 38; patriotic messages by, 44, 45, 47–48, 78–79; presidential power's increase under, 45–46, 119, 123, 150–53, 162, 191–200, 202–3, 208, 217–18, 252–77, 293; rhetoric of, 47–49, 59–60, 290; and Saudi Arabia, 213; secrecy of, 46, 120, 124, 125–26, 210–12, 293–97; speechmaking by, 47, 80, 119, 193–95, 259–62, 265, 267–70, 273, 275, 291; state of emergency declared by, 41–42; tax cuts of, 83, 85, 121, 126, 255, 258, 259,

262–63, 265, 266, 271, 282; on terrorism as especially immoral, 4, 7–8, 10, 12, 290; on tolerance, 57–58, 80; travel destinations of, as president, 262, 269; on War on Terrorism, 38, 46, 118–19, 162, 192–95, 208, 267–69, 283, 290, 292; at World Trade Center ruins, 54, 268

Bush, Laura, 44, 58

Bush at War (Woodward), 288, 290–91

Bush v. Gore, 157n.3

Byrd, Robert, 123

Cable News Network, 50, 51

Campaign finance reform, 271–72

Canada, 51, 243, 273

Capital punishment, 125, 150, 152–53, 162

Card, Andrew, 257, 258, 283

Carter, Jimmy, 47, 72, 256, 300

Casualties: of 1993 World Trade Center bombing, 143; lack of tolerance for American, 121; in 9/11 attack, 37, 281; in Oklahoma City bombing, 143; in Pearl Harbor attack, 291

Catholicism, 43–44, 107, 113

Censorship: in Civil War, 98–100; in Iran, 51; after 9/11 attacks, 40, 156, 174–75, 181; in response to French Revolution, 103, 161; Supreme Court on, 147; under wartime presidents, xi, 95–133, 181. *See also* Free speech; Propa- ganda

Centers for Disease Control, 240

Central Intelligence Agency. *See* CIA

Change, organizational, 237–38, 243

Chemical weapons, 120. *See also* Weapons: of mass destruction

Cheney, Lynne, 44

Cheney, Richard (Dick), 41, 46, 191, 257, 264, 283, 290

China, 50, 110, 111, 285; Kuomintang government in, 137; Mao's takeover of, 137, 144, 148–49; U.S. spy plane forced down in, 263–64

Christian Coalition, 55, 124, 129n.24

Churches. *See* Religion

CIA: budget for, 215–16; failure of, to prevent 9/11 attacks, xii, 235–51, 278–80;

under Homeland Security Department, 119, 203, 246; internal culture of, 235, 240–41; in Korean War, 111; new powers of, under GWB, 124, 214. *See also* Information: sharing of

Civic participation, 65–69, 78. *See also* Federal government: trust in; Sacrifice; Volunteerism; Voting

Civil liberties (human rights): Americans' valuing of, 47–48, 121, 161; Kissinger's record on, 294–95; Lincoln's commitment to, 99–100; vs. national security, xi–xii, 95–188, 191–234, 282, 292–300; in Nazi Germany, 110; in the South, 99–100, 126, 138, 140–42; terrorism as curtailing, x, 64, 79–80, 191–234; wars as curtailing, xi, 95–133, 292–300. *See also* ACLU; Censorship; Civil rights movement; Free speech; Secrecy; Tolerance; Xenophobia

Civil rights movement, 75, 114, 117, 120, 141

Civil War, 95–100, 107, 109

Civilians: as easier to kill than soldiers, 12–13; killing of, by terrorists, 14–16, 20–23, 48, 118; killing of, in wars, 4, 8, 15–18, 20–31, 38. *See also* Innocent people; Soldiers; Victims

Clark, Ramsey, 117, 125

The Clash of Civilizations and the Remaking of World Order (Huntington), 284–86

Clear Channel Communications, 40

Clinton, Bill, 46, 54, 255, 256, 274; administration of, ix, 201, 258, 264, 298; community service ideas of, 42, 77, 82; and judiciary, 146; and patriotism, 76–78; speechmaking by, 259, 260, 262, 298–99; and terrorism, ix

Clinton, Hillary Rodham, 41, 54–55

Clinton v. Jones, 146

Cluster bombs, 16–17, 29

CNN, 50, 51

Coast Guard, 122, 206, 243, 245–46, 248

Cold War: anticommunism in, 71–72, 110–14, 137, 144–45, 148–49, 161; curtailing of civil liberties under, 95, 110–14, 117, 125, 126, 135, 137; foreign policy

58, 79, 123; and FBI, 239; under GWB, 119–20, 123, 125, 201, 214; pursuit of radicals by, 103, 106, 112–14; in World War II, 108, 109. *See also Specific attorneys general*

Just-war theory, 5–6, 8, 14, 15–16

Kean, Thomas, 295–96
Kennedy, Edward, 255
Kennedy, John F., 38, 39, 47, 71, 114–15
Kennedy, Robert F., 117, 118
Khatchadourian, Haig, 13–15
King, Martin Luther, Jr., 75, 118
Kissinger, Henry A., 294–97
Koran, 57, 286. *See also* Islam
Korean War, 110–15, 126, 146, 149
Korematsu v. United States, 144, 145
Krugman, Paul, 127
Ku Klux Klan. *See* Vigilante groups
Kuwait, 84, 289
Kyllo v. United States, 147
Kyoto Treaty, 264, 272

Labor unions: federal employees, 83, 122, 210, 213, 293; spying on, in Cold War, 113; around World War I, 101, 105, 106; in World War II, 71, 110
Law: as basis for balancing power and democracy, 138–39; denial of, to prisoners at Guantánamo Bay, 79–80, 123, 151–52, 214, 273; denial of, to prisoners before military tribunals, 150–52, 162; and GWB, 79, 193, 214, 264, 272, 273, 283–84; innocence as defined by international, 14–15; and terrorism as a crime, 79, 153. *See also* Constitution; Geneva conventions; Judiciary; United Nations; *specific cases*
League of Nations, 105
Lebanon, 120
Liberation movements. *See* Freedom fighters
Lieberman, Joseph, 42, 46, 217
Lincoln, Abraham, xi, 95–100, 104, 105, 107, 109, 110, 113, 125–27
Lindh, John Walker, 53, 123
Lindsay, Lawrence, 84, 216
Link, Arthur, 103–4

Los Angeles Times, 78
Lott, Trent, 209
Loyalty oaths, 97, 112, 128n.12

MacArthur, Douglas, 111, 113, 115
Mail, 79, 102, 106, 176. *See also* Anthrax attack; Email
Maryland, 96–97, 117
Mass media. *See* Media
Materialism. *See* Consumption
McCain, John, 42, 217, 272, 293
McCain-Feingold campaign finance plan, 272
McCarthy, Joseph, 112–14
McCarthyism, 71, 113–14, 144–45, 161, 162, 210. *See also* Loyalty oaths; "Red Scare"
McClosky, Herbert, 161, 181–82
McDonald's restaurants, 50, 52–53
McGranery, James, 113, 125
McGrath, J. Howard, 112, 125
McGrath, Judy, 56
McNamara, Robert, 128n.17
McPherson, James, 96
McWilliams, Wilson Carey, 72
Media: calls for tolerance by, 58; changes in programming by, after 9/11 attacks, 40–41, 44; on GWB-Gore election controversy, 257, 258; GWB's use of, 260, 268, 283–84; and Iraq War, 215; on Korean War, 111, 116; 9/11 coverage by, x, 39–40, 143, 149, 191, 291, 296; and Powell, 283–84; support of, for GWB's policies, 123–24; Taliban's rejection of, 48; and terrorism before 9/11, ix; U.S.'s influence through, 51–52, 284; on Vietnam War, 116; on War on Terror, 123–24, 217–18, 292; in World War II, 107, 109, 110; World War II generation's depiction by, 40, 76. *See also* Advertising; Censorship; Popular culture; Propaganda
Middle East, 254, 271, 275. *See also specific countries in*
Military, U.S.: assistance by, to countries that violate human rights, 214–15; for police work and spying, 126, 212; service in, 72; size of, under GWB, 121;

Reagan, Ronald, 42, 52, 256, 257, 294; and Iran-contra scandal, 72–73, 211, 212; rhetoric of, 59, 71–73; wars under, 72

"Red Scare," 106. *See also* McCarthyism

Religion: and conscientious objection, 109; participation in, after 9/11, 43, 78; in public life, 50; social services provided by organizations of, 83, 255, 260; spying at houses of, 124, 162, 176. *See also* Catholicism; Fundamentalism; Islam; Jews; Secularism

Repression. *See* Censorship; Civil liberties: vs. national security

Republican Party: Civil War riots against, 98; on communists in federal government, 112; defectors from, 265, 266; in election of 1862, 97–99; in election of 1920, 106; in election of 1948, 112; in election of 1952, 114; in election of 1964, 115–16; in election of 1966, 118; in election of 2000, 254–55; in election of 2002, 47, 56, 83, 122, 282, 283, 297; and foreign policy, 56, 83, 116; free-market views associated with, 126; and MacArthur's firing, 111, 113; unequal sacrifices favored by, 72, 83, 84, 86; around World War I, 104–5; in World War II, 110. *See also* Trade; *specific Republicans*

Revenue. *See* Taxation

Revolution. *See* Freedom fighters

Rice, Condoleezza, 283

Ridge, Thomas, 82, 119, 203, 248

Robertson, Pat, 55–56

Roosevelt, Franklin D., xi, 42, 70–71, 85, 105, 106–10, 125, 127; curtailing of civil liberties under, 95, 106–10, 126; Japanese internment under, 80, 107–9, 137, 144, 145, 161; and Supreme Court, 145

Rosenberg, Ethel, 145

Rove, Karl, 257, 258, 260, 283

Rudman, Warren, 280

Rumsfeld, Donald, 283

Russia (Soviet Union; U.S.S.R.): in Afghanistan, 72; American cultural influence on, 51; American treaties with, 264, 272; Bolshevik Revolution in, 101; in Cold War, 48, 110–11, 144; as nuclear power, 111, 115; repressive terror in, 137; and Soviet Union's collapse, 73, 76; in World War II, 25, 107, 110, 148. *See also* Communism; Putin, Vladimir

Sacrifice, wartime, 64–92, 121, 127; not asked of citizens in War on Terrorism, x, 64, 65, 85, 121, 192

Safire, William, 124–25

Salamon, Lester, 246

Saudi Arabia, 213, 286; as Gulf War funder, 84, 213; 9/11 hijackers from, 213, 280, 286; refusal of, to fund Iraq War, 84; U.S.'s corporate ties to, 294

Schaar, John, 71

Schaffer, Ronald, 105

Schultz, George P., 217

Searches: by authorities, 79; public's view of, after 9/11, 175; "sneak and peek," 120, 162, 178, 179; Supreme Court on, 135, 147–48, 156; under USA Patriot Act, 119, 120, 200, 201–2. *See also* Email; Internet; Mail; Wiretapping

Secrecy: of GWB's administration, 46, 120, 124, 125–26, 210–12, 293–97; of Homeland Department's information, 204; Kissinger's, 294; of military trials, 79–80, 109, 212; in Reagan administration, 73, 125, 212; and "shadow government," 210; of USA Patriot Act's applications, 120, 199, 200

Secret Service, 57, 96, 122, 206

Secularism, 50, 55–56, 79, 285–86, 288. *See also* Religion

Sedition Act of 1918, 102–4, 106, 107, 113

Senate (U.S.): in election of 1862, 97–98; in election of 2000, 254–55; in election of 2002, 47, 83, 283, 297; and federal judges, 134; Jeffords's role in, 265, 266; and 9/11 investigation commission, 295; on preemptive strike against Iraq, 122; report of, on 9/11 intelligence failures, 279–80; on War on Terrorism, 119, 197–98. *See also* Congress; *specific committees*

Taliban, 53, 55, 58; in Afghanistan, 119, 126, 288; on West vs. East, 48, 49, 51

Taxation: cuts in, under GWB, 83, 85, 121, 126, 255, 258, 259, 262–63, 265, 266, 271, 282; federal contracts for those with shelters for, 122, 209–10; increases in, in Civil War, 96, 100, in Korean War, 111, 114, in Vietnam War, 116, in World War I, 101, 105, in World War II, 108, 110; information on forms submitted for, 124–25; war's need for increases in, 84, 85, 121, 127. *See also* Budget (U.S.)

Telephones. *See* Wiretapping

Television. *See* Media; Popular culture; *specific networks*

Tenet, George, 278–79, 283

Terrorism, x–xi; American associations of, with Islam, 57; in American South, 99–100, 126, 138, 140–42; condemnations of, seen as hypocritical, 3–4, 7–9, 31; as crime or act of war, 12, 79, 126, 153; definitions of, xi, 4–18, 24, 136; dual targets of, 6, 7, 10, 11–18, 136; as especially immoral, 4, 7–8, 10, 12, 119, 290; Falwell and Robertson on causes of, 55–56; GWB doctrine on, 121; inadequacy of some governments to control, 137, 139; as national or personal threat in America, x, xi, 163–77; nations as committing acts like, 9, 31; as not associated with a single nation, 117, 119, 126, 148, 149, 152, 162, 182, 241, 288; as not subject to military defeat, 79; as not the most important issue in the U.S., 7–8, 247, 267; question of justifying, x–xi, 3–34; and Reagan, 72–73; and Saudi Arabia, 213, 280; vs. war, 20–29, 126. *See also* Assassination; Counterterrorism; September 11, 2001, attack; Terrorist groups; Victims; Vigilante groups; War on Terrorism; Warlords

"Terrorism and the Argument from Analogy" (Wallace), 24, 26–27

Terrorism Risk Protection Act, 212–13

Terrorist groups, x, 5–6, 12. *See also* Al Qaeda

Thimerosal (chemical), 209

Time magazine, 46, 210

Tocqueville, Alexis de, 68–69

Tolerance, 48, 56–57, 80, 102, 109, 197. *See also* Democracy; Neighborliness; Xenophobia

Torture, 123, 212, 214, 215, 285

"Total Information Awareness" project, 124, 125, 211–12

Totalitarianism, 136–38

Trade: agreements for, 216–17; sanctions against, 196, 200; as U.S's post–cold war foreign policy goal, 76, 85, 121, 193. *See also* World Trade Center

Trading with the Enemy Act of 1917, 103

Transportation Department, 246

Transportation Security Administration, 206

Treason, 96–99, 107, 112–14. *See also* Espionage Act; Sedition Act

Treasury Department, 196, 216

Truman, Harry, xi, 71; curtailing of civil liberties under, 95, 110–14, 117, 125, 126; government reorganization under, 193, 204, 242, 243–44; Supreme Court and, 146, 147

Tyco scandal, 272

United Nations (UN): Gulf War's sanctioning by, 74; on Iraq and weapons of mass destruction, 120, 122, 215, 283; and Iraq War costs, 84; Islamists' view of, 50; and Korean War, 111; and nation building, 215

United States (U.S.): allies of, in Gulf War, 83–84; allies of, in Iraq War, 281; as becoming a security state, xii, 111, 123–27, 135, 299–300; founders of, 67–68; hatred for, 49–53, 281, 284–89; 9/11's effects on people of, 37–63; as nuclear power, 111, 114, 115, 128n.17, 144, 149, 196; political divisions in, 53–56; as privileged country, 286–88, 300; slavery in, 96–97, 99–100, 141; as supreme power in the world, ix, 74, 76, 129n.20, 300; terrorist attacks on, before 9/11, ix, 12, 118, 143–44; unilateral actions of, under GWB administration, 79, 120–22, 194–95, 208, 264, 272–75, 283–84, 291–92, 300; as vulnerable to terrorist attacks, x, xi, 65, 163–71, 278–302; after World War II, 71; World War II bombing of cities by, 23, 25. *See also* Civil liberties; Federal government; Popular culture; Public; September 11, 2001, attack; War on Terrorism; Weapons; *Specific offices and branches of government and presidents*

United States v. Drayton, 147

U.S. Criminal Code, 9

U.S. Northern Command (Colorado), 124

Unity, Americans' sense of, after 9/11, xi, 39–40, 60, 65, 171

USA Patriot Act: concerns about civil liberties under, 199–202, 293; features of, 38, 119–20, 153–55, 195, 199–201; lack of debate about, 293; likely judiciary responses to, xi–xii, 120, 134–59; as likely to change American politics and society, xiii, 198–202, 217–18; passage of, 120, 162, 195–96, 198; presidential power under, xii, 162, 197–200, 217, 293; public's view of, 160–88; secrecy concerning, 120

U.S.S.R. *See* Russia

Victims, of war or terrorism: families of 9/11, as demanding investigation, 293–97; government compensation to, 82, 196, 197, 200; as innocent, 3–4, 6, 8, 9, 12–31; intentional vs. indiscriminate killing of, 13, 15–17; as not understanding terrorists' goals, 20, 28, 30; protection of corporations from lawsuits by families of 9/11, 82–83, 202. *See also* Hostages

Vietnam War: and Johnson, 114–18; and Kissinger, 294; lessons from, 216; opposition to, 76–77, 116–18; and patriotism, 71, 76, 85; secrecy in, 73; spying in, 162. *See also* Gulf of Tonkin resolution

Vigilante groups, 100, 103, 109, 140

Violence. *See* Terrorism; Wars

Volunteerism: costs associated with, 81–82; after 9/11 attacks, 64, 78, 85; as patriotic activity, 72, 76–77, 80–82, 269. *See also* AmeriCorps volunteers; Civic participation

Voting, 72, 75, 140–41. *See also* Elections

Walzer, Michael, 23–29

War Advertising Council, 71, 124

"War convention," 24–25

War Department, 98. *See also* Defense Department

War on Terrorism: vs. civil liberties, xi–xii, 7–8, 95–188, 191–234, 282, 284, 292–300; color-coded alert system for, 279; congressional authorization for, 197–98; consequences of, xiii, 191–234, 278–302; consumption, not sacrifice, asked of citizens in, x, 64, 65, 85, 121, 192; difficulties of telling whether we're winning, 182; as driven by politics as well as security issues, 281, 282, 296–97; enemy in, not always identifiable, 117, 126, 148, 149, 152, 162, 182, 241, 288; GWB administration's reputation as riding on, 56, 252–77; GWB on, 38, 46, 118–19, 162, 192–95, 208, 267–69, 283, 290, 292; lack of debate about, 46, 84, 125, 151, 162, 199, 208–9, 218, 282, 292, 299; length of time of, 38, 127, 152; need to reflect and debate responses to, 282, 288, 291–92, 300; no end to, 38, 127, 152; no single nation as object of, 118, 148, 149; and sacrifice, 78–86; U.S. media on, 123–24, 217–18, 292; U.S.'s allies in, 281, 291–92. *See also* Afghanistan; Budget (U.S.); Civil liberties; Homeland Security Department; Iraq War; Mobilization; Prisoners of war; Soldiers; USA Patriot Act; Weapons

Warlords, 137, 139, 216

Warren, Earl, 145, 147, 148, 156n.2

Wars: dissent permitted in American, xi, 95–133; dual targets of, 12; as having an end, 100, 126–27; killing of civilians in, 4, 8, 15–18, 20–31; limited, 74, 111, 115, 120; as morally justifiable, 4, 20–